Innovations and Entrepreneurs in Socialist and Post-Socialist Societies

Innovations and Entrepreneurs in Socialist and Post-Socialist Societies

By

Jouko Nikula and Ivan Tchalakov

CAMBRIDGE
SCHOLARS
PUBLISHING

Innovations and Entrepreneurs in Socialist and Post-Socialist Societies,
by Jouko Nikula and Ivan Tchalakov

This book first published 2013

Cambridge Scholars Publishing

12 Back Chapman Street, Newcastle upon Tyne, NE6 2XX, UK

British Library Cataloguing in Publication Data
A catalogue record for this book is available from the British Library

ISBN (10): 1-4438-4237-0, ISBN (13): 978-1-4438-4237-2

TABLE OF CONTENTS

ACKNOWLEDGEMENTS

First of all, we would like to thank the Aleksanteri Institute for inviting Ivan as a Visiting Scholar in Spring 2010 - without that this book might never have come true. We are also grateful to Vladimir Vladov, who proofread the text with very high professionalism in a very short period of time. Irina Todorova kindly gave her permission to use one of her works for the book cover. Finally we want to thank the administrative staff of Cambridge Scholars' Publishing for all of their help and support while we prepared the manuscript.

FOREWORD

This is an unusual book, comprising the edited interviews with entrepreneurs from Bulgaria, Estonia, Macedonia, Latvia, Lithuania, and Russian Karelia. Representing two distinct regions of Eastern Europe – Balkan and Baltic countries, the interviews reveal both unique patterns and striking similarities in entrepreneurial activities during the administrative economy of socialism and the period of post-socialist transition towards market economy and democratic government rule. The book partially approaches the form of readers containing exemplary business stories on entrepreneurship, published by some of the leading business schools in US and some other countries.[1] However, the interviews presented are much more than that – in fact they are exciting life histories, through which the remarkable (often tragic) post-World-War-II history of small nations in Eastern Europe comes to life.

Socialism emerges in the selected stories not as a steel-armoured, non-modern control society, but a societal formation of its own in which market-type of relations also functioned, albeit in a strange and distorted form. An economic reality is revealed that goes beyond the simplified version of totalitarian society where the main characteristics are a single-party society with one official ideology, centrally directed economy, strictly controlled media, and strong state security forces, militia, security police, and army. True, all these did exist, but in addition to that the reader will find heroic entrepreneurs from the circles of the economic nomenklatura that were able to shake – even if temporarily – the very ideological basis of this society, bringing to life new industrial sectors, new organizational forms of making 'business', and unique innovative

---

[1] Such as Nick Tart's & Nick Scheidies's book on *What it Takes to Make More Money than Your Parents: 50 Interviews with Young Entrepreneurs* (Wise Media Group, 2010) or Brian Schwartz *50 Interviews: Entrepreneurs Thriving in Uncertain Times*, interviews with successful entrepreneurs in a variety of industries, etc. There are a number of Internet based sources in the field, such as the Harvard Business School online collection of interviews with leading entrepreneurs (see http://www.hbs.edu/entrepreneurs/), http://www.50interviews.com/, or http://www.entrepreneurship-interviews.com/blog/. The blogger Cristian Dorobantescu, an entrepreneur from Eastern Europe, also carried out and published a number of interesting interviews on his web page (http://entrepreneurs.about.com/od/interviews/Interviews_with_Entrepreneurs.htm).

products. They succeeded (or failed) not just because they found ways to get around the administrative system and devised informal ways of 'getting things done', but also because they used the system's own mechanisms, thus deflating some of the well-established notions of socialism.

The stories of start-up entrepreneurs that emerged during the post-socialist transition also challenge some of the key neo-liberal principles and recipes, dominant for more than twenty years in the social sciences, among international experts, and in political circles. A typical example of this trend is Simon Johnson's and Gary Loveman's book *Starting Over in Eastern Europe: Entrepreneurship and Economic Renewal* (Harvard Business Press, 1995), where by studying a number of successful (and failed) entrepreneurs in Poland, in sectors such as shipbuilding, clothing, consulting, food, banking, and publishing, the authors recognized the emerging new private businesses as the main engine of economic renewal throughout the region and as a key factor for improving the international competitiveness of post-communist countries.

However, as some other studies have shown, this was not universally valid throughout Eastern Europe. It becomes clear that the reformers and a large part of the academics had a distorted and one-sided understanding of the structural features of the socialist societies, of the nature of enterprise in these societies, and of the ramifications these two had for the history and forms of development in post-socialist societies. They completely ignored the 'hidden program' of a specific wing of the former Communist nomenklatura that opportunistically used the dominant neo-liberal model, promoted by the Western experts, in order to implement a policy aiming to suppress the newly emerging economic agents (such as foreign investors, authentic entrepreneurs, etc.) and to impose their own rent-seeking and assets-scraping strategies that eventually transformed their former political power into the economic power of the new oligarchic groups. This happened in most of the so-called 'second-wave' countries of EU enlargement (Menske & Weber 2001), where the "political wing" of the communist nomenklatura preserved (although partially) its influence - the clash between the political nomenklatura's 'hidden strategies' and the 'official neoliberal program' of transition introduces tragic overtones in some of the entrepreneurial stories in the book.

To help the reader better understand these processes and 'see' what we – the authors of the research projects for which these interviews were conducted – were able to see in the stories presented in the book, a detailed theoretical introduction is given. It outlines the different research traditions in studying entrepreneurship in Eastern Europe in the fields of economics, sociology, political science, economic history, and science and technology studies.

The current views on Communism are still dominated by the theory of totalitarianism, involving concepts that predominantly focus on the static structures of the totalitarian/authoritarian power, as based on a rigid hierarchy, centralization of state functions, state-directed plan economy, and all-embracing control mechanisms. In this perspective, the communist society enjoyed a restricted space, where, under state-control, autonomous actions and bottom-up initiatives were discouraged. Only lately has this view been challenged by historical and sociological studies on the so-called 'second economy' and communist entrepreneurship (Romsics 2007, Bundzhulov 2003, Mozny 2007, Szeleni 1994).

These studies revealed that during the decades after WWII the 'indigenous' way in which innovations were outlined by the agents of socialist economies involved the notion not of entrepreneurship but of *technical progress*. This concept, however, reduces the role of entrepreneurs and considers technical changes as external to the economy proper, i.e. as an 'exogenous factor'. The process of innovation was conceived of as a rational process, subject to socialist planning. Interestingly enough, up to the late 1970s the notion of technical progress was dominant in Western neoclassical economics as well, where innovations were also treated as 'exogenous' to the economic system. Many leading post-WWII economists shared the views of the late Schumpeter about the gradual disappearance of the entrepreneurial function in capitalist market economy, where the increasing dominance of large corporations was allegedly transforming innovations into a routine activity of salaried employees (Langlois 1987). We believe this was one of the key reasons for the specific 'blindness' (or rather bias) in recognizing the role of entrepreneurship in the former socialist economies and its effects on the process of transition.

In contrast to these assumptions, we claim that the socialist society, by its very nature, produced and maintained structural features that gave rise to entrepreneurship and that have influenced the way in which private entrepreneurship has evolved in many post-socialist countries. Our claims are supported by some recent works by a group of economic historians, such as Karen Freeze, Valentina Fava, Riika Nissonen, and some others. During the last fifteen years they made valuable case studies of the innovations in the socialist economies, which questioned the earlier studies, carried out in the framework of the neoclassical paradigm (Amann and Cooper 1982; Hewett 1987, Berliner 1988). We also found support in the pioneering research on the socialist enterprise carried out by Simon

Clarke in Russia immediately after the fall of Communism (Clarke 1994, 1994).

After 1989 the economic models of *post-socialist transition* can be broadly classified into two large groups - neo-classical liberal models and neo-statist models, both sharing the traditional market-state opposition. For the neo-liberalists, the state is an end in itself and is destined to be forced out of the field of economic activity and out of the theoretical schemes of analysis (Kosolowski, 1992; Sachs, 1996), while for the neo-statists, the establishment of a powerful and coherent state is the sole alternative to the weak markets, an efficient means of resolving the problems they have generated, and a reliable tool for reforming the entire society. The two approaches clashed during the first years of Eastern European transformation. However, the 'neo-liberal fallacy' (Hirszowicz, Mailer, 1994) was dominant, perhaps because it equated the triumph of capitalism with the triumph of the market. It took notice only of the market revolutions of Reagan and Thatcher (Stark, 1992), overlooking the industrial transformations in Germany, Japan, and France, which were neither solely market nor hierarchical ones. According to J. Kornai both models of post-socialist economic transition failed to take into account the set of practical problems required for normal operation of a market economy:

> "...Once the laws are satisfactory, the key question is to ensure they are observed in a disciplined way. This requires that law courts administer justice quickly and efficiently and penalize breaches of contract and lapses of financial discipline. In warranted cases, courts have to declare firms insolvent, and if necessary order their liquidation. Lawyers are needed to represent debtors and creditors professionally, officials to implement court decisions and conduct auctions, personnel and institutions specializing in reorganization and liquidation, and so on. Socialist countries, before the start of the market-oriented reforms, possessed no trace of this kind of apparatus, which functions traditionally in developed market economies." (Kornai 2000: 1596-1597)

Since the mid-1990s, however, the so-called *path-dependency approach* became prominent, especially after the work of David Stark and Laszlo Bruszt on the so-called 'recombinant capitalism' established in Hungary in 1990s. As they put it, there is little sense in the idea of transition in the East European economies as a 'rational design of [new] economic institutions', simply because the capitalist economy and its institutions are not the outcome of a rational design (like the communist Utopia). The evolutionist approach, based on the concept of path dependency, has the heuristic advantage of examining what is happening here and now as a constant activation of the existing (available) organizational forms, institutional mechanisms, social relations and products, used by the actors to answer immediate practical dilemmas" (Hausner, Jessop, Nielsen, 1995; Stark & Bruszt 1992, 1996).

Another promising research avenue was the *techno-economic networks* approach developed in the field of social studies of science and technologies (M.Callon, B. Latour, J. Law), whose notions of emerging and stabilised techno-economic (or socio-technical) networks allow tracing the complex web of cognitive, technological, economic, political, legal, etc. relationships in the process of innovation and its evolution. Applied to the economic realities of socialism and post-socialism, it provides rich resources for going beyond the market-state opposition, and for taking into account the science, technological, and institutional base of the studied societies.

These two research traditions, the recent studies of economic historians, the critical reading of the classical ideas of Joseph Schumpeter on innovations in non-market economies, and the original model of the communist 'Sacred and Profane', developed by Finnish sociologist Markku Kivinen, became the key sources of theoretical inspiration for the authors' researches on post-socialist entrepreneurship, pushing us to leave the privileged position of *observers that already know the outcome*, and to try to revive the 'open end' situations, in which the past actors had striven to achieve their goals and realize their strategies. The original synthesis of these ideas into a general model about socialist and post-socialist entrepreneurship is presented in the introduction of the book. It simultaneously challenges *the common way of conceptualizing entrepreneurship* as something that is related only to production of goods or selling services/goods (i.e. the concept of innovation/innovative action); *the commonly held belief that there were no entrepreneurs under socialism*, or if there were, they were just black-economy swindlers and crooks (i.e. a belief that expands the range of entrepreneurs to include Party and KGB structures and others); and *the commonly held idea of post-socialism as an antidote of socialist order.* Viewed through this model, the data reveal a new picture of post-socialist transition, which appears richer in real-life opportunities and astonishing new developments…

Ivan Tchalakov, Jouko Nikula,
Sofia-Helsinki, September-November 2012.

PART I

INTRODUCTION

The idea of this book arose somewhere in the spring of 2010 when Ivan Tchalakov was a visiting scholar at the Finnish Centre for Russian and Eastern European Studies, University of Helsinki. During the regular joint lunches, we discussed our research interests and research histories and discovered that we shared the same research interests – and research history. Ivan had studied the emergent class of entrepreneurs in Bulgaria and Macedonia and I had studied the same class in the Baltic countries – Estonia, Latvia, Lithuania, and Russia at their later stages. What made a distinction between us was the starting point: while Ivan's studies were based on the theory of socialist entrepreneurs as a group distinct from the ideological or political nomenclature, my studies were based more on customary notions of entrepreneurs as products of the waste- and shortage-economy, informal practices and networks (blat relations, corruption and others) or grabbers of joint property in obscure privatization operations. Another difference was in our views of the core functions and competences of the entrepreneurs - for Ivan the core of entrepreneurship was creation and dissemination of innovations in the sense of Schumpeter, while for me the key issues were sustainability of the business, penetration into new markets, and ways to succeed in competition (through prices, quality). This explained also our difference in the search for relevant conceptual tools to account for the rich empirical data collected.

However, the point that we shared was the understanding of socialism as a social formation that was not a steel-armoured, non-modern control society, but a societal formation of its own where certain market-type relations also functioned, albeit in strange and distorted forms. This introduction presents the results of our efforts to bring together our conceptual frameworks for a better understanding of the (post)socialist entrepreneurship. There is no doubt that the stories told to us by the interviewed entrepreneurs go beyond any conceptual frame. Yet our understanding of these stories and the societies their heroes lived in may provide the reader with one more perspective on (or way of looking at) them.

* * *

The socialist system collapsed in Europe (and Russia) some twenty years ago. The "revolutions" in former socialist countries were, in a sense, accompanied by neo-liberalism, the Reaganist and Thatcherist ideology, which had been sweeping through Europe and USA since the mid- 1980s. In this thinking, the causes for economic problems were seen to be the Big State, the established structures of regulation of economy (publicly-owned enterprises, trade unions, etc.), the welfare state; the "cure" was to curtail these. There was also a longing for "fundamental values", such as the worth of the individual, the importance of ambition, pursuit of personal wealth (even in China), and localism. The neo-liberal thinking with regard to the socialist countries was deeply rooted in a simplified version of totalitarian society according to which its main characteristics were a single-party society with one official ideology, a centrally-directed economy, strictly controlled media, and strong state security forces, militia, security police, and army. This would imply that the Soviet-type societies were tightly controlled and homogeneous unities in all socio-economic respects, oppressed by the Party. In a Soviet-type society, the argument goes, individual preferences and initiative were strictly controlled or banned. Collectivism prevailed in all spheres of life – in housing, in work, in culture. When this centralized collective began to dissolve, this happened through a number of processes, as illustrated in Janos Kornai's (2010: 2) description of the key processes of the Great Transformation:

> "The 'Great Transformation' is an ensemble of several processes. Firstly, there were changes in the political domain: the transition from a single-party dictatorship to a multi-party democracy. Then there were changes in the economic domain: the predominance of state-ownership was replaced by the predominance of private ownership. Associated with the transformation of ownership forms, the relative influence of various coordination mechanisms also went through radical changes. The impact of centralized bureaucratic control became much smaller, and the influence of market co-ordination and other decentralized procedures increased dramatically. These profound political and economic changes, associated with several other changes, jointly meant the change of the system, i.e., the transition from socialism to capitalism".

It was exactly these things that the IMF and World Bank advisors proposed: a complete dismantling of collective, state ownership and withdrawal of the state from the regulation of the economy. Only through marketization, liberalization and privatization was it possible to "produce" the optimal economic structures, boost entrepreneurship via creation of a viable stratum of small and medium-sized enterprises, and guarantee the smooth development of democracy.

Our starting-point is that the reformers and a large part of the academics who analysed the socialist society, have had a completely distorted and one-sided understanding of its structural features, of the nature of enterprise within it, and of the kinds of ramifications these two matters had for the history and forms of development of entrepreneurship in socialist and especially in post-socialist society. For us the socialist society, by its very nature, produced and maintained such structural features that gave rise to entrepreneurship and have influenced the way private entrepreneurship has evolved in many post-socialist countries.

The introduction is structured into seven parts. We begin with a brief discussion of the key obstacle faced by any social study of past events that pays attention to the indigenous actors' point of view – controlling the asymmetry between the worlds these actors were living in and our privileged position of observers who *already know* the outcome of those events.

The second section outlines the strange similarity in the ways Marxist political economy and neoclassical economics considered entrepreneurship during the decades after WWII, i.e. as a sign of the imperfection of the corresponding economic system, as something that plays an auxiliary, compensating role. We present the main features of the socialist society and economy (including the social relations within the socialist enterprise), which fostered the evolution of entrepreneurship in socialism and the forces that maintained its development.

The next three sections (3-5) deepen our understanding of the specific political, economic and cultural patterns that emerged and stabilized in the former socialist societies as a specific form of modernity, patterns that have a bearing upon the process of post-socialist transition. Sections 3 and 4 provide a critical reading of Schumpeter's implicit theory of economic development in non-market economies, which is juxtaposed (section 5) with an outline of the indigenous structure of power relations in communist economy, with their specific tensions and dynamics. Taken together, these three sections propose an original conceptual frame that significantly modifies the 'compensating' or 'auxiliary' notion of socialist entrepreneurship.

Section 6 explores the related 'cultural matrix' of former communist societies. It reveals the code of socialist 'Sacred and Profane' as a motivational ground underlying the actions of the former communist nomenclature and ordinary economic agents.

This is an important step, for it displays this code as radically different from the 'Sacred and Profane' of capitalist societies, thus providing the resources to think about its transformation during the post-socialist transition and its influence on the behavior of the interviewed entrepreneurs.

Section 7 briefly outlines of the transitional paths of Bulgaria, Estonia, and Russia during the last two decades, thus providing the reader with more resources for interpreting the interviews.

The Asymmetry that Makes the Study of (Post) Socialist Entrepreneurship so Difficult

During the decades after WWII the 'indigenous' way innovations were outlined by the agents in socialist economies was the notion of *technical progress*. This notion, however, reduces the role of entrepreneurs and considers technical changes as external to the economy proper, i.e. as an 'exogenous factor'. The introduction of innovations was conceived as a rational process, subject to socialist planning. Interestingly enough, up until the late 1970s the notion of technical progress was dominant in Western neoclassical economics too, where innovations were also treated as 'exogenous' to the economic system.

There are striking similarities in the way technical changes were considered in neoclassical economics and in socialist political economy, which equally shared the so-called 'diffusion model of innovation' (Callon & Latour 1986). This model assumes that any (technical) innovation possesses 'internal' properties and that there exists a 'social' resistance against diffusion of a given technology or artifact, so that the clash between innovation's own momentum of development and the resistance to it, leads to a certain delay in its introduction. Underlying these assumptions is the general 'philosophical' principle of *the asymmetry between past events*, which can always be explained by their (in)efficiency, profitability and necessity, *and the present situation*, which is always enigmatic to a certain extent. More than twenty years ago the new sociology of innovation emerged precisely by questioning this assumption, and by posing the questions: How to understand innovations in their 'proper present', before history has judged with its standard schemes of reasoning? How to analyze and trace innovations before they became efficient, profitable, and indispensable?

We believe these questions are relevant also in studying entrepreneurship in former socialist economies and the period of their transition towards capitalism after 1989 – here too we need to leave our privileged position of *observers that already know the outcome*, and to try to revive the 'open end' situations in which the past actors strove to achieve their goals and to realize their strategies. As a number of studies have shown, it is not possible to judge between several competitive projects, on the basis of our knowledge about states of technology, type of economies and markets, or laws of physics – the states are changing, market are created, physics is constructed (or revolutionized). Hence, in their emerging and polemic state, innovative products and services are 'under-defined', vague and unclear (Hughes 1983). Yet it is at this 'under-defined' stage that the most important decisions about the destiny of the innovation are to be made – where is the money to be borrowed from, what is to be researched and developed, what marketing strategy is to be elaborated, etc. And this is precisely the environment *entrepreneurs* are faced with, including the socialist and post-socialist entrepreneurs. The interviews we collected in this book provide rich evidence of this challenging 'real-world' environment that the (post)socialist entrepreneurs were living in.

Were the Socialist Entrepreneurs at all Possible?

The Disappearance of the Entrepreneurs in Modern Economies and their Reduction to Auxiliary, 'Compensating' Economic Agents

In his seminal paper on *Entrepreneurship and Management*, Alberto Martinelli provides a compelling – if brief - historical outline of the concept, pointing out the importance of the three 'classical' interpretations of entrepreneurship in Karl Marx, Max Weber, and Joseph Schumpeter.[1] He stresses that Marx "…does not distinguish between the owner of capital and the entrepreneur, and does not offer much insight into the specific features and behaviour of entrepreneurs as collective actors" (Martinelli 1994: 477). Although Marx provided vivid descriptions of the role of the bourgeoisie at the earlier stages of capitalism, much of which could be considered as true entrepreneurial activity, the latter was not

[1] It is beyond the scope of this introduction to analyze the early contributions to economic theory of *Cantillon (1755)* and *Turgot (1776)*, who first related entrepreneurship to the acceptance of the risk and uncertainty inherent in economic activity, or of *Jean-Baptiste Say (1803, 1828)* and *John Stuart Mill*, who introduced the distinction between entrepreneurial function and supply of capital. See also the overview by Tyson, Petrin, and Rogers (1994) of the definitions of entrepreneurship and their relevance for the study of early post-socialist economic realities, especially Jones's and Sakong's (1981) study of Korean entrepreneurship.

considered as something distinct in the large theoretical scheme of capital accumulation and growth. His analyses in *Das Kapital* of the automatic machines and the transition from manufacture to the factory system of production does not leave much room for the entrepreneurs either, considered by Marx as 'managers' or supervisors of production processes as opposed to the workers. This specific interpretation laid the ground of a tradition where, under the notions of 'socialisation of production', of the 'alienation of labour' and its 'reverse appropriation' under communist society, the specific entrepreneurial function was largely neglected. *For many decades entrepreneurship as a concept practically disappeared from the textbooks of Marxist political economy, and it was never used in describing the socialist economies.*

In his economic analysis Max Weber retained much of the basic Marxist assumptions, pointing out, however, the cultural factors that distinguished capitalist entrepreneurs from their earlier predecessors; among these factors were "...rational and systematic pursuit of economic gain, calculation based on economic criterion, the relation between trust and credit, and subordination of consumption to accumulation, etc." (Martinelli 1994: 487). In his famous analysis of the Protestant ethic and in other writings, he managed to provide a much more concrete and detailed picture of the role of individuals in shaping the behavior of the capitalist class as a whole and in the functioning and development of modern institutions of capitalism.

It was Joseph Schumpeter (1912), however, who decisively linked the entrepreneurs with innovation, defining them as risk-takers, relatively independent of inherited property, and introducing new combinations of the factors of production, thus breaking the static equilibrium of the circular flow of the economy. He stressed that "...even if a businessman is owner of the capital, his function and position are not those of a simple provider either of money or of the physical means of production. *This is the profound error (which dates from Adam Smith but which was stressed by Karl Marx) of seeing nothing else in the activity of a captain of enterprise* (italics ours). Rather it is comparable to the role of a military commander; the businessman is essentially a worker who is the leader of other workers." (Schumpeter 1991: 403)

Yet the ideas of Joseph Schumpeter have never been accommodated in the neoclassical economics that gained momentum after WWI. After the so-called 'neoclassical synthesis' with Keynesian macroeconomics, the latter became the dominant economic paradigm in Anglo-Saxon countries from the late 1940s till the 1970s. Hence the explanatory power of the concept of entrepreneurship slowly faded in the Western part of Europe and North America. These theoretical developments went hand in hand with the rise of managerial capitalism and the expansion of the large corporations, which sharply reduced the role of individual entrepreneurial efforts. With the gradual establishment of monopolistic or oligopolistic markets in each industrial sector during the decades around WWI, authors like Rathenau (1918) described 'organisierte Kapitalismus' as based on de-personalization of property and as covering the same path as did the modern state, while Berle and Means (1932) claimed that the separation of ownership and control was an irreversible trend including the rise of the modern corporation, considered as an 'organized social group based on interdependence of different economic interests – those of owners, employees, consumers, and the controlling group (managers)' (Martinelli 1994: 488). Referring to this period, A. Chandler described the major trends in the economy as *transition from family to managerial capitalism*, powered by technological innovations, larger markets, international competition, industrial concentration, vertical integration, etc. (Chandler 1977). The Western societies also witnessed increasing involvement of governments in steering economic activities, especially after the experience they obtained during WWII (see Reich 1991, ch. 4).

The result was the gradual 'disappearance' of the entrepreneur in economic theory on both sides of the Iron Curtain. Barreto pointed out that "...with the advent of the modern theory of the firm, the economics lost track of the entrepreneur, [because] the framework assumptions – especially those of perfect rationality, does not allow for a consistent implementation of the entrepreneurial behavior. The role of the entrepreneur was reduced to a 'static, passive and therefore redundant economic agent within a self-running firm" (Barreto 1989:84). In the decades that followed WWII, the 'heroic' entrepreneur appeared in mainstream economics in the paradoxical from of a *sign of underdevelopment and/or distortion of the markets*. As Martinelli put it, the dominant development economists at the time

> "... shared the idea that pure entrepreneurial profit would be the smoothly corresponding reward that market conditions require and make possible. This approach assumes that factors of production are relatively mobile; that producers, consumers, and resource owners have knowledge of all the opportunities open to them; that risk and uncertainty are minimal; and that the influence of social institutions is neutral. The policy implications of this approach for development strategy are: let the market work, remove the barriers of traditional society, and entrepreneurs will appear from everywhere. When the above assumptions are relaxed and market segmentation, ignorance, impeded factor mobility, and pervasive administrative controls appear, the 'extraordinary' role of the entrepreneur

becomes apparent, as does the need to analyze more carefully the factors that can favor his formation." (Martinelli 1994:485)

Hence, it was believed that little room was left for true entrepreneurship in the developed Western economies of the mid-20th century, dominated by large corporations. Joseph Schumpeter himself called this process 'march into socialism', stating that "...the perfectly bureaucratized giant industrial unit not only ousts the small or the medium-sized firm and 'expropriates' its owners, but in the end it also ousts the entrepreneur and expropriates the bourgeoisie as a class, which, in the process, stands to lose not only its income but also what is infinitely more important, its function. The true pacemakers of Socialism are not the intellectuals or agitators who preached it, but the Vanderbilts, Carnegies, and the Rockefellers." (Schumpeter 1942: 134)

This was the context in which socialism as an economic system emerged in the decades after WWI; coupled with the tradition of Marxist political economy, it left no room for entrepreneurship as a conceptual tool for understanding the processes in the emerging administrative economies. The classical account of Janos Kornai in his "Political Economy of Communism" illustrates this: in his orderly theoretical scheme, the concept of entrepreneur is simply not needed (see Box 1 below).

It is interesting here to provide the comment by Wlodzimierz Brus about the evolution of the notion of 'enterprise' in socialist administrative economies. According to him, when the foundations of the socialist economies were laid down in the 1920s and early 1930s, the "enterprise was elevated to the status of the main link in the system of management... but *without actual possibilities for taking allocation decisions...* [It is] an organizational unit designed to *implement*, in the most accurate way possible, decisions coming from *above* in the form of obligatory targets and plan-determined resource limits." (Brus 1988: 100) Hence the author concludes that, under the socialist economic system, the enterprise as an organisational unit "...does not exercise the entrepreneurial function: it does not make choices either about objectives or means, and it does not bear the resultant risks and responsibilities" (ibid). Quite in tune with the predictions of the mainstream neoclassical economics of that time, Brus relates *the scope for entrepreneurship under socialism inverse to the degree of administrative regulation, as a sign of its imperfections and distortions*, and he finds *only relative differences* between administrative and (corporate) market economies.

Box 1 - *Janos Kornai about key features of the socialist non-market economy*

According to Kornai, the ‘classical socialist economy’ that took root in Eastern Europe has several interrelated characteristics:

1) The *common political structure*, whose distinguishing features are the inseparable political power of the ruling party, the reciprocal infiltration of party and state, and the suppression of all forces that distance themselves from or oppose the party policy; all these features legitimized by communist ideology.

2) The practical implementation of the principle of *supremacy of the state property*, imposed by the political structure, since “the inseparability of power and concomitant totalitarianism are incompatible with autonomy which exacts private property." The disappearance of the phenomenon of "business secrecy" constitutes a substantial after-effect of the supremacy of state property.

3) The specific constellation of co-ordinating mechanisms, *administrative co-ordination being the most essential component.* It consists of (a) elimination of free enterprise; (b) elimination of autonomous market agents and competition among them; (c) centralization of decision-making and information; (d) domination of hierarchical dependence (of vertical relations over horizontal).

4) The three distinguishing features of classic socialism have an immediate effect on *the interests and motivation of the economically active persons* - this, Kornai claims, is the fourth major characteristic. It gives rise to a number of typical phenomena such as planned contracting, striving for quantity, paternalistic behaviour of the people of high standing, soft budget constraints, weak reaction to prices, etc.

The socialist economy can be explained by these factors – the character of the governance, official ideology, prevalent state property, and administrative co-ordination. However, once they emerge, the factors gain independence and start in turn to influence and modify one another. Kornai calls this sequence of four elements (factors) ‘explanatory chain’. Their interaction results in several lasting economic phenomena that are typical of classical socialism, the most important of them being *forced growth, deficit of manpower and hidden unemployment, economy of chronic deficit, specific role of foreign trade, etc.* (Kornai 1992, part II)

The Nature of Socialist Economy: Not Only Command, but also a Waste- and Shortage Economy

What was the economic context in which the socialist entrepreneurs emerged with their 'compensating' functions? In the system of 'classical socialist economy', outlined by Kornai, the emphasis was on extensive growth, i.e. maximal use of resources (labour, land), and not intensive growth, where growth is realized through increasing productivity. There was a lot of free labour and the productive capital was underutilized. According to Nove (1969), as the Soviet economy developed, it simultaneously became increasingly complex and increasingly difficult (or even impossible) to plan economic activities. This led to deficits and contributed seriously to development of the shortage- and waste economy.

In this context Simon Clarke defines the socialist enterprise as "a primary unit of Soviet society and the basis of the social and political power" (Clarke 1993b, 7). It was also a kind of *hub that nurtured various forms of informal economy and blat relations*. In the socialist enterprise the most important issue for the director was reproduction of the production process by constantly struggling and negotiating with central planning authorities over the financial, labour, and other resources. Marketing was not an issue for him, because markets were secure and regulated by the same central planning authorities. Enterprises produced goods according to orders and had no authority over the prices or the marketing of their products. The emphasis on quantitative growth meant that in investments as well, the main attention was paid to extensive reproduction of the means of production – enterprises invested in new machines, new production facilities, *but not in measures that would have improved their competitiveness in terms of product quality or skills of their employees*. This was the result of the fact that all the revenues of the enterprise went to central planning authorities, who distributed money according to past performance and future planning of production targets. Competition over the resources between different branches of economy and within the branches was fierce, and to guarantee their success in this competition, the enterprises were forced to overestimate their needs, underestimate their targets and hoard all possible resources. The result was a dislocation of many resources, ruptures and other forms of bottlenecks in the production processes, which in turn increased the power of the high-skilled employees to demand higher wages and more fringe benefits[2].

---

[2] See Nove 1993, Kornai 1992

In Clarke's account the third significant feature of the socialist enterprise was its nature as a means of authoritarian paternalism. The enterprises took care of almost all aspects of the life of their employees and many of those of the community where enterprises were located, in exchange for loyalty and consent to the demands of the management and Party. Enterprises gave employment, provided housing, health care, leisure and in many cases also provided a variety of consumption goods. However, the production of consumer goods was grossly underrated until the late 1950s – early 1960s, and serious problems in distribution of these goods existed until the collapse of socialism. The enterprises sponsored local community schools, sports activities, they built and maintained roads, provided transport services, etc. The trade unions functioned as a broker between the enterprise management, the Party, and the employees, negotiating on wages and benefits, and taking care of the distribution of benefits, where seniority and loyalty were important criteria.

The Sources of Informal Proto-entrepreneurship in Socialist Society

In the shortage- and waste economy, enterprises had larger autonomy to meet their target plans and recruit labour and other types of resources for sustaining the production process. Wlodzimierz Brus outlines two types of such 'compensating' entrepreneurial activities: 1) The manipulation of the superordinate level of economic administration in situations of 'imperfect knowledge' – i.e. the centre has to rely on information supplied by an interested party: if an enterprise is rewarded for plan fulfillment and punished for under-fulfillment, it tries to hide its capacities (in order to receive a less demanding target) and exaggerates its needs (in order to get a more generous allocation of labor and material inputs); 2) Informal transactions between enterprises themselves – i.e. the mismatch between supply of and demand for production factors is corrected by enterprises arranging swaps, which only go against the rules of vertical channels of allocation (Brus 1988, 101). In organizing necessary inputs, the horizontal and largely informal network ties became stronger and more important. This meant that the economy as a whole moved gradually to "grey" or even "black" zones of economic activity. The shortages of goods and services[3] nurtured different forms of the second economy, such as petty

[3] The Bulgarian sociologists Andrey Bundzhulov notes that the official system of distribution, which was counterpoised to the 'second networks' and blat, was not uniform and homogeneous. The communist nomenclature created two systems of

trading, hidden incomes from unofficial jobs, or intra-firm barter (Sik 1995, 10). Finding niches and taking risks represented proto-entrepreneurship and were logical and necessary products of the economy that wasted resources and suffered from shortages of most consumption goods.

Socialist proto-entrepreneurs were an inevitable substitute for an official economy, because they diminished the bottle-necks in the distribution of resources and goods and therefore they were, at least unofficially, accepted. The actors who negotiated and took care of the exchange of resources between enterprises were *tolkachi*, a special group of lower management whose main task was to barter for materials they needed. Nell (2006) does not regard them as entrepreneurial because "…*tolkachi* were filling the gap in supply of inputs for state enterprises to fulfil their plan targets. Hence, the origin of this activity is the plan – not the entrepreneurial drive of these middlemen" (Nell 2006, 4).

Yet the researchers have found another group of informal and 'systemic' entrepreneurs – the so-called *tzehoviki (цеховики)*, who secretly manufactured consumer goods and used their networks to get goods from the shops and markets. In the economy of shortage this attempt to satisfy public demand brought them huge profits. However, they had very little chances of reinvesting their profits because they were constantly crossing boundaries by acquiring necessary raw materials through theft or corruption. Also, the fact that they were using state shops for private transactions on a large scale could get them a long sentence in prison. Therefore it was a very risky yet fabulously profitable business. These "entrepreneurs" used all their power to mitigate risks, for example through bribes to get entry into the Party hierarchy and maintain mutually

---

distribution – official and unofficial. The former was apparent, encompassed all individuals and operated at a relatively low level. By Western criteria, it was ineffective both in terms of quality of the services and standards. To meet its own needs, the 'apparatus' created an additional ("special") system of distribution, *the system of privileges* – special shops with high-quality merchandise, specialized hospitals and rest homes that provided better treatment, comfortable flats in elite residential neighborhoods, privileges in obtaining higher education, traveling abroad, etc. Bundzhulov goes even further and distinguishes *three systems/levels of distribution* – 1) a system which caters to the needs of the apparatus; 2) an official system of distribution for the general public; and 3) official privileges for certain social strata [managers, Stakhanovite shock-workers, etc.] or regions (Bundzhulov 2006: 403). The difference between the first one and the other two is that the system of privileged distribution *is off the record – "the privileges of the apparatus are secret, they are not known to the public"* (ibid)!

beneficial ties with local Party leaders. In a sense, they were a win-win phenomenon, because for entrepreneurs themselves the shortage and waste economy created good grounds for profitable business. They were profitable also for some parts of the Party apparatus and the state administration, because the existence of *tzehoviki* depended to a great extent on the benevolence of a range of inspectors and law-enforcement officials and, naturally, on the amounts of roubles that these officials received from the *tzehoviki*. Being unofficial, these entrepreneurs were naturally at the mercy of unofficial "security entrepreneurs", i.e. racketeers.

At the level of everyday life the Soviet-type economy forced most citizens to spend a lot of time and energy to find goods that were in short supply. This required organizing complex systems for exchanging goods and favours with the members of their social networks. This "private entrepreneurship of shortage" (Srubar 1991) gave birth to various forms of social networks between different social groups (workers/managers; managers/Party officials, etc.) and to an "economy of favours" or *blat* (Ledeneva 1998), which were complementary to the 'official' social organizing in the Soviet economy. Rehn and Taalas (2004, 237) argue that "*the Union of Soviet Socialist Republics might be seen as the most entrepreneurial society*" (italics original). True, the Soviet citizens (like the citizens of other socialist societies) were extremely innovative in finding new economic opportunities in the face of uncertainty and other obstacles (shortages of goods, threat of legal penalties, etc.), but it is also true that *blat* systems did not enhance the well-being of the community or region, not to mention the state. They were mainly about individual exchanges; usually there was no money involved, but a service was exchanged for another service or goods. Rehn and Taalas argue that *blat* had many positive impacts on the socialist economy; it increased flexibility and fostered trust and reciprocity between the members of the network, which entailed active participation and contribution from their members. (Rehn & Taalas 2004, 244)

Some sociologists studying the former socialist societies generalize the 'blat' phenomenon by introducing the notions of *second networks* emerging *on the borderline between the deficit of power and the deficit of goods*. The second networks (as opposed to the 'first', official relationships), they claim, may be regarded as a fundamental phenomenon of socialist society, a phenomenon defined as an 'exchange of goods and power'.[4] These networks do not duplicate the socialist state but are its opposite:

---

[4] See also Elemer Hankiss' notion of 'second society' (Hankiss 1988). Using Claus Offe's idea about the two basic organizational principles operating in advanced capitalist societies to outline the differences between West European capitalist and

"In [socialist] society, there are real hierarchies besides the formal ones, because with an exchange of goods for statuses, it is normal to have central and peripheral points. Therefore public hierarchies emerge, which compete with the official ones and have an increasing influence over them. In this sense, we can rightfully define this process as colonization (Ivo Mozny)." (Raychev 2002, p. 4).

Hence, similarly to the developments in the Western countries since the 1970s, where, with the rise of neo-liberal economic theory, individual economic initiative and the role of the innovative small and medium enterprises were recognized as a key engine of capitalist economic development,[5] in most socialist countries the reformist rulers openly supported the forms of bottom-up 'socialist entrepreneurship' as a remedy for the inherent shortcomings of the administrative economies and as part of the ongoing process of economic reforms. Just a few years before the 1989 velvet revolutions in Eastern Europe, Wlodzimierz Brus wrote:

"...In the closing decades of the twentieth century, in most of the 'real socialist' countries (this is still the designation used in official Soviet language to describe the countries ruled by Communist parties), a frantic search is going on to find tools to revive the entrepreneurial function... This is true not only for countries like Yugoslavia where the search is already almost 40 years old, or Hungary, which introduced the (then) 'New Economic Mechanism' in 1968, but also in the two giants and ideological standard bearers of the communist world: China, where reforms have been in full swing since the end of the 1970s, and the Soviet Union, where from the platform of the Communist Party's XXVII Congress and from pronouncements of Secretary General Mikhail Gorbachev, the repeated calls for socialist entrepreneurship can be clearly heard." (Brus 1988: 99)

East European socialist societies, he defines "the second economy" as additional to the administrative economy and "only loosely integrated into it", and not as a substantial – if complementary – part of it (ibid, p.18). It appears as a weakened version of the capitalist market economy that emerges inside the administrative one as its alternative. [We are indebted to Katalin Miklossy for pointing our attention to Hankiss's work.]

[5] See Kurzner's notion of entrepreneurship as a process of discovery and his critique of the neoclassical notion of 'maximizing behavior' and the economic importance of other typically entrepreneurial features of the economic agents such as alertness, creativity, risk taking (Krizner 1997). See also Florida and Kenney about the role of financial innovation such as venture capital that created new opportunities for the individual entrepreneurs and, since the 1970s, made start-up companies and small and medium enterprises one of the key drivers of innovation and economic development in US and other Anglo-Saxon countries (Florida and Kenney 1988).

The "mundane entrepreneurship" experiences under socialism proved to be crucially important in establishing an enterprise, because many enterprises operated in the "grey area", where formal rules and practises did not exist. In this operational environment enterprises utilized the *blat*-type networks for gaining knowledge about buyers, sellers, and money. Many of the new enterprises continued to fill the gaps in the provision of services and consumer goods; enterprises bought and sold used cars, pirate computer programmes, metals, tobacco, etc. Social networks with foreigners and foreign companies proved to be a vitally important precondition for a successful business; they provided entrepreneurs with starting capital, know-how and open doors to foreign markets. As noted earlier, for many entrepreneurs the enterprise was not just an opportunity to get rich, but a way to cope under very insecure economic and social conditions or even to avoid poverty. In the turbulent early years of post-socialism the entrepreneurs frequently changed their branch and type of enterprise. Typically, they started as owners of micro enterprises and gradually accumulated capital for a more serious business.

We would argue, however, that the *blat* positive impacts did not extend beyond the personal networks and, on the contrary, *blat* relations fostered closed social networks and limited trust or reciprocity, while creating and reproducing an attitude of suspicion towards the "outsiders". The complex networks of *blat* did certainly play an important role in the establishment of private enterprises already during late socialism and during the first years of transition, when a large number of small and medium-sized enterprises were established by utilising social networks of friends, family members, and former colleagues. Yet the legacy of *blat* made difficult the establishment of larger business networks and of trusting relationships with those outside the 'friendship circles' and eventually the overall increase of trust as precondition for an efficient capitalist economy (see also Hsu 2005, 314-323).

Below we will consider in more details the different forms of entrepreneurship that took place in the former socialist countries in the late 1980s and, after 1989, with the legalization of private ownership, were transformed into true capitalist enterprises. Yet to understand how this painful transformation took place and the largely unexpected difficulties the post-socialist entrepreneurs had to face, we need to expand still further our understanding of the functioning of socialist societies and their economies. The understanding of socialist entrepreneurship only as compensating the 'failures of the Plan' cannot explain these difficulties or the specific dynamics of socialist economic development. Two critical issues are to be discussed here: 1) the ability of communist leaders (the nomenclature) to fulfill the entrepreneurial function, hence to serve as the main engine of innovation and 'forceful growth' (Kornai) in the earlier stages of socialism, and 2) the specific 'Sacred and Profane' as the immediate basis and horizon of economic actions in socialist society. Both the social strata of the nomenclature and the socialist 'sacred' did not disappear overnight after the fall of Communism, and this fact had major effects for the process of transition.

Joseph Schumpeter's Forgotten Ideas about Communist Leaders as Entrepreneurs

With its publication in 1912 (and especially its revised English edition in 1934), Schumpeter's *The Theory of Economic Development* shed new light on the mechanism of economic development in the capitalist market economy, preparing the advent of the economics of technical changes as an autonomous economic discipline (see Rosenberg 1976, Nelson and Winter 1976, Dossi and Freeman 1988).[6] In an earlier article, one of us argued that Schumpeter's theory about the role of entrepreneurial activity as the driving force of economic development in the market economy contains major premises, concepts, and explanations that provide important keys to understanding the development in non-market economies as well, more particularly, the economies with centralized planning and state ownership in Eastern Europe, Russia, China, and some other countries (Tchalakov 2003). The first argument supporting this claim is the fact that Schumpeter explicitly compares the market economy with private property with non-market economies without private property, and he expresses in passing some ideas about the mechanism of economic development in what he calls 'communist' economy. Secondly, Schumpeter's theory is relevant to the study of rapid industrialization (in fact 'industrial transition') in most of the former socialist countries, since it is not a theory of equilibrium, but of *development*, and "development", "progress", "leap", "catching up with", etc., were not only ideological slogans, but the core of the economic efforts of socialism. As Janos Kornai points out in his *Political Economy of Communism*, what he calls 'forceful growth' is "the

[6] A few years later Frank Knight (1921) introduced the important distinction between risk and uncertainty in economy as a tool for distinguishing the truly entrepreneurial behavior. Martinelli adds to this line of development the contributions of Israel Kirzner, made many decades later, who defined the entrepreneurial competition as a discovery process and stressed the role of alertness, creativity, and judgment as inherent features of entrepreneurship and economic action in general (Martinelli 1994: 485-86).

type of growth typical of the system", one of the fundamental features of classical socialist economy (Kornai 1992: 193).

In brief, the main findings of Schumpeter's *The Theory of Economic Development* that bear on the problem of economic development in market economies could be summarized thus:

- The distinction between 'circular flow' and 'development' is fundamental for the capitalist economy. In the former, the economic system functions in a 'static' state, as a 'routine' along the beaten track of 'past cycles'. 'Development' signifies a specific class of economic changes - the radical, abrupt changes in production.
- The source of development is the 'functioning in a different way', i.e. the introduction of innovations (new combinations). Because the new combinations are always more profitable, a key aspect of 'economic development' is the competitive elimination of the old forms of production. This process of 'creative destruction' is a fundamental trait of capitalism.
- The introduction of innovations is impossible without the function of the entrepreneur. The only contribution of entrepreneurs is their 'will and action' in channeling the existing production resources along new tracks. But the entrepreneurs could not implement new combinations without resources, i.e. they must have
- Access to capital - already existing or created ad hoc; this explains
- The essentially different role of credits when the economy functions in a regime of development. Creating means of funding 'ex nihilo' (through an abundance of credit tools) and thus ensuring credit to entrepreneurs, the banker seems to 'suck value from the future' into the present economic cycles, and hence makes them more dynamic.

On the basis of this orderly theoretical scheme, Schumpeter considers the following *specificities of the innovation processes in the non-market (socialist) economies*:

1) The important difference concerns the *entrepreneurial function.* This specific combination of 'will and action' is a type of leadership; it demands qualities possessed, as a rule, *by a limited circle of individuals*. This leadership is needed not only to break the routine and tradition, but also to overcome the adverse reactions of the social environment in which the new combination is carried out: the resistance of endangered producers ousted from the market

by the new combination, winning over consumers, finding allies, etc. Precisely because these are rare qualities, providing the possibility for *every potential entrepreneur* to possess [though temporarily] the resources necessary for the implementation of new combinations, i.e. access to credit, was a key condition for economic development.

In the *Theory of Economic Development* Schumpeter quotes two cases of non-market economy: a) the isolated kingdom where all the means belong to the lord, b) the isolated communist society in which the central authority possesses all commodities and labor resources and determines all commodity values. What is common to both of the two cases is that *some individuals enjoy absolute control* over the means of production. They expect no production cooperation, nor do they provide possibilities for making profit to other economic agents. So the problem of access to resources necessary for carrying out the new combinations "... does not exist in a non-exchange economy even if new combinations are carried out in it; for the directing organ, for example a socialist economic ministry, is in a position to direct the productive resources of the society to new uses exactly as it can direct them to their previous employments". (Schumpeter 1934: 68) Hence follows the assumption that 'communist leaders' or the 'central organ' can play the role of entrepreneurs *directly*, without using bankers as middlemen. In the case where the banking system is formally preserved but is controlled by the leaders, the latter combine both functions: of entrepreneurs and of bankers.

2) This leads, however, to the *narrowing down of the social basis of entrepreneurship*. The direct and absolute control on behalf of the communist leaders over resources deprives the remaining economic agents of the possibility to carry out independent entrepreneurial activities. They are economically unable to become entrepreneurs. Having in mind that only a limited circle of individual possess the qualities needed to become entrepreneurs, the narrowing down of the social basis has major long-term effects on the rates of innovations and hence on the rates of economic development in a communist economy.
3) The direct control by the communist nomenclature over the necessary resources creates *an essentially different situation as regards risks and the speed of introducing innovations*. In the market economy the entrepreneur must first persuade the banker and gain his confidence before getting the necessary credit. The conjuncture on the credit market has a strong impact on the rates

and scope of entrepreneurial activity. In socialist non-market economy all this is non-existent. If he so chooses, the leader may always supply the necessary resources, even risking thereby to hold back or worsen the living standards of the other social groups.

4) Another important consequence is the *disappearance of the phenomenon of 'creative destruction'*. In a market economy with private property, the profit comes to the entrepreneur only after it has made its way through competition - it is not only competitively distributed among bankers and owners of capital, but its very existence stimulates the next waves of surrogate entrepreneurs who, attracted by the initial success and monopoly profit, imitate the First Innovator, 'steal' a bigger or smaller portion of the profit, until they fully exhaust it (the new combination has 'aged'). The communist leader's direct control over resources in a non-market economy does away with competition and economic agents related to it – the bankers and other autonomous entrepreneurs.

There are two consequences for the socialist economic development stemming from this. On the one hand, the fusion of the functions of entrepreneur and banker abolishes barriers before the quick introduction of innovations. On the other hand, however, it also takes away the pressure on sectors working under old combinations. Schumpeter maintains that in socialist economy new and old combinations can exist in parallel and profit may be distributed among them. The complete restructuring of the sector on the basis of the new, more effective combinations is a matter of authoritative, administrative decision, rather than a competitive pressure.

Why did these ideas of Schumpeter about the entrepreneurial function of communist leaders (the nomenclature) have so little influence on subsequent economic analyses of these economies, up until 1990, when they were first applied by Peter Murrell in 1990? In my view there are important reasons for this.

Let us take for example the account of the 'inherent' deficiencies of the administrative economies' capacity for innovation, as discussed in Amann and Cooper's (1982) book on *Industrial Innovation in the Soviet Union* (see also Berliner 1988; Kornai 1992):

> "… This fundamental problem of harmonization is evidently and exceedingly a troublesome one in all societies. In Western countries it is ameliorated to some extent by the fusion of science and production within large industrial firms; many of the problems still exist but the close proximity of the two sides induces some modification of behavior… In the Soviet context neither the structure of incentives, nor the organizational framework encourages harmonization of scientific and industrial

> objectives. Soviet industrial enterprises tend to play only a minor role in research and development... [and] by far the largest proportion of industrial R&D is carried out by specialist institutes which are separate in both an organizational and geographical respect from industrial enterprises… What this can mean in practical terms is exemplified vividly by the case of the AKESR range of industrial control instruments. The initial research was done in Moscow; the experimental plant was set up in Smolensk, 380 km to the West; preparation for production began near Kazan, 1200 km from Smolensk; and the final manufacture plant was located in the Western Ukraine, 2200 km from Kazan." (p.15).

When reading such texts, the reader is left with the tedious impression that they completely miss their target, finding *only relative differences* between administrative and (corporate) market economy, referring to the mysterious instances such as 'deeper sociological reality', or transferring the opposition between the two system to a political and ideological ground.[7] Having fallen into a similar situation, in his study of Eastern European foreign trade Peter Murrell articulated the problem in the following way:

> "…Much of the discussion of the properties of the socialist economies, both academic and popular, is cast in terms that are directly derived from the standard paradigm of Western economics – the set of ideas that economists call neoclassical economics… By applying neoclassical theory in an empirical framework, I sought to discover the characteristic features of socialist economic behavior, but as the analysis proceeded, it became clear that marked differences between the two types of economic systems were not a significant element of the results derived from the traditional economic models. Once the empirical analysis stepped outside the confines of these models, however, distinctive features in the behavior of the socialist economies became apparent… In explaining the results of the

[7] "From the 1930s to the 1950s, distinguished scientists with Marxist sympathies – like Bernal, Blackett and Joliot Curie – argued persuasively that public ownership and central planning were better able than the capitalist system to mobilize R&T for economic and social progress… Indeed, one former economic advisor to President Eisenhower wrote the book entitled *The Price of Freedom*, in which he argued that the pluralism of the capitalist system could not hope to compete with the centrally planned system in mobilizing resources for investment, education and ambitious technical advance." (Pavitt 1995: 44) The so-called redistributive theory of socialist economy also fails to provide a convincing explanation of the observed phenomena in socialist technological development, maybe because it also shares the basic assumption of neoclassical economics (see Szelenyi, Beckett and King, in Smelser and Swedberg 1994, pp.234-251).

> empirical analysis, I have sought refuge in a Schumpeterian theory of economic behavior." (Murrell 1990, pp. 3-4)

Peter Murrell's book was one of the signs of the revival of interest in Schumpeter in economic literature in the West and was part of the 'vogue of entrepreneurialism' (Shmulyar-Green 2009, 42-43; see also Swedberg 1998). More recent empirical studies of the real functioning of communist economies during the decades between 1917 and 1989 have confirmed most of Schumpeter's ideas, adding some new elements to the original model, such as *militarization of the economy*, *specific patterns of foreign trade*, *economic functions of the secret intelligence services*, etc. (see Hanson and Pavitt 1987, Murrell 1990, Kornai 1992, Revol 1994, Tchalakov 2003b).

Yet there are two other aspects of these economies, which Schumpeter's model fails to take into account, but which are of crucial importance in understanding entrepreneurship under socialism and post-socialism. His failure is related to Schumpeter's *1) neglect of science and technologies as a key source for innovation* and 2) *his perception of "communist leaders" as a homogeneous group.*

The Missing Link between Invention and Innovation: From Emerging to Stabilized Techno-economic Networks

Schumpeter's model takes for granted the source of innovation (invention, discovery). He notes that "... it is no part of entrepreneurial function to 'find' or to 'create' new possibilities. They are always present, abundantly accumulated by all sorts of people. Often they are also generally known and being discussed by scientific or literary writers. In other cases, there is no need to discover them, because they are quite obvious." (Schumpeter 1934: 87). This assumption ignores major aspects of the relation between the process of discovery and innovation. Recent studies in the fields of the economy of technical changes have revealed a close interdependence between public investment in science and education, and the heavy 'infrastructure work' that mediates assimilation of relevant discoveries into the economy. This process unfolded after World War I and even more after World War II, when new industrial branches emerged on the basis of the latest scientific and technological achievements. So we have to take into consideration the links between production of new scientific and technological knowledge and its integration into the economy, simply because a large part of the entrepreneurs had academic titles and working experience at universities, research institutes, and industrial laboratories. *The socialist economies emerged in precisely these conditions* and it is no coincidence that, for several decades, "mastering the latest achievements of science and technological progress" was both a basic ideological slogan and the immediate practical task of these economies.

The mechanisms of 'translation' between technological solutions and the logic of the market, advanced by the *techno-economic networks* (TEN) approach,[8] are based on the understanding of scientific and technological knowledge as a unity of three interrelated elements: 1) codified knowledge (objectified in scientific texts, formulas and diagrams); 2) technical artifacts (scientific equipment) that corroborate this knowledge; and 3) skills embodied in scientists and engineers as the ability to use scientific texts, operate scientific equipment, and interpret and compare data and texts. The development of sciences and technologies implies the establishment and maintenance of a network of interrelated local research centers (laboratories), among which the above elements (scientific texts, artifacts and accomplished scholars) circulate as mediators. This expensive process is in constant need of large investments. The traditional view of scientific and basic technological knowledge as a universally accessible "public good" is thereby changed. *Only through the local level of investments can this knowledge become a public good* (Callon 1994). One can benefit from the announcement of a new scientific discovery or a new patent only if one has been prudent enough to invest in relevant workforce and equipment at the right time. Hence the development of science and technologies resembles an oligopolistic market where only those can "appropriate" the results of research who maintain a high level of investment in science and related industries.

The analysis of the initial development of socialist economies shows that their key strategy was to copy and diffuse innovations that had already proved successful in the developed (Western) countries, rather than to develop their own, original scientific and technological products. The 'transfer' of entire industrial branches became the main form of innovation activity. There were few attempts to introduce original innovations until the next, 'mature' stage of the socialist economy. The inference that "*technological progress in the classical socialist economy entails only the copying of innovations in the advanced capitalist states*" (Kornai 1996:

---

[8] The TEN approach is part of *actor-network theory* (ANT), an influential trend in the social study of science and technology, developed since the 1980s. More on ANT at http://www.stswiki.org/index.php?title=Actor-network_theory_(ANT) and http://www.lancs.ac.uk/fass/centres/css/ant/antres.htm

278) implies the need to create conditions for the simultaneous transfer of the three interrelated elements of science and technologies.

Very important in explaining this process is the notion of *"state of the techno-economic network"* (Callon 1996) and the distinction between *emergent networks* (emergent configurations) and *stabilized networks* (consolidated configurations). When new radical innovations are introduced (when new techno-economic networks emerge), knowledge and skills are in rivalry and can be appropriated – here the codified statements (publicized discoveries or patented engineering projects) that come fresh from the laboratory are externally contestable just like any other commodity and are *not* commonly accessible to all. Instead of separate and well established artifacts, competent people, and a codified text ('information') accessible to the entire scientific and engineering community, we have a fused set of 'statements+instruments+embodied skills' as a unique 'form of life'. Initially this set exists in only one specimen, and in order to transfer the innovation you have to reproduce the set in its entirety. As this process advances, however, mutual interests become stable and the networks intersecting them spread out and solidify, whereby the statements gradually become 'public goods' accessible to all. The emerging configurations are transformed into *stabilized networks*!

The stabilized techno-economic networks reveal a different world, in which many places possess the same instruments and people with similar embodied skills, all available and open to mobilization. They help communicate meaning and utility to the statements that circulate inside the network. Within such a configuration scientific statements are a public good and we have a kind of 'universalism inside the network'. In this structured and stabilized world "…the programs of the different economic actors (corporations, governments, etc.) precede action and set its size and shape. To some extent, they are mutually replaceable because the actors know each other's objectives and mobilize similar competences. Every program engages a certain amount of resources and can establish a relation between them and the expected objectives. The expectations are rational: the actors possess identical capabilities and, therefore, their estimates of the consequences of the action, the program, etc., are similar. As a result, the behavior of the competitors becomes predictable…" (Callon 1996, 51).

For the people socialized in the former socialist societies, this citation sounds rather familiar – objectives and priorities are clear-cut and definite, resources can be estimated and programmed. But why 'programs'? We can safely call them 'plans': *five-year plans, annual plans, etc.* These plans could then be reduced to tasks, and behind each task is a set of actors, each with their rights and responsibilities. This can be illustrated by

Lenin's well-known definition - "*Communism is Soviet power plus electrification of the whole country*!" which, after the October Revolution, was applied in his GOELRO plan for all-encompassing electrification of Soviet Union.

When a socialist country is building its industry, it is actually in a situation that can be defined *neither as an emergent nor as a stabilized network.* On the one hand, its industry is not yet part of a "long and stabilized network", and here information, skills and artifacts are yet to be established. On the other hand, however, the process of their establishment differs significantly from the emerging networks, because the artifacts, skills and information are already known, even though in foreign countries. Hence, in the industrializing socialist society the three elements must be "transported" together. However, along with this, socialist entrepreneurs were saved from the risk of not knowing exactly what should be transported, what behavior "leads to identifiable results", etc. In a way they resemble the 'second movers', the surrogate entrepreneurs in capitalist economy that are copying the original innovations.

It is precisely at this stage, in the conditions of 'clearly defined goals' and 'predictability of resources' that the advantages of administrative coordination over the market in terms of mobilization and control of the resources are displayed. It is the time when the removal of the inherently capitalist barriers to entrepreneurial activity produce positive effects – the communist elite enjoys freedom of action that is not possible in the capitalist economy: the adversaries of the system, and hence competitors, are ruthlessly crushed; due to the communist propaganda, most of the working people are "disciplined and ready to make sacrifices" in the name of the "bright future". Most importantly, the leader knows in advance the industrial path to follow, i.e. it is possible to plan!

It might be that *the socialist project was possible precisely because of the specific situation in the countries peripheral to capitalism.* The catchphrase "Communism is Soviet power plus electrification of the whole country!" fully communicates the essence of this project. In the course of thirty years (1874 – 1904) a galaxy of inventors and industrialists made numerous experiments (Edison, Westinghouse, Tesla, Siemens, Gantz, etc.) and huge resources were spent, until electrification stabilized in a form that has remained unchanged ever since: alternating and *not* direct current, generation of power at the source of raw materials, and long-distance electricity transfer along high-voltage transmission lines, daytime consumption (through AC electric engines) to make up for the evening demand (for lighting, etc.), etc. (see Thomas Hughes' *Networks of Power*). It was only after those thirty years of experimentation was accomplished that a Lenin could step forth and pronounce the famous phrase encouraging millions of people to perceive the rightness of the course and follow it.

With the establishment of Socialism after WWII a peripheral European country like Bulgaria or Soviet Estonia could not profit from scientific and technological learning unless it had invested previously in its own science and technologies and had built its own industry to 'appropriate' the relevant scientific and technological knowledge possessed by an oligopoly of developed industrial countries. These smaller countries had to: 1) train a large number of specialists, competent engineers, and researchers; 2) set up laboratories, engineering departments, and information infrastructure; and 3) build their own industrial facilities. After these investments were completed 'all of a sudden' the scientific knowledge published in literature became useful and industrial espionage became important: now there were specialists capable of deciphering the stolen formulas or copied designs, R&D units to do reverse engineering work, and industrial facilities to produce the prototypes. In these two countries the process that made this possible lasted for almost two decades, from the late 1940s to the early 1960s.

Now we are able to outline a specific linear dynamics of socialism, and to Kornai's two-phase development of socialist economy (the stage of 'forced growth' and that of decelerated development, stagnation, 'zastoi') we should add *an initial phase of creating the necessary infrastructure* (educational, scientific, technological) prior to the phase of "forced growth" (Tchalakov 2002). This is the stage of the country's integration into the global technological-scientific network of the developed industrial states, which makes it possible to capitalize the innovations introduced in the developed countries and gradually become economically more or less comparable with them. These countries seemed ready to enter upon the next stage of economic development, when they were going to rely on their own original projects and innovations as well.

The Internal Divergence of Communist Leaders

Contrary to what Schumpeter describes in his model, the communist nomenclature appeared to be split into different camps not only vertically, but also horizontally. The dividing lines between and functions of, the different groups varied during the different stages of evolution of socialism. Hence the entrepreneurial behavior of the leaders varied - the internal struggle and constellation of forces between different camps of the communist nomenclature strongly influenced the speed and direction of economic development. The recent developments in the so-called 'historical sociology of socialism' have revealed an interesting dynamics of socialist economies, *the pendulum movement* from total dominance of administrative coordination (i.e. taking away power from mediators like commodities and money) to the rise of 'second networks' (i.e. weakening the power of hierarchies and partial restoring the power of commodities and money) and then back again (Bundzhulov 2002, 2003, Deyanov 2003, Mozny 2003, Raychev 1985, 2003, Tchalakov 2003, 2005).

The Bulgarian sociologist Andrey Bundzhulov points out that the expropriation of capitals that followed the October Revolution "changes the very essence of power: from anonymous, fluid and dispersed, as Foucault describes it (Foucault 1986), it becomes the personified and robust power of the big Apparatus". Following Janos Kornai, he adds that power is now concentrated in a homogeneous and transparent ('superconductive') political structure, whose focal point is Stalin. However, Bundzhulov claims, Stalinist power is 'modern', in the sense that it is based on Party, Ideology, and Plan, extensively uses modern technologies, and maintains the modern institutions it has inherited – state, school, industrial enterprise, prison, etc. (Bundzhulov 2002). In fact, the socialist society incorporates many of the achievements of capitalism and, by re-defining them, it manages to establish complete control over (almost) all fields of social life and turn them into mere 'resources' for the execution of the socialist Plan. These transformations have far-reaching consequences and impact upon the possibilities of introducing innovations in the economy.[9]

According to Bundzhulov there was a difference between the initial communist project of Lenin and the subsequent Stalinist model, a difference that is of crucial importance for the way innovations were introduced in the economy. The Stalinist model, he claims, created tension within the communist nomenclature! Unlike Kornai, who considers the communist economic elite as just one part of the all-encompassing administrative system (Kornai 1992, pp.338-341), Bundzhulov argues that *the division between 'economic' and 'political' nomenclature (Party nomenclature in the narrow sense) was a key feature of the Stalinist model.* As it often happens in social sciences, he found the best formulation of his thesis in a literary work - the novel of the late Soviet writer Anatoliy Rybakov, *The Children of Arbat*:

[9] In the next section we describe some of the key aspect of the specific socialist modernity or rather deviance from the "modernization path" (see Kivinen and Nikula 2006).

> "... Lenin was aware of the importance of the apparatus. However, he chose to strengthen the state apparatus because he needed its support to perform as head of the government, while Stalin relied on the Party apparatus.... Stalin introduced strict control over the state apparatus (which executed primarily economic functions) through newly fledged Party structures. The Party apparatus had to control all other apparatuses in the country, including the economic one, and above all the one in industry, because it had the most independent, educated and pre-eminent cadres." (Rybakov 1987, pp. 250-251, p. 266)

To put it briefly, in Lenin's model the Party apparatus complements the role of the state and the economic apparatuses, while in Stalin's model the latter is controlled by the party nomenclature. Alex Nove defined the essence of the change in the following way:

> "Men of rank in the Soviet Union happened to be identifiable through the appointment system, which was developed by and under Stalin… A British analogy would be administrative civil service, except that the Soviet list, like the power of the Soviet Party, is all-embracing. It covers officers of the Party itself, civil servants, ministers, mayors, secretaries of musicians' societies, censors, trade union officials, generals, managers, editors, and collective-farm chairmen. No matter who is supposed to appoint or 'elect' them, a Party committee (in all important instances *the personnel department* of the central committee) is in fact the body which hires and fires [italics ours]" (Nove 1981: 51).

However, when analyzing the nomenclature, Bundzhulov uses Pierre Bourdieu's sociological theory and 'extended' notion of capital to describe the actors' behavior in various social 'fields'. In the socialist society it is the political (not the economic!) capital that plays a fundamental role and promotes the "nomenclature" as the main power group in society:

> "The nomenclature… is formed of circles whose significance is determined by the extent of their access to the political capital. Within the framework of this general premise, the different circles have a privileged access to different resources: economic, ideological, organizational, cadres, information, etc. They intertwine and interchange, compete and enhance each other". (Bundzhulov, lecture 2)

As seen already from Nove's outline above, the privileged part of the nomenclature is the *political (Party) nomenclature,* comprising organizational (personnel) and ideological departments plus State Security services as their 'right hand' (in every socialist country the secret police was directly subordinated to the top political leadership). Among them the organizational departments play a leading role, since they concentrate the whole information about the cadres (inquiries, personal and service records) and control them.

The key distinction is between the economic and the political nomenclature, for empirical studies reveal that here was the main conflict in the socialist society. According to Bundzhulov, the cause of this conflict was not the "nature" of the socialist system, but the specific mutation of the original Leninist model. In this model, it was not the "apparatus" as a whole but only part of it – the economic and especially the industrial apparatus of 'independent and highly accomplished grandees', which was able to carry out innovations (new combinations) in the economy. On the contrary, Stalin, with the intent to restrict the 'excessive' power of the economic nomenclature, built a special party apparatus to duplicate it: next to the economic nomenclature were the political (in the narrow sense, organizational/personnel and ideological) departments of the Communist Party, which guaranteed the system would stay integral and would be 'transparent' (that is accessible to the ruling top at every point). Hence this new division inside the nomenclature stretched in parallel with the administrative hierarchy from top to bottom – now the differences and even split within the nomenclature emerges at every level of the hierarchy and not, as Kornai put it, only between the lower and the higher levels (see also Grossmann 1963: 118). Hence, starting from their 'invention' by Stalin in the late 1920s and until the end of socialism in Eastern Europe, the economic and political nomenclatures were often in opposition to each other, which sometimes escalated into severe conflicts. The dynamics of their relationships took the form of *pendulum oscillation between a strengthening of administrative coordination* (i.e. the deactivation of the modern mediatory structures - commodity-money relations and market, bourgeois law, and democracy, the bourgeois mass media, the bourgeois forms of life) that the political nomenclature stands for, and *introduction of 'reforms'* (i.e. the partial restoration of some of the elements of the capitalist economy and society, often disguised under ideologically acceptable terms such as 'personal' and 'cooperative' property, relaxing the mechanism of planning, providing greater 'freedom' of enterprises, etc.), pushed forward by the economic nomenclature seeking higher efficiency. (Bundzhulov 2003, Romsics 2007)

The history of socialism witnessed several attempts of the economic nomenclature to emancipate itself from the control of the Party nomenclature, and of their representatives to act as real entrepreneurs for their own sake (which is the main reason for its pendulum swing). The reforms also expand the social base of entrepreneurship by empowering ordinary peasants, workers, and technical intelligentsia, etc. to launch their own economic activities. As we will see in the stories given below, many of the post-socialist entrepreneurs gained their initial experience from the last wave of economic reforms and successfully transferred and developed this experience in the conditions of the emerging market economies. However, going too far with the reforms was a threat to the communist project Stalin put forth and to the dominant position of political nomenclature, which in turn increased its resistance to reforms and eventually swung the pendulum back. In the history of the Soviet Union we can distinguish several oscillations between launching of reforms and the subsequent hardening of the regime – Lenin's NEP and Stalin's regime, then the reforms introduced by Khrushchev and the reverse movement during the Brezhnev era, then Gorbachev's perestroika and the failed putsch in 1991. Similar pendulum dynamics of economic reform could be identified in other former socialist countries of Eastern Europe, and even in China[10].

The pendulum swing illustrates Schumpeter's idea that only communist leaders are in a position to foster economic development. However, having revealed the intricacy of the socialist hierarchies and the socialist system of distribution, *the historical sociology of socialism makes some rather futile attempts to explain the phenomenon of economic development under Socialism.*

As we pointed out above, according to Schumpeter, the entrepreneurial activity of the communist leader in the socialist economy may be regarded as a *third production factor*, along with labor and natural resources (the land). Given their direct control over the production factors, communist leaders who have introduced the new combination in the economy are *fully entitled to the whole profit* and do not have to share it with anybody else. Consequently, with the start of development and the large-scale introduction of new combinations in the economy (this happened in all socialist countries that started out from a relatively low level of development), the ruling elite obtained one more source of support for its economic policy – the communist leaders began to consider themselves as the real motive force of development (after forcefully depriving the autonomous individuals of this right) and *fully entitled to the lion's share of the profit.*

However, in the beginning of the 1970s, the rates of economic growth started decreasing and a decade later they fell below zero. At this point of history the internal differences between the various segments of the

[10] From Mao's cultural revolution – to Deng Xiao Pin & Zhao Ziyang reforms - to 1989 events (tightening of the regime) – to 1992 Deng Xiao Pin travel in South provinces and new wave of reforms. (see Zhao Ziyang 2009)

nomenclature (and the complex and contradictory relations between them) surfaced. To explain the events, we need radical changes in the Schumpeterian model of the economic development of non-market economies. If we stay with his initial model, the separate political nomenclature that Stalin had established appear absolutely unnecessary for economic development. The economic nomenclature could structure and reproduce itself quite independently. Meanwhile it can recruit people from the enterprises and universities and promote in the hierarchy those Party members who have proven successful in introducing innovations and in the development of the economy. After the imposition of the Stalinist model it appeared that *the economic nomenclature, just like entrepreneurs in the capitalist economy, faced certain limitations to their activity*. However, restrictions here were not imposed by bankers and competitors, but by the political nomenclature (i.e. the Communist Party's organizational and ideological departments, and the NKVD/KGB as their 'right hand').

In a grotesque way, the functions of the Party nomenclature resemble those of the bankers in capitalism. On the one hand they keep the economic apparatus under control, lest it begin to appropriate all the entrepreneurial profit for itself; on the other hand they penalize this apparatus in case of a failure of innovations, which is the socialist equivalent of bankruptcy for the private entrepreneur. On multiple occasions, upon failure (to meet the deadlines for implementing production capacities and products, to achieve the planned parameters, bad quality, etc.), economic leaders had to answer to the respective Party organs and often to the State Security. After being charged with negligence and 'wasteful practices', or, even more dangerously, with 'appropriation' and 'economic sabotage' (*vreditelstvo)*, hundreds of managers were sentenced to prison, especially during the first decades of Socialism. This process continued during the entire socialist period, as witnessed by the archival documents available now.

Presumably, during the first stage of accelerated development, this constellation had been advantageous for both the economic and political nomenclature - the economic apparatus needed the organizational and ideological apparatus in order to secure resources for the infrastructure and launch innovations in entire branches (something that Stalin did in his time); there were things that economy by itself would have failed to do: 'temporary' overexploitation of the peasants, a large-scale literacy campaign, creation of ample opportunities for secondary and higher education, development of research and information (libraries) infrastructure, scientific and technological intelligence, mobilization to observe labor discipline, etc. However, by the end of the period of 'accelerated growth' and during the third phase of decelerated development, the situation changed – the administrative system based on the Plan, on Communist consciousness, and on open or hidden Terror, began to slip, and the need for original innovations became indispensable.

But what does 'original innovation' mean? - It means that the future course of industrialization is not known in advance! Could anyone in the mid-1950s have possibly proclaimed: *"Socialism is Soviet power plus computerization of the entire economy!"*? It did become possible to say this and someone did say it, but… about 20 years later. For in the mid-1950s nobody was certain of this, not even in the developed West.[11] This, in turn, made it possible for cybernetics to be declared a 'bourgeois science' in the USSR, and deprived the few grass-root enthusiasts of the possibility of experimenting and opening the way for the implementation of the new technology into the economy.

In explaining the economic development in late socialism, a key question emerges: What happen to the nomenclature *in situations where it no longer had where to copy innovation from* and the socialist entrepreneurs found themselves in an insecure world of *emerging configurations*? Empirical analyses actually provide an answer to the question: *the nomenclature openly splits apart and the contradictions between its contingents come to the surface.* Then the official hierarchies block the economic development and a struggle between the separate wings of the nomenclature ensues. It also appeared that the earlier stages of industrialization, when the economic apparatus was controlled by the Party nomenclature, had negative long-term effects on its motivation for the kind of risk-taking that became much needed in the third phase.

Summing up the analysis so far, we can point out that during the first two phases of development of socialism (in 'initial phase' and that of accelerated growth in Kornai's model), the nomenclature as a whole monopolized the opportunities for entrepreneurial activity, but this occurred in a situation, in which it was clear enough where the economy had to go technologically - namely, it had to catch up with the developed capitalist West. In these phases there was little risk and growth rates were high. Gradually, however, the two systems drew closer and socialist economies entered their third phase. In terms of technology and organization of industrial and agricultural production, by the late 1960s

---

[11] However, the managers of IBM, DEC, and of several other private companies *believed* in it, because they detected an opportunity for real profits. Taking the risk, ten years later they made the new knowledge and new computer technology 'universally valid'. (Kidder 1981)

and early 1970s socialist countries had nearly caught up with the developed Western countries. But also during this period, crisis phenomena began to grow in socialist economies, precisely because in a system where the initiative for economic renewal could only be taken centrally, the dominating administrative system greatly hampered the opportunity for spontaneous local innovations.

This assertion must be accepted somewhat tentatively, since there were important differences between the different socialist countries with regard to their general level of scientific and industrial development. Karen Freeze, for instance, reveals the remarkable story of the design of a unique spinning machine that employed a spindleless technique and was created in the darkest days of Communism in Czechoslovakia:

> "... The irony in the creation of this machine is that we are talking about a unique project embodying superb management practices, applied decades before they were articulated in Western business schools, talented people, as well as the advantages of the command economy. This is also a history of pragmatism overcoming ideology, where technology diffuses on both sides of the Iron Curtain at a time when it seemed shut tight." The machine was called BD-200, the initials standing for the Czech term "bezvretenovane dopradani", meaning spindleless spinning with 200 spinning headstocks. The world debut of the machine was in 1967, when it won a tough competition with the leading European and Japanese firms. This machine conquered much of the textile industry for yarn production; it tripled productivity, facilitated work, and improved the working conditions of thousands of textile workers throughout the world. In the next decade the export of these machines supplied three fourths of the revenues in hard currency of Czechoslovakia. (Freeze 2007: 250).

Such examples serve well to illustrate the inability of socialist economies to implement original innovations on a mass scale and to impose them on a long-term basis on the markets. In this respect the reforms undertaken by the economic nomenclature had but one economic purpose: empowering the local agents, i.e. expanding the circle of potential entrepreneurs. As our 'triple' theoretical framework revealed, however, this move was not just 'restoring (or reintroducing) the principles of market economy'. Due to the massive 'infrastructural work' in building the techno-economic networks of modern industries, carried out by 'socialist entrepreneurs' from the economic nomenclature, the socialist societies – perhaps with the exception of the ones that had been the most developed prior to the imposition of socialism (Czechoslovakia, East Germany) - appeared radically transformed. They faced new, unprecedented challenges, and it was up to history to judge whether the simple empowerment of the local economic agents was enough and whether the decades of totalitarianism had not damaged the very core of economic behaviour.

In the next section we go deeper into the 'cultural matrix' of former communist societies as a motivational ground underlying the actions of the nomenclature and ordinary economic agents; this discussion will aim at outlining the specific connection between entrepreneurial activity and the socialist 'Sacred and Profane' as radically different from the 'Sacred and Profane' of capitalist societies.

The Sacred and Profane of Socialist Modernity

As we pointed out above, one of the key points stemming from Schumpeter's implicit theory of economic development in the non-market economy of communism was the assigning of entrepreneurial profit to the communist leaders. Based on more recent analysis carried out in the framework of historical sociology of socialism, we modified this point by stating that *not* the nomenclature as a whole, but a specific part of it – *the economic nomenclature* – were the real agents introducing the innovations into the economy and hence the bearer of this profit. Is the entrepreneurial profit, however, the same key motivational force of their efforts to introduce innovations in the economy, as it is for the capitalist entrepreneurs? Also, does the collective and the strong sense of adherence to the Communist Party have a bearing upon the individual action of socialist entrepreneurs? *And more generally – was the economic development in socialist society (and its key categories of ownership, profit, consumption, etc.) backed up by the same values and 'moral sense' as those in capitalist societies?* If there was a difference, how did it influence the entrepreneurs' behavior during the post-communist transition?

The widespread understanding of the nature of the socialist society is that it was modern, but in a different way. Let us look at the Parsonian understanding of modernity as an industrialized society in which modernisation plays an important role. For Talcott Parsons the Soviet Union represented a radical rationalization of the ultimate values, which resulted there in the disintegration of hereditary power, the decay of the domination of religion in society, rapid industrialization and urbanization, the expansion of education, and modern citizenship in the form of a wage worker society. The non-modern features of the socialist (Soviet) society included the power monopoly of the Communist Party, which undermined one of the cornerstones of modern society – parliamentary democracy. The political suppression applied in the economy was also a deviation from the "modernization path" in socialist society. The restrictions for research and education and selection of labour force according to non-meritocratic criteria were also clear evidence of the non-modern nature of this society.

In analyzing the Soviet type of modernization, we can start from the conceptual differentiation between the Sacred and Profane of Socialism made by Markku Kivinen. According to him the sacred element includes all the elements of the Modern in the socialist sense, and the distinction between the sacred and the profane can be summarised in terms of a set of fundamental contrasts.

Sacred	**Profane**
Science	Religion
Progress	Backwardness
Development of the forces of production	Poverty
Urban	Rural
Working class	Bourgeoisie
Party	Czar

Kivinen notes:

> "The Bolshevik faith in science derives from the Enlightenment. Just like the thinkers of the Enlightenment, the communists believed that the world was open for science to conquer. The achievements of the natural sciences and engineering were hailed as true miracles of science. But this requirement of scientific control was to extend to every aspect of social development as well. It was upon such a scientific foundation that the crusade towards a more advanced and affluent society was to be based. The key to achieving affluence was the development of the forces of production. This called for industry. People had to move into the cities, into the realm of civilisation and out of rural stagnation. The working class was the new dominant class that was to gather further momentum with industrialisation and urbanisation. At the vanguard of the working class, fighting for progress was the Communist Party, which brought together the spontaneous working class and science." (Kivinen & Nikula 2006)

In some important aspects the socialist modern did not differ that much from the "bourgeois" modern as defined by Weber, Durkheim, Marx, and many others after them. The *force behind social development was science*, which dismantled the role of religion, gave basis for the development of forces of production, increased people's level of knowledge. The greater development of the forces of production increased well-being, eroded poverty, and narrowed the gap between rural and urban; it promoted urbanization and an urban way of life.

To understand the stories that (post) socialist entrepreneurs are telling us, we have to reveal (at least partly) how this basic cultural code of Communism was 'translated' into their daily activities. In his analysis Kivinen points out the essential need to relate this cultural level (the "basic cultural code of Soviet civilization") to structures and strategies at other levels, such as class interests or power, but also to the field of economy. This is not an easy task, he points out, since the 'sacred' thus defined "...was in constant flux throughout the existence of the Soviet Union. *All sacred things were accompanied by a negative of problematic shadow*: demonization of reality, chaos, consumption, the peasant way of life, the nomenclature and the new middle class, and the NKVD. Since the strict duality that is typical of Russia lived on in the Bolshevik sacred, these shadows represented *a non-neutral area. They became taboos.* Hence the structure of Russian culture can be represented in the form of a triangle, the angles of which are the profane, the sacred, and the negative sacred, or taboo." (ibid., p. 184) The basic distinction between sacred and profane was complemented by the awareness of the tensions and problematic relationships between the socialist cultural code and its implementation in real social life with the resulting taboos.

What brought these taboos into existence were the *unintended consequences* of the implementation of the Bolshevik project. Initially these could have been passed and ignored, but with time "...as Parsons assumes, unintended consequences also unfold into complementary structural forms and institutions (Parsons and Shils 1951). Alongside the actual sacred there develops a specific complementary instance (an unthematized area or unintended structural feature" (Kivinen 2002, 185). Hence, taking into consideration the structures and institutions that emerge for the purpose of dealing with these unintended consequences, provides a peculiar complementary 'taboo' reality in each of the six sacred codes. The political process in Soviet type of societies, Kivinen claims, unfolds in the "strained field between the actual sacred and the complementary instances":

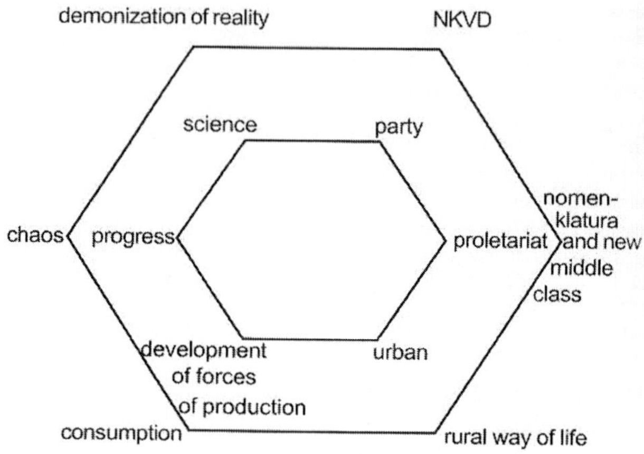

Figure 1 – The Bolshevik project and its distortions. From: Kivinen 2002, p.222

What are those aspects of socialist sacred and profane, and the taboos accompanying them, that bear upon the actions of socialist entrepreneurs, providing the underlying values of these actions and engendering the threats they must respond to?

We will start with the *collectivity* as a key aspect of the proletariat as the dominant, ruling class in the socialist society:

> "In the family, in the workplace, in the party, everywhere the proletariat represented steadfastness, discipline, collectivity… In general collectivism was an important value. Soviet ideology attached to collectivism such emotions as altruism, comradeship, friendship, devotion to the immediate environment and neighbours – and even democracy. *Making sacrifices for the collective has been one of the key themes of socialist realism. One of the biggest sins has been do stand up against the collective….* As early as the 1920s the main view in the party was that the threat of bourgeois and petty-bourgeois influences was ever-present… *any 'deviation' of way of life could be considered as bourgeois or petty-bourgeois."* (Kivinen 2002, 209-2010)

As the collectivity was an important part of the Bolshevik 'sacred', this entailed that individualistic economic endeavour could hardly be praised in this society. Just the opposite, the hero Pavel Korchagin's self-denial and total sacrifice for the collectivity in Nikolai Ostrovsky's famous novel *How the Steel Was Tempered* (1934) became an iconic model for the first generations of revolutionaries – workers, professionals, managers, Party leaders. "It is hard to deny their sanctity", Kivinen stresses. Obviously the cultural code that motivated the actions of those who planned and fulfilled the major steps of Soviet industrialization, creating the entire new industrial branches in the country involved the following: they served the Party and the working class, they fought poverty and bourgeois enemies, they developed the forces of production and promoted the progress of their communist fatherland. They considered their own personal achievement as a contribution to the development and progress of their country, to the glory of the Party and the Communist Revolution.

Closely related to collectivism is *modesty* in one's personal life and consumption. This often grew into real asceticism, especially during the first five-year 'plans of the development of the people's economy', where the scarcity of resources put the fulfilment of production needs first, while personal needs and consumption became secondary:

> "For the first generation Bolsheviks, the only source of real happiness was their participation in political work and production. The new virtues of proletarian collectivism were 'solidarity, unity, the subordination of specific interests to group interests'. As the main accent in the development of the Soviet economy was on heavy industry and people were called upon to work harder and to make further sacrifices with no promises of any rewards, this was a political choice whose roots lay in this kind of collectivism." (Kivinen 2002, 199)

Although in the decades that followed, especially after WWII, the ascetic attitudes were relaxed, "...the pursuit of individual happiness remained a somewhat problematic and delicate issue throughout the Soviet period... consumption and success appear at least as problematic issues on which people are expected to be at least modest" (ibid, 203).

Hence the entrepreneurial socialist strata consisted *not* of bold individualists who each sought their own personal profit as a guarantee for returning their loans and providing resources for further development of their enterprise. They were also different from the owners and managers of the perfectly bureaucratized giant industrial unit in the capitalist West Schumpeter claimed they were the 'true pacemakers of Socialism' – if socialist entrepreneurs from economic nomenclature gained, they gained as a group, and it was always possible they might be dismissed and prosecuted for various reasons – production failures, unfulfilled plans, excessive self-esteem, not following the political line of the top leadership:

> "...Although Soviet factories had a one-manager system (which Kaganovich described by saying that when the manager does his rounds on

> the shop floor, the earth must tremble), even managers could not feel safe. One of the deviations attributed to the managers was their bureaucratism. As many managers tried to contain the effects of the demonization of reality at their factories or to reduce the chaos caused by the Stakhanovism movement, the "beloved leader" himself would intervene (sf. Filtzer 1986, 199). Any specialists who tried to prevent the Stakhanovism movement from below, he said, would have their teeth kicked in. And he was not speaking rhetorically". (Kivinen 2002, 209)

This was the strange world the socialist entrepreneurs from the economic nomenclature lived in: believing they were serving the Party and the working class, working in tension, in quiet or even open conflicts with their comrades from the organizational and ideological departments and the NKVD, enjoying some privileges, which, however, were often just a little more than the remuneration of the best workers in their factories. Yet as socialist societies evolved, the tensions between its sacred and the taboos stemming from the unintended consequences of the Bolshevik project gradually changed the environment the socialist entrepreneurs of the economic nomenclature worked in – they found themselves on the same track as the 'blat' entrepreneurs from below, compensating for the failures of the 'Plan'.

Consumption, so important for 20th century capitalism and its welfare states had a dubious meaning in the Soviet cultural code. That was exactly what happened in the Soviet Union, especially after World War II and until the late 1970s: Soviet society became Westernized. Consumption patterns changed, Soviet-type societies became increasingly linked with the Western countries, and the Soviet-type middle class (managers, engineers, teachers, doctors, etc.) grew rapidly. These processes provided a basis for various types of entrepreneurship both within the Party and among the people. The years of Stagnation did not stop the entrepreneurial activities, they only changed their form and a larger part of these activities went underground. Finally, Gorbachev's reforms together with (relative) emancipation of economic nomenclature made a significant share of the informal entrepreneurship formal and officially accepted, and accelerated the process of disintegration of the centralized economic system, including from within the Party. After the collapse of Socialism, entrepreneurship did not newly arise together with the newly founded enterprises and according to Western advice – no, entrepreneurship was already there in full swing. The transition severely shook the operational and economic basis of entrepreneurship by dismantling almost the whole institutional basis on which the enterprises and the whole economy had operated. This social and economic turmoil revamped the entrepreneurial setting in most countries and did not differ very much from the experiences in Asia or Latin America, except for the pace of the changes and the fact that most of the processes were taking place concurrently. Gradually, however, the new basis for entrepreneurship was created, and turmoil was replaced by a strengthened social and economic regulation of entrepreneurial activity.

Entrepreneurship during the Posts-socialist Transition

Below we outline some key features of post-socialist economies, based on the *theoretical traditions outlined above*. We believe this outline will help the reader by providing a meaningful non-orthodox framework, and allow a better understanding of the data presented in the selected interviews.

The Strange World of Post-socialist 'Fluid Modernity'

The post-socialist transition completely changed the ideological and social basis (nature) of society. The Communist Party, which was supposed to possess the ultimate truth about society and represent the avant-garde of the social forces in society, was pushed to a marginal position by the transition and "thrown off the track of the sacred code" (Kivinen & Nikula, 2006). The symbolic power relations between the social classes were turned upside-down: the working class became virtually a taboo in social discourse, and the position of leading force in society was taken over by the middle classes. Among the middle classes of post-socialist society it was the entrepreneurs, owners of small and medium-sized firms that were believed to guarantee social stability and to create a pluralistic, wealthy society, based on the values of personal freedom, individualism, and decentralization of economic power (Brzezinski and Fritsch 1995).

In this context Zygmunt Bauman speaks about *fluid modernity*, which has taken over the previously existing solid modernity. According to Bauman, the embodiment of fluid modernity is the neo-liberal economic and social policies that were adopted in most post-socialist countries in the 1990s. In the new stage of modernity the sole engine of modernization and of development of the forces of production are believed to be the structures of the market economy – and not the Party, or Science, or the working class. The market economy Utopias are often based on the same kind of binary oppositions as Bolshevik projects: they too are defined by complete negation and demonization, this time, of the socialist era. (Kivinen & Nikula 2006) In the same vein as in the Bolshevik ideological project, the neo-liberal ideological project produces its own non-intended consequences, profane features, and processes. In the case of the Bolshevik project these features consisted of growth of nomenclature, of middle classes, of consumption, and the increasing influence of the secret police. In the case of neo-liberal project the individualization that was supposed to be the cornerstone value of new market-based liberal society, turned out to be mere egoism, devoid of respect for others, devoid of political, ethnic, or social tolerance. Competition has decayed into market authoritarianism and the domination of big conglomerates that control the whole value chain and the small producers or small and medium sized enterprises. Innovation and science have in many countries been crushed under the imperative of profit, which is evident in the high rates of brain drain of academics and the low wages of those who choose to stay. Consumption – previously one of the main features of the profane in Soviet society, and seen in it as the cause of growing petty-bourgeois values and way of life – has turned into a key element of the sacred in the conditions of fluid modernity of post-socialist societies. Bauman argues that Socialism lost the competition for satisfying needs, and that consumption has acted as a vehicle of fluid modernity. Paretskaya (2010) argues that middle class values had already begun to arise among Soviet citizens in the 1960s, when it became evident that ideological fervor was no longer enough to legitimize the socialist society; there were increasing signs that people wanted to be consumers. As a consequence, individualist values gained ground and led to Soviet consumerism, and to urban middle class patterns of consumption with strong Western influence (youth culture, mass media, and a "consumerist" way of life).

Another unintended consequence of neo-liberal project was the behavior of former political nomenclature, including security services' officers. Paradoxically, they interpreted neo-liberal project as chance to preserve their power, if not on ideological but on purely economic ground. Hence considered from the point of view of entrepreneurs, the post-socialist transition appears as a hostile environment of rent-seeking and assets-scrapping capitalism. After the 'velvet revolutions' in 1989, in most post-socialist countries the economic developments that followed were heavily influenced by the hidden program of this specific wing of the former communist nomenclature, which opportunistically used the "Neo-liberal Sacred' to implement a policy aiming to suppress the newly emerging economic agents (such as foreign investors, authentic entrepreneurs, etc.) and steer the economic processes in the direction it desired. This program, however, did not succeeded in all sectors of the economy. We could tentatively define *two complementary principles*, which, taken together, help differentiate the sectors 'conquered' by the representatives of the post-communist political nomenclature from the sectors in which 'authentic' entrepreneurs have a better chance to develop.

The first principle is the overall *profitability of the sector.* The political nomenclature as defined above, focused on the most lucrative sectors, such as production of mass consumer goods for the domestic market (tobacco, alcoholic beverages, including wine, petrol derivatives, pharmaceutical products, cosmetics and household chemistry, etc.), or on trade that delivers such goods (especially import), as well as on sectors that still have competitive advantages on the international markets – ferrous metals, wood and wood processing industry, heavy chemical industry, electric power industry, etc. Here we should add service sectors such as telecommunications and tourism, although their specific characteristics have led to some long-term constraints for pure rent-seeking strategies. Only a few very strong multinational companies have been able to limit to a certain extent the power of the political nomenclature in these sectors, often with the help of Western governments and after making serious concessions. However, the *low-profit sectors* - those producing manufactured goods or providing services for which there is a relatively limited demand; those having low prospects for export; those requiring significant investments and expensive maintenance; those with a long return cycle of profit, etc. – remained relatively free for entrepreneurial initiative.

The second principle is *the inherent resistance* (or more precisely rigidity) *of the sector to the rent-seeking and assets-scrapping strategies.* The political nomenclature may also be considered as a newcomer to the economy and from this point of view we can distinguish between *sectors with 'low entrance' and 'high entrance' barriers.* The former did not require specialized know-how or they implied know-how similar in kind to that possessed by the representatives of the political nomenclature (for example trade with consumer goods and petrol derivatives). In these sectors the representatives of the nomenclature have easily taken command positions and have been able effectively to manage their new business. The traditional industries of mass production like ferrous metal, heavy chemical industry, etc. should also be included in this group, because here the ability to control low-skilled employees (both in production and in the system of distribution) was a key asset, and it was relatively easy to sustain mass production of an acceptable quality. Usually the output here consisted of low-tech products that did not require special maintenance or the development of special services for customers. In addition to that, in these sectors the violation of the existing regulations, industrial standards, intellectual property rights, etc. was not punished, for the government institutions were submissive, and hidden control was exercised over the system of justice.

However, there were also sectors with *high entrance barriers*, in which the very production process and specificity of the products required specialized knowledge, and hence, the use of skilled labor and management; in these sectors the maintenance of trust between producer and his customers (or between service provider and his clients) was crucial for business. In the majority of such cases it was difficult for the political nomenclature to develop a sustainable business – for example in IT industry the most successful business of its representatives was to re-sell abroad the sophisticated equipment of electronics plants, imported previously with great effort across the embargo imposed by the West.

These processes varied among the East European countries, which made it difficult to identify this trend and prevented scholars from discovering early enough behind the neo-liberal rhetoric the indigenous synergy between economic and political processes that had been taking shape. The research task became even more difficult with the EU integration process started in the late 1990s, which involved institutional arrangements and policy prescriptions that added new variables of change to the specific political and economic situation in these countries. The Bulgarian case we outline below sheds light on the development in some other former socialist countries, as could be seen from some of the interviews taken in Latvia, Russian Karelia, and Former Yugoslav Republic of Macedonia.

Post-socialist Transition in Bulgaria

Here the rent-seeking and assets-scrapping capitalism originated from the events that had taken place during the last decade of socialism, a time marked by intensification of the struggle between the two key wings of communist nomenclature – the political and economic ones. With the reforms that had been gradually introduced in most socialist countries since the 1970s, the dominant positions of the political nomenclature were challenged by the increasing power of the *economic nomenclature*, i.e. the 'cadres' managing the economy - from the lowest position of directors of enterprises, through the managers of the large vertically integrated state 'combines', and to the heads of economic ministries and their officials. This nomenclature developed its own sense of unity, its own 'industrial ethos' and managed to establish itself as a group opposed to the political nomenclature.

From this point of view *the history of the higher echelon of the Bulgarian Communist Party was marked by several big clashes between these two wings, in each of which the political nomenclature overcame the economic one*. This happened first at the end of 1960s with the dismantling of the legendary economic cartel "Bulgarian Sea Fleet" (former TEXIM), when the founder and chief manager of the cartel, Georgi Naydenov was prosecuted and sentenced to jail under false accusations. A similar clash occurred in the beginning of 1975, when Prof. Ivan Popov – the man who had initiated the successful development of electronic industry and had later been made Deputy Prime Minister and a member of Politburo – was dismissed from all his positions and sent as Bulgarian ambassador to Switzerland. The high reputation of these men in Bulgarian society, especially among industrial managers, threatened the power of the Party's organizational and ideological departments, including the top leadership of the country. However, the economic nomenclature soon recovered and by the early 1980s it managed to create a special organizational structure, the Bulgarian Industrial Economic Association (BISA), which copied the structure of the Japanese Federation of Industrial Branch Organizations. BISA became very popular thanks to its initiatives aimed at optimizing economic development. It backed the attempts to relax administrative control, to allow small-scale private property in industry and agriculture, to enforce foreign economic relationships with Western corporations, etc. Remarkably, one of these initiatives was to boost the development of small and medium enterprises and to allow them greater autonomy in comparison with other socialist economic organizations. Some of these SMEs resembled Western spin-off firms – they operated using indigenous innovations or licensed Western technologies.

However, on the eve of the radical changes in November 1989, the economic nomenclature was once again defeated. In December 1988 Ognyan Doynov – a Politburo member, the most popular economic leader in the country and highly respected among Bulgaria's Western economic partners - was dismissed from Politburo. His removal was a sign that the same would befall his followers in the economic, state and Party apparatuses. Although a member of Politburo of the Bulgarian Communist Party and similarly to Prof. Ivan Popov, as a typical representative of the economic circles, Doynov never identified completely with the Party nomenclature. His memoirs contain a short section entitled "Some Injustices", where he reveals the system of repression against the economic nomenclature and discusses his attempts to defend punished directors of industrial enterprises. Todor Minkov, one of the economic leaders saved by Doynov, would later say: *"The truth was that in places where things were going well, State Security* (Bulgarian KGB) *always intervened and compromised the cadres"* (Doynov, 2003, p. 155-168).

So, unlike Hungary, it was the political nomenclature – whose representatives in their vast majority saw the economy through the optics of old Marxist political economy and lacked specific industrial managerial skills – that was destined to carry out post-socialist economic transformation in Bulgaria. Instead of opening the door to foreign investors, empowering the most talented industrial managers, and promoting the spirit of entrepreneurship among the economically active population, which for more than 50 years had been deprived of the possibility to become entrepreneurs (with property rights and fair access to credit), the representatives of the political nomenclature did just the opposite. They adopted a *strategy of converting their political capital into economic one* and successfully used the neo-liberal model promoted by the Western experts to suppress emerging entrepreneurs, to push out the socialist industrial managers from the positions they still possessed, and to impose their own rent-seeking and assets-scrapping strategy. This strategy included a number of interrelated measures:

- Gaining control over the country's financial system by appointing trusted people in the now independent bank system;
- Keeping the share of state property in industry large enough, while dismantling former vertically integrated structures (state combines) and establishing stringent control over the industrial managers of separate enterprises (via the bank system, by appointing trusted people, by means of specially created criminal groups, etc.);
- Exploitation of the state-owned plants by compelling their managers to buy raw materials and other supplies at higher price from specific suppliers and to sell their production at lower price to specific distributors;[12]
- Not allowing penetration of foreign capital for as long as possible;
- Suppressing the emerging independent entrepreneurs in other social groups by limiting their access to credit and forcibly pushing them out of the most profitable sectors;
- Controlling the legal system by appointing trusted people as magistrates, by introducing special legislation, and by cutting off the legal system from public control and accountability.

---

[12] The same process was observed in the last years of USSR and the early 1990s in Russia. The researchers call this process 'siphoning off' of profits from state enterprises through private commercial and financial intermediaries (Clarke & Kabalina 1994). See more on this in the next section.

The process of restitution, launched in 1992, that returned the property nationalized in 1947 to the former owners was slow and incomplete, and it was successfully used as an ideological cover for the real economic processes that were taking place. Worst of all, *the restitution mentality promoted by this process was practically identical with the economic philosophy of the political nomenclature.* It also implied rent-seeking capitalism; focusing public attention on the possession of property (most of which consisted in outdated material assets) instead of on the opportunities for making money through new ventures and on the related emancipation of banking from the political system through creation of conditions for fair access to credit.

By preserving its control over the new 'independent' public media, the former ruling elite consciously discredited the emerging patterns of entrepreneurial activity. They continued to spread the atmosphere of distrust towards private initiative and equated it with some sort of semi-criminal activity. Few positive examples of successful entrepreneurs managed to creep into the media.

Having accumulated significant financial and economic strength, however, it seemed that, similarly to their Russian and Ukrainian counterparts, the emerging Bulgarian post-communist oligarchy – as a result of the 'conversion strategy' of the former political nomenclature – would take complete control over the economy by privatizing the remaining lucrative economic sectors such as chemical and power industry, ferrous and non-ferrous metallurgy, and some others. Yet the internal conflict with the younger generation of Socialist Party leaders that came to power in the mid-1990s, excluded the emerging post-communist oligarchy from the process of mass privatization, so that some key industrial assets fell into the hands of foreign or previously unknown local economic actors. The political and economic clashes that followed, combined with grain shortages and high inflation, led to the mass civil unrest in the winter of 1997, to preliminary elections and a new democratic government, which in a few months closed down the 16 'drained' private banks, introduced a currency board, and launched the second wave of mass privatization. In few years only the share of state ownership in the economy fell from over 70% to below 30% and this seemingly ended the domination of the ex-communist political nomenclature.

However, it soon became evident that the former domination was replaced by a fairly similar in its effect 'democratic domination', where the anti-communist 'democratic' government exercised strict control over the privatization process and economy as a whole, favoring its own party apparatus. The state and political institutions were again used for the enrichment of a specific politically engaged group. After that, little changed under the next two consecutive governments, those of the ex-monarch Simeon Saxe-Coburg-Gotha and of the three-party coalition that succeeded him. In each case the initial hopes for a new (political) beginning soon waned and the governments continued to serve the selfish interests of powerful economic groups, each (partially) controlling certain sectors of the economy.

Hence the results of our research have shown that the initial 'conversion' strategy of the political nomenclature and other politically bound economic circles that followed did not succeed on a full scale. As evident by some of the interviews, some sectors provided sufficient conditions for entrepreneurship to emerge develop and grow. Their representatives came from different backgrounds – R&D centers in industry, industrial managers dismissed by the political nomenclature in the years before and after 1989, descendants of the former capitalist class that had regained their family property through restitution, or simply talented people with an entrepreneurial spirit who seized the opportunity for business in the new economic conditions, where private property was after all legally admitted. Being relatively invisible during the first years of transition and passing through great hardships, these entrepreneurs gradually increased their economic strength.

The integration of Bulgaria into the European Union that took place in 2007 has been an important source of changes in the country's post-socialist political system towards better democratic standards of governance, including some changes in the relationships between the political and economic spheres. Political and economic conditions emerged that allowed for the 'authentic' entrepreneurs from the local micro, small and medium enterprises to develop. Being relatively invisible during the early years of transition and passing through much hardship, these entrepreneurs gradually increased their economic strength. By uniting their efforts in newly founded branch associations, together with the emerging organizations of civil society, the newly established, (relatively) autonomous state agencies backed by EU institutions, and some (still limited) circles in legislature, in the last few years they have begun to exert pressure on the political system to change the established model of rent-seeking capitalism.

As result of these developments, today Bulgaria did not form oligarchic structures powerful enough to establish total economic and political control, like those in the Russian or Ukrainian cases. Nor have these Bulgarian structures become significant international economic players. Hence the country's economy entered a prolonged equilibrium between the *authentic entrepreneurs* on the one hand, and, on the other, a *'middle-sized oligarchy' connected with the former political nomenclature and newly emerged politically tied groups*. To these we should add the group of steadily increasing *foreign companies* in Bulgaria. They usually follow their own strategies, but it could be generally said most of them are on the side of the authentic entrepreneurs. Whether or not these processes will finally lead to the establishment of the *heterarchical type of democracy* (Bruszt 2001) is still unclear. Yet it is worth studying them, while simultaneously elaborating a theoretical framework able to explain the different developmental paths simultaneously available in the field, a framework that cuts across the economic, political, legal, and other fields of society.

The Last Years of USSR and Post-socialist Transition in Russia

In the Soviet Union similar processes started in the mid-1980s as a result of Gorbachev's economic and political reforms. The laws[13] that were supposed to boost consumer goods production and improve the productivity of the Soviet economy paved the way for "initial privatization" of productive capital through cooperatives and leased state enterprises.

These laws made possible the rapid and spontaneous (first wave) privatization[14] of state property – the process that Clarke & Kabalina (1994) and others have described as siphoning off of common property. The result was an intense proliferation[15] of private small and medium-sized enterprises. Clarke (1992) defined three types of spontaneous privatization in the Soviet Union during the period 1985-1989. The *first* of these were the private appropriation of property and financial assets of the Communist Party and the Komsomol by Party officials and the involvement of the 'new democrats' in the private appropriation of urban property; but these trends did not play a substantial role in the overall development of the economy or production. The *second* type took place through cooperatives and leased enterprises when managers transferred

[13] Law on Individual Labour Activity (1986) , Law on Cooperatives (1988)

[14] Clarke & Kabalina (1994, 2) note that "some kind of 'privatization' was implicit in the program of perestroika from the very beginning, as a necessary condition for any kind of economic stabilization."

[15] According to Radaev, the number of cooperative firms grew five-fold between 1988 and 1991.

profitable parts of state enterprises to their private ownership. However, this form was also not important, most of these firms being very small. The *third* and maybe most important form was the process of the siphoning off of profits from state enterprises through private commercial and financial intermediaries. These firms were the basis of most of the private fortunes created under the perestroika. These processes contributed to the development of many unintended consequences, such as the increased deficit of consumer goods: many cooperatives concentrated their operations in areas of quick and high profits, i.e. in illegal economic activities like smuggling. The lack of free markets resulted in a constant lack of materials, spare parts, financing, etc. (i.e. institutional failure). The economic role of cooperatives was very small, and two out of three of these were state-owned. (Liuhto 1998, 4)

Closely related to the Law on Cooperatives was the Law on State Enterprises which would free enterprises from the centralized control of various ministries. The state enterprises could be "privatized" in various forms: they could become independent state enterprises or independent divisions of state enterprises (Kiselev1990, 1). The state enterprises would imitate private enterprises – they would seek profits, become self-financing, and fill up the gaps in consumer good provision. They were free to make their own plans, decide what goods to produce, set prices and wages independently. Moreover, the workers were given the right to elect the managers. This reform likewise proved half-baked and led to many unintended results: enterprises remained highly dependent on the state sector for supplies, a situation that fostered the growth of the unofficial, "grey" sector of the economy when they tried to secure the necessary supplies. Enterprises were also dependent, and relied on, state orders, which meant that there was no need to improve the quality or find new buyers. This law legalized the de facto control of the managers of subsidiary firms over the state enterprises. As Clarke and Kabalina note, "enterprise managers saw privatization as the means of securing their economic independence and relative prosperity, which at that stage, was the almost universal concomitant of such independence." (Clarke & Kabalina 1994, 4)

In the privatization process that started in Russia shortly after the collapse of socialism, the Russian government, guided by advice from Western financial institutions, adopted the strategy of privatization to the labor collective. Sutela (1991) claims the main aim of this was to ensure rapid privatization; secondly there was a belief in the need to break the ownership position of the branch ministries in order to make the transformation irreversible. According to Clarke, for enterprise directors privatization was a means to legally ensure their independence and power over their enterprises. In order to guarantee optimal results, the "industrial nomenclature pressed increasingly strongly through a variety of channels, including Parliament and the official trade-unions, for privatization to the labor collective (or workers-management buyout) (Clarke & Kabalina 1994, 5)." This strategy was also supported by neo-liberal economists, for whom ownership as such was not the main issue. The demands of the enterprise directors were fully accepted in the privatization program of 1992, which kept the enterprises in the hands of the labor collective by allowing the latter to buy a majority (51 %) of the shares at a nominal price. The final stage in cementing directors' power and creating powerful oligarchs started in 1994 when the group of wealthy businessmen acquired a strong political leverage through a deal whereby oligarchs gave Yeltsin's administration financial support for the electoral campaign in exchange for temporary control over the biggest and most lucrative Russian enterprises (Shmulyar-Green 2010, 204).

The means used to acquire the majority of shares was through FIGs (financial-economic groups), established by industrial and financial managers and other members of the former Soviet elite. According to Shmulyar-Green, the financial elite - owners of large commercial banks - was the most powerful group in the FIGs and could dictate the terms of the country's economic development (Shmulyar-Green 2010: 205).

Evolution of Private Entrepreneurship in Late-Soviet and Post-soviet Estonia and Latvia

The evolution of Estonian entrepreneurship can be seen as an example of academic entrepreneurship: according to Venesaar (2006, 275), the researchers of the Estonian Academy of Sciences, Institute of Economics, were the first in USSR to start elaborating standards of economic activity for small enterprises. These designs were later tested in the new private enterprises. According to Venesaar, these experiments were a basis for "the resolution by the USSR Council of Ministers to permit state-owned enterprises to be founded in all the Union republics." (ibid) Liuhto (1996, 120) also considers that Soviet Estonia played an exceptional role in the Soviet economic reforms, because "*several experimental reforms were tested there from the 1950s onwards, until the disintegration of the Soviet Union. This 'guinea pig' role in these experiments brought Soviet Estonia and her enterprise sector slightly closer to the market economy mechanism than other Soviet republics*." One of the first experiments was the foundation for private entrepreneurship, which operated in 1985-1987.

Workers' cooperatives were the first steps towards private entrepreneurship in Estonia during the late 1980s and by 1987 there were more registered cooperatives per capita in Estonia than in any other Soviet republic. The boom of registration of organizations began in the end of 1991, and by the beginning of the following year the total number of enterprises was more than 35 000; by 1995 the total number of registered enterprises was over 83 000. However, a large share of these enterprises existed only on paper (the so-called shoe-box firms), and most operating and active enterprises were micro enterprises that employed only 1-2 persons. The fact that a large part of the enterprises did not pay any taxes and that the unemployment levels remained strikingly low during the years of rapid privatization indicate that a significant part of economic activity took place in the grey areas – illegal forestry, smuggling alcohol and tobacco, stealing and mediation for precious metals, moonlighting, and other forms of black economy.

The impact of joint ventures in late-Soviet Estonia was rather small in the beginning (as it was in the USSR in general), but with the passing of the Decree on Joint-Stock Companies, their numbers grew explosively from a mere 82 to 1100 within the following two years[16]. Even though the relevance of private or semi-private entrepreneurship in Estonia remained rather modest in economic terms, these reforms were significant in paving the way for genuine private entrepreneurship. After the two countries regained their independence, the Estonian and Latvian governments adopted the insider-privatization strategy: "the nationalist-oriented policies in relation to the large Russian speaking minority meant that the period of supporting broad employee takeovers of enterprises was very short" (Myigind 2000). Before independence employee takeovers implied that control was taken away from the central authorities in Moscow and passed to the Baltic Republics, "but as soon as this goal was accomplished the priority was to strengthen the position of the titular population and to find the most efficient ownership structure" (ibid). In the "small privatization", 80 % of small firms in Estonia became employee-owned and seven large enterprises were sold to employee ownership. Insider advantages were curtailed from 1992 onwards and discarded completely a year later (Myigind 2000, 5).

In Latvia the privatization started a year later than in Estonia and the small enterprises were privatized partly by municipalities and partly by the management of the enterprises. Similarly, in the privatization of large

[16] "In April 1989 Soviet Estonia had 26 registered foreign-owned companies, meaning one company per 60 000 Estonians, whereas the Soviet Union had at that time one registered joint venture per 800 000 people." (Liuhto 1996, 122)

enterprises the employees were favored for a short period of time, after which privatization was decentralized under the sector ministries. As a result, the majority of large enterprises were leased to insiders and only a minority of them was genuinely privatized before 1994, when the Latvian government adopted a similar strategy as that of Estonia. In both countries privatization took place through tenders, where investments, price and job-guarantees were the most important criteria (Myigind 1999, 5-6). Estonia used privatization of large enterprises as a means of acquiring foreign investments and in the tender process foreign capital had a strong position, because it had better access to capital, far better management skills, and established international business networks. By 1993, foreign owners had already privatized some of the largest enterprises in Estonia, and by the end of 1998 they had taken over one third of the enterprise assets included in the large privatization. During the years 1996-98 in Estonia the foreign share of purchase in privatization was 56%; in Latvia that share was 34% in 1995-1997. (Myigind 1999, 17)

So, unlike Russia, and similarly to Bulgaria, *the privatization of productive capital in Estonia and in Latvia did not lead to the formation of strong national oligarchs that could exert strong political influence.* Instead, political considerations led to a rapid (and almost complete) dismantling of the former Soviet production structures. In addition to political considerations, the fact that both Estonia and Latvia lacked domestic capital to carry out the necessary restructuring of the economy contributed to a strong position of foreign capital in the Estonian and Latvian economies.

Insiders got a strong position in many smaller enterprises and especially in those that were less capital-intensive and less lucrative in the eyes of foreign investors. A large share of newly created private enterprises was born as spin-offs of former larger units or through auctions of enterprises in the service sector. Former specialists and managers invested their privatization shares in woodworking, repair shops, bars, and stores. Firms were established by utilising social networks - friends, family members, former colleagues, etc. Many entrepreneurs started their business under very difficult and challenging circumstances: the banking system was underdeveloped and therefore loans were very difficult to obtain and interest rates were very high. In addition, many aspects of institutional development were only starting. The main obstacles in the development of entrepreneurship were the unclear legislation and the lack of information and training in many crucial issues, such as marketing, business finances, or supply channels. Entrepreneurship was also made very difficult by the lack of trust, security, and the uncertainty as to future developments in various spheres of society (political, economic, legal, etc.). On the other hand, many of these factors facilitated the development of unofficial entrepreneurship; since laws were lacking or underdeveloped, no rules existed for many issues of ownership of resources or premises, and legal control was random. During the first years of transition firms were generally very small and required very small starting capital, on the other hand, many firms operated in the "grey area", where formal rules and practises did not exist. Social networks proved to be a vitally important precondition for a successful business – networks provided entrepreneurs with starting capital, knowledge, and open doors to foreign markets.

The excerpt from an interview with a sawmill owner illustrates the ways in which many rural specialists became private entrepreneurs.

A furniture factory in Northern Estonia
The furniture factory houses the premises of the headquarters of the former collective farm, which was privatized in 1993. The director of the factory is the last director of the collective farm. He was trained as a mechanics engineer, but in vocational school he also learned the basics of carpentry. During the de-collectivization, the property of the farm was divided into separate units and those units were then privatized by employees of the farm. The director privatized the sawmill of the collective farm and he obtained the employees together with the sawmill: "*The one who started with some department, he would also take the people that used to work there... it was compulsory; it was in our reform plan. And so that firm started, in the beginning there was no need to have workers from outside*"

The "Wild West capitalism" phase of Estonian and Latvian economies gradually faded in the late 1990s when the different kinds of enterprise support systems started to evolve, which included more strategic planning, and stronger government intervention and services for businesses. This process would not have been so successful without the accession to the EU and the implementation of pre-accession programs like PHARE (Kuura 2006).

PART II

DIFFERENT ROUTES TO ENTREPRENEURSHIP: THE CASES

Five Groups of Entrepreneurs: a Short Outline

Our sample includes a total of 23 interviews from different periods of time (the earliest were taken in the mid-1990s, and the latest, in 2007-2008), different locations (Bulgaria, Russia, Estonia, Latvia, FYR of Macedonia), and related to different histories. We can divide these 23 interviews in separate groups according to certain characteristic features. In our original design for the book, we outlined the following axes:

1) survival vs. (innovative) development and growth;
2) high-tech vs. traditional businesses
3) narrowly focussed business vs. differentiated ones

However, after analysing the interview data, we noted that though some of the dichotomies above are valid, there are other divisions very crucial for our theoretical argument about the different origins of entrepreneurship. Entrepreneurship is not just something that happened in the post-socialist space after Socialism collapsed, and it had not resided only in factories or service companies, but it had also grown within the (management of) socialist enterprises, in the Academies of Sciences with their laboratories, and even with the support of the state. Hence, the first group of entrepreneurs in our study are those that had already been acting in an entrepreneurial way during the years of Socialism. Some of them were "stifled" by the administrative system, while others survived and managed to guarantee the survival of the enterprise they were running by relying on their extensive networks within the former socialist space and in "Western" countries. These interviews comprise the two subdivisions of the first group what we called '***socialist entrepreneurs***' – those from an ***earlier generation*** and those from ***the younger generation,*** who, on the basis of their experience accumulated in the framework of the former (giant) socialist enterprises successfully managed to transform their former companies into real capitalist ventures. Other crucial elements of their success were maintaining the core of the labour collective and specialization in core product(s) - the managerial strategies of the former Soviet firms rely on strong paternalism, where the common interests of the workers and the enterprise are emphasized in the spirit of social partnership (Clarke, 2004).

In any case, this fact does not necessarily testify to the strength of the Soviet traditions in the sense of path-dependency; but there are many overlapping reasons for the reproduction of these practices. Firstly, it may merely reflect the weakness of many localities to maintain the necessary social services, infrastructure, etc., due to weak financial resources of the local governments. Secondly, efforts are made to divide the labour into core and fringe groups, where the high-skilled labour force is indispensable for the enterprise and is therefore able to dictate its own terms for consent to work, while the fringe groups of the labour force are easily replaceable with cheaper and equally unskilled labour when the need arises to cut costs or to rationalize production. Thirdly, strong paternalism is a sign of the employees' low trust in the trade unions and strong trust in the enterprise management to provide them the necessary services and wages.

The second group represents the ***entrepreneurs who started their enterprise as a completely new, private enterprise***. Their assets in undertaking entrepreneurship were personal enthusiasm, ambition, and very skilled planning and development of business. The social networks have played a role for these entrepreneurs as well, but in their case these networks were narrower and more intense – relatives, friends, school-mates, etc. Many of these entrepreneurs display the classical features of the entrepreneur: innovativeness, personal austerity, and rational calculation are part and parcel of their business philosophy. For these people the "modern" capitalist managerial strategies represent the "norm": skilled labourers are valued and their contribution to the success of the company is rewarded with adequate salary, but most social benefits and services are "outsourced" to the public sector and their services towards the community are set on a market-relations basis, and not as social partnerships. The fringe labour force is minimised through a maximum degree of mechanisation. Thus, these entrepreneurs may provide some benefits for the employees and even for the local community, but only on a voluntary basis, and not because they feel obliged to.

A third group of ***entrepreneurs took advantage of the business opportunities they were given or that they seized during the privatization***. For them cost-efficiency is the key issue: they produce cheap products, utilize low-skilled labour, and do not seek new markets for their products or try to improve their products, not to mention innovating them. For this group, networks are not very important for the development of their businesses. The (survival) managerial strategy here is the most traditional patriarchal way of controlling without supplying care: the entrepreneurs try to keep their work force loyal by means of threats. They give low wages, very weak or no security of employment, and constantly threaten to replace the current labour with new. Also, they provide almost no services to the local community due to their weak financial position; hence they have a very low rating in the eyes of the local or regional administration.

The fourth group consists of ***entrepreneurs who started their enterprises within academia*** – they have turned their cultural capital into a commercial product. For them the choice of becoming entrepreneurs has usually been involuntary. Entrepreneurship has been a strategic choice in the face of looming economic crisis and unemployment in the academic sphere. Very few academic entrepreneurs made a conscious decision to draw profit from their research work, but as Ivan notes in the beginning of the interviews with two of his cases: "… the stories presented below reveal another specific form of entrepreneurship, which we called *'institutional entrepreneurship'*, but they have some common features with the *phenomenon of intra-preneurship*, known from the studies of entrepreneurs inside large corporations. It emerged under conditions of radically reduced public funding for research, and thanks to their operational autonomy, some directors of institutes or heads of university departments organized their research on an entrepreneurial basis in order to cope with the shortfalls of the transition." In these enterprises the labour collective is more like a community of colleagues or peers rather than having a manager-employee relationship, and this special relationship affects the managerial strategies as well; decision making is decentralized and based more on consensus than on formal agreements. The core of the labour force, the part that is crucial to the economic success of the firm, is highly skilled and well-paid, while the fringe labour force is kept down to a minimal size and treated in the framework of employer-employee relationships. As the last case in the group reveals, this type of entrepreneurship can develop only in a favourable institutional environment; when this environment changes for the worse, there is always the possibility to spin-off and establish one's own company.

The final, fifth group are those **entrepreneurs whose business is gradually disintegrating**, despite their efforts to keep their firms floating through product modification, cost-cutting, or other measures. In the interviews presented here it is difficult to find a common pattern behind their decline or failure, but certainly the harsh economic situation, weak legislative basis, and lack of appropriate institutional support for the start-up companies have contributed to their failures.

A. Socialist Entrepreneurs

A1. Earlier Generation Socialist Entrepreneurs from the Economic Nomenclature

Valter Udam. The story of one of the most talented agricultural managers in socialist Estonia, who managed to establish profitable and very successful kolkhozes and initiated the idea of transforming the kolkhozes into an agricultural complex through vertical integration: production of crops and animal breeding, industrial processing of production, and its marketing via an own chain of stores. This is a story of a man who looked upon the obstacles imposed by the administrative economy as a challenge and as something to be changed.

Ivan Popov. This is the story of one of the most successful industrial managers in socialist Bulgaria, who initiated the development of entire new industrial branches in the country and applied true capitalist methods, even as a member of the Communist Party Politburo. A talented mathematician, in the early 1930s he left his post as assistant professor at Sofia University, Bulgaria, to study electrical engineering in Toulouse, France. Upon returning to Sofia, he established his own company for maintenance and production of electrical apparatuses and laboratory equipment. In the early 1940s he became an engineer at the AEG plant in Budapest, Hungary. Back in Bulgaria in 1950 he made successful carrier as director of a large electro-technical plant and university professor, to become in 1963 Chairman of the Bulgarian State Committee for Science and Technical Progress. Here, among other activities, Popov initiated the accelerated development of Bulgarian electronic industry that during the 1970s produced about 40% of computer technology in former COMECOM (Run and Utt 1990) and was appointed Minister of Electronics, and later Deputy Prime Minister and member of the Communist Party Politburo. After a conflict with some influential members of Politburo he was dismissed in 1975.

Former kolkhoz leader from Iecava, Latvia. The interview with the Latvian man, who was chairman of the local kolkhoz for almost 40 years, between 1951 and 1987. He was born in Russia in a farmer's family; his father and brothers were deported to Siberia in 1933 as kulaks and he had to struggle for survival. Sent to Latvia with the Russian army in 1945, after demobilization he remained there, began farming for an orphanage, and was later appointed chairman of one of the first kolkhozes. In the interview he tells the story of his work as chairman and comments on the economic and political changes after 1991.

A2. Younger Generation of Entrepreneurs, Who, on the Basis of their Experience in the Framework of the Former (Giant) Socialist Enterprises, Successfully Steered their Companies into the New Economic Realities of Post-socialist Transition

T. Ltd. An engineering company specialized in thermal power technologies and machines – water heating, power boilers, and related equipment. The company is successor to the former applied research units on thermal power stations – the "Thermal Technology" Department at the state enterprise *Automation and Modernization of the Power System,* established in 1967. In 1979 the enterprise was transformed into *Industrial-Scientific Enterprise TECHENERGO*, which in 1988 became *Industrial-Scientific Combine* with a special *Technological Research Institute (NITI).* In 1990 the "Thermal Technology" Department at NITI was established as an autonomous public company, owned by the Bulgarian state. In 1993 the company became a state-owned Limited Liability Company. It was privatized by *Energoremont Holding* in 2004, and specialized in design, repair and maintenance of (electric) power facilities.

G. Ltd. A company producing coated electric cables. It was established in 1968 in a middle-sized regional centre of a mountainous region and continued its operation as a state-owned company till 1996 when it was privatized under the 'mass privatization' scheme. In the last years of socialism some modest investments had been made in new technology, which together with the good management of its director (who preserved his position from 1987 till the privatization in 1996) helped the company survive during the difficult years immediately following 1989, and even to achieve economic stability in the mid-1990s.

M. Co. A company specialized in composite industry. It was founded in 1990 by the former director of a large composite plant in former Yugoslavia, and initially consisted of a handful of engineers and university professors. They started working as consultants in composites industry, and later turned to building electronic components and designing machines for production of composite items for different industrial branches. The founder of the company worked sixteen years in the production of various equipment for the Yugoslavian composite industry and has more than 30 years of experience in the composite industry. The activities of the company can be divided into two groups. The *first group* consists in designing and manufacturing machines and auxiliary equipment, such as filament winding machines, prepreg machines, prototype fiber placement machines, etc. The *second group* of activities includes machines and so-called computer controlled machines for processing different kinds of materials such as marble, steel, aluminum; also included here are laser, plasma, and water-jet cutting machines. The company employs 20 engineers, 5 doctors of science, and 10 manual workers.

N-Techno A/S. Situated in south-western Estonia, the company was founded in 1991. The roots of the company were in the state-owned company that provided technology for agriculture. The production profile was very versatile at that time, but after privatization the company specialized in manufacturing hydraulic cylinders and metal constructions. Currently the company has 75 employees and its turnover in 2010 was MEUR 3,5.

B. New Innovative Entrepreneurs

E. Cosmetics and Sons Ltd: specialized in perfumery and cosmetics. The company was founded in 1991 by a medical doctor and currently provides employment to about 80 persons. For certain period in late 1990s and early this century it was the only Bulgarian company producing its own brand of perfumes.

R. Ltd: specialized in essential oils production and in cosmetics. The company was established in 1992 by a retired accountant in a public transport company, his son, and two other partners. Having first starting with petrol business, after being pressured by an organized crime group, the company switched to cultivation of roses and rose oil extraction, eventually becoming one of the biggest producers and exporters of essential oils in Bulgaria.

K-wood A/S: Situated in south-west Estonia. The firm produces construction materials, mainly planed timber. It was established in 1997. At the time of the interview it employed 25 persons.

T-wood A/S: A woodworking company, also situated in south-west Estonia. It was established in 1990 as a cooperative. It specializes in glued timber and employs 180 workers.

A-heat A/S: A company in south-west Estonia, which imports and installs heating equipment. It was established in 1997 after its owner had gained experience working for a Finnish company in Estonia that operated in the same field.

A&B Software: A Russian software company established by a young Russian software engineer who had initially worked in an institute of the

Academy of Sciences. After changing several employers and the bankruptcy of his first own company, he now manages a successful company operating in six countries.

Killey, Cable TV entrepreneur: A young man from Tanzania, after graduating in radio and TV technology in a Bulgarian technical university, established his own cable TV company in a small Bulgarian provincial town. The initial success was followed by a period of hardship during which he adapted his business strategy to the changing economic environment.

C. Surviving Firms

The A-Service Company produces and repairs diesel and electric fork-lift trucks. It is located in the Plovdiv region. The company was previously part of the socialist industrial combine BALKANCAR. One of its main plants was 'Record' Machine Works in Plovdiv, which once produced tens of thousands of diesel trucks annually, exported to COMECOM and other countries. A few years after 1989 the BALKANCAR combine collapsed, after which numerous private companies were established upon its ruins. At the time of the interview the company employed about 130 people.

J-sewing S/A: The company is a subcontractor for the large Estonian garment industry. It is situated in northern Estonia. It produces blouses for men and women. The company started in 1990 with 30 employees and by the time of the interview it had 50.

K- radio plant: During socialist times the company was part of a large production association that comprised four enterprises. In 1991 the plant was transformed into a cooperative with 400 members. At the time of the interview the company employed about 40 workers in radio production and 14 persons in services.

D. Institutional Entrepreneurs

Two Stories of Entrepreneurship from Bulgarian University

A female university professor who is simultaneously conducting three different activities: teaching, scientific research, and running a small production laboratory that commercializes some applications of her scientific achievements. The main application is the production of diagnostic test strips for fast analysis of biological liquids.

A male university professor running a laboratory for mathematical chemistry and selling original software under the lab's own trade mark to large multinational companies and government agencies worldwide.

Both laboratories operate on the premises of the university. In the early 1990s the first lab employed 10 persons, but during recent years the number of employees has been reduced to 4. The second lab has had steady development for more than twenty years and currently employs more than twenty people on the scientific staff plus several technicians.

R Electronics: The company was created in 1990; before that it was part of the Institute for Technical Cybernetics and Robotics (ITCR) at the Bulgarian Academy of Sciences (BAS). By the end of the 1980s this large institute split into several smaller institutes, one of which became the Institute for Applied Cybernetics at BAS. The department carried out R&D on industrial computers, and later on personal industrial computers. The company was established as a private firm from the very beginning.

E. Declining Firms

L-apparel A/S: The company is situated in north-western Estonia. During Soviet times, it used to be a department in a large production association producing consumer goods such as women's clothes and handbags. The company started as a cooperative in 1990 and was transformed into a joint-stock company in 1992. Initially it employed 80 persons, but at the time of the interview only 3 remained.

Firm P: Established in the spring of 1991 as a high technology firm specialized in R&D, it originated from the 'Parallel Processors' Department of the former Institute of Microprocessor Systems (IMS), and in late 1980s its team designed some of the hardware for the Soviet space shuttle "Buran". Originally the company employed 40 persons, out of which only 8 remained at the time of the interview.

AV Joint-stock company: The company is located in Russian Karelia, close to Petrodzavodsk. It was founded by two brothers on the basis of a forestry company and it grew rapidly into multi-branch firm with tourism as spearhead activity and other branches supporting the growth. The company was well-received by the Republican administration and it implemented a lot of community projects, like foot-ball stadium, church and others. At the time of interview the company employed 200 people.

A private farmer in Mindunai, Moletu district, Lithuania. This is the story of an energetic and enterprising woman. She and her husband left the capital Vilnius and started their private farm on the land of their parents, which had been returned to them under the Law of Restitution of Land. The story is one of courage, persistence and hard work; she remains unvanquished despite the many blows she has suffered.

Earlier Generation Socialist Entrepreneurs from the Economic Nomenclature

This group of three interviews presents the entrepreneurial efforts of socialist economic managers – one of them (Prof. Ivan Popov) was a typical industrial manager with background from capitalist Bulgaria and Hungary before and during the WW II, while the other two (Walter Udam from Estonia and Iecava Kolhose's chairmen from Latvia) operated in agriculture and related food processing industry. Because of their economic achievements and innovation introduced - whose scope sometimes comprised entire industrial branches, Ivan Popov and Valter Udam have been promoted to the top levels of communist political hierarchy. Yet all three cases provide rich evidences about both exceptional opportunities and inherent barriers to innovation under the administrative economy, and about the values and 'cultural code' that motivated the entrepreneurs from economic nomenclature described in the Introduction. We believe the reader will be impressed by the scale and scope of the activities of Popov and Udam and will notice as well the bitter taste of their stories which – if in a different way – is also present in the reflections of the Ieacava Kolhose leader.

1. Valter Udam

Tallinn, Estonia, June 7th 1999
Interviewers: Ilkka Alanen, Jouko Nikula, Rein Ruutsoo
Interpreter: Helvi Pöder

A Short Introductory Note

Valter Udam worked in leadership positions in the Tallinn and Tartu Komsomol organizations, as Secretary of the District Committee and also as inspector in the Central Committee of the Estonian Communist Party. From 1971 until 1990 Udam was representative of the Supreme Soviet of the ESSR. He has been recognized as one of the creators of the Agro-industrial Complex and he published a number of articles on agriculture; he also wrote plays. He died in a car-accident close to his home in March 2001.

My name is Valter Udam and my first profession is agronomist and the other is from that theater studio. When I got out of the army I had to go register myself at the Army Commissariat, but the secretary of the Komsomol had already made an agreement with the Commissariat that if any sportsman came, he needed that person to be a director of the sports department (I am also a veteran athlete). At that time the Komsomol acted in sports as well. And so they took me there in the Komsomol, I could not go to [work in the] theater and later on I could not work as an agronomist.

From the Komsomol I went to the Party and so on. I wanted to tell you why I already had three professions, why I went to Party work; there I had no profession at all, but because I came from the army, they took me in the Komsomol. The First Secretary of the city Party committee at that time, Mr. Madre, said to me: “Listen Valter, one lousy actor more or less, but I need you to be the director of the sports department”. And he took me in the Komsomol and later in the Party.

I was a farmer’s son and used to work there and later it [the farm] was liquidated. Father and mother worked in a kolkhoz for 10 years and they did not get a single cent, there were only the norm-days which were counted and nothing was received from that work. The first ten years were very bad and when the Khrushchev thaw came and when Tõnurist was Minister of Agriculture he was almost fanatical, he started to say that we could not get the farms back but life in kolkhozes could be improved, more human. And for that [goal] I worked 35 years and fought in Viljandi, Pärnu and Võrumaa. During the war I worked in Valga county, then in the Tartu area. And three times I left everything in Tallinn and went to rural areas. I was in Võru, also in Viljandi and in Pärnu. I had the opportunity of just sitting in a chair in Tallinn, but I went to the county [rural areas]. Three times we moved from Tallinn with our family. In the county I was my own master. I could decide, fight, and act – I was like the general of an army. But in Tallinn – there you had to bow to Moscow all the time. In the beginning the bosses were Russian Estonians and Russians. I left Tallinn because during Soviet-times they listened a lot to Moscow, but in the countryside the First Secretary of the region could do what he wanted, as long as the economy was fine. When I was First Secretary in Pärnu, I accumulated 36 million rubles of profit from agriculture, and from the whole Agro-complex, 46 million – that would mean one billion today. It is the same billion (crowns) out of which the government makes the additional budget. Yes, at that time I had profit from agriculture. We invested 10 million in schools, 5 million in canteens, shops and other such things, and in culture. I was able to arrive in Tallinn any day [I wanted] and kick the door of Mr. Käbin with my foot, because I did not ask for any money. I just asked for construction materials, I was the master of the region and in Viljandi we also had profit – some 20 million or more.

Those 20 million rubles is nowadays about 400 million Crowns – you have to multiply by 20. This was the reason why I was brought back to

Tallinn – and I went back. Tallinn bowed to Moscow just in the same way they bow to Brussels nowadays. And they translated those 80 000 pages of advices and regulations of the European Union. Even now I would like to move to rural areas, where I could make decisions by myself.

- *When did you obtain those millions?*

In the 1970s and 1980s. In the beginning the kolkhozes were very poor, but I was talking about the 1970s and 1980s.

- *May I ask a more detailed question? If I understood correctly, this agricultural…complex, which we are talking about, was a national (republican) organization. And the leader of that organization was a distinguished Party person, or what? And this person had a lot of money?*

The question refers to the Agro-industrial complex. It was a special formation which was constructed on my initiative; I was in a way the father of the idea. It started from Estonia and from Viljandi in Estonia. It was a united state cooperative, because sovkhoses also joined in it.

- *They joined voluntarily?*

Yes, at a general meeting where they voted on this matter. Joining it were kolkohozes and sovkhozes, the state institutions, and in addition also the dairies.

So, why was it an Agro-complex? Simply because the processing industry also joined it – dairies, meat factories and trade, together with forestry and fishing. So, we can really say that it was an Agro-complex.

They produced agricultural products themselves and processed them and also provided services for agricultural workers.

I was the chairman of the Commission of Estonian Agro-industrial Complex, in the Presidium. But in Viljandi I started it as an experiment, then continued in Pärnu and later the whole of Estonia shifted to it. Coming to today, if we had that complex now, then it would not be that a farmer should sell milk for one crown per liter. I go to the store and pay 5 crowns for that liter of milk. But we had that complex, we produced by ourselves, processed everything by ourselves. Because it was an experiment and since the profit was good in Viljandi, it was applied in Pärnu as well. I went to Pärnu also because I was told that Viljandi is very fertile and it is easy to succeed there, you cannot fail. But take another place, much worse. Well, I went to Pärnu and got better results there than in Viljandi.

- Here we heard, in the beginning he (U) told us about a person who held a leading position in the Party and there was a lot of profit made and they had to negotiate over those profits and resources. So, there was money, but they had to have the resources – labor, technology, infrastructure, etc. But who was the key person there and what kind of a person was he and how were those negotiations conducted? You were Party Secretary and the father of the Agro-complex?

Yes, I was

- But the founding of that organization was done by the Party leadership, you did it as a Party Secretary, didn't you? So was it thanks to you as a person or you as a Party Secretary that the Agro-complex was established?

Well now, this is how it was, as Mr. Tuulik says in my book that I (Udam) was a county leader at that time, officially he was the First Secretary of the Party Committee, but I also had the duties of county leader. Things were not decided in the Executive Committee but in the Party. That is naturally not a just comparison – the county leader then and a county leader now, they are totally different things. Nowadays a county leader does not amount to much at all, he is just a stooge for the government, fulfills government orders. But the First Secretary in Soviet times, he operated and was highly responsible for a large economy.

Why did I become the "father" – the researchers in Estonia and the Soviet Union had an idea that allowed us to create an agro-industrial complex, but they needed a madman who would say "I will make it real" and would take responsibility. So I went, my hat in my hand, to meet Mr. Bronstein, Mr. Tõnurist, researchers, and said to them "let's do it in Viljandi". In the Estonian Academy of Sciences there was a research committee on Agro-industrial Complex and I went there as well, because I had made my own studies there and cooperated with them in the same group, and so I offered my own district for this experiment. And since I realized the experiment, I was called the father, but it was the researchers who invented the complex.

- Tõnurist was Party Secretary for agricultural issues?

Yes. In the Supreme Council I was the chairman of the agricultural board, but in the Academy of Science I was only a member.

- *So this experiment began in the 1980s or was it earlier?*

The experiment began in 1975 – I was three years in Viljandi and in 1978 I moved to Pärnu. It so happened that in the beginning they decided "let's experiment in Viljandi and then expand it to the whole of Estonia". In three years we proved that it worked, but the leadership of the Estonian SSR did not want to approve the expansion. They did not want it yet, they said "let's experiment in another district, in a more difficult place". Then I went to Pärnu for three years and only after that they were ready to make the decision that the whole of Estonia should adopt the system. It was made in 1982 or 1983, then it became an all-Union system. And then they let it sink.

- *In what sense?*

If I now say something, I am a district level leader from Soviet times. And I of course was very critical towards the men at state level. For me there were nothing but bad things, but certainly there must have been something good too. I was very critical towards them, except Mr. Tõnurist and Käbin listened to him. Tõnurist made all those things, and Käbin let him act. But when Mr. Väljas came, he sacked Tõnurist and it changed the situation. I had the full support of the agricultural department of the Central Committee. In that department were all the agricultural experts and their working language was Estonian. I went to Party work when Tõnurist became Secretary for Agriculture, I went to Võrumaa. And there I got such experience that when I went to Viljandi as First Secretary, I was completely sure that the district would be successful. And it was the same with Pärnu. In my books I write that even in Soviet times one could defend the interests of Estonia and that the leader could be human. At district level everything was done in Estonian and at the Ministry of Agriculture there were Estonians, the Estonian mind and spirit was there and they could promote the interests of Estonia. For the others it was more difficult – the people in the ideological department of the Central Committee were not completely bad, but they were more dependent on instructions from Moscow. The whole agricultural line – from the bottom up to the top, was in the hands of Estonians and they defended the Estonian issues.

Tõnurist had been an agricultural consultant during the first independence of Estonia and he had the training. He used to say to me that "If I told you all the instructions and advices that I get from Moscow, you would say I've gone crazy. Therefore I tell you only 10 % of the advice Moscow sends here. It shows what kind of a chain there was, what was transmitted and what not. Because there were Estonian-minded people in the Ministry, the orders from Moscow could be ignored if things went well. And in Estonian agriculture things were pretty good, so there was no reason to attack us. I was called many times to the Central Committee for ideological reasons, since I was the First Secretary, but I said that we had just received a ticket for good work and we had made a profit of 30 million. But if we had bad ideology, then the people would work badly and I could not get all those bonuses and medals for good work. So, ideology cannot be bad as long as the work is good. Mr. Ristlaan, who was a complicated and devious person, I had good relations with him, because he invited me to talk with him. At the bureau I was called bad names and he stood by and took care that I was not punished, even though I received a lot of accusations, but not serious ones. Later he clapped me on the shoulder and said, Valter you are the internal dissident in the Party.

- *What were the ideological accusations you were charged with?*

Two times I received a reminder, which is the first punishment, the most merciful one. Then later it was nullified. The accusation was that the First Secretary talks too little about ideological matters and works only on agricultural matters, in the Agro-complex, with farmers, tours around the kolkhozes, but does not advise Party secretaries there, but talks with cattle breeders, engineers and such. Another accusation was that the Agro-complex had its own board; I was on that board and that caused such a scandal that a first secretary could be a member of that board, since Udam is then also an employee of the Director of Agro-complex. There were a lot of problems and I was asked to resign from the board. In Pärnu I was again a board member and I was told that I was the servant of the Agro-industrial complex. But in fact the Agro-industrial complex was my servant.

There were a lot of accusations; for example when they held those days of political lecturing, they asked what was lectured about. That Udam talks about milk, economy, money, but says nothing about the Secretary General and what Brezhnev had done. In those days there was a rule, that 25-30 % of the lecture should deal with the Secretary General, but this Udam, he starts right away talking about economy. Yes, there were lots of accusations...

After the experiment in Viljandi proved a success, delegations from Russia started coming, there were delegations every week and I was asked to speak. Then we made tours with Tõnurist all over the Soviet Union. Researchers had quite good proposals. There was a scientific conference in Moscow; I spoke there, then in Leningrad, Kiova and Tbilisi. Mr. Bronstein was also with us – Tõnurist and Bronstein were theoreticians, I was the practical man. The Agro-complex was discussed at the conferences; Moscow understood that agriculture and processing, trade, all that should be united into one. The department of agriculture of the Central Committee invited me there to speak during the Brezhnev period. That department supported me. At the time when I constructed the Agro-complex, Gorbachev was Secretary of Agriculture. So, I spoke at the Academy of Science with all the researchers around me and they supported us and then they made many films about it and my articles were published in Moscow journals. Also, one dissertation was written on this topic. But the Bank, the planning organ and the Ministry of State Treasury were all against it – the main pillars of the state were against it.

So, there was a conflict, because we had money, but the bank and planning organ were obstructing it. Then they started to accuse me that I did nothing but travel all over the Soviet Union; I also visited Finland and other countries, and I neglected the Party work.

I attended all-Union conferences more than ten times. That idea of Agro-complex, I learned a lot about it in Finland as well. When I was in Helsinki, they had their so-called "agricultural days", organized by the Social Democratic Party of Finland. That was in the 1970s. In ten days I was shown more than 20 farms and they explained to me that this farm was a member of a cooperative milk industry and slaughterhouse. And another thing is that they (the Finns) have a united ministry of agriculture and forestry – not separate ministries. So, the producer is tied to the processing industry. So, we learned from Finland as well, the idea comes from Finland. Another root [of the idea] was the fact that during the first independence of Estonia we also had cooperatives of which farmers were members. So, we did not invent the idea out of nothing.

We made an Estonian model of our own, but we borrowed something from Finland, something from the First Independence and then it was born as an experiment. In Finland and elsewhere it was based on private property, with us on state ownership, and we combined the state farms and kolkhoses.

- Were there any problems caused by the fact that kolkhozes had more autonomy than sovkhozes or because the dairy was a state enterprise?

Sure, there were a lot of problems; in Moscow they did not understand.

They did not use our model; they had separate complexes for sovkhozes and kolkhoses. And they did not allow combining dairy and meat industry into an agro-industrial complex. So, they accepted the idea, but made many complexes instead of one unified complex. In our district we had only one. In Russia they could have 4-5 complexes in one district, but I wanted them all united. When Gorbachev was still Agricultural Secretary, he supported our model, but after he became Secretary General, he could not withstand the resistance of the financial department, planning department and the bank. He had only two supporters in Politburo and therefore he lost. And therefore it failed in Russia. I demanded that in the managing body of the Agro-industrial Complex there should be farmers, but in Russia the power was given to processing industry and the Union of the Agro-industrial Complex was headed by some musician, who did not know anything about agriculture but who had made a good career in processing industry. They made him director and naturally it failed. Also, my proposal for the director of Estonian Agro-industrial complex was disregarded and the director of the agricultural technological unit was nominated. The most qualified person was selected to be vice-director. And the governing board was enlarged and made very big. I was not listened to anymore.

- *Why was that?*

Because the processing industry took over the power in the Union of Agro-complexes – in the Soviet Union those guys took over power and the same happened in Estonia too. In 1983 Gorbachev invited me to see him, when the experiment in Pärnu was still running. There were 11 men from all over the Soviet Union present and Gorbachev fully supported our model. The President of the Academy of Agricultural Sciences told us that everything was correct, but the Planning Committee and Financial Department were against us. An important role was played by Käbin, because when he came to power after Karotamme, I was disappointed. Käbin was an Estonian Russian and carefully obeyed Party orders. However, twenty years in Estonia had made him good, he had adjusted to the local circumstances and he started to support locals (Estonians). Tõnurist could always talk him over. And the reason why he did not pass on the orders from Moscow was that he had started to think like the Estonians. And the reason why the Agro-industrial Complex failed was partly the fact that Käbin was removed from power and was replaced by Mr. Väljas. If Käbin had stayed in power, Estonian agriculture would not have degraded.

- *What was the reason for the resistance of the Planning Committee, Bank and financial organizations. What was their justification, considering it was a functioning system, why were they against it?*

The problem arose then... when I started to work in agriculture.

I went everywhere with my hat in my hand and begged for money, but now we had our own money and I demanded there be a bank of our own for agricultural producers. We made a profit of 36 million, but we could not use it, because the planning committee plans all the possible bureaucratic hindrances there. The minister of the State Treasury and the bank do not give any support for it. And then, being constantly worried, I put [the problem] on the theatre stage in a play in which I complained how these organizations prevented its operation, how they obstructed agricultural producers to use their own money. We did not ask them for a single kopek, we had our own kopeks, but we were not allowed to use them. Then this play, "Responsibility", was soon translated into Russian and a legal accusation was sent to Moscow. It was before Gorbachev. They phoned Mr. Ristlaan and me and argued that the First Secretary was destroying the supporting pillars of the state, that the representative of the Planning Committee was depicted on the theater stage and made fun of, as well as the representatives of the Bank and the financial organization. Moscow demanded the play be banned. But Mr. Ristlaan told them that "Mr. Udam is not my employee, he is a member of the Central Committee and the chairman of the agricultural commission in the Supreme Council". Then they phoned at my home three times, my wife answered the phone, but she does not understand Russian. They phoned three times and said that the play would be banned. If it had been written by some writer, it would certainly have been banned, but I was not his employee. In the eyes of Gorbachev I was already one of his allies. I visited him, and his colleagues had visited Pärnu – and then there was a command to ban and to sack me. The vice-director of the ideological department phoned many time from Moscow. However, I was not sacked and the play was put back on stage. And a week later Gorbachev came to power. And he took guys from the agricultural department as his allies, the ones I already knew. And then another guy whom I also knew phoned me and said "Valter Jaanovits, this is a very good play and it talked about reforms before the actual reforms (perestroika and glasnost) took place".

Then my play was officially translated into Russian, Ukrainian, and the Russian Cultural Ministry made copies of it and sent it to all republics of the Union. Then it was made into a movie and also a radio play. It became very famous all over the Soviet Union and this was when Gorbachev came to power.

- *But still, what arguments did the Planning Committee use to oppose the system?*

The basic principle was that the basis of the state is the plan, while I demanded that responsibility be given to the Agro-industrial Complex and a right use be made of its own financial resources. And that banking bureaucracy be reduced, I also demanded a bank of its own for the Agro-industrial complex. I also demanded that the Planning Committee should not pressure us with those financial limits. We went to Novgorod, Moscow, Pihkov to buy things and actually we had a "black account" in every kolkhoz. Otherwise it would not have been possible to live, if you had 36 million and you were given only a little part of those resources and you could not use all that – the quotas were so small - and that was the reason for the black account. In that play of mine I tell a story about how a load of cement is transported from Kunda and a man from Pärnu Agricultural Technological Complex goes to Kunda, because he does not have any cement. He drives after the lorries from Pihkov, those lorries are taking the load of cement from Kunda to a storage in the Pihkov District Agricultural Technological Complex. The load is then loaded on Pärnu lorries and taken back to Estonia – only via Pihkov. Money talks and that was the way it was done.

Mr. Polinitski from the ideological department said to me "Mr. Udam, you are dismantling the three basic pillars of our society. These are the three basic pillars of Soviet society – the Planning Committee, the Bank, and the financial organizations".

I replied to him, that yes, that is true, but they need to be reformed. In Soviet times they said that the chairman of a kolkhoz could go to jail without legal process and that was true. And as a Party Secretary I saved them from court by saying it should be stopped. The planned economy was a strange thing; it would be decided we should build something, but there were never enough resources, for example there might be only 70 % of the necessary construction materials. The other 30 % had to be acquired through tricks and through black accounts.

The black account was not big enough for the needs, it was merely a kind of pre-payment resource, it could be used for various expenditures, representation, and some of it was given as bonuses, and we also used it to take care of personal relations. For example, we paid kolkhoz leaders in Pihkov so they would be willing and ready to transfer some resources from one pocket to another. So, the black account was important but it was not that big. The organization committee of the Central Committee and all the bureaucrats demanded that the First Secretary should be against them.

- *Against whom?*

Against the black account, that people should obey laws and that I should support those three pillars of Soviet society. Here it was so, that if you wanted to promote the development of the district, you should support the Chairman. Those were the main conflicts in Soviet society, and the main concern of those three pillars was that we could not accommodate the Agro-industrial Complex as, ideologically and theoretically, a kind of free-market zone within Soviet society. We would have had our own bank and a free market economy within the Soviet society. The Soviet strait-jacket tightened. It gave a push later, when the model of Economic Autonomy of Estonia was being made, when we drafted the Farmer Law, I was the only salaried employee in the Supreme Council. From all that the Economically Autonomous Estonia was born. I am not saying that I was some kind of theoretician in that, no, I was still a practical person. The idea of Economically Autonomous Estonia could not have been born if we had been poor, if we had not had our own money. Because we were sure that we could manage our own economy, our level of competence was so high. My contribution in that program was the agrarian program, the experiences from Viljandi and Pärnu provided good examples.

- *This was sometimes around 1985?*

One very important point was that in the year before I left Pärnu the private farms started to appear. Then, under my leadership, a model was made for reorganization of the district agro-industrial complex into an agricultural cooperative. It was supposed to cover the whole Pärnu region. All farms belonged to it. I made it the year before I left. I had permission to reorganize the Agro-industrial Complex into a cooperative as an experiment. Everybody was to be given a chance to join it – kolkhozes, private farms, all. Also private property could join it – if all that had been given the chance to come true, the Estonian agriculture would not now be suffering as it is (1999). It would have been very difficult to close down the agro-industrial cooperative, like they did with the Agro-industrial Complex. The person who replaced me did not want to realize my model and Estonian agriculture lost because the cooperative was not established. In Pärnu we had already started a process where sovkhozes were transformed into kolkhozes and large kolkhozes were [divided into] smaller ones. I received from Mr. Sauli permission to make such an experiment in Pärnu region and also dairies and slaughter houses joined in that cooperative. But when I was transferred to Tallinn, the person who came in my place after me did not want to even hear about my model. He was not directly against it, but he delayed it and then began the Singing Revolution and the Agro-industrial Complexes were completely dismantled. And later the kolkhozes were also closed. If I had had one more year in Pärnu, the plan would have been completed. I was sweating when I got the permission from Mr. Sauli – if I had asked from Moscow, I would never have gotten it. Mr. Sauli was a brave man in some sense. Here in my book there is a chart of the organizational structure of the cooperative, it was already negotiated in the Party Committee and in the council of the Agro-industrial Complex. The project was ready – also the farms were there, 60 farms were to be part of the cooperative. But Mr. Raidla, who replaced me as the first secretary, did not want to realize the plan.

Mr. Raidla was a lawyer and I was a farmer. He was a lawyer and was in no hurry to establish the cooperative. Nobody had any idea that the agrarian program in the Economic Autonomy of Estonia program would be rejected and the kolkhozes would be liquidated. But the agrarian program was a program which was approved by the Americans and also the Finns, we exchanged experience. Every week delegations visited me, I was called bad names for this, I gave interviews every week and every week I would write an article for some all-Union newspaper. That was what I proposed then, but it was not done. Now we are in a situation where we have only 25 % of the amount of pigs we used to have and more than 50 % of the cows have been slaughtered. Even though large-scale production is much more efficient and productive. This is what the Finnish farmers also say. Large production should have been shifted directly to the market economy; by that time kolkhozes had grown very large and we formed economically autonomous departments. For example we divided one large kolkhoz into three - cowsheds were also much too big then, but that was the all-Union model. Why did they make such large farms in Estonia, the plans came from Italy and America. The Estonians did not invent them. Another thing was that in the Soviet Union there was a decision that if the farm was worth more than a million, the state would pay for it. And that was the reason for the very big farms and cowsheds. The Soviet Union gave us every year 100 million currency rubles for selling milk and meat to Russia. 500 000 tons of milk products and 70 000 tons of meat we sold to Russia; with that you could feed 1,5 million people.

The Soviet Union paid us 300 million ordinary rubles and 100 million currency rubles –at that time it was comparable to a dollar. We got 100 million dollars. In current currency that is 1,5 billion crowns, one-tenth of the Estonian annual budget.

So in the 1980s we began to break down large-scale production into smaller units. We began to transform sovkhoses into kolkhozes. I should add that those 100 million currency rubles made it possible to use Swedish and German machinery on large farms.

- *What kind of relations was there between Party and local council, between executive committee and the Soviet government?*

That depended quite a lot on the persons; I had good relations with the executive committee. In Estonian agriculture there were carts drawn by two horses and a plough and other machines. On a middle-sized farm there were usually two horses. My and Tõnurist's philosophy was that two men could pull agriculture forward, the First Secretary and the director of the Agro-industrial complex. A third person will not be pushed aside, but he has mainly symbolic power. He is a representative of Soviet power, the village council did not have any rights, two men had to draw the wagon. This what we did with Mr. Rahula in Viljandi and with Mr. Soasepp in Pärnu, but we maintained our relations with Soviet power, we considered it a [mere] symbol. When I left Viljandi, they organized a feast in my honour and the people said that not a single time had anybody seen Mr. Udam to pound the table with his fist or make a fuss about Party power or anything like that. No, they said I was always cheerful and even-tempered, mainly joking about that. I had no problem with the chairman of the executive committee either; everyone has his own role to play. In drama school I was a student of Mr. Panso, who used to teach us that theater is life and life is theater and also that a leader must fit into his role. He has to come to terms with local people. Why did I move three times? Mr. Panso said to me: "If you, young man, remain bent down already at a young age, you will remain like that for the rest of your life, so stand straight". He gave me a marvelous education for life and later I visited Paris and Italy with Mr. Panso. Sadly enough, it turns out that those who were bent down before Moscow in Soviet times are bent down before Brussels today. I took Mr. Panso's lessons seriously in Viljandi, Võrumaa and Pärnu and I became proud and unscrupulous to some extent – I did not previously prepare my speeches for Central Committee meetings but I went on stage and started to talk, I criticized the interpreter and there was a conflict. When I was nominated Hero of Socialist Labour, the proposal did not come from Estonia, but from Moscow, because I was a frequent visitor there. Mr. Väljas proposed another person, the secretary of Paide. But I had become unscrupulous and arrogant, and that was not allowed. I talked in sessions about state plans, demanded a bank of our own and explained, and never prepared a text beforehand but went and spoke my mind. Some things, naturally, I forgot and there were disputes with Mr. Väljas. But our speeches and reports went to Moscow and the results were to be known. I did not listen to anybody in Estonia and became egotistical – fame spoiled the person. Two Finnish journalists promised to translate my texts and publish them in the Finnish journals; this was done, it caused a lot of difficulties.

There was a period when many kolkhoz directors were sacked and I offered them jobs. All of them were very good at their work, but they had problems with Estonian state leaders at that time – there was a case of drunken driving, cases of black accounts and others, but I helped them when they were dismissed. There were sons of kulaks also, because a son of a kulak is a good leader. All those chairmen of the best kolkhozes in Estonia, those red barons, all of them were children of large farmers from the time of Estonia's first independence. No ordinary peasant was capable of being a kolkhoz leader. As a leader I did not follow any formulas, the most important thing was that the person was working and how he was working. That was the reason for the success of Viljandi and Pärnu. That is why the chairmen of kolkhozes were sons of kulaks – those red barons. It is shameless to call them red barons, because their fathers were sent to Siberia and they have already suffered from that. Let's take Mr. Lind, a guy from my home village, his father was a municipal director, a son of a big farmer, who was already on the list of those to be taken to Siberia, but the Party organizer at the village was a drunk and the father bought his freedom with a piglet. So the Party organizer took his name off the list because of the booze. He had the right to do so. If I had followed Party orders when recruiting workers, there would have been no success in Viljandi or in Pärnu.

- *Could you tell us about the time of the Singing Revolution, why your model was rejected at that time and how it happened in fact?*

We may say that during the Singing Revolution they started to write in journals that it was the Party that had created the Popular Front. That was true to a certain extent. I was First Secretary and at the same time I was a delegate to the first congress of the Popular Front. When I left Pärnu Mr. Raidla became the First Secretary and I was elected delegate to the Popular Front. Well, all the power at that time was already in the hands of the Popular Front. Then five men were selected for the Supreme Council; Savisaar, Väljas, Põldroos, myself and one more. And then they took over the whole power in the Supreme Council. Savisaar wrote all those projects and gave speeches and started to take over the whole power, they had a big influence in the Supreme Council – 80 – 90 % of them were Estonia-mind. They got into it and then there was the declaration of Independence and all the changes in the Constitution. Savisaar played a big role but Väljas was also important, since he was the First Secretary. He was not the Chairman of the Supreme Council, but there was a proposal that he should become Chairman because there were so many Russians in it and for them Väljas was still the First Secretary. So, Väljas was chairing the session even though power was already in the hands of the Popular Front. It was clear that the declaration of independence was a fact; all the Estonia-minded persons supported it unanimously. But there was a need to show to Moscow that the Russians also supported it, supported the language law and all that. And since the First Secretary chaired the session, he had authority. The role of Mr. Ruutli is exaggerated, because if Moscow had wanted it, the First Secretary would have been the first to go. At that time the Farm Law did not allow private ownership of land – it was only a transitory law. The progressive part of the Party joined the Singing Revolution; they did not regret or wish for Soviet Power. I also went in that direction, but in relation to agriculture I would have acted more wisely. The whole world witnessed the Supreme Council of Estonia approving the Declaration of Independence unanimously. And Moscow witnessed it too. A couple of Russians were against it. Later they understood what it meant and started to organize demonstrations and meetings. At that moment Väljas had only a symbolic power, but in the eyes of Moscow and the Russians he was still the First Secretary.

- *What were the differences between the two groups – Popular Front and Estonian Congress – in relation to agricultural reform, and what were the consequences?*

I would say that in the Popular Front there were more pragmatic people. At that time it was clear that economic autonomy requires full independence of Estonia. But they supported a gradual process – first economic autonomy within the Soviet Union, and they accepted the Union Treaty and then Savisaar and others said that this was a transitory period. But the Patriotic Party and Estonian Congress demanded full independence at once, no transitory periods – they did not want to hear about a gradual process. That was the difference, both wanted independence. Even now Savisaar thinks that we should have good relations with Russia, cooperate with it, our markets are there and a lot of raw materials are there. But the Patriotic [Party supporters] they want to turn their backs to Russia and go towards Europe. But in reality both were fighting for Estonia. I supported a compromise that the Popular Front and Estonian Congress should cooperate. I was also a member of the Estonian Congress, I was in their list, registered myself in Pärnu, both I and my wife. I was in both, in the Popular Front and in the Estonian Congress. It is paradoxical. Savisaar had difficult times as head of government – they say that we had food coupons then. Well, when Savisaar became Prime Minister, we went to a market economy with a crash, all the prices were let free, but the prices of agricultural products were kept low for 7 months. Then the mania began and coupons followed. And Savisaar said that he could not free the agricultural prices, because people needed food. If he had freed them, prices would have skyrocketed without any coupons. But he regulated them for 7 months. If all the prices had been freed, the stores would have been full, because we produced more than we could consume, we ate twice as much meat and milk as we consume now. Now our shops are full. There have been a lot of false accusations in the newspapers; in fact he did the right thing then. But his mistake was that he did not explain to the people why he did what he did. But if he had stayed in power, the kolkhozes would not have been destroyed. We cannot go to a market economy while agriculture remains in socialism, because all the prices in stores were regulated. But raw materials, services, machines and other things, all those increased and that was a heavy blow to agricultural producers.

- *But the liquidation of kolkhozes only started when Laar's government (the Patriotic Party government) came to power, is that true?*

Yes, then the decision was made that all the kolkhozes be liquidated and in each county was created a liquidation board. I have made a comparison that just as farms had been liquidated in Soviet times, in the same way were kolkhozes liquidated now. The task was assigned to municipal Party organizers in both cases – there was a need to carry out a forced liquidation, people had to be explained to why it was being done. I read in the Moscow archives about the collectivization and there they said it was voluntary, but in reality it was done through force. Now we learn likewise that the liquidation committee started to work and there were demands that meetings should be organized and people were forced to vote, but the liquidation committee acted like the Party organizer in Soviet times, they used exactly the same methods to liquidate kolkhozes as they liquidated the farms back in Soviet times. Naturally part of them disbanded immediately, part of them are still in the process of being dissolved, they built agricultural associations and did not dissolve immediately, but a majority of them dissolved completely.

Our agrarian program in the Program for Economically Autonomous Estonia was a transitory-period program, we wrote that large-scale and small-scale production should go side by side and the future should then show which was to remain, the farm or the company. Prime Minister Laar rejected that program completely, but it was meant for the transition period. We argued that small and big are mutually dependent, small farms do not have machines or buildings and if the kolkhoze were dissolved there would be no production buildings and nothing, only the land. Laar believed some kind of miracle would happen. 80 % of farm owners were city dwellers. But when they were preparing that agrarian program, we made a survey in Pärnu, which showed that if we created at first 300 farms and gradually made more, as many as there are willing persons, and those who start farming immediately should not be obstructed, and the kolkhoz should give them land. And then they would work together and later life would show which was the right form and survived. I fought years for this coexistence, but here in Tallinn they said no, no, the big ones must go, kolkhozes must be destroyed. Mr. Raig wrote that as soon as kolkhozes were destroyed, small farms would start mushrooming. Well, kolkhozes were destroyed, there was also rain, which did bring a lot of mushrooms, but not so many farms. And now those farms are closing down because it is not possible to produce at these prices - you are paid one crown and in the store you must pay 5 crowns for the same product, while middlemen take 4-5 crowns in between. Well, that was not only the mistake of Mr. Laar as Prime Minister, the same policy was continued later, but Mr. Laar made the decision.

- How was your program accepted by the Popular Front, did Mr. Savisaar understand your aims?

Savisaar was one of the leaders behind the Economically Autonomous Estonia Program. I wrote the agrarian part and he accepted it also. Then he became Prime Minister and could not keep an eye on that agrarian program. He told me that he was aware we could not maintain socialism in agriculture, but then he did not dare to make decisions about it, he knew that if he liberalized prices, they would skyrocket immediately. I guess he did not guess that there would be Mr. Laar who would destroy the kolkhozes, because Savisaar never accepted forced liquidation of kolkhozes.

2. Prof. Ivan Nikolov Popov

Sofia, Bulgaria 1996; three consecutive meetings on May 8th, June 21st-22nd, and August 20th.
Interviewer: Ivan Tchalakov

A Short Introductory Note

Prof. Ivan Popov was electrical engineer and professor at Sofia Polytechnics, a key figure in the development of electro technical and electronic industry in Bulgaria in the years after 1945. He made remarkable carried as industrial manager and university professor during 1950s and 1960s, to become Minister of electronic industry, Vice-premier Minister and member of Bulgarian communist party Politburo. He was dismissed from all his positions in 1975, and after short period as Bulgarian ambassador in Switzerland he spent the rest of socialist period till 1989 away from the economic affairs as Chairmen of the Federation of Science-Technical Unions. Ivan Popov passed away in year 2000 at age of 93.

Early Years

We were three children in the family – I was the eldest, then my brother Emil Popov, three years younger, and finally my sister Irina. I was born in 1907 [in Veliko Tarnovo, the medieval capital of Bulgaria], and when I was at the age of five, my father was mobilized in the army and from 1912 to 1918 he fought in the wars (first the Balkan Wars, then in WW I). So my mother – a small, thin woman, raised us by herself. As I grew up, being 'head of the family' I had to help my mother. During the war there was rationing and I was to stand in queues for bread and other basic goods. How afraid I was of those queues! - People were tripping over each other. Being shy and thin like my mother, sometime I was almost trampled... Once in the queue I was beaten by the cadets from the military school. When my mother saw this she pounced on them and with her nails bloodied their faces - then I understood what a mother is and how she loved me ... Honestly speaking, when I watched my mother during those war years and even after that, how she struggled alone to raise us, I swore never to allow such things to happen again.

In 1918 my father was demobilized from the army, and soon after that our family moved to Sofia. We bought a house in Knyazhevo, one of the suburbs of the city. When in high school, I became member of a small Marxist circle – there was a young man coming every other week to report about the political situation, international policy, etc. This man was linked with Marko Fridman, a member of the group that on April 16, 1925 blasted St Nedelya Church in Sofia.[1] So this young man was caught by the police and he confessed everything, including about our Marxist circle, how he was giving lectures to us, that we collected money for the famine in the Volga basin in Russia, etc. So we were also apprehended by the police… How cruel people were in those times – I, a 16-year old boy, was put in heavy iron chains for forty days – me, the big enemy of the state, almost a kid. Our trial was in a hall near the Military Cllub, at the corner of Rakovska Street and Russki Boulevard. I was sentenced to 2 years in prison. When I left the prison, I had to complete high school privately, as an independent student. Then I entered Sofia University.

While a student, I discovered I had a special talent for math – I had never known that before. But it became evident that my mind was built in such a way that I could think very quickly and easily understood the matter. I published several papers abroad, and wrote several booklets on different matters in math. So after I graduated university I was invited to be an assistant to Prof. Lyubomir Chakaloff.[2] I told him: "You know my file, how could they possibly admit me as assistant professor?" – "Do not worry, he said, I'll take care of it." So for one year I was his assistant at the university, and then I left for France, I became a student in "electrometallurgy of non-ferrous metals" at Toulouse Polytechnics… I had a good salary as assistant professor at Sofia University, so I saved up some money, which was enough for me to live in Toulouse during the first year.

I graduated in France with the highest grades in the group and I won a scholarship for the obligatory practical assignment in industry. I chose three enterprises in Paris, where I learned a lot! I was in the firm *Siequi,* owned by four brothers, French Jews, but the name was not French, maybe they were originally from Greece or some other country. David, the eldest brother and director of the firm, was the first in the world to succeed in producing a spot welding of a Duralumin resistant to sea water and used in hydro-planes. While other companies used for this purpose some special additives, chemical compounds that were corroded by sea water, David

[1] One of the major terrorist attacks against the Bulgarian bourgeois authorities after WW I, carried out by the communist resistance. As a result, 150 people of the country's political and military elite were killed and around 500 were injured (see http://en.wikipedia.org/wiki/St_Nedelya_Church_assault).

[2] http://en.wikipedia.org/wiki/Ljubomir_Chakaloff

managed to do such spot welding using only an electronic scheme – they would seek the 'zero'-point of the sinusoid and make the welding precisely at the moment when it started climbing upward. I saw there for the first time the application of electronics in these processes, a marvellous application. They made sea water resistant welding instantaneously using no chemicals!

The *Siequi* brothers dispersed in all directions – only the youngest one, Mario, remained in France to run the company. The others headed branches of the company in USA, in England, etc. In each country they had a monopoly position in the field; no other company knew how to weld aluminium this way. But I left the firm to continue my practical assignment in another company, the French branch of the Swiss firm *Oerlikon*. In all these companies where I was apprenticed I learned a lot, for example what production discipline means. Also, there was a seminar in one of these firms, where every week they would discuss the latest achievements in the field of electro welding.

- You mean that they were evaluating the potential of every innovation and scientific results in the field?

Yes. There I saw how French people discussed these matters – when you are reporting, the others are not arguing personally against you, but they were analysing your report objectively – how for example an Australian patent could be used, or a US patent, or a patent from South Africa. They were discussing whether they were valuable or not, how could be applied, etc.

During that period I wrote a letter to the department of electro welding in Braunschweig, Germany. They were editing the journal "Elektroschweißen", in German, a world renowned journal. I wrote to the professor there that I would be glad to go and see him personally, pointing out that I had graduated electro-metallurgy of nonferrous metals in Toulouse. He invited me and when I came and we discussed the latest achievements in our field (we were talking in French), he realized I knew some things better than he did. He asked me – "Where did you learn all this?" I told him about these seminars in the French companies at which I was on a practical assignment, about the discussions there, and said to him "You have the same technical literature, about patents etc., you are receiving all the news but you are not reading it this way, you are not analysing it the way the French companies do, when 20 smart brains are discussing the value of a given patent, both from the practical and theoretical point of view". Yes, there I realized the importance of objective scientific analysis of the patents.

Entrepreneur in Bulgaria during the 1930s

When I returned to Bulgaria in 1934, I needed something to start with. To have a welding machine was the most important thing, the transformer being the key part of it. So I made one together with my brother Emil, who was executed in 1943.[3] We found an excellent transformer-plate [special plate for transformers] at the storage facility of the Swedish company *Boeyler*, near the Alexander Hospital, where my father was working at the time. The plate was rather rusty, but we cleaned and polished it and we made a very good transformer, an exact copy of the model of the Swiss company *Secheron* [the company still exists; see http://www.secheron.com – I.Tch.].

So finally I had a good welding machine and started working with it. Very soon, however, I realized I could not work as a welder – my hands trembled as in Parkinson disease. My hand would tremble and I was unable to make good welding – you need first to produce a spark, to draw away the electrode a little and then to bring it back close. But my hands trembled and I could not control this. What was the reason? – The doctors were helpless. It was not a big trembling, otherwise I am a healthy man, but enough to spoil the welding work…

So again the same question arises –"What to do?" … I registered a firm in my name and thinking what its profile should be, I concluded - without knowing all these economic schools, it should be something that is made by hand. So I established a workshop called "ELPHA" – from "Electrical, Laboratory and PHysical Apparatuses". I rented two rooms near the transformer station on the corner of Iskar and Konstantin Stoilov streets, behind the Sofia City Bath. There was a small square there and our workshop with these apparatuses was there – laboratory equipment, electrical equipment.

I had two secret associates in the workshop – the first was Nikola Genadiev, whose father Pavel Genadiev owned a lead mine located near

---

[3] Emil Popov was the wireless operator of a local resistance unit working for Soviet intelligence during the WW II. The group leader was Alexander Peev ('Boevoy'). Emil was arrested on April 15, 1943 but managed to escape during the arrest. He was captured again on July 12, 1943, sentenced to death and executed on November 22, 1943 in Sofia, together with Alexander Peev and Ivan Vladkov. (source: http://calendar.dir.bg/inner.php?d=28&month=11&year=2010&cid=&sid=&eid=3732).

the town of Panaguyrishte.[4] I knew him because we had graduated math at Sofia University, and he was naturally gifted in technology. He was a very clever and a hard-working young man. His brother Assen Genadiev graduated chemistry; he did some valuable work too. The second associate was Peter Paunov, assistant professor at the Faculty of Physics, Sofia University. He was also a very practical man. Both were secretly helping me, they did not declare openly they were my partners. But we divided our tasks, so that each of us knew what he was responsible for, while I became a kind of official owner and manager.

Before long Peter Paunov left the workshop – it was too difficult for him to combine the two types of activities, professorship at the university and our business. But Nikola Genadiev remained with me – skilful, clever, honest boy, I relied very much on him. Indeed, we ran the workshop together… My brother Emil also helped us, and we also hired a young woman. Her name was Maria Moldovanova, she had graduated physics at Sofia University. Later she became a full professor, one of the founders of silicon semiconductors production in Bulgaria.

When we established our workshop I barely had any capital. So I took a loan of 20 000 Bulgarian levs from the Popular Bank in Sofia. I used it to buy a lathe, a very good lathe, a drill – a relatively big one, and another tiny little lathe for fine details. I think that was our whole machinery, the rest of the work we did manually. There was scarcity and hardship in the beginning…I did not have enough money to rent a flat for myself, so using wooden boards and beams we built a loft in one of the rooms of the workshop. During the day we used it as working place too, but in the evenings after planning the tasks for the next day, I cleaned it, unfolded the mattress and slept in the loft. I was eaten by fleas, it was terrible! Every month, when the term to pay the credit instalment in Popular Bank approached – wow, what a rush there was to collect the money! Yes, I suffered a lot, but eventually my idea about this workshop worked out well, and I succeeded. We established ourselves in the market and there was growing interest in our services.

With the approach of WW II, importing electrical and laboratory apparatuses became a complicated matter. Especially after the beginning of the war the Bulgarian laboratories had much trouble getting the

[4] Hariton, Nikola and Pavel Genadiev are from a famous Bulgarian family from the town of Bitola, Macedonia. Ivan Popov's associate Nikola had the same name as his uncle and was son of Pavel, the youngest of the Genadiev brothers. During the interwar period Pavel became one of the biggest Bulgarian patrons of the arts and was editor of the journals *Artist* and *Library*. In the late 1930s, however, he lost most of his fortune and the family declined financially.

necessary equipment from abroad. So the number of orders to my firm grew. I even managed to stop [make unnecessary] the import of some apparatuses – I copied some of them, and others were of our own design. For example, we produced centrifuges for biological experiments, items for physical laboratories, machines for water distillation, high-precision thermostats, etc. ELPHA became so popular, that we got orders from the Rockefeller Institute for Contagious Diseases in Sofia, from the Bulgarian National Bank, etc. Gradually we created a team of high-skilled workers that did an excellent job. Later I used this experience when we created the Bulgarian computer industry. By the early 1940s we were able to compete with established firms importing equipment and chemicals from abroad, and our firm often prevailed in the tenders (at one point I was even offered money not to participate in the tenders!).

Seeking to expand my business, I bought a license from the Hungarian company *Agrolux Co.* for household electrical heaters (for water and other purposes) and launched its production. The heater was relatively cheap and sold well. But when we redesigned the heater as an electric ring, where the temperature was higher, we found that sometimes it became conductive and potentially dangerous for the users. So we put a claim to the Hungarian firm that the heater did not correspond to the licence we had bought. Meanwhile, I red in a journal about a German patent for a different type of insulator called *cohezam*. Together with my brother Emil we experimented with it and found that it was much better than the kaolin-based material the Hungarian firm was using. So I wrote a letter to the firm saying that now we were able, in turn, to offer them a better solution. Soon the Hungarian firm invited me to go to Budapest and to try to introduce the new insulator in their plant.

So I went to Hungary, leaving ELPHA to my father and my associate Nikola Genadiev as technical director.

Engineer in Hungary during the 1930s

In Hungary, initially I could not learn Hungarian because I found all these young engineers in the plant who were speaking to me in French in order to exercise their language skills. I felt well, of course, but after a year I realized I didn't understand a word of Hungarian. "What an idiot you are!", I told myself, and soon after that I left the plant and entered the AEG branch in Budapest. I was recommended by a Hungarian professor in engineering – Belatini Braun. He was from an aristocratic Hungarian family, obviously with some German strain. Prof. Braun worked at the Istanbul Polytechnics in Turkey, and came back to Budapest during the summer period only. He took me under his patronage and had spoken with AEG about their hiring me.

However, already in my early stay in Hungary I become acquainted with a French woman living in Budapest. We became acquainted in the train during one of my trips to France. When she was a student in the Sorbonne, she had made the acquaintance of a Hungarian colleague studying there and had married him. So this man brought this young, freethinking girl into a conservative Catholic Budapest family, where they prayed every morning, she had to kiss the hand of his mother, etc. She barely survived one day and told him: “We should go to live alone, or I'm leaving. I cannot live in such a situation!” This Hungarian seemed a little weak-willed, otherwise a very good person and smart – he did not agree and stayed with his parents. And she left and began to support herself by giving lessons in French.

So gradually we fell in love and I married her. Before coming to Hungary I had been married in Bulgaria and was divorced – why and how is not important. But my French wife appeared to be a very bright, very talented woman. She wrote and published two novels and three other books in France, they were translated also into Bulgarian, and when she died she left the manuscript of another book.[5]

So when I moved to AEG plant, I really improved my Hungarian to such an extent that I was able to make speeches to workers, though with lots of mistakes [he laughed]. It was important, however, that they understood me. Because while in AEG, French was of no use – with the exception of the manager, who was a Belgian, nobody spoke French. I was often called by the manager to talk to him in French, but I was afraid not to say something wrong – because already by the early 1940s he was telling me “Our cause is lost, we lost the war!”

So I stayed nine years in all in Hungary. But during my first years in AEG something very bad happened… I learned that my brother Emil Popov had been arrested in Sofia and that he was going to be sentenced to death, that he would be shot [the events took place in the spring and summer of 1943 – I.Tch.]. It was a very hard experience for me, I loved my brother. When I learned this, my nerves got on edge; I prepared my suitcase, a bag with everything necessary, toothpaste, etc., so as to be

[5] The name of Ivan Popov’s wife was Hélène Bannerot. Ivan Popov had two of her books published in Bulgarian – a volume of her selected short novels (1997) and her novel *Les amours de l'atelier Mirette* (1999). He gave me copies of these books at our last meeting on April 21, 1999. The novel *Les amours de l'atelier Mirette* was published in France in 1958 by Editions *Seuil* (http://livre.fnac.com/a95554/Helene-Bannerot-Les-Amours-de-l-atelier-Mirette)

ready if they came to arrest me because of my brother. Because I helped my brother a bit, not very actively, but ... He got a radio transmitter, the Russians call it 'ratzia'. It was given to him by Krustyo Belev, a novelist from the city of Varna. When he gave it to my brother, he and Borislav Djakov (brother of the well-known Bulgarian physicist Emil Djakov[6]) tested it and realized that the transmitter was rather weak. So they decided to make their own transmitter.

So I was looking for materials for them in Hungary, that was how I helped them, nothing else. Still was I afraid I could be arrested because of that. So I kept my suitcase next to the back door of AEG, to escape easily if they came to arrest me. As I said, I was afraid somebody from my brother's group might say something about me. But nobody came – maybe because in 1943 there was no longer a Bulgarian embassy in Budapest, they had all fled. The [front of the] war was approaching. So knowing there was still a Bulgarian engineer working in AEG plant, many Bulgarians in Hungary came to me asking for help…

About that time they overturned Admiral Michael Horthy from power. His wife was Jewish, his government did not persecuted the Jews, who were about 600 000 in Hungary. In fact most of the Hungarian trade, medicine, construction, design, almost everything was in the hands of Jews. But when the Hungarian army was defeated in Russia - they lost a heavy battle at Voronezh and when they retreated they completely destroyed the city… That is why they kick Horthy off. And very soon the Jews were registered; they began to collect them… I proposed to these fellows – there were many Jews among the engineers in the plant, to try to go to Tito, to escape in the mountains of Yugoslavia. But they did not want to. And I yelled: "You will regret it bitterly! Don't you see what is happening - all of you will go to the ghetto and then be burned in Auschwitz!" They rejected my words, they did not believe... Almost all died, only one or two survived.

Our AEG plant was producing two main items. The first was a special device for the German "Stuka" ground-attack aircrafts. It was manufactured with enormous precision by special Swiss-made lathes. The second item was a coal furnace-mill for electric power plants. It was also something very modern at the time, though for the low-power plants, about 60 kilowatts. So when the Russian troops were approaching Budapest, I met with one of the senior technicians, his name was Meyer, to

[6] Emil Djakov is Bulgarian physisist, who together with academician Georgy Nadjakov established technical physics in Bulgarian. The BAS Institute of Electronics is named of his name (see more on http://ie-bas.dir.bg/Presentation.htm)

decide what to do with the plant. In fact I was one of the few engineers left, since the manager and most of the other engineers had escaped to Austria together with the German troops. We learned that they were planning also to evacuate the equipment to Austria. We even knew when they would do it. Since these were very expensive Swiss machines, we decide with Mayer to dismantle some of their small key parts, thus making the machines unusable. We decided to hide the removed parts among the iron castings - we had lots of iron castings in the plant. So we hid them between castings and we made a list where each part was. When next day they came to evacuate the equipment, they saw it was damaged and took nothing.

When the Germans left Budapest, there was not a single bridge intact, not a single tramcar, or car, or train running. They destroyed everything. The Hungarian solders took off their military uniforms and put on civilian clothes. When the Russians took the city, they knew Hungarian solders were there and checked everyone in order to take the solders as prisoners of war. The Russians would block the streets, take the people and question each man where he had been previously. And many people were arrested and sent to Russia. One of our engineers disappeared one day and later we found out he had been sent to Russia to work in a railway factory.

So eventually I remained the only engineer in the AEG plant and I had to manage it. I went there every day, remained with the workers even if there was nothing to do – just to be sure I'm there and able to react if something happened. During the battles for Budapest one day an air bomb dropped, penetrated the roof and the floor below, reached the second floor and exploded. But the plant was very well designed – with large thin windows, like an exhibition hall. The windows exploded taking the shock wave away, while the machines remained practically intact. I ordered the workers to cover the broken windows with wooden plates and that was all. And so we kept the plant in order, no robberies, and no lootings.

One day, however, I stayed at home – there was sporadic shooting in our part of the city and it was not safe to walk in the streets. By noon someone knocked on the door – there was a Russian officer with a few solders asking if I was the AEG engineer. I said 'yes' and they said I should go with them to the plant. My wife began to cry, I tried to calm her…

So they put me in their jeep and drove me to the plant. I found there an enormous man, a Russian general, sitting in the manager's office. "Are you Ivan Popov?", he asked. "Yes", I replied. "Who is managing the plant?" – I said I am the only engineer left, there were no others. Then he asked me if it was true that it was me who arranged the damaging of the machines, so that the Germans were unable to evacuate it. Obviously he had been talking before with the workers and Mayer told them about that. So I confirmed. "Are you able to restore the machines and put them back to work?" – I confirmed again. "Tell me more about yourself!" he asked again and I told him my story – that I was a political prisoners in the 1920s, that my brother was executed in Bulgaria as Soviet spy, etc. "Well, the general said; now we are deciding the destiny of this plant. I am appointing you director and from now on we will communicate with you!", and he pointed to one of his officer, captain Shelentzov was his name. He said he would be my contact person and they gave me a telephone number to call when necessary. That was how I became director of the plant.

Soon after that we resumed the production – now we manufactured an item for the Soviet tanks. It was similar to those for the "Stuka" aircrafts, but not so accurate. Still it was a sophisticated product and complex enough. We worked in fortified conditions; the main entrance was constantly locked, with an old truck blocking the iron doors from inside. We were afraid a lot since there were no special guards in the plant – indeed; there were several attempts by other Russian officers to enter the plant searching for valuable items. Every time I was to negotiate with them, and to call captain Shelentzov to intervene. Yet gradually the situation became calm and I remained as engineer in Hungary till 1950.[7]

Coming Back to Bulgaria as Manager of Nationalized Electro-technical Plant

Then in 1950 I returned to Bulgaria together with my French wife. I was appointed director of the *High-voltage Plant "Voroshilov"* in Sofia, it was a well-paid job, everything developed well, and we bought an apartment. It was not a very big one, but together with my wife we designed and outfitted it, so it became a cosy and convenient home…

The *High-voltage Plant* I was manager of in fact consisted of twelve workshops scattered all over Sofia. These were former private workshops and small factories, nationalized in 1948. It was almost impossible to visit them all in a single day. We had a lot of problems, especially with the former *Bergmann* factory, now part of the plant, producing pipes for

[7] According to his collaborators, in 1945 Ivan Popov was appointed director of the *Hermangyoy* plant, where he remained till 1949. It is not clear enough if this was the same AEG plant, renamed after 1945. According to the same sources Ivan Popov returned to Bulgaria in late 1949 (Dimitrova, M. *The Golden Decades of Bulgarian Electronics*, Trud Publishing House, Sofia, 2008, pp. 96-97).

electric cables.[8] Because of the asphalt there was a fire in the factory almost every other month. Its manager Marko Shopov, a very good man, was complaining constantly "We cannot prevent accidents when working with such materials, paper and melted asphalt – at the least accident and it immediately ignites!" This was a single case; there were accidents in other workshops too – here a wall would fall, there the machines would break down, fire again… Eventually I prepared my small suitcase from the war period in Hungary, seeing what the situation was. It was during the Chervenkov Stalinist regime, tough times. So I put the suitcase in my office and said to myself "You will be arrested before long!"…

Then our plant grew and we became *High-voltage Combine ELPROM*, where all electro-technical plants in the country were united in one. I was appointed general manager. The problems, however, continued. I remember the plant for electro porcelain in the town of Nikolaevo, eastern Bulgaria. It was a real disaster there – twelve people from the management were to be tried for sabotage… This plant was built using German technology - trophy equipment taken by the Soviet army. The equipment was provided directly to Bulgaria, not even going through the Soviet Union first. The machines were German, but the technology of high-voltage porcelain insulators was Soviet, designed by a professor from Leningrad (Saint-Petersburg), with detailed documentation in which the entire process was described. So we launched production – first the mixture was prepared and then we poured it through cloth filters to expel the water, making the mixture semi-dry. The mixture consisted of three elements put together in a large rotating drum with porcelain balls - clay, quartz and... I can't remember the third one. When mixed well in the drums and then passing through the filters, the dough-like mixture went on slowly drying, and then the forms were covered with glaze and entered a tunnel furnace in which different areas had different temperatures. It was a long process that was managed electronically. That is how I realized again the benefits of electronics… And then suddenly defects started to appear.

We had bought a test station to check the ready-made products. Our initial intention was to produce 20 kilovolt insulators; we did not dare to go to a higher voltage. But when tested, none of the produced insulators withstood the voltage! We fired the technician there, put other people on the job, but defects continued - we were unable to produce a single series able to withstand 20 kilovolts. We checked everything – the heating gas in the furnace, the recipe, the workers' qualification… Nothing was wrong,

[8] These were the old paper pipes, coated with asphalt as an insulator. The pipes were installed in homes and other buildings, the electric cables were placed in and thus the buildings were electrified.

hence it followed that the reason was the lack of discipline in production. But where? People from the economic police decided it was sabotage, a deliberate damaging of production, and started their own investigation. I too was among the suspects.

So I had to go to the plant and stay there until the problems were solved. Eventually we discovered there was a young woman in the night shifts working with the balance and pressing the buttons, determining thereby the quantities of kaolin, clay, etc. to be put into the mixture. The volumes were defined according to the recipe and then she recorded in a special notebook what she had put into the mixture. She recorded as it should be according to recipe, but in fact she put in the mixture as she pleased. So the recording did not correspond to the real composition of the mixture. She was caught on the spot, and then she started crying… We replaced her and suddenly the problem was fixed, we reached the required specifications! I stayed a few more nights together with the local managers to make sure the things were all right. Prior to that we had changed five or six directors of the plant, and 12 people – including me - were brought to justice.

The problem was to impose production discipline in the newly built plants. I will tell you later the problems we had in electronic industry. But here in the *Elprom* combine I learned something about financing the investments that I later applied to electronic industry too. Our combine was subordinate to the Ministry of Electrification (electric power), which each year decided the total amount of money to be invested in different projects – dams, power stations, etc. This included our combine – early in the year we knew how much money we would get for investment. However, none of the enterprises at this Ministry fulfilled the plans. So early in the fall when our Minister Kimon Georgiev [former general from the Bulgarian royal army who helped the Communists Party take power in September 1944 – I.Tch.] saw his money would be lost – i.e. we would not fulfil the investments plan - he re-allotted it to those who could expend the funds. That is how I got additional money for investments, in fact as much as I wanted, and every year I managed to build a new plant in my combine, each plant made up of just three design elements. For these three elements I was helped by the director of the *Factory for Building Structures* in the city of Stara Zagora. His name was Gospodin Velikov, a very talented man. It was my idea, but Mr. Velikov's factory implemented it - as I said, he was an ingenious builder! Whatever he undertook worked out neatly. The factory was completely automated, as far as the conditions of those times permitted, and manufactured nice products, cheaply and quickly enough. Later Velikov became a PhD, but remained director of the plant. Because the plants were built using only three structural elements, it was easy to expand them if necessary – we just removed one of the walls at the other end and then moved it further as much as was necessary. So the plants grew without difficulties.

But I would like to tell you something: wherever I have built factories, myself - whether in electronic industry or in machine-building industry, everywhere I was taken to court and there was a court proceeding against me. Why? – There were always people denouncing me to Todor Zhivkov [The First Secretary of the Bulgarian Communist Party – I.Tch.]: "Ivan Popov this, Ivan Popov that!" ... Then I had to prove that it was not true, that I was innocent, and that these were lies.

Take, for example, the electric tube factory in the town of Sliven. There we, *Elprom* combine, inherited by the Nationalization Act a private enterprise called *BELFA* (from Bulgarian ELectrical FActory). They produced electric tubes, importing almost all the necessary elements. At one point we realised it would be cheaper to produce these elements here, so we built a new plant. But when the production of the new plant increased, a problem arose. Producing electric tubes requires perfect conditions – absolute cleanliness, no dust, everything must be pressurized… So we produced large quantities of tubes, but when you screwed it in, it lit up for a little while and fired once, crack, and it all went black. That is why we called it “black plague” in the tubes. There was something wrong with the technology - obviously air or dirt was entering from somewhere into the tubes; maybe the metal had not been cleaned inside as it should have. We suffered great damages… and State Security again put me on trial for sabotage!

But then I put our science into production… It was the 1950s and in Sofia Polytechnics there was already a *Department of Metallurgy*. The professor there seemed nothing special, but there was a very capable assistant, his name was Mirev. He helped us a lot! Otherwise I sent many other scientists to this plant to look for what caused the “black plague” in tubes. They all found it was because the air in the tubes had not been cleaned enough. However, nobody could say where the dirt came from. There was a huge cleaning vessel for the air, made of glass, and only Mirev proposed to replace this vessel with one made by metal, by simple iron sheets. The physicist at the factory, his name was Stefanov, rebelled: "How can you use the iron plate!? Great shit! You could not purify the air with dirty iron sheets, there are pores inside, there is dirt, etc." So he went to the Central Committee and complained. Still Mirev argued that nothing bad was going to happen. So I was summoned again by the police, the investigator questioned me, etc. Eventually I was indicted in two cases...

I remembered then I knew the director of the *Tungsram* plant in Budapest. I had lots of connections there and I wrote him a letter. No, rather I arranged first for the *BELFA* physicist Stefanov to visit *Tungsram* and see how they worked. I was not angry at Stefanov – he did what he believed, that was what he had studied at university, that you can't clean the air in dirty metal vessels. I sent Stefanov on a specialization in Tungsram for one month. And one day someone knocked on the door of my office – the *Elprom* chief manager's office. I went out and saw Mr. Stefanov. He says: "Comrade Popov, excuse me for all the trouble I caused". "Excuse for what?" I ask him. "Well, in this huge Hungarian plant, which we will never reach in size - they supply the whole Soviet Union, the vessel in which the gas is purified was from metal plate! Comrade Mirev was completely right! Please excuse me!" And he was begging to be forgiven, etc. Of course, I thanked him for this – he saved me from the trial (laughs).

Well, but this was only one of the cases. I was still indicted in another case – the so-called "3% return" that I had introduced. I had ordered the traders that, when the client buys a tube from the shops or grocery stores, in each tube box there should be a note with the date and signature of those who had produced it. If the tube burnt out at first use, the client gets a second lamp for free. So the tube traders were allowed to substitute [items] for these notes. There was a lawsuit against me about this order. So I wrote to *Tungsram* again, asking whether they gave a guarantee with which a defective lamp can be replaced. My colleague from *Tungsram* confirmed, and in addition he wrote that in Hungary they gave not 3% but 5% - this was an old factory, with long experience! I immediately translated the letter, the Hungarian Embassy certified that everything was authentic, and I brought it to the investigator. When he saw it he said "Hm, you get off again!" I was saved again...

One day, however, I had just come back from a mission abroad[9] when they told me my wife was seriously ill. She had cancer… Some doctors said this was not cancer, but did not find the cause. Then in Third City Hospital a heart disease specialist, a Jewish woman – her name was Tamara Pilosof, she decided that we must explore my wife and see what she was sick of. Tamara had graduated medicine in France and she somehow had sympathy for my wife. She gave us her own room, the doctor's office – they put in another bed for me and I took care of my wife. Six months I watched her slowly dying... It was then that her second

[9] Later in the interview Ivan Popov remembered this was after he returned from a conference in the Technical University of Ilmenau, former German Democratic Republic.

novel was published.[10] So I was alone at her burial. She was a very intelligent person, that's all I can say… (His eyes fill with tears, and we remain silent for a while.)

- Tell me, please, about your professional contacts in DDR, the conference at Ilmenau, etc.?

The colleagues in GDR liked me very much indeed… They invited me several times, I helped them a lot. So I became an Honorary Doctor of the Technical University in Ilmenau. However, during one of my stays there I fell sick. I had some illnesses since my stay in jail in the 1920s that I never managed to cure. And while I was ill in Germany, Vibi – the secretary at the university's international relations department, looked after me. She saw that I did not feel well, and she arranged for my stay in a hospital at Erfurt - famous for a doctor there who was a great professional. I stayed there and he treated me - "Everything's fine, everything's fine, says the doctor, it's just that your battery is exhausted!" I worked too much, he meant. This is how I met Vibi, my last wife, she was German.

Meanwhile the Germans in GDR were building a large electro technical research institute near Berlin. It was the only institute in our camp [CMEA] that had a machine for testing large transformers that could withstand high voltage of lightning, of sudden short circuit, etc. The institute was brand new, built in a bare field. The director of that institute had left – he did not defect to the West, he was Austrian, when his term expired he wanted to go, did not want to stay in GDR anymore. So when the Germans saw I was working in this field and I was dealing with all these things, they asked me - through our government – if I could go and run this institute. This happened in the late 1950s… They asked me to manage this R&D unit. It was a very important research centre, the only in our socialist camp (CMEA). The colleagues from GDR sent an official request to our Government and I was given permission to go but only for three years, without a pension, without a salary here in Bulgaria, entirely

[10] Obviously these tragic events took place in 1958, when the French publishing house *Seuil* published Hélène Bannerot's novel *Les amours de l'atelier Mirette* we mentioned above..

at the expense of GDR.[11] That's why since 1989 I have been fighting to get a German pension, for those three years... It cost me a lot of efforts, but eventually it was arranged, these days I am waiting for the final approval. If I get the pension, I will publish the last novel of my wife Hélène. I will publish it with my own money…

Head of Bulgarian State Committee for Science and Technical Progress; the beginning of Bulgarian Electronic Industry

When the three years in GDR passed, I returned to Bulgaria and I was appointed President of the *State Committee for Science and Technical Progress* (SCSTP). I came in touch with the Bulgarian electronic industry because of the position I held in SCSTP.

The development of electronics in Bulgaria started after we bought a French licence for production of germanium transistors and germanium-based semiconductors in general. A modern plant was built in the town of Botevgrad near Sofia. There was nothing there at the beginning, but gradually there emerged a team of scientists and engineers who mastered semiconductor technology, even though based on germanium and not on silicon. They acquired the necessary knowledge and skills and later they were able to go on to silicon semiconductors. There were several clever scientists in Botevgrad, I remember in particular Yordan Kasabov, who established his own Institute of Microelectronics here in Sofia. In 1966 he designed the first Bulgarian electronic calculator (called ELKA), based on germanium semiconductors. This was on the eve of the integrated circuits, so these machines, though small, were packed with several layers of plates full of transistors. Now everything is on a single integrated circuit, but this was not possible in the beginning. And that is how my struggle began; it was here that I entered electronics…

---

[11] Ivan Popov was appointed vice director for science at the Institute for High-voltage Technology near Berlin, GDR. There he also headed an international team on electric distribution transformers, designed under his methodology. For the successful implementation of these transformers in industry Ivan Popov was awarded the National Award for Science and Technology of GDR. (recollection of Prof. Georgy Barbutov, who worked at this institute as a research engineer during the same period (Dimitrova 2008: 98)

- So the experience gained in Botevgrad was later transferred to other plants, like the computer memory device plants in Stara Zagora, Plovdiv and some other cities?

Yes, just to say a few words about the first ELKA calculator designed by Kasabov. In 1966 there were three such types of electronic calculators in the world - not in Europe, but in the world! The first was ANITA, a British one based on silicon technology, the second was IME, an Italian one, and the third was our ELKA (the name came from ELectronic CAlculator). There were no other desk calculators produced in the world, only those three! So it was a real [technological] achievement.

We signed a contract with a French company that manufactured typewriters. They gave us the technology to produce small and portable electric typewriters to be integrated with the ELKA calculator. In turn, they were to market our ELKA in France. The French liked our calculators… Everything went well in the beginning; we mastered the production of the calculator typewriter device, and supplied the first batches of calculators in France. Very soon, however, the calculators started to show defects. I told you, they were rather complex machines, packed with several layers of electronic plates. So the French company complained that our ELKA had flaws, some broke down and the French technicians were unable to fix it even after replacing the plates…

Twice I sent a team of 4-5 engineers to fix things there, they repaired the machines, they found out what the problem was and fixed it. One of them even defected to Switzerland; he did not return to Bulgaria. Yet defects continued and so did the complaints from France… Eventually I went to France and approached their Communist Party, its Central Committee. Of course they knew me, since I was also a member of the Bulgarian Communist Party Politburo, so they respected me ... And I honestly told them: "Please give me a capable engineer who is familiar with electronic components and calculator design. Please give him to me even for one month – just to have him open our eyes and find out where we are wrong!"

The French comrades sent an engineer, a Jew, a very gifted engineer – you know, among the Jews there are some very good men, very honest and very good-natured men. He came here and never returned to France – he married a Bulgarian woman and remained in Bulgaria. Some years later he died in a tramcar accident here in Sofia… So when this man came to Sofia, he said: "I want to visit the production plant!" It was in the town of Silistra, in the north-eastern part of the country, near the Romanian border. He went there, stayed a few weeks and then returned. "I know what the problem is, he said, *your workers are not wearing gloves*. They are working with bare hands, but some of them…" I was very surprised to learn from him that there are people whose palms are always sweating. And that sweat remains inside on the solder joints of the electronic components… The sweat is like a chemical salts that corrode the solder joints from the inside! So you will never understand where your defect is, everything is covered over. He said: "Your staffs have to work always with gloves, gloves made of a special synthetic material with holes in it, for ventilation, but a worker should not touch the metal."

We immediately bought such gloves from France, introduced them in the factory and the last batch of 500 ELKA that had been exported to France were brought back to Bulgaria – we redesigned them and sent them back again. In about two months the calculators again showed defects. And I realized that something was happening in the plant. Because otherwise we were testing the devices as all companies in the world did – we imported special Japanese equipment and, just as they were doing, we subjected every new product to different temperatures, bumps, etc. In spite of all the severe testing there were still some defects, though at a lower rate.

As there was nothing else to do, I decided to go to the production plant personally. For I had sent several of my assistants to check on the spot, but in vain. Thus time I went myself. When I entered the huge production hall where the women were soldering the joints of the electronic plates, I immediately noticed that two of them bent down and put on their gloves. *So they were working without gloves and put them on now, seeing I was there!* I immediately summoned them and told them: "Do you know that you're fired! Dress and leave the plant! You caused us enormous troubles." So I fired them and told the others what they had done, what troubles they had caused for the country and how they had damaged the country's name in industry, and, most importantly, that the defects cost us millions of US dollars.

However, some weeks later the first secretary of the Communist Party regional committee in Silistra called me: "Comrade Popov, he said, the two girls are suing you, and the public opinion is set against you. The girls will file suit in court to be paid compensation. Please, restore them to work, in another place if need be!" Hearing this I went directly to Todor Zhivkov [the top communist leader of Bulgaria – I.Tch.] and I told him the story, and about this call from the Regional Party Committee. Shortly thereafter, a major national conference was held in Sofia. There the Prime Minister Stanko Todorov made a report on the economic situation. And he related this case at the conference - how an economic minister, a member of the Politburo could not dismiss two undisciplined workers whose negligence had resulted in the loss of millions of dollars for Bulgaria and the country's name as a manufacturer was damaged. Because ultimately the Frenchmen gave up on us, they cancelled the contract, and there was no more export! That is how it was - we are still slouches in production, otherwise we are smart people, I have said it many times!

Later I put one of the two women workers on a parliamentary committee when the Germans invited us – she was to travel with the members of the committee to see how the Germans worked and why people have confidence in their technology. You know - everything lies within us, everything depends only on us as persons… We Bulgarians are capable people, very capable, but we are slouches, undisciplined. We are terribly undisciplined, that's it.

Establishing the International Frame of Bulgarian Electronic Industry

At the same time I pressed the Soviet Union to establish a special commission on computer technology among our socialist countries. Together with former Soviet minister of Instrument Equipment, Mikhail Evgenievich Rakovski (who later became first deputy chairman of Gosplan) we decided that we needed to create a commission, an intergovernmental committee on computer technology among the socialist countries. However, this committee was to be outside of CMEA and it should not be subordinated to CMEA - otherwise there would be too many people getting involved, most of whom did not understand the matter! While we needed an organizational unit devoted only to computing, of course approved by the governments of CMEA countries. It was to be a 'standing committee', chaired by Rakovski. I was vice president, and practically I was suggesting to him many of the ideas our committee was to deal with. So he and I were the creators of this commission, the Standing Committee[12], so to say.

[12] It was finally named Inter-Governmental Commission on Computer Technology (IGCCT), established by *Multilateral Governmental Agreement on the Development, Production and Application of Electronic Data Processing Equipment*, signed in 1969 (see Crane and Skoller 1988, Rand Corporation; see also *Soviet and Eastern European Foreign Trade,* Vol. 24, No. 1, Integration in the CMEA (Spring, 1988), pp. 18-36)

- It is still not quite clear for me why you created it outside the structures of CMEA?

Because the committee would be subordinated to many people, while, when separate, we - the men from electronic industry - would be the bosses. I recall we prepared a list of different products that an information-computing centre is made up of - such as processors, memory devices, monitors, printers, input devices, etc. We described all these items and the list included 105 articles from the smallest to the largest item. So we had the list of devices needed, at the computer technology level of that time, of course.

So these 105 products needed to be produced in SMEA – this was imperative in the Cold War situation... We thought here in Sofia with my people about what to embark on and we decided to take only four of them. While the colleagues from the other SMEA countries were loaded with five, six, ten and even more products... Imagine it meant to be able to produce ten items of computer technology, imagine how many people you needed for development work alone! And if a single item does not work, you will be accused, you will be held responsible, both personally and as a country. So we took only four. But four, which are among the most important in value – memories (magnetic disks and tapes) and two more items, I will tell you when it comes to my mind, I forget it now. So we took these four and set a lot of smart people to work on developing them.

Prof. Angel Angelov, a close associate of Ivan Popov, later director of the Central Institute of Information Technology in Sofia:

"...We had to choose our priorities and propose them in Moscow at the session of the Inter-Governmental Commission on Computer Technology (IGCCT). Ivan Popov organized a kind of brainstorming together with Prof. Borov, Mihail Krimkov, Gudelkov, and others. We went down to the first computing centre the country had just bought from IBM - an enormous hall with over 100 devices. Of all those devices, we chose four, which, in the final account, amounted to more than 50% of the cost of the entire system: one type of processor, magnetic tape and disk memory devices, and one printing device. When I was leaving for Moscow, Ivan Popov said: "If you don't obtain these specializations for us, don't bother to come back!" (From an interview with Ivan Tchalakov)

About the same time I managed to establish relationships with Japan. Similarly to the French license, before I became chairman of SCSTP Bulgaria had already bought from Japan a factory for electronic components (capacitors), built in the town of Kyustendil (in western Bulgaria, near the Serbian border). The factory was bought from *Imanichi*

Co., a company located in Tokyo. The owner of this company was a very capable engineer. He had left the big computer company *Fujitsu* where he had previously been employed and had established his own company producing capacitors only, nothing else. But it was fully automated and produced very high-quality capacitors. So we imported equipment for a similar plant in Bulgaria, but the Japanese could not put it into action. The owner himself came here, his engineers came several times too - they struggled with the machinery, made a lot of changes in it, but in vain. Time was running out and we lost a lot of money - instead of producing capacitors, we continued to buy them from abroad. When the owner came to Bulgaria again, I told him: "Look – firstly, we have a lot of [financial] losses, and secondly, you also suffer moral damages because you cannot fulfil the contract. Thirdly, the same thing might happen to you at home. You are a new entrepreneurial company that bears your own name, and when the other companies realize that you cannot put your equipment into action it will be a big blow for you. So it's better that you take back the equipment and send us a new one." And he agreed, who knows what [financial] losses they sustained… Then he invited me to visit his company in Japan to see the production site, etc.

That is how I established contacts with the big Japanese company *Fujitsu.* At that period the boss of *Fujitsu* was Mr. Vàda[13] - I did not know why, but Vàda liked me, perhaps because of my frankness. I was honest, and he was honest… (Popov smiled.) He had come to work as director of Fujitsu from the military; they had been working previously for the military industry. So people like him made decisions in a military manner: exactly, in pace, rigorously.

I invited Vàda to come to Bulgaria. He came and saw our factories, one of which was the factory for computing devices in Sofia. We had not yet mastered computers on silicon transistors. However, when Vàda saw in Botevgrad the machines that we had bought from France, the germanium-based semiconductor technology, he said: "Do you know how little you

---

[13] Tzunesuke Vàda was born in 1887 in the small town of Aza, Yamaguchi prefecture. He graduated Kobe High School of Trade in 1909 and entered the *Furukawa Company*, where he worked for more than 70 years. *Fujitsu Co.* was created in the beginning of the 20th century as a subsidiary of *Furukawa*, specialized in telephone and communication technology. Starting as a simple employee, Mr. Vàda went through the entire hierarchy of the company to become its top manager. After WW II he was president of *Fuji-Electric*, then of *Fujitsu Co.* When Ivan Popov contacted him, he was president of the *Fujitsu* board of directors. In 1970 Mr. Vàda was given one of the highest Bulgarian medal "Madara Horseman". He died in 1980.

need to move on to silicon-based technology? You do not need to buy new licenses ... Now we are moving on to silicon technology and if you agree, we will give you this technology in return for a modest reward". And we agreed. They, *Fujitsu*, were on the threshold of silicon circuits, on the threshold of introducing integrated circuits.

The reward was that we agreed to buy twenty of their medium size main-frame computers. These were not very big computers, the boards of the silicon diodes were composed of small squares containing all necessary elements - capacitor, transistors, transformer, etc., and everything was on this small square board. In fact this was what at the next step would be transformed into integrated circuit ...These machines were on the verge of the contemporary machines in integrated circuits, it just took several years to turn these small square boards into a single small integrated circuit.

So we agreed to buy twenty of their machines, he sent people here to install them and also he took some of our engineers in *Fujitsu* to train them. He also delivered automation equipment to us - some very interesting automation processes were introduced in our factory here in Bulgaria, with the equipment he installed.

- *You mean the Computing Machinery Works here in Sofia?*

Yes. And thanks to him, with these twenty machines we created twenty regional computing centres, called Regional Data Computing Centre (TIC in Bulgarian). As I said, these twenty machines where what we paid for our transition from germanium to silicon technology, plus the experience we gained. Something very important - Mr. Vàda did not ask payment for the training of our engineers! We just bought the machines and installed them. But he set them working, having previously trained our people ... That is how I became acquainted with the president and the founder of the famous Tokai University – a private research and educational institution in Japan, because part of our engineers, invited by Mr. Vàda, were trained in this university, and the other part were trained in *Fujitsu* itself. I will tell you about our relationships with Tokai later.

During the negotiations with Vàda, I told him frankly that we would like also to conclude a license agreement with Fujitsu to produce memory devices on magnetic tape, but we insisted that the license cover both the Bulgarian and Soviet markets, i.e. to be able to sell the devices in the Soviet Union. We said that, when exporting to other countries, we would pay additional fees, but for Bulgaria and the USSR the license was paid for by the purchase of these 20 main-frame computers.

Prof. Ognyan Tzarnorechki, leading researcher at the Central Institute of Information Technology:

Ivan Popov went to Japan to the company *Fujitsu* and we talked about purchasing their license, documentation, and know-how to produce their "Facom" magnetic tape memory device. At the same time, however, he began to collect R&D teams here in Bulgaria. He sent his assistants to look for relevant specialists able to carry out a certain amount of R&D work. For example, specialists in linear motors from the factory in Troyan – they called them, saying, "How much money do you want to build the linear motor of the device?" One of his assistants came to me and said, "Can you do the magnetic tape roller?" I guess it was that way everywhere, I'll tell you how it was with me.

At that time I was senior researcher and scientific secretary of the *Institute of Plastics and Rubbers* in Sofia. I had a lot of work and initially refused his offer. Then the assistant said: "What you said about your current tasks is irrelevant – Comrade Popov was told you are the person who could do the job and he wants a contract with you personally. He is ready to pay all you need."

In the late 1960s there was a law that a state employee could not get additional payment larger than six monthly salaries. Added to this was the fact that as director of the institute I could not have a personal contract – it had to pass through the Council of the Institute and it was a long procedure. So we were six people in my team and I calculated six-month salaries for all of us thinking he will not accept such a big sum of 4000 BGL (about 2500 USD). But he just asked: "How much time do you need to fulfil the task?" My answer was we would do it in one year. A few days later the same man came again with a positive answer. But I still hesitated and said that we made new calculations and realized we would need not 4000, but about 6000 BGL. He called Ivan Popov from my office and after a short talk with him said: "Mr. Popov wants to see you personally!"

When we met, Ivan Popov said to me: "Here is your offer - now I am signing for 8000 BGL instead of 6000 you proposed, but you will sign that you will do the job for six months instead of one year. And as a member of the Politburo of the Bulgarian Communist Party, I promise you will get this money personally, you may pay no one." It was very tempting offer and finally I signed.

I know that this was the way he also ordered the R&D work for the electrical step motor, the aluminium frame, for all the mechanical parts of the tape memory device – i.e. all the mechanical parts, which were very difficult to produce. I will show you the roller that I made - this is a small roller, which actually pulls the tape. And friction is very important – there must be no slips, etc., one of the most demanding products. The electronic components, you can put them in your pocket, you can lie about it, steal it, etc., but not the mechanical parts! So in six months he got the entire prototype of the "Facom" magnetic tape memory device. Then the so-called international trials on prototypes of those 105 items of computer technology had been scheduled and experts from all CMEA countries gathered to evaluate the products each country had developed. This happened somewhere in the fall of 1969... When we met at these trials, all Bulgarian R&D specialists who had been visited by assistants of Ivan Popov said to me: "We underestimated the work we did! It was hard work, it cost us lots of efforts, but eventually everything was done ..." And they all said we got ripped off by Ivan Popov; he paid us much less than the value of the work we did. That was how Ivan Popov made us work 12 or 15 hours a day, but we were all glad that we managed to do it. (From an interview taken by Ivan Tchalakov)

During these negotiations I was impressed with the Japanese way of thinking, the way their minds work. Here is an example. I was in Japan with Mr. Angel Angelov, Bulgarian trade representative in Tokyo... We sat down to negotiate: I myself presented our proposals. Every time I made a proposal for a clause in the contract, the Japanese withdrew - they were 20 people for the two of us and each time they spent about half an hour in the next room talking among themselves. We only heard the sound of conversation and then they came back with a decision. They never decided alone, they always consulted on the decision collectively!

The Japanese psychology is very interesting indeed. I recall, we started negotiations early in the evening and finished at 4 am - the key point was about our insistence to consider the Soviet market as our own, as part of the Bulgarian market. We told them: "You will not be paid anything for the Soviet market!" Because if we did not have the Soviet market, we would go bankrupt in two days – electronics was an expensive thing, we would be ruined if we paid the Japanese for our exports to the USSR, and we are such a small country... The negotiations dragged on. At one point Angelov said: "Do you know why they behave this way? They think you will get exhausted and you will bend ..." - “Ha!” I replied him. They can’t pull that trick on me!"

- *And you continued the negotiations until 4 a.m.?*

Yes, till 4 a.m.! And then came Vàda, and the others went with him. "We accept, he said, to include the Soviet Union as part of the contract with Bulgaria! We accept ... " And then, with a distorted pronunciation, he started to say something in English ... I did not understand. I asked Angelov, "Maybe he is criticizing me?" - "Forget it, I'll tell you later," replied Angelov. "Tell me what he said!" - "I'll tell you later – he is an angry man talking nonsense." And then Angelov told me privately what he had said: "Yes, you should know that now we agreed with you. But you should know also that the yellow race is much better than you and one day you will be beaten! "… What shit! He was agitated inside, he was angry - because previously Vàda had been a senior officer at the Japanese military technical services… Anyway, we signed the contract. Nevertheless, Vàda later helped us a lot!

We had finished our work in Japan and returned to Bulgaria. As I told you, out of the whole range of 105 articles comprising a computing centre at the time, we chose only four. There was the Special Committee (IGCCT) meeting where we insisted on these four articles as Bulgaria's specialisation in electronics, and eventually we got them. For each item there were at least several countries that were working on their own prototypes. Eventually only one of it was to be selected for production – that was the aim of specialization. Yet, even though we got such a small number, you need research and development on these devices, you can't do it otherwise! So a year later, at the next Special Committee meeting, we tested the prototypes of the tape storage devices – the meeting was in Minsk, Belarus, at their large computer research institute.

Of all countries in CMEA, the GDR competed most with us – [East] German competitors appeared for all four products we had selected... They had made a big factory in Jena, and also built a large institute for computer equipment there, including optics departments, etc. I have visited this institute, everything there was made with very expensive equipment and materials ... So at the tests in Minsk our competitors from GDR submitted their computer memory devices on magnetic tape, and we submitted our device. The Committee also took the sake of comparison a similar device produced by a Western firm... And it became clear that our device - an exact replica of the Japanese machine – was the best and it won the competition! We had all of them beaten! So the Special Committee granted us the specialization on tape memory drives. The Germans were dying of grief – they had thrown so much money on it… What they did with this institute later I do not know. The device itself was rather complicated – the electronics components, the duralumin frame, etc. It was very, very expensive…

I won against the Germans several times, although I married a German woman (smiling). Just to give another example, the Hydraulics factory in Kazanlak. In the field of hydraulics the situation in CMEA was similar to that in electronics – there was a special CMEA committee established, where all producers of hydraulics in CMEA countries came together, each presenting samples of their products. So the committee was to compare the products and to decide which country would specialize in what product. It appeared, however, that Bulgaria had only two items to present, both far below the parameters of those produced by our competitors in CMEA. We had to do something about it! Then at short notice we decided to get a few articles from BOSCH - you've probably heard of it, one of the best companies in the world. We took some of their hydraulic elements and manufactured exact copies of them. Our engineers and technicians worked around the clock, day and night! And finally we succeeded; we got these items into production. When we went to trials and presented our products, our GDR colleagues grew pale – they did not believe we were producing it, because our products were much better than their own products! Indeed, they were exact replica of BOSCH products, but already mass produced in Bulgaria. But the colleagues from GDR did not believe us and insisted on opening the products and seeing what was inside, looking for the brand name of BOSCH on the elements... For at the time BOSCH would put its brand name using a laser beam that did not damage the item but made the company name visible. We told them "No problem, open it!" They found nothing and it became clear that we were able to manufacture it. That is how we gained CMEA specialisation again…

Building the Bulgarian Electronic Industry's Backbone

Getting back to electronics - winning a specialization in Minsk enabled us to build these electronic plants; each specialized in a particular area.[14]

- How was it possible to build seven plants simultaneously, with such verve, you said?

It was decided.

- Were you the one who suggested it?

Yes, but it went through Politburo, it was approved, etc.

- You ran all these plants; did you copy everything from the Japanese? Did our scientists here at the Academy help you at all or not?

We copied the disk memory devices from IBM. But our scientists initially had created the first Bulgarian computer[15] and hence I started

---

[14] Under the direct guidance of Ivan Popov, in 1969 simultaneous construction began of *seven plants* (!) for electronic equipment - four plants for computer memory devices, situated in Plovdiv (magnetic tapes), Stara Zagora (magnetic disks), Veliko Turnovo, and in the village of Dragor, near Pazardzhik. These plants produced finished products and were supplied by specialized factories for magnetic heads (in Razlog), mechanical structures (Blagoevgrad), and printed circuits boards (PCB) (in Ruse). To this list we should add the previously constructed plants for semiconductors (Botevgrad) and computers (Sofia).

helping them when I became chairman of SCSTP. It was done at BAS by prof. Lubomir Iliev, mathematician, and another younger Bulgarian mathematician, Blagovest Sendov. These two men initiated the machine and when it was ready, we decided to present it in Moscow, at the first exhibition of the achievements of Bulgarian industry held in 1964. I still remember Sendov telling funny stories about how it was done – they completed it the evening before the exhibition, it ran for a while then broke down, next day they had it working again, it worked a little while, and that was how they saved our face... However, this machine was important mostly for learning cite, it helped them to grow as a team of developers ... This was the first team, while the second team came from telecommunications, their leader, Angel Angelov, had specialized in DDR where he worked for the *Posts, Telephone and Telegraph* (PTT). Angelov's project was aimed at computerization of communications. So with these two teams we created the Central Institute of Computing Technology (CICT), which began large-scale research in electronics. These things are well known, but the seven plants were indeed built under my supervision...

I had a conflict on these issues with my deputy, associate professor Bogomil Gudev, he was vice chairman SCSTP. He reasoned this way: the people capable of doing some R&D and production work in electronics were only available in Sofia, the capital. Hence we were to build a very large and modern computer plant in Sofia, and CICT next to it. I opposed this line of reasoning - I said we should put these plants wherever there were experienced technicians and engineers in general, not just in electronics. What was important was to have proof that they were able to handle complex equipment. And such capable technical staffs was available in several major cities - Plovdiv, Stara Zagora, Silistra (where the ELKA producing plant was in operation already), Ruse, Veliko Turnovo, Pazardzhik. Besides, Bulgaria was not a big country – most of the sites were within 200 km from Sofia.

We built these Computing Machinery Works with three concrete elements, three prefabricated elements only, no more - "Tak, tak, tak", presto ... Their back walls were removable, because as the plants grew, the walls were moved further, you could do it several times when needed.

---

[15] The first Bulgarian computer *Vitosha* was created in 1962 at the Institute of Mathematics, Bulgarian Academy of Sciences, with the help of Prof. Victor Toma and his colleagues from the Atomic Institute in Bucharest, Romania. (see the picture of the Vitosha computer at: http://en.wikipedia.org/wiki/File:Vitosha_Computer.JPG; about Prof. L.Iliev see http://www.computer.org/portal/web/awards/iliev)

Also, none of the infrastructure was above the ground - no cables, no pipes above the surface, they were all placed underground, hence you can redesign the plant freely as you like. And it proved to be awfully cheap… The Russians liked this design scheme a lot and they took drawings from us ... However, they built nothing.

There were two reasons to put these plants on the periphery of the cities: first, to be away from the noise, air pollution, etc., second - once a person came to spend the shift, there was nothing around to entice him [away from work]. Because that was the weakness of our technical staff, the people were still not very disciplined... I had issued an order that, once the worker entered the plant, he should not leave it until the end of the working hours. They said they were like prisoners… You come in, go to lunch through the tunnel, you cannot leave the plant and go out in the city, you are shut up like a convict inside. … And we kept absolute pharmaceutical cleanliness - our plants were immaculately clean and proper! Especially the semiconductor production – entering there, workers were first cleaned with blown air at the entrance and stripped almost naked, then they put on special clothes, special shoes! And when they left, they passed through the locker room and took off their clothes for washing. Maybe I was a bit too harsh…That was it – I never saw cleaner factories than ours anywhere, such cleanliness, Draconian! Later I saw I had not been mistaken, I had done it the right way.

- Professor Popov, it would take several generations of workers to establish such technological discipline as it happened in Germany and other Western countries...

No! Why do you think that? It can be done! Why was it possible to have such strict discipline during my administration? - It is quite simple… One day I was summoned to the Central Committee of the Party ... We had a factory in the town of Yambol, it was in the early 1950s and I was still director of *Elprom*. The Party secretary called me and said: "Comrade Popov, let us introduce ourselves." I presented myself and asked: “Why did you call me?” - “We have many complaints from your employees”, he said. “Why?” I asked again. “Well, here are the orders for punishment you issued!” He pulled out an envelope with 10 orders for punishment, not more. “Why do you punish these people?" I told him just this: "I punish them for negligent attitudes towards their working duties. But why they did not give you my orders of promotion and awards? While the punishments are 10, those are 100", I said. “True?” He asks. "It is true; please ask to see how many people have rewards." "Sorry, he said, you are free to go, forgive me for bothering you" ... That's how it is, we need rules!

- Let us go back to the Fujitsu case, after you got the agreement to manufacture their machine for Bulgaria and USSR. How did you organize the production here in Plovdiv?

When we decided to make the plant in Plovdiv, we found there a small plant for electrical machinery, yet equipped with quite good premises, on the river bank of the Maritza river. We changed the profile of the plant and expanded it. We appointed as director an engineer, his name was Varnov. Since the magnetic tape memory device was a rather complex machine, there was large collaboration with several other plants in the country. They supplied Plovdiv with components - mechanical frames from Blagoevgrad, magnetic heads from the Razlog plant, etc. So the plant in Plovdiv was assembling the final product and did its adjustment and testing.

Now I can see the difference between the managers – Varnov was a good man, but he would constantly complain: this was lacking, that was lacking. I was spending most of my time helping him supply components from the Western countries or from the USSR. He was obviously a man who waited for everything to come to him by itself... This was not the case with Vasil Nedev, the manager of the magnetic disk memory plant in Stara Zagora. He rapidly got into the job – he would go by himself to the Soviet Union, became friends with the directors there… I was not envious of him, on the contrary – I encouraged him. He governed everything in his plant that is why the work there went very well.

When the plant in Plovdiv was opened Vàda, the *Fujitsu* manager, came - I took him there to see our production lines... I was afraid about the tape devices, because we had copied his machine down to the last detail!

- Without buying a license?

No license – eventually we decided not to buy a license, but to have a long-term contract with *Fujitsu* for purchasing only a particular number of electronic components. So we just copied their machine changing something inside – in the Japanese version there was a huge, very large capacitor. Our engineers from CICT replaced it with a much smaller and simple capacitor with a very clever scheme, different from those of *Fujitsu*.

So we went with Vàda to Plovdiv - he entered the workshops, watched, went back and forth, looked around silently. Finally we faced the tape memory device at the assembling line - he should have recognized the

Fujitsu device for sure… He looked at it - only the capacitors were different. Then I said, "Well, Mr. Vàda, we made the utmost efforts to hide our work from foreign firms, but we did not manage. So you copied our device…" As I said that, he burst out laughing: "Ha-ha-ha..." He was an interesting person, Vàda, a very honest man...

- *And he was not angry that you had copied their machine?*

No, no. He and I became great friends. At my suggestion Todor Zhivkov awarded Vàda with the order of Stara Planina for foreigners with great contributions to Bulgaria. I remember the medal was given him by the President of the Bulgarian Parliament Kulishev, son of a famous anti-fascist hero. After the ceremony, the journalists and other people, mostly women, surrounded Vàda and asked him questions - "Mr. Vàda ..." He interrupted them saying: "I know what you are going to ask me. Everywhere they ask me the same question: how I reached this age, more than 80 years old, and I'm still alive and in good health. Well, I'll tell you, but I'm not sure you will broadcast it! "- "Why, we certainly will!" they replied. "Well, let's see: my simple recipe is that I do not keep any poisons within myself. Whatever is on my mind, even if it might be unpleasant for others, I always say it, I do not keep it in me. And secondly, I defecate regularly!" They all went - "Ah!"… "I told you that you would not broadcast it?" he laughed...

Vàda had a great sympathy for me personally and many times we were in contact on different issues... But then he died [in 1980 – I.Tch.]. Yes, honestly, I have great respect for this man... (His eyes become moist). I do regret that we, the Bulgarians, later spoiled our relations with *Fujitsu*. Some dishonest people spoiled them. There was a professor, his name was Nikiforov, director of the Bulgarian National Bank - he did that.

Our plans were for *Fujitsu* to help us expand the functions of regional computing centres, established previously. They were linked to the Ministry of Supply and their main task was to report the movement of goods and raw materials within the economy. The Ministry was headed by Nikolai Zhishev, former regional Party secretary of Burgas. He did a very good job, organizing things Japanese style, but unfortunately the system covered only unsold products - every time some factory was looking for a scarce commodity, the electronic system would say: "In plant so-and-so, there are reserves in such-and-such quantities." Also, the system covered only the national and regional supply, but not the lower level - nobody there knew what the stocks were there at the present moment. So the idea was to use *Fujitsu* technology to expand the system and cover all plants and factories.

However, Prof. [Veselin] Nikiforov, as vice president of the State Committee of Planning fiercely opposed – he said this was rubbish; it would be useless, etc. Nevertheless we signed the contract with *Fujitsu*, where it was stated that the contract was valid till a certain date, and then it was to be renewed. So Nikiforov did everything he could not to renew the contract, sending memos to me, to Todor Zhivkov, etc. Eventually he waited for the term of the contract to expire and immediately informed the Japanese that Bulgaria would not renew it. That is how the trouble happened…

The Japanese people are honest, even though it might seem to us their thinking is a bit primitive - I mean that their managers do not decide by themselves, do not trust anyone, but always work in a group, having endless talks before they finally decide. I had other friends among them such as the founder of Tokai University; I forgot his name [Shigeyoshi Matsumae - I.Tch.]. When he came to Bulgaria, he fell ill. I spent several days with him at one of the Government resort stations in the mountains - I looked after him as I had for my wife, checking his temperature, his medicines, etc. I had experience when my wife was fighting the cancer ... So he was very grateful and he liked the country too. Many of our specialists were trained in his university free of charge, at his expense. So the Japanese are not just honest, but also sentimental people... I remember him once saying: "We are not the most intelligent of the yellow race - Koreans are much smarter than us, they quickly understand things, and show more decision, etc. We are a bit slow... ".

- I would like to ask you to make an assessment based on your many years of experience in the industry. Bulgaria began forcefully to develop its industry in 1950s and later had good achievements, such as yours in Elprom combine, then in electronics and other industries, our industrial goods were well situated on the CMEA market... But why did the country fail to win a place in the global market? Why not at least in some industrial sectors, with certain products? Was there anything in the socialist system itself, then, which prevented this from happening?

Why do you say "global"? - We were on a par with the global level in the products we produced! Many of them had global-level quality. But how in those times could you export freely to the West? - It was very difficult. Well, it was possible if... The President of the industrial managers in France opened my eyes. We had several meetings with him and finally he also somehow took a good attitutde to me. So at one of the meetings he said, "Would you like me to speak sincerely?" I answered him: "That's exactly what I expect from you!"

So the President of French industrial managers said: "You will never be able to export to the West!" "Why?" I asked him - "Because you are doing stupid things (bêtises)! For example you had here a trade office in Paris. It was located at X Street, far away from your embassy. But your country closed the office and moved it to the same building as your embassy. Look what happened after that decision of your Government: the orders to your enterprises from France decreased by 50%. Why? Because the French businessmen do not like to mix trade with politics! When you tell a businessman that he must go to the Bulgarian Embassy to sign a contract or purchase such and such a thing, he usually refuses to do it. Because that is politics!"

You see our main mistake? - Moreover, the Frenchman said that the rent we were paying for the trade office was a token sum: “You had a very nice trade office with all amenities ... In France we have a law that after the conclusion of the lease contract it cannot be touched. Having such a cheap rent meant that our Government offered yours this office as a present for another 10 years!”… And what did our government do: the Bulgarian ambassador bought a house on the left bank of the Seine. He lived on the top floor and they refurbished what had previously been a stable into a consular office for issuing visas. The Bulgarian trade office was also located there, a place to which nobody wants to come ... how silly.

Here is your second mistake, the president said: “You may think that, in creating a common market here in Western Europe, we strictly observe its rules. Not so! If your representatives go to a French industrialist and offer him the same quality that he bought from Germany with delivery of spare parts on time, good service, etc. but less expensive – he will abandon the Germans and will buy from you. That’s what you should do! But do you have a good service here for the Bulgarian firms offering their products?"- “No!”, I told him. "That is correct, he said, when I led a delegation to the Plovdiv International Fair last year I really liked some of your lathes, our merchants liked them too. But here is what happened - I went to the plant producing these lathes, ZMM firm in the town of Troyan, and asked them the price – it was much cheaper than the Germans’. "How long will it take you to produce 40 pieces?", I asked - They grew pale, "Four years," they said ... While the Germans have them ready in stock! And you do not have any spare parts or else you cannot make fast delivery. So you just do not know how to trade! The only ones who know how to deal with the capitalists are GDR companies - they have made a separate company here in Paris, they have a warehouse for spare parts, etc."

- Do you think this was unknown to our politicians and our company managers?

They knew it, but they did not invest in such things… We simply did not develop the right way. That was how it was; the president of the industrial managers spoke some other bitter words about all of our mistakes and stupidities... So we killed our export to France, it just died.

The Removal of Ivan Popov from the Management of Bulgarian Economy

Nobody but Bulgarians have such a proverb: “The poor man saw the rich man was prospering, yet was still provided with assistance. The poor man went and asked for assistance too and they said to him: "Ask whatever you want, but you should know that whatever is given to you, twice as much will be given to the rich man." He thought for a while and then said - "Take away one of my eyes!” i.e. the rich man would have both eyes taken away...

I was warned when I returned permanently to Bulgaria from GDR: "You will see the bill [to pay] in no time!” For every computer or electronic equipment plant I had built I was tried in court for mismanagement, ‘sabotage’, etc., but eventually somehow I managed to prove myself ... That’s how it was. What I regret most is that there were men that I liked and trusted, and who suddenly showed themselves as a completely different person ... I cannot understand such people!

- Please tell me something about Todor Zhivkov’s role in the creation of electronic industry and more generally about his role in the economy?

Zhivkov was a very precise man, a man who stuck to principles. Accuracy is something very important - in France they say that the politeness of kings is expressed by their accuracy. When the king came on the exact minute, he showed his respect for you, he was polite to you! Zhivkov was also eager for new things. But one of his bad features was that once he targeted someone - then God help that person! When he set his mind against someone, he was done for! Furthermore, he was not very honest; there was a bit of pettiness in him.

Two people contributed most to my dismissal from government and from the Politburo of the Central Committee – Gyudzhenov, from State Planning Committee, and Penyo Keratsov, who was secretary of the Central Committee. Jealous men, they attacked me and Mariy Ivanov, the minister of Machine Building and an excellent manager – instead, they sent him away as a diplomat… I had many conflicts also with Tano Tzolov, a prominent member of Politburo. He was easily annoyed and had several brain strokes... Yet I remember our last meeting in his car when he asked me to take his son to work in my office to teach him accuracy and business precision...

- *How were you dismissed from Politburo and the Ministry of Electronics?*

This happened in 1975. I knew some things that most of the other members of Politburo were unaware of. I was reporting on a new five-year plan for heavy machine building and I offered lower growth rates than in the previous five-year plan. Tano Tzolov became angry: "Why do you propose lower rates, how do you dare propose that in Politburo? See our annual growth rate till now – Bulgaria is already ahead of most socialist countries, only Romanians set higher rates, but it is not clear if they fulfil their rates or not! "

And then I said: "I know some economic trends are not very good. The Western countries are on the verge of a crisis, it will reflect badly on us. We would have no orders, and hence no [currency] revenues, so it would be better to plan a slower pace of economic growth." However, my comrades did not accept it and the majority voted for higher growth rates. A few years later, when I was already dismissed and I was sent to manage the Bulgarian Science and Technology Unions[16] I phoned Stoyan Ovcharov, candidate member of Politburo and responsible for economic development, who still respected me. I asked him about this issue, and he said: "I will come to see you." So he came to my office and at the end of the conversation he said: "The current economic situation is very bad – we have huge debts, we cannot pay them." I called also Vasil Kolarov, the governor of the National Bank - he confirmed it.

During the last years before I was dismissed, being Vice Prime Minister, I was responsible both for machine building and electronic industries. Shortly after the vote for the new five-year plan, and without asking me, Todor Zhivkov proposed separation of machine building from electronics. This happened when I was reporting on some current activities

[16] Bulgarian Science and Technology Unions (STU) were professional organizations of engineers and applied scientists, controlled by the Communist Party and playing a complementary role in social and economic life. Ivan Popov remained head of the board of these unions for almost fifteen years, till 1989. There he promoted the idea of creative thinking, of establishment of centres for new ideas, etc., and supported innovative activities of engineers, having, in fact, no resources and means to influence the real economic development of the country.

to Politburo and Zhivkov asks me: "What about the new investments in heavy industry?" I answered him that the five plants we had built in this sector were enough – the heavy industry plant in the city of Ruse was developing well, as were likewise the new metallurgical plant in Debelt, the machine building plant "Vaptsarov" in Pleven, the chemical engineering plant in Haskovo, and one more. “How could we pay if we build more new plants?” I said.

However, they all insisted on new investments! I knew the world economic crisis was coming, that we had no resources, so I proposed to them: “Let us put all parameters of the five-year plan in a mathematical model to simulate it on a computer. Then we will see if the results are close to your forecast or not.” In the mid-1970s there were only two data centres with powerful enough computers able to do these calculations – the computing center of Gosplan in the USSR and one in the GDR. It was possible to arrange making the simulation there. However, all other members of Politburo were in a rage, they were all against it. Todor Zhivkov got angry and shouted: "You are the only member of the Politburo, to whom a special committee will be appointed to investigate your political activity from the very beginning!” Then he said he would separate machine building industry from electronics.

I said that I agreed in general – electronic industry was developing very well, yet before this separation should happen, we needed to develop some intermediate units - electronics had to enter the banks, the post offices, and the telecommunications. We still had not done anything in this direction, plus the fact that we had still not implemented electronics in industry on a mass scale. It would take time before such a separation should be made.

However Todor Zhivkov insisted: "No, I will separate the two industries!" and suggested Toncho Chakarov to be the minister of Machine Building and for Electronics - Yordan Mladenov. I agreed about Toncho – he had enough experience. But as for Mladenov, I was against – he had no experience in managing production on such a scale; because he came from the Institute of Radio Electronics, and he did not understand the situation in the computer industry.

The meeting was over; we had to leave when an assistant came and told me I was invited to Todor Zhivkov’s office in the State Council. It was very close by, just the next corridor. I went there and I saw Zhivkov was by then in a good mood. He offered coffee and said:

“- I was emotional a bit, please excuse me. Do your work and don’t worry.”

Everything I do, I replied to him, I do it for Bulgaria. And I cannot repeat constantly "This is what comrade Todor Zhivkov said, that is what Todor Zhivkov said" ... That's my nature."

Todor Zhivkov went grey in the face and looked towards me a bit above my head. The moment he looked up this way, I realized that I was done for. Because I'd already seen this gaze before, for other comrades...

Epilogue

When later [after 1989] I was summoned as witness at the trial of Todor Zhivkov and Milko Balev, at the trial against them in the court, I defended him. I told the judges that he personally made only minor decisions, but otherwise for everything important he had asked for approval in Politburo, and every one of us would give his written consent. Then Madame Dokovska, his lawyer, came and told me, "Mr. Popov, my compliments!"

So... at first I was President of SCSTP (1960-1971), then in 1971-1975 I was Minister of Mechanical Engineering, Deputy Prime Minister and member of the Politburo. After 1975 I spent some time in the State Council as Vice-President for the Environment, and after less than a year, in August 1976, they appointed me president of STU (Scientific-Technical Union), and there I remained until the end, till 1989.

3. Former Kolkhoze Leader in Iecava, Latvia

Iecava, 27th March 2000
Interviewers: J. Nikula, I. Alanen and R. Ruutsoo

- Are you an ethnic Latvian?

Yes, I am Latvian, but I was born in 1918 in Novosokolniki, Pleskava District in Russia in a farmer's family. My father owned 21 ha of land. In 1927 we left that land because our parents were afraid they might be deported to Siberia. However, my parents and elder brothers were deported - in 1933, when I was 15 years old and nobody wished to give me a job. It was a tough time in Russia due to hunger. So, I was pressed to attend the teacher courses for nine months. Then, for two years I worked as a teacher. But as I had graduated only 6th grade, I went to Novgorod where my brother was the director of a school and I graduated the 7th grade there. Then I returned to Novosokolniki and began working at the depo. In 1940 I was recruited into the Soviet army. I was supposed to be recruited in the army back in 1938, but as I was Latvian that year they did not recruit me. And I was in a construction battalion. Because Russians did not trust Latvians and they did not wish to entrust them with any weapon. So, I was building a railway with a spade. In 1941, the war began. I was in an artillery battalion. In the autumn of 1944 I was in Poland and then there was given a command that all Latvians should return to Latvia. We were three Latvians in the battalion, Brants, Lapins, and me. Through Warsaw, Minsk and Moscow we arrived at the railway station in Vishin Volochok, Kalinin district. There was formed the 121st Latvian regiment. So, I got to Kurzeme. But I did not participate in any battle there because I arrived in Kurzeme in March 1945 and the battles were already over. So, the war was over and in 1946 I was demobilised.

- And you stayed in Latvia?

Yes. The fields that were owned by my parents in Russia were destroyed during the war. I began work as a steward in an orphanage in Baldone. It owned some fields and cattle and they were under my responsibility. In 1948, I was elected leader of Baldone pagasts. In 1949, a kolkhoze was established in Baldone. I had to organise also the cutting of woods, because every pagast had to fulfil its plan. In 1950, I was ordered by the Communist Party to move to the Iecava kolkhoze. There were three kolkhozes here initially in the Iecava pagasts – Zalite, Iecava, and Upesciems, but later we united them in one and it was named after Stalin. I did not like that name, but some man from KGB said that if I didn't agree they would consider what to do to me.

- I would like to know what was the general mood, people's attitude, what were the practical problems?

Those people who were poorest and lazy were rather willing to establish kolkhozes. But those who were successful and strong farmers and who could secure their living by themselves [were against]. The impetus that stimulated the establishment of kolkhozes was the deportation in March 1940. Very many farmers were deported to Siberia. So, we established the kolkhoze here too. In 1951 I was directed to agronomy school in Zalenieki, Jelgava District, because I did not have any education. I studied there for three years. In 1954 I graduated from that school and returned to Iecava and I was elected again as director of the kolkhoze. So, till 1987 I worked as the director.

- How big was your kolkhoze? Could you describe the development of your kolkhoze?

In 1950, when I was elected director, it was a rather small kolkhoze: it owned 3000 ha of land. In 1951 when we planted winter crops and clover as well, we had a yield of 13 tons of clover and got a good profit. We also grew potatoes, grain, flax, which we did not wish to grow, but in accordance with the plan we had to. We also had green houses. Later we built a workshop for plastic production. After the uniting of kolkhozes we had as many as 6000 ha. But the land here in our kolkhoze was rather poor compared to neighbouring kolkhozes. There was an agronomist in our kolkhoze and he was a Baptist. But Communist Party members reproached me for employing him. But he was very good specialist.

- How was it politically possible for a Baptist to be holding a position of leadership?

I took that risk and it was my responsibility. There was one other similar case: some man had returned from Siberia and nobody wished to employ him, but I did. He is still living here in Iecava.

- And the local Communist Party did not protest?

No, there were no protests from the local Communist members because they were interested that there would be good workers in the kolkhoze.

- I know that kolkhoze leaders had to be members of the Communist Party. How big was the Communist Party's influence on everyday life in your kolkhoze?

It was rather powerful. There were strong requirements towards Communist Party members and that of course did not have any negative impact on the economy: they had to work better, to improve the quality, etc. And therefore also the economy of the kolkhoze improved.

- I am also interested about how the Communist Party influenced who the team leader would be, and about how the ideological questions were discussed at the kolkhoze meetings, and so on.

There was no big difference whether a worker was in the Communist Party or not. People had to be responsible for their work and then there was no difference between those who were and those who were not in the

Communist Party. In everyday life there was no separation [made between the two].

- *If you and the Communist Party secretary were of different opinions, did he have more power to make the final decision?*

The local Communist Party had made the decision to dismiss 6 or 7 employees. I took their decision and went to the central bureau of the Communist Party in Riga and said to them that if they could find some Communist Party members who were as good specialists as those 7 people then I would dismiss them. As they could not offer me anybody, those 7 people continued to work in my kolkhoze.

- *What were your relations with the vice chairmen who at the same time were representatives of the Communist Party and did not have to be elected?*

We had a plan for maize. In 1962 it was very rainy. And we made the decision to plant not only maize but to mix it with beans. As the summer was wet, the maize did not grow, but the beans did. And when we harvested we had a lot of fodder for cattle. And we succeeded precisely because we had not complied with that plan.

- *And what happened then?*

Some man from the Ministry arrived and he was just wondering why we had enough fodder for our cattle while other kolkhozes did not. I answered that we had not followed his plan and he did not ask me any more questions. As I said, there was one more case, some man who had returned from Siberia and he wished to work in our kolkhoze. Usually the board of the kolkhoze made such decisions. But the people in the top ranks of the Communist Party and KGB were against it. Their main argument was that he was not devoted to the Soviet regime.

- *Were there any punishments if you did not comply with the Communist Party?*

Yes, there were reprimands.

- *Which time was the tensest in the relations between the Communist Party and the others?*

In the very beginning, in 1950, when I began to work in the kolkhoze, Communist Party members just said that they too have to do only their work. They did not influence my work much. There was an organiser of cultural life in the kolkhoze – he was also one of those people whom nobody wished to employ. He had organised an event were people from the whole republic had arrived and he had organised also a trip to Estonia. We spent overnight in some school. There was a man among us who knew Russian and he explained [to them] where Latvia is and those people trusted us. We visited some farms, which were already mechanised at that time. When we came back to Iecava, we built similar farms here and they became the bases of our production and economic development.

- *Could you compare the situation in Estonian and Latvian agriculture then?*

The economic growth in Estonia was more rapid. Also they had those mechanised farms earlier than we did. They were first introduced here three or four years later.

- *What could be the explanation?*

I think that the support for agriculture was better. Because when we entered Estonia we saw that roads there were better and not so many bushes as here. Maybe it depends also on the people themselves but maybe there was such a command from the top to keep everything in order…

- *Were you satisfied with your local agricultural bosses?*

I received some support from them. When we went to Kazakhstan, our Party Secretary chose me [to go with him] as a representative of agriculture. And that man told me that he had helped some kolkhozes a lot: they had built many buildings and so on. I asked if he could help me. He asked what I wanted. I said that we wanted to build a house but we did not have construction materials. And he gave the order and so that building was built here. We did all the amelioration with our own money.

- *There was an anti-nationalist campaign at the end of the 1950s and all the leaders were changed. It had a strong influence on culture. How did this influence agricultural policy?*

I did not feel it. I did not have time and I was responsible only for my fields and farms. I attended some meetings. I heard about it, but I did not experience it here.

- Weren't people afraid they could likewise be accused of employing deported people or believers?

Of course, people were afraid. Therefore I was also reproached that I employed those people. I received some reprimand. It was not announced loudly, it was just written down in my card. It was their obligation. But on Iecava kolkhoze it did not have any impact.

- What was the kolkhoze's development? Was it smooth, or were there some ups and downs?

On June 30, 1954 I was elected chairman. At that time they took milk to Riga by a simple cart; but by autumn we bought a big dray. It happened in half a year. It didn't seem like much, but it was a good beginning. Initially we had some 100 cows, later we had as many as 2000 cows and all three trucks were not enough to take all the milk to the dairy. We had built big drying sheds and produced fodder. We had arranged workshops and green houses.

- You had access to a market but there were plans that you had to fulfil. If you could produce more than was indicated in the plan did you?

Yes, there were plans, but we could produce more and sell it on the market. The main measure was how much you produced per ha…

- As I understand, you get a better price on the market. It means that it was in your interest to reduce the plans and to enlarge the capacity and sell freely. Did you manage to do such things?

I could not influence in any way that plan. It was only in 1950 that we sold milk on the market. Later there was no such need anymore.

- What happened, if those plans were not realistic?

I do not know how it was in other kolkhozes, but we did not have any problems. The total land area in 1965 was 3600 ha, but in 1972 it was 5550.

- Was it possible to sell freely on markets all the time or was it just something temporary?

No, it was only in the beginning of the 1950s. Later, when shops were full of produce, it was not important anymore to sell produce on the market. It was not profitable anymore to go those 60 kilometres to the market. And meat and grain were distributed. The price of milk was 13 kopeicks. Now it is 7 santims.

- *How was the privatisation of the kolkhoze carried out, when did it begin and what were the results?*

About stealing during perestroika – we call it privatisation when everybody grabbed everything he could. Some four people came to me and were asking about Tiesnesis and other people. They wished to find who had stolen some items. But they had to leave without any results.

- *How did the division of the kolkhoze happen?*

Every employee received his shares. Those who were leaders got the better items. Old people had shares but soon there was nothing to privatise anymore. Somebody had shares for 200 lats and there was nothing to privatise for such big money. So, they had to sell their shares for 50 santims. And many people did not get anything.

- *Who had devised that share plan?*

It was the state's plan. When Godmanis was our Prime Minister, a regulation was passed that all the kolkhozes' property must be evaluated in shares. Initially we still had the Russian rouble, but later our national currency was emitted and we got 1 lat per 200 roubles. For example, if I had 1000 roubles I received 5 lats. I had 1000 lats in Baltija bank, but it went bankrupt and I got back only 140 lats.

- *How was it possible that the kolkhoze property was already divided before the official stage of privatisation? How was it possible, it being collective property?*

When the USSR broke up, there were quite a few people who foresaw how the process would continue and they grabbed the best things step by step. Some collective stuff was evaluated cheaper than it actually was and later it was sold for more money.

The kolkhoze property was divided into units and there were organised offers. And those who made better offers had the right to buy it first. Sometimes there were difficulties in collecting the needed shares. Formally they seemed to observe the law but there was stealing.

Those who had power chose those objects that they wished to get – some green houses or workshops. While ordinary people did not understand the process and sold their shares cheaply.

- How did the leaders avoid auctions?

There were organised auctions, but ordinary people simply did not understand the process of auctioning.

- Are there still any remnants of kolkhozes?

There are, but not very many. Could be around 10…

- I think that the main mechanism for stealing was that people who knew what were the best objects, were able to buy cheaper shares and agreed with other bosses that they would not fight among themselves?

It is difficult for me to answer such a question because I did not participate in the privatisation process. But I think that such things could not happen in our kolkhoze. I think that there had not been such agreements among our leaders.

- How much did they fight? When several people made claims for some valuable asset such as sawmills?

I said already that I did not participate in privatisation. I do not know such cases when there were any fights.

- Another mechanism of stealing was by manipulating bookkeeping, some new machines were evaluated at a lower price than they actually had.

There may have been such cases but I really cannot say that it ever happened in our kolkhoze. Our bookkeeper was strict. I think that she would not agree to such manipulations. I show you that house. Local people do not have enough money to buy it and rebuild. Then some German arrived here in Iecava and he wanted to buy it. But he could not, because he did not have land property here. Then the kolkhoze chairman bought it and then sold it to that German. Of course, nobody knows how much money he received after this deal.

- If we divide people in several groups: the leadership, then people working in offices (they were close to leadership), and the third – the people who ran practical business. Which group was in the best position, which won in that privatisation process?

I cannot say that any of those groups in general was a winner. Those people, who understood what was happening and who could foresee the future a bit, those people began to act and they gained. Ordinary people and old people who did not have communication means, telephones at home, they were just sitting at their homes and did not know anything and did not think about any privatisation at that time. And they also did not get anything.

- We have the impression from other interviews that some leaders were absolutely honest but they could not always control what was happening in the departments, for example, in some workshop, where there were good possibilities to manipulate bookkeeping and to change the names of machines so that in the end would be able to buy good machines at a cheap price.

Yes. Mechanics could take away some spare parts from machines. I know that 7 motors were stolen from a dry-house and it could not function anymore. And there was a worker in some workshop: he had not worked there for very long but enough for him to steal everything there.

- Was it during de-collectivisation?

It was around three years ago. The previous manager of the workshop was a really honest man, but he fell sick.

- And during the kolkhoze time, weren't there such criminal acts?

Maybe there were some criminal deviations. But as we would have to pay a lot for a lawsuit, nobody wished to begin a process [in court]. And we were also not sure that those who acted illegally would be punished. It was difficult to prove guilt.

- Why did those persons who found that something had disappeared not go to the police?

As I said, it was difficult to find out who did it. And I doubt that anyone would have liked to begin the lawsuit. The leaders changed often and there wasn't strict bookkeeping everywhere. So, the new leader could never know what was supposed to be in his workshop. During kolkhoze times, there was strict bookkeeping – every building and tractor and so on had its number. But when de-collectivisation began, all those documents were lost.

- How did you receive Latvian citizenship?

I did not go anywhere to get it. It was insulting. When I lived in Russia I was an outsider because I was Latvian – nobody wished to recruit me in the army and so on. When I moved to Latvia and had worked here for 47 years, I even had a birth certificate that my father is Latvian, but I could not initially receive Latvian citizenship. Only in 1998, when I was already 80, was I called to the municipality council and I received my Latvian passport. And I had to pay 1 lat for that.

- How did you feel when people were shot during those days and many of them were not Latvians?

Of course, it was also painful, but on the other hand the question was - what would happen further on? If I had known at that time what the future would be – empty buildings, uncultivated fields – then I would have had another attitude. I did not know that everything that we had built would not be needed anymore. When going around Latvia we can see how overgrown and weedy the fields are… Miserable. We had invested a lot of money in land amelioration. At that time there were still large fields of 60 to 100 ha. But now everybody has fields of 6 to 30 ha and if some farmer does not take care of his fields, others suffer too.

- How big a role did culture play in such a small place? Did people try to restore traditions? Did they remember history and restore cultural monuments? Was there any cultural awakening here?

I began to work here in 1946. I remember that at that time we would still celebrate Midsummer Day. I remember that we went around the fields, singing songs and looking if they were cultivated and clean. Around 1960 this holiday was banned. And I did not understand why. Because it seemed to me that there was nothing wrong with that holiday. People were just enjoying their work, summer, and the result of their work. But later we began to get together again... If I had lived here before the war as well, I could compare. I can speak about the time of the kolkhoze. I said that we lived like one big family. One of my neighbours had a birthday. There was a canteen in the kolkhoze. I went by horse to his home and brought him here. All the kolkhoze's collective was there and we celebrated his birthday together. There was such a tradition from the 1960s till the 1980s. But later we stopped it.

- I have a question concerning the period before the liquidation [of kolkhozes]. There was a time when the former chairmen and leaders were called "red barons". What was the situation here?

Yes, there was such talk here as well. I too was called a red baron. When some acquaintance called me he asked my wife if the red baron was at home. I had worked here for 40 years. But at times people also called me an idiot, because during those years I had not taken anything for myself. The kolkhoze chairman that succeeded me built a new house during those 4 years of governance. While it took me 40 years to build my house. He also has 2.5 millions in some German bank.

- How was it possible? How did that chairman get so much money?

It's just talk. I do not have any proof. The chairman was clever enough. He also bought some old hotel in Riga. They had destroyed everything there and sold it. He went to Germany with lorries of the kolkhoze and sold everything there. And then he built his big private house.

- In the beginning he would need money for his own business. What could be the explanation? Could he get it from the kolkhoze?

Of course his salary was not enough. Similarly, our Prime Minister Skele made 29 million.

- How did Communist Party stop working here? Had people taken it to their hearts? When did it begin to lose its power?

If it hadn't been for all those transformations, the Communist Party would still exist. When I became a pensioner, I stopped paying membership fee. It was in 1989. And I did not go to meetings anymore. But such persons – like a tractor driver who had studied in the Party school and after that had become Communist Party Vice-Secretary – they had taken it to their hearts. Now that man is unemployed and those years he worked as Secretary are not taken into account when his pension is calculated.

- Didn't you feel that you had lost something important?

I do feel it. The First Secretary of the Communist Party in Bauska District was Lithuanian and his brother was a professor in some institute. His brother had received Latvian citizenship rather soon. But that ex-vice secretary could not get it for five years. But he had not worked for himself in the Com Party. In the time of the Com Party I could speak from a tribune and express my opinion. But now - whom can I tell anything? Now everything is done through money.

- And at that time, did people listen to you?

Yes. Not always, but with respect to some practical issues they listened. I did not orient myself well in political issues.

- What is your attitude towards those people who were members of your party and who are now making big money in other parties?

There is a saying that when a fish begins to rot it smells from the head, but it is clean at the tail. The same happened also in the Party – its head – Gorbachev and others in Moscow began to smell, but the cleaning was carried out here…Some people still continued to believe in those ideas. But let's live and see who was right. Just look at what happened in Russia. It is such a big country, but it has been totally ruined…

I did not pay too much attention to politics and tried not to get involved in any political activities. Still, during the kolkhoze time all pensioners were provided with food – 2 kg of meat, 30 kg of potatoes, milk they could get freely. And if somebody died, 70 roubles were allocated for the funeral. Pensioners too could not foresee the outcome of all these transformations. At that time they could live on their pensions – 32 roubles; they did not have to buy food.

- But if it had been possible to foresee, for what would they have voted?

I do not know. But I would not like to experience all that again.

- Would people agree to live again in the old system?

Not everybody, of course. Many have received their own lands and houses and they can live rather well. But if somebody has to live in a flat and his fields are 5 to 10 km from the house, then it is rather difficult.

- Then the arguments are more economic than political?

Yes.

- But is there any political argument that Latvia would not be an independent state anymore, but would be in some union again?

It is difficult to say. Many are saying now that we were in the Soviet Union and that soon we will be in the European Union and that nothing will be better there. Nobody knows what would be the outcome.

- *After de-collectivisation different firms were established. Could you tell me about them? What has been their fate?*

A green house was created. But they have difficulties paying for gas. And also the price of their produce is low. Most of the employees have been dismissed. There was also a joinery created. But now it has stopped working because there is not enough work. There is a pig farm but they also have difficulties selling their produce. There is some joint stock company that is engaged in cattle breeding. They have some machines, cattle, and a drying shed. But the drying shed was shut down and until spring comes, they have no money to cultivate their fields.

- *I understood that all the big cowsheds went bankrupt?*

If they are not bankrupt then they are declining. Their workers are looking for jobs in other enterprises. Some of those enterprises are still producing, but in small quantities.

- *Could you describe how many cows and employees they have?*

I do not know precisely. There is not enough food for cows. All the agricultural activities are related. There was a fodder manufacture here, now it is shut down; the dairy is shut down, the spirits manufacture, where it was possible to get grains for fodder, also shut down, a bakery shut down, a sauna also shut down. I wonder how agriculture exists at all.

- *Do you know of any successful farmer?*

There are two good farmers. One of them had been an economist, another – a zoo-technician at the kolkhoze.

- *What kind of farms are they?*

They are not very big farmers. They have some 3 cows, a couple of pigs. But both of them are good specialists. They too used to work in the kolkhoze system and thus they can compare the situations. There was a man who was a brigade leader in the kolkhoze – he also created his private farm specialised in vegetable growing. He got a good yield – around 200 tons of flower cabbages, but simply could not sell them. And he also didn't have an appropriate storehouse. Finally he had to go to the hospital because all those problems caused some mental problems. Now he is back and is considering what to do and how to farm – he had taken a loan and has to repay it.

- *Can you tell us about any really successful farmer?*

There are no such big and successful farmers here.

- *What is the future for entrepreneurs in the context of EU?*

I do not know. [Prime Minister] Skele said that only big farmers would receive support. Then maybe they will develop. But what will small-scale farmers do? They will have to go bankrupt.

- *I wonder why in Latvia the results of agricultural reform are so different compared with the situation in Estonia, where several big farms are still developing.*

It's also due to our governments changing so often. During this period of time we have already had 6 governments. During the governance of the first Prime Minister, Godmanis, the emphasis was put on trade with non-ferrous metal and as a result, everything was stolen – machinery and wires. There were firms that bought up non-ferrous metal in Iecava too. Some children stole my aluminium bowl. In the night time kilometres of electric wire were stolen and then they were sold abroad. Three bells were stolen from the graveyard. To my mind, even during the war our agriculture was not destroyed so much as in these 10 years after 1991. Many people dropped totally out of the system. Many of them started drinking. There was an article in a newspaper about two men who had drunk too much and they were arrested due to their behaviour and taken to be sobered. One of them died because they had drunk bad-quality alcohol.

- *I have heard that 15% of the children in the countryside who are at obligatory school age do not attend school. And there are a growing number of illiterate people.*

The situation is similar here. During the kolkhoze time, if any children did not attend the school, teachers informed me about that and then I called those children and their parents to meetings. The children listened to me and felt guilty. But now – children do not go to school and nobody takes care of it.

- *I think that it is a very sad and dangerous situation. Could you describe what the parents' attitude is? I think that alcohol is not the only reason...*

Yes, alcohol is not the only reason. People are rather poor here and they do not have enough money. Many children also live rather far from the school. During Soviet times there were regular buses and children could go easily to the centre. But now many bus lines are closed down and children will not walk those many kilometres to the school. Many smaller schools, which were closer to their houses, were shut down and liquidated. And of course, many parents drink.

- *Have you had any discussions with those parents who do not have enough means, how do they describe the situation? What is their self-esteem?*

I have not talked with them. I have just heard. But, of course, they feel very badly because they cannot help their children. If all those enterprises that were liquidated during these years worked, there would be more tax money that the municipality could use for such costs. Where can the municipality get any additional money?

- *But the leaders of the municipality know the situation and are worried about it, but they just don't have the means to help?*

Yes, they know the situation, but they cannot help. Also, old people lack money to pay for their flats. Some people here were thrown out of their flats, because they were not able to pay for them. And many children are sick with different diseases.

- *Do you see any light in the future?*

Even sociologists working in various institutions do not have any answer to such a question! Some order should be established. I think that commerce should be developed. Some time ago we used to sell flowers and vegetables in Russia. Our Prime Minister Skele built his house with the money he earned in such a way. But now – farmers grow potatoes but they cannot sell them. All those big complexes that were working and producing in the times of the kolkhoze should restart working.

- *What is most important for farmers? How to help them strengthen their enterprises?*

First, they should know what to grow, where and at what price they could sell their produce. In this way they could plan. I told you about the farmer who could not sell his cabbages. There was an option that if you cannot buy one pound of fuel per 1 pound of milk then there are real difficulties. Milk costs 6 or 8 santims now, while fuel is 40 santims. And farmers do not have horses.

- You said that in the kolkhoze all employees were like a big family. Now, when everything has been destroyed, does ethnicity play any role when people want to co-operate?

People co-operate not based on ethnicity but on neighbourhood – neighbours plough land together and stand together. As I see, everybody helps everybody. I remember our big canteen in the kolkhoze where 350 people of different nationalities ate together. There are no big differences between nationalities.

- And the fact that some of them are [Latvian] citizens and others are not, does not play any role?

No, it does not. But, of course, in conversations everybody will express his or her opinion.

- Some ethnic Russians said that they were scared of the Latvians. What do you think?

There is a reason to be scared. Many of them have been living in Latvia since the 1950s and many of them participated in construction and building everything here. And now they do not even have the right to elect the local government. They are not trusted.

Younger Generation of Socialist Entrepreneurs, who Successfully Steered their Companies into the New Economic Realities of Post-socialist Transition

This group comprises four interviews with two Bulgarian, one Estonian and one Macedonian engineer, who gained experience as industrial managers already in the in 1980s. Starting their careers in the reforming administrative economy of socialism and having clear ideas about its inherited defects, they profited from the radical political and economic changes in 1989-1991 period to transform (or create anew) their former enterprises at new, capitalist ground. Yet they all are not typical neo-liberal heroes of capitalism. Their entrepreneurial 'style' still preserved some of the core values of socialist managers, such as a softer version of collectivity, a kind of modesty in personal consumption, preserved sense of social partnership, etc., all blended with the imperatives of economic efficiency, aggressive market behaviour and continuous investing in new technologies and in improving the competences of their companies' personnel.

The specific characteristics of this group put it in a kind of intermediary position between those of *earlier generation socialist entrepreneurs* and *new private capitalist entrepreneurs*. We hope that reading and comparing their stories the reader could get some genuine insights about the vanished economic realities of socialism and about the compelling, often contradictory realities of post-socialist present our heroes had to cope with.

4. Interview with the Executive Director of "T" Ltd.

Sofia, Bulgaria, September 2009
Interviewer: Ivan Tchalakov, project "Current's Power', *Riskmonitor* foundation, Sofia

Short Introductory note

T. Ltd is an engineering company specialized in thermal power technologies and machines – water heating, power boilers, and related equipment. The company is successor to the former applied research units on thermal power stations – the "Thermal Technology" Department at the state enterprise *Automation and modernization of the power system,* established in 1967. In 1979 the enterprise was transformed into *Industrial-Scientific Enterprise TECHENERGO*, which in 1988 it became *Industrial-Scientific Combine* with a special *Technology Research Institute (NITI)*. In 1990 the "Thermal Technology" Department at NITI was established as an autonomous public company, owned by the Bulgarian state. In 1993 the company became a Limited Liability Company, owned by the state. It was privatized by *Energoremont Holding* in 2004, and specialized in repair and maintenance of (electric) power facilities. I, the executive director, worked as deputy director of T. since its establishment in 1990, and in 1993 Mr.I became director of the company.

- How was your company established?

During socialist times we were part of a much larger organization – *NITI* and *TECHENERGO*. The famous *Energoproekt* Institute was even bigger, as many as 3000 people. So there was specialization and the state favored this type of organization, since we had no economic autonomy. For example, we did not possess our own bank account; there were unified cost and labor tables that you could not exceed. I soon realized we should change this. Because, under the old type of organization, we were not allowed to take on and to control the entire process: from the initial design of the power unit, through its construction, and down to setting it in operation. I mean the control over the entire chain of activities - under socialism this was not allowed for us, the design engineers. So already in the late 1980s, while in NITI, I claimed that taking control over the entire process is the future of our engineering work. We had a lot of discussions with my former boss, R. G., friendly discussions in the presence of the company staff – he spoke, I replied, these were long debates. My point was that we should change the old way (old organization of work)... In 1993 R. left us and established his own private company under almost the same name – *T. Engineering*, and we remained *T.* only. However, all contracts and other assets remained in our firm. Now the company consists of 40 people, and this number has remained the same since the very beginning. Not a single person has been fired, relocated, etc. During all these years the staff was pretty stable.

- You were founded as a small, 'neat' company and have remained such ever since...

Yes, and we continue to be a 'neat' company. Unfortunately, some of us are getting older, some have already retired. So we are now looking for younger people, we need novices to learn the trade. Now, being part of a larger corporate structure helps too – if we have problems, aid comes from the Energoremont holding.

- Is it correct to say that Energoremont holding is similar to the former state-owned economic combines that were dismantled in 1991?

Yes, it is very similar. But before privatization we worked the same way… When we were a state-owned company for 15 almost years – do you think that I could go complain to the Power Industry ministers M. Kovachev (2001-2004) or I. Shilyashki (1998-2001) about my problems? – This was unthinkable! The most I would have achieved by asking them for help was getting dismissed on grounds of my inability. I never counted on the state during our existence as a public company - we did not get a penny from the state.

Since 2004 we are private company - I am not an owner or co-owner, but a manager under a contract. When we got privatized, because the people from *Energoremont* knew about us and what we were doing, they came and asked me – "Would you like to work with us?" So we bargained, discussed the conditions… I insisted that we as a company should keep our operational autonomy. This means that decision making on the commercial matters should stay within the company – I bear the responsibility for the contracts, etc. Well, I don't mean I can sell company shares, of course. We are working together with *Energoremont's* CEO and the holding obtains some of its contracts thanks to the fact that we, as an engineering company, are also taking part. For example recently we carried out the modernization of Fifth Thermal Power Unit at *Republika* Power Station – it had to be redesigned, a plan for its reconstruction had to be calculated, etc. We did it as a design, and *Energoremont* holding with its construction and repairing companies carried out the project.

- I know that T. Engineering got a contract with "Puente" thermal power plant (TPP) in Spain; they supplied them with a new combustible installation for lignite coal...

They trumpet everywhere about this contract, but the fact is that the contract was signed first with our company, *T.* But the former director R. G. later transferred it to his private firm, when he left us... So these assets belong to *T.* – it is not fair for a private company, which emerged out of our firm, to count such assets as its own. Those people, who are now in the firm (R.G. passed away a few years ago), they deserved nothing; the contract in question is entirely the merit of our firm *T.!* Recently we renewed with the Spanish partners - the latest bank order for 380 000 euro came just a few days ago. So enough about these impostors from T. engineering!

The more important fact is that we changed our profile: from a design company we became an engineering company offering complete solutions in power industry, 'under lock and key'. Maybe my previous experience helped here – before joining NITI, I had worked 17 years as an engineer putting in operation the industrial installations in electric power. There you see the final result [of the design work] – and I knew perfectly every design of the installations we put in operation. And there were often errors in the designers' work. But when the installation did not work, it is not the designer but the engineers like me who were blamed... This period was a great schooling for me.

So I came to NITI and later when I became deputy of R. G., T. Company was established. There I said: "*We should change the way we work, we need to combine design with engineering activities and construction work!*" It is not possible for the 'muscles to guide the brain', as it was under socialism – in those times we would design a project that was applied N-times, and we were paid only once while those who were applying the project were paid N-times! So the workers from the construction company received their salaries for N number of applications, while we, the designers, only once for the initial project. So to get more money we had to design a new project, i.e. there was no multiplication of the results of our work... And I said to the company's staff: the only way to survive and to get enough money is to engage ourselves with the entire process. We should stop supplying our designs to other companies – no transfer of drawings, no design contracts! We are supplying final solutions, completed installations, and if someone needs another power unit or other installations, he should order it from us again.

It does not matter that we would be applying the same or a (slightly) modified design, this is company know-how. Because the intellectual and industrial property rights belong to our company – we learned the laws, and managed to defend our know-how. In TTP *Maritsa-East 2* we made eight boilers, working as subcontractors of the Japanese company *Mitsui*. Interestingly enough, no one mentioned this in public – there was not a single news announcement in the Bulgarian media that the boilers providing steam for the Japanese turbines had been established by Bulgarian company *T.!*

- *Does it mean that your company has preserved and developed the Bulgarian technology for burning low-quality lignite coal, as designed in the late 1960s by Prof. Nikola Todoriev and Rumen Ganchev? And was it true that they got the idea from German engineers, who built Kozani TPP in Greece, based on lignite fuel too?*

Initially the Germans were far ahead in this technology. Their deposits consist predominantly of black and brown coal – with a small proportion of ash, but high humidity which makes it difficult to burn. So it has to be enriched and dried before burning. The first German steam boilers had fire-grates; just like in the stove, but the grate moves forth and back, the burnt coals fall down and the new ones come from above. Later they introduced the whirlwind or vortex burners, where the flows of air and coal clash in the whirl. The problem with these burners is the high resistance of the flow, but when high-quality flow is used the process is pretty efficient. However, when you have low-quality lignite, as in our Maritza-East deposits, the volume of gases needed is four times more and this type of burners do not work.

Then, for the Kozani TPP, built by the former *Reinbraun (*now *RWE*), the Germans invented the so-called 'fan-mills burning chamber'. These chambers took large amounts of high-temperature gases from the chimney to dry the coal and then the fan-mills crumble the coal together with the air. So they put several such burners into one chamber, positioning them along the tangent of an imaginary circle so that the different jets would mix the air and the fuel. When in the right proportion, the jets form a common torch and the coal burns very efficiently.

Where is our know-how, where is the innovation of Todoriev? When the Germans designed the new boiler, they used a rather straightforward approach - one main burner consisting of a dust-concentrator, which separates most of the coal mass and focuses it in the lower part of the burner so that a kind of enrichment takes place. In this specific zone of the burning torch, about 50% of the gases are concentrated, and in some narrow areas even 85%, so that the fuel power increases correspondingly – from 1500 kcal it becomes 3000 and more kcal. So, the burning chamber works properly.

The contribution of Todoriev and his team (including my former boss R. G.) was that they improved the process, allowing even lower-quality coal to burn efficiently, as was the case with the extremely poor Bulgarian lignite. They designed additional burners, where by a cascade of coal particles they achieved still greater concentration of coal dust – they managed to split the jet into 3 or 4 parts with gradually increasing velocities. Now here, in our company T., we further developed this approach after we noticed that these velocities were not a random value – in the initial model it is taken as random, but in fact the jet velocity is closely related with the size of the dust particles, which vary significantly. There are particles of different mass coming from the fan-mills, so that, having the same energy at the exit, they have different velocity, especially compared to the gas particles. So we designed the burning chamber in such way that, by carefully locating the burners, we achieved a calculated burn, whereby the particles reach the centre of the flame zone at the same speed, thus increasing even more the efficiency. When some years ago I explained to Todoriev the design of our last model boilers, he said he saw we had gone deep enough into the process – 'deeper then we went at the time', he said.

So we preserved and developed the ideas of Todoriev and R. G., but you can't say that it is just a 'know-how'. I mean something rather pragmatic here, not just the 'know-how' basis of this technology, we are developing some other things as well. You know that in many cases it's the details that matter, not just the principles – for example, we managed to redesign the existing boilers at TPP Maritza-East 2 in such a way that we increased their productivity and they were able to supply enough steam to the new Japanese turbines. This was something more than just 'applying the know-how'.

- How was it that you, as a state-owned company, survived during the difficult years of the 1990s and till your privatization in 2004? I mean that one and the same private firms are winning most of the tenders in the Bulgarian power sector so that some people now are talking about hidden links between these firms and the political establishment?

We survived because of one thing - lot of work and a serious attitude to our duties. When we say that we will do something, we do it, and so far we have not failed. As a company we have never been attractive for privatization, because we possess no material assets, only our brains. So when the gentlemen from *Energoremont Holding* came to us in 2004 they grasped the situation – I honestly told them that if we did not come to an agreement, we would move to another company. But instead of 40 people, only 6 of us would move, doing the same amount of work. So they agreed and accepted our conditions.

Why did we succeed during all these years? – Because, as I said, we changed the organization of our work just in time. We were the first company in our field to switch from pure design work to the execution of a completed project. So we learned how to hire subcontractors, to control them and to be responsible for the entire process. That is how we succeeded in multiplying the results of our (design) work. While those people from the *Energoproekt* institute continued in the old way…

- When I interviewed the former minister of Power Industry from the early 1990s, he said just the opposite – "The tragedy of Energoprojekt was that its heads of departments established their own firms and privatized the institute piece by piece!"

Yes, but what did they do? They split the institute into different teams (collectives), so when a team wins an order, they demand 30% for the firm, and the bosses (heads of the departments) manage the rest of the money. There is no way such an organization will work! They attempted to offer this way to our company, but I said to my people – so long as I am the manager, this will never happen!

The reason is simple: there might be a task for 50 000 euro, for example, but taking this task we are making a breakthrough and then because of it we are taking an order for 5 million. So if one team in your company is working on a prestigious, but less paid task that, however, opens the door for another team to get routine, but highly paid work, you as manager should not allow each group to stay within the money they earned. At first this looks illogical, but the reason is that in Bulgaria people are still paying for the 'iron', for the material stuff, and not for the ideas, for the design work. So the highly qualified designers are paid little money, while the ordinary engineers and workers took the big money. How can one work this way? But this is precisely what happened in *Energoproekt!*

– You mean the R&D, the design projects are risky, less paid, but they introduce the innovations which later open the doors for larger projects, though at times simpler and routine ones?

Yes, in Bulgaria R&D and design projects count for nothing! So if you specialize in engineering projects alone, i.e. a given task to be adapted to specific conditions and requirements assigned by the contracting authorities, you cannot survive with the money from such projects. And we survived as a firm because I never allowed such a division inside the firm! So my people know very well: every contract is important and must be fulfilled, there is a person responsible for each contract, but there is also a manager of the company who decides for everyone where they will work.

- I noticed in my interviews with some engineers in the ICT field, but also in some other fields, that when an engineer gains self-confidence and becomes well-known, he is tempted to think he could manage alone, and he tries to become independent and establish his own company... How did you manage to keep the company staff all these years, so that you remained a team? Was it the very specificity of your work that helped?

I succeeded, because I never thought to take more for myself at the expense of the others… You see, millions and millions worth of money passed through my hands, so I should have been a millionaire by now, but I am not. And my people, they see this…

- You mean there was some king of ethics in your management...

Of course! The partners I am working with in the company – these are my colleagues with whom I began my career. You have to preserve their trust, not cheat them… so that you will be able to count on them. This is an established style of work, a kind of rearing that allows none to behave otherwise.

- Could you tell me about some of your most important projects during these years?

Yes, our first big project was TPP Varna.[17] The task was to convert the boilers from black oil to natural gas. It was technically possible, but in addition to that we had to reconstruct the entire installation according to EC standards, since the boilers were designed according to Russian standards. We changed the configuration of all power units. The contract was initially for one boiler, then for two more, and so on till the end. Now the boilers are burning 60 cubic meters of natural gas per second. The people there were happy.

Working on this project, we completed the conceptual design to convert TPP Varna to a new type of fuel – high-quality coal from Indonesia or something like that. In this way all ecological problems would be solved. We initiated this work, believing it was important. Unfortunately, no one from the government paid attention to it.

This is our 'know-how' – I had to explain at length to some people called power engineers that it was not possible for low-quality lignite from Maritza-East to be burned in Varna and high-quality imported coal to be burned in Maritza-East – each type of coal needs a different, specially designed boiler. And this is our business; we call ourselves 'kotlyari' [equivalent to 'cauldroners' in English].

The next project was at Maritza-East[18]. The three big TPP there had constant problems with burning this low-quality lignite coal – first the stability of burning, then the clinkering of the burning chambers, which reduces the boilers' power – instead of 240 MW it falls to 210, 205 MW and even lower, which is a huge loss. TPP Maritza East 2 organized a tender and we were the only Bulgarian company that took part in it. The task was to be completed entirely by us, i.e. not just the design, but also real work on the boilers.

- You mean [you were to] carry out the preliminary study, technical design and then its realization?

Yes, I applied at the tender in presenting our previous results, then I found a subcontractor to carry out the metal work – where everything had

---

[17] With its 8 power units and total installed power of 1200 MW, TPP Varna is the biggest in the country. It uses imported coal.

[18] This is a large lignite coal basin in South Bulgarian, on the left bank of Maritza River.

to be clear beforehand, including where the supply would come from, the ignition with black fuel, everything down to the smallest detail.

- Was this the way you worked before, in NITI and Energoproekt? And maybe what helped you was the fact that in the beginning you had worked as a construction engineer putting the installations into operation?

Yes, there hadn't been such practice before.

- Well, then where did your 'know-how' for steering the entire process come from?

Hmm… there is no know-how here; we arrived at this way of working not of our own will...

- What do you mean?

Just that! ... The contracting authorities are looking for final solutions, not just designs… That is why I say this [new] way of working was not an end in itself, we arrived at it not of our own will…

For example, the contracting authorities said: "Here, in this boiler there are four burners. I want you to change it so that the boiler will have eight burners. In addition to that the burning chamber should not form clinker, should keep full load for one year, and it should be guaranteed it will preserve its energy conversion efficiency, etc." There are other benchmarks too – for example the temperature should not go above a certain level, etc.

So what did I do in this case? – We went back to the company, we sat down with my colleagues and analyzed the things one by one. We looked at the assignment; we found some errors in it… First we conducted diagnostics – although we are familiar with these matters. Then we roughly specified the materials to be used, saw what the completed object would look like, then made a precise specification of the needed material and equipment compiled. I sent faxes to the [potential] subcontractors – one, two, three… They sent back their offers, I selected the best one, and then I added the insurance, equipment expenses, labor cost for the assembly work, etc. When I put all this together, I added our profit and my offer to the contracting authorities was ready.

- So you proceed like a businessman, in spite of the fact that you come from an "applied" research institute?

We have been working this way since 1993… I had insisted on this way of working to my former boss R. G. even before that, but he had refused! "As an engineering company we should deal only with the project, with the design work!" he insisted. "We are going to die from hunger!" I replied. And before we turned to this way of working we had a very difficult period of time. However, when we finally switched to the new way, the firms that specialized in construction and repairs work objected – 'Why these people from T. Company interfere in our work and are taking our business!'

- So that is how you won your first project at TPP Varna?

Yes, Varna was delivered 'under lock and key', then Maritza-East was delivered the same way, we did a boiler at TPP Ruse, another one at TPP Bobov dol…

But what happened at Maritza East? We redesigned the boilers at TPP 2, where the new Japanese turbines were installed. The task was not only to replace the burners, but to respond to the higher demand for steam the new turbines required. Hence the burning chamber had to be redesigned with different parameters. We calculated all this, manufactured it and assembled at TPP. And when we completed the work, my former boss R. G. came with his private firms *T. Engineering,* copied everything and installed it at TPP 3. However, his employees were so stupid that they did not assemble the boilers properly, so their boilers had many problems… Eventually the Italians[19] kicked them out! During the same period we were redesigning the boilers at TPP Maritza East 3 – they are still very pleased with our work… And now – the cherry on top of the cake: Australia and Indonesia! We got contracts there, they invited us …

- As far as I know, Australia possesses large reserves of lignite coal…

Yes, their lignite has 100% humidity, but only 2% ash, unlike our lignite at Maritza East, which has 50% humidity but 15-16% ash! So their lignite is better than ours. I will show you a letter we received from *International Power*, which owns these TPPs, both in Spain and in Australia... *International Power* is a British company, and some years ago they came here to Maritza East, while we were working there. At that time

---

[19] Italian company *Enel* became owner of the TPP 1 in 2002.

the German company *Babcock Borsig* won the tender for TPP 3, but soon after that they went bankrupt and were replaced by *DSD,* another German firm. *DSD* had no experience with this type of lignite coal TPP, so they came to TPP 2 where we were installing the new boilers. They saw our work, noticed that the boilers were working without clinkering, keeping their power. But because we were an [unknown] Bulgarian firm, they hesitated. A year later they said – these are the right burners! However, it will be *T. Engineering* and not *T. Company* that will fulfill the task. The firm of my former boss! This was an outrageous lie! We fought in court, however they used bribery, the court was constantly postponing the decision, up until now… You understand.

However during these events *International Power* sent the director of one of its Australian TPP, which uses similar lignite, to check the situation here and to verify whether our burners were working as announced. They wanted assurance before bidding in the tender for TPP 2 at Maritza East. So this Australian director came to the TPP, looked at the boilers and reported – 'Yes, here the Bulgarian company has managed well!'

Three years later I got a fax – from the same Australian director. He wrote he was impressed with our work at TPP 2 and he asked for us to consult him on problems they had with their boilers! They had decided that the know-how already existed and they would try to use it. So we went there and found an antiquated TPP, worse than the Bulgarian TPPs, with very bad economic parameters. I said this honestly to them and that we were able to help. Now there is a project going on, under the heading of ecology. Next year is the beginning.

Meanwhile, another Australian TPP found out we were there and they also invited us. After the talks they said they wanted us to supply the burners for their boilers! I told them – why from Bulgaria, the transport is too expensive. Their director insisted – "Nikolai, he said, don't be silly, the transport will be about 1% of the costs!"

- *You mean they are going to order these burners here?*

Yes, everything for our projects we produce here, at *Energoremont Holding*. They have five plants and they fulfill our orders. But look – a burner is a heap of laminated iron, there is nothing special in it. What is important is the design! I tried many times to explain this to the expert at the Bulgarian patent office – 'Why are you referring me to Patent Law? The patents are something important, but among them there are a lot of crazy things – a spoon with a hole, for example. And people are often patenting without paying attention to whether it is useful or not. But copyright is something different – you have it also when you are using ready-made elements! This is something the judges in Bulgaria are still unable to understand – that something new is made out of known elements, but which is genuinely new and has never operated before. It is the same as with an architect – he is using well-known materials, bricks for example. But this does not diminish his copyrights, because his [new] conception is in the way he combines these bricks or other well-known elements. The situation in our field is intolerable – your competitors are taking you burner, assembling it anew, and they consider that they have the right to produce it!

- Which means that in fact you have problems with Bulgarian judges when you have to defend your copyrights in court?

Yes! When we eventually go to court, there is endless evasion – this way and that, because the same things can be presented in a number of ways. We can complain higher up in Brussels, as was the case with *T. Engineering,* although at that time Bulgaria was not yet an EU member. Anyhow, this is all behind us, in the past…

I told you about Indonesia – they organized a conference there, the topic was burning ecological coal, because they have only high-quality coal, almost without any sulphur. So the Americans who owned these mines organized this conference. We were also invited – we knew one of the organizers from our work for TPP Varna, where we designed the conversion to this type of coal. Our project was not realised, but that is another story – why did they allow a shake of the bag to come here and direct our development [he meant the Czech power company CEZ, which had recently bought TPP Varna]…

- Mr. Nabatov, a retired expert from the National Electricity Company, told me that those managing the sector today don't care about preserving the existing traditions...

He is right, they don't care because accidental people are heading the power industry today, starting with Ivan Shilyashki, who was absolutely unknown when he was appointed Minister… Only later did I realize he had been my fellow student at the Technical University, but he was such a dud that no one remembered him. Maybe they appointed such a man on purpose… Not to mention the directors of power plants – so many talented and established people were fired!

To conclude my story, after we were privatized in 2004, we got a project for TPP Deven at the *Solvay* chemical plant near the Bulgarian Black Sea port of Varna – this was a structure of about 500 tons designed by us for a new fuel supply. We had never had such a project before, but we made it in cooperation with *Energoproekt*. The project comprised the entire process, with real construction work and putting it into operation. When we got such a specific task, as was the case here, we looked for subcontractors – for example we don't developing the automatic control systems in the company, so we buy the control systems from other firms. These are firms with which we are in good relationships, we allowing them to make profit… We take our part, so we support each other…

- You said you were ready to enter Australia and Indonesia, but what about the European countries?

We are already in Spain. Here is a letter in which they ask for our consent to work on improving the ecological parameters of one of their TPPs… The latest hit is that most EC thermal power stations are renewing their ecological licenses, i.e. the gratis period in which they were allowed to operate above the ecological norms. Now the time is approaching when they have to comply with the norms – for example the entire process of improving the ecological parameters for Maritza East TPPs starts again. *T. Company* is ready with new schemes for reducing the emission from TPP – because during the gratis period we succeeded with the new burners at TPP Deven, at the *Solway* plat, where we competed with *Babcock* and other firms. So we managed to reduce the emissions there by 30% and more!

Look at the materials from the conference in Indonesia - here is the organizers' definition of low-quality coal: 'below 5000 kilocalories and humidity above 30%'… I don't know whether I should laugh or cry – because in Maritza East we work with coal of 1500 kilocalories and 55% humidity! And when we tell them this, they stand there gaping … So we are accumulating more and more valuable experience.

- T. Company having such achievements, the big Western firms would maybe like to buy it?

Why? They don't need us – they could perfectly well do their job by having us as subcontractors…

5. The Former Director of the *G. Ltd.* Electric Cables Plant

October 23rd, 2004 - Smolyan, Bulgaria
Interviewer: Yuliana Goranova
Selection of the firms, questionnaire design, and supervision by Ivan Tchalakov under the project "From Networks to Networks", The Open Society Institute – Sofia, Bulgaria

- How did you arrive in this enterprise? What was your career as engineer and manager?

I became a student at Technical University in Sofia with a stipend from this plant. After I graduated, I came back to the plant as brigade leader in the so-called Department 300, [dealing with] extrusion. A year later I became a deputy director of the plant and in 1987 was appointed director.

- Could you say about some people in the plant they were your teachers?

Some of the first directors of the plant, whom I found when I came here, I learned a lot from them. Such as Deltcho Gegov, who is now deceased, but also many managers and engineers. Each of them gave me something in different periods of my career. Unlike art, in the production business it is difficult to point out a single person as your teacher…

- How did the plant develop during those years?

The plant was established by government decision in 1968 and the first production department for coated electric cables was opened in 1975. During the years that followed the plant was equipped with different machinery that expanded the type of cables produced. Till 1980 the plant was part of the former Cables and Wires Combine, together with two older plants in the towns of Burgas and Sevlievo. Then it became an autonomous enterprise, still in the framework of the same combine. Until 1989 the plant functioned as a typical socialist industrial enterprise, there was no substantial modernization after its opening – this is a rather traditional type of production, not like electronic or military industries where renovations were regular. Till 1989 there was only one modernization of the plant, for about 5.5 million Bulgarian leva – 3 million for construction works and 2.5 million for equipment. This is a rather modest investment for a plant with annual production of about 25 million Bulgarian levs [about the same amount in USD – I.Tch.].

The plant had a good position both with the industrial customers and households – it specialized in so-called 'light type' cables, used in buildings, radio-transmission, in the household appliances. The bigger types of cables used in power industry, telephone networks, in machine-building industry, were produced in Burgas and Sevlievo.

Initially the plant was equipped with the second-hand machinery taken from the two other cable plants, in Sevlievo and Burgas. However, after 1975 and especially in the early 1980s new equipment was introduced, including some very good machines from reputed Western companies. Hence until its privatization in 1996 the plant was relatively well equipped. *(Assessment by the current director of the plant, appointed in 1999. Interview taken in 2004)*

From a technical point of view, by the late 1980s we were processing about 6 500 metric tons of copper and selling produce for about 25 million USD annually. There were about 400 people working in the plant in three shifts. The production was not very sophisticated, but we satisfied the needs of industry and households for certain types of cables. By 1989 the plant was in a good financial state, without serious debts to the banks, its production was well-known on the market and valued by the customers.

- *What were your relationships with foreign partners?*

Till 1989 these relationships were managed by the centralized system of planning. They decided what part of our production would be for export, and what part for the domestic market. They made the balance of the needs and the output and our entire production was distributed according to the planned quotas – every plant was able to buy such quotas and, based on it, we demanded a corresponding amount of raw materials from our suppliers. The relationships between enterprises then were predetermined by the annual and five-year economic plan – it stated how much you would buy from whom. For example, a given enterprise was allowed to put up to 2 million linear meters of cables in their products, containing no more than 5 metric tons of copper (as a strategic commodity, copper was controlled). Hence this enterprise was able to buy a certain amount of cables in the frame of this quota. The quota was divided in three-month periods, etc. From a financial point of view these relationships were rather good – most of the customers were paying on time the planned quotas, so that our plant had a good reputation also among its suppliers. In the plan system there were guarantees that every one of our customers would pay for the cables supplied – either the bank was allocating some money, or they were transferring the money from other sources if the revenues were delayed somehow.

- Did you manage to preserve these relationships after 1989, and after privatization?

This system existed till 1989, maybe also in 1990. Then it collapsed and was dismantled. New economic agents emerged – the private firms. Some of the former partners, especially those exporting to USSR and other COMECON countries, sharply reduced their orders. Hence most of our former partners practically disappeared. In 1991 the centralized system of trade with industrial goods was dismantled too and the former "Regional Trading Companies" ('commercial bases') were shut down. Those were among our biggest customers – for example the so-called TERSNAB (Regional Supply) state-owned commercial enterprises, buying cables for the industry in southern Bulgaria – ceased to exist. They were replaced by new private firms, some of them established by the employees and managers of the former state commercial enterprises. They took the trade with electric cables in their own hands. Till 1990 we were also selling cables directly to about 50 big industrial plants, but they too practically disappeared, especially those in electronic, electro-technical, and machine-building industries.

- What about your relationships with ministries and other government institutions? Were there attempts made at political intervention in your plant, in the way it was managed?

Practically no; till 1989 and part of 1990 there was only partial political intervention – simply because then the Communist Party was the ruling party and this was written in the country's constitution. The Party intervened directly in the investments, in the planning, in the selection of cadres, etc. After 1990 the influence of the Bulgarian Socialist Party (as the former communist party was renamed) in the industrial enterprises diminished - maybe there was still some influence, but indirectly, via the people who sympathized with it. But there was no official intervention anymore. Every managerial contact in *G. Ltd* was approved by the corresponding minister or his deputies. Hence the Ministry was controlling our plant indirectly, via the managing staff they appointed. But direct centrally-planned orders disappeared – now, based on our resources such as machinery, employees, raw materials, we at the plant have to decide what to produce, to whom it is to be sold, at what price, etc. We have to look for customers, to negotiate with them, etc.

Box 5 - The breakdown of Government's control over the economy

... Control was weak. It can't be strong when you have seven thousand enterprises.

- *You mean that between 1989 and 1995 the directors, though appointed by the ministries, were in fact the true rulers [of enterprises]?*

Yes... At least as far as the operative leadership was concerned, but even in the area of investments they were almost absolute masters. Both in terms of their behaviour and mentality, and in terms of their action... The managers' rights, according to the typical contract they concluded with the respective ministry, were pretty big, almost unlimited. Some state officials were in the board of directors of enterprises as representatives of the state as owner of the assets... Most of them just received their remuneration without participating in the board meetings; but even when they did participate, they soon forgot about the interest of the state... There were many abuses [of the property rights], on a large scale.

- *Is it normal for the state to require some profitability from its enterprises? You require it from the enterprises in your Investment Fund?*

There were no specific requirements. There were no such in the regulations that existed then, and there was no way we could directly demand such a level. The most that could be done was, when exercising surveillance over a given public company, to say: "Well, you've had large losses, something here is not in order"... You see, in the 1970s or even the 1980s the economy was simply a planned economy: then the management by the state was much more direct. The state had resources to control, in fact there was mainly control without incentives: party organizations, economic police, if necessary court and prosecution [laughing]... After 1989, especially after 1991 when the enterprises were transformed into limited joint stock companies, they became independent in their operational management! There was no direct instrument at all to make them work better. Besides, the goal was privatization, after all. The bad thing was that during this period many companies were destroyed.

- *This went on six whole years...*

Even more than six years, because some of them are still state-owned today (laughing)." (Former Minister of Economics in the ly 1990s, now managing an investment fund, Tchalakov and Hristov 2005)

- The years of directorship of the plant in 1990s were known as a 'golden period' – your employees had good salaries, bonuses, festivities... How would you describe the relationship between the management and your employees?

Generally speaking the plant was in good shape because we took adequate steps to change the previous system. Facing the sharp decline in the number of our customers, it was clear enough we could not function the way we did till 1990. In the former COMECON Bulgaria specialised in certain types of production and our cables were put in items produced in large series for the entire COMECON market. When this market collapsed, the plants were unable to realize their production, so they stopped buying our cables. What remained was the local household market, but till then only 1-2% of our cables had been intended for this market – copper was a strategic resource and they did not allow selling it to private persons abroad. So we suddenly had lots of cables produced without customers and in a short period we needed to find new customers for it, including abroad, where we had limited experience.

We managed to reduce the number of employees because the economic system that existed in the early 1990s allowed us to keep the 'Salaries' fund at a certain level independently of the number of employees – this became possible as part of the economic reforms in the late 1980s. Provided we had achieved certain parameters of production, we were able to keep the share of salaries – for example you have a sale of 10 million, then you could pay for salaries 1 million and it does not matter if you hire 300 or 150 people on the staff. So in the early 1990s our production dropped by three times – we processed 2100-2200 tons of copper annually, but the people were twice less and those remaining had twice bigger salaries. We were also allowed to export and we reached a percentage of 30% of our cables sold abroad. So when you have good salaries and a just system of evaluation of the contribution of each employee, the people are generally happy.

Yet there were important changes in personnel relationships in the plant, for during Communism the income pyramid was reversed, so to say – the highly-qualified workers received the highest salaries, higher than those of the top management and key engineering staff. Those in managerial positions – deputy directors, heads of department, chief designer, chief machinist, chief technology officer, head of maintenance shop, etc., and their salaries could approach the salaries of the qualified workers taking into account the additional payments at the end of the year. After 1989 we put the pyramid back on its base – the management personnel and key specialists received much higher salaries, which corresponded to their responsibilities. These changes normalized the internal relationships in the plant – instead of managers being paid a salary of 300 Bulgarian leva (BGN) to control workers with salaries of above 500 BGN! The best workers now had incentives to become brigade leaders and deputy heads of departments, because this was the only way now to get higher salaries. Before we made this change, if a head of department was dismissed for some reason, it might be that he would be getting more money as a worker than as head of department! Or if you see a good worker and you offer him to be made brigade leader or deputy head of department, he would often refuse – "Why should I take more responsibilities for less money?" he asked. Because he received 400-500 leva as a worker with fewer responsibilities, and if you appointed him head of shift group or deputy head of department he would get 220 or 250 BGN maximum!

Hence, turning the salary scale back and putting the employees' salaries in relation with their education, qualification, skills, and with the responsibility they carry, we normalised the situation. Now the leader or specialist gets good money and when you assign some obligations to him, he has a choice – either he should work as he is supposed to, being well paid for that, or he should leave. There were no other options anymore for him – the old schemas allowed him to get good money for little work done. So if a person does not meet our expectations, there are plenty of others to replace him. This had very positive effects on the organisation of work.

Outside the plant there were many state-owned companies that were literally robbed by their managers; they were plundering the enterprises they managed! I mean both the top management and the lower level managers. Instead of focusing their energy on developing their companies, finding a niche on the changing markets and holding it, many managers of state-owned companies created their (hidden) private companies and began to suck out the state companies they managed – they drained its assets, transferring it to their private companies – machinery, raw materials, sales, part of the profit, almost everything... When the money disappears, your enterprise can hardly function, and this is especially true for traditional industrial companies. If you are in a modern high tech business and those you are selling your products to trust you, they may agree to finance your business in advance. But in the traditional industrial business this rarely happens, so that you have to preserve the resources and to use them in the company's interest and in the interest of the people working in it. That was missing in many public companies; their management [and groups behind it] just stole the money, leaving their personnel on minimal wages, often going unpaid for 5-6 months. Soon it became impossible to work in such plants…

- How did your own workers react to these changes?

In fact there was no trouble at all – since our company was not in debt, and we reduced the number of personnel according to our sales, the wages were paid on time… There was trouble in the enterprises having large [investment] credits that they became unable to serve. There were plants with 20, 30, even 50 million Bulgarian leva investment loans, and they lost their markets and had no produce anymore. Plus, the fact that part of the investment was not fulfilled so they were unable to launch the new products they planned. These enterprises were literally ruined in the early 1990s!

Of course, when you have kept some of your customers and you are producing your goods, you often need operational credit and that was difficult to find too. But our company was less concerned; somehow we managed to produce without such credits…

The last issue was the political interference in companies' work. You know, during the 1990s the Socialist (ex-communist) and Democratic parties came to power in turn several times and they often changed the management of the public-owned enterprises. We had some luck not to be fired, maybe because we kept at equal distance to all political parties while collaborating on issues of general public interest. I cannot explain why they kept me as director till the privatization in 1996, but it is true that in most public enterprises the 'political broom' was sweeping their directors every year, sometimes even every six months… *G. Ltd* was one of the few in which there were no such changes. But thinking back on this issue now, I can say that here in our town this process was less pronounced – there were other directors who also preserved their positions till privatization – for example the directors of the Instrument Plant, Rodhope Textile Plant, etc. The reason was that most of our enterprises were in a difficult situation, had meagre profit, so there were no big appetites for them at national level. Maybe there were still some interests at regional level, but somehow not strong enough. This was not the case with big public companies that were still profitable, like the Burgas Petrochemical Plant, cement or chemical plants, etc. There was much less to steal from plants like *G. Ltd* or Rodhope Textile.

One thing that protected us from political interference was that we never took sides with any of the political parties – for example when the Democratic Union came to power in 1991 many people then said 'Hurrah! Democracy has come!" and they consciously began to instigate people in one direction or other. However, when the Parliament decided political parties were to leave the enterprises, everyone was free to go to whatever party he liked, but outside the plant - there was no place for political debate at the workplace anymore. So political organisations in the company were dismantled and I did not tolerate any political presence there. Maybe this line of behaviour helped too, because if you play with a given political party and for example help it financially during the election campaign, those who lose the elections usually come to power in the next elections and then they take revenge... They will say – "Last time you helped us lose the election, now we will help you not to be director anymore!" This is how I reason now about that period.

- *So what happened with your plant during the transition?*

Well, when the Parliament passed the Mass Privatisation Law in 1995, our plant was in very good economic shape, relative to the Bulgarian conditions, of course – we had no debts, we were well established in the market, we had already built our distribution network which realized our products. So we earned our money and the plant had always been profitable – we invested part of the profit, even though in the framework of our relatively limited resources. I would have preferred more investment, but I never allowed myself to invest money from the turnover, because we might then be unable to finance our production. So our company was economically sound and there were practically no serious problems in it.

Till 1996 there was no big investment in material assets and this was understandable – no one knew who would be the owner, so who would be crazy enough to invest in something that would be bought by buy someone else. The plant had good economic results, good marketing strategy, they also organized the first distribution network. They had a good social policy, where the largest part of the profit was distributed among the employees in the form of different types of bonuses. Viewed from the present-day point of view, this was not so good, because if they were invested the profit in new machinery instead of in salaries, our current investments would be much lower. That period brings back good memories to the workers, who say "Hey, boss, if you knew what money we were getting before 1996!" And I usually reply "See how much fewer machines were bought then!" *(*Interview with the current director of the plant, 2004*)*

According to the Mass Privatisation Law our plant was put on the list for privatisation with 67% of its shares. It was to be sold through so-called 'privatisation bonuses"[20] – by the fall of 1996 there were already five or six tenders carried out and about 5 privatization funds had acquired shares of our plant, none possessing the majority share. They had between 7 and 18% each.

- As far as I know, there was an attempt made to organize a 'Worker-Managers Partnership' and to privatize the plant under workers-management buyout schemes, described in the Mass Privatization Law. It seems to me that this failed?

Yes, we made an attempt to buy the remaining part of shares. According to the Mass Privatization Law, up to 25% of the company could be privatized through the workers-management buyout schema. Hence we registered such a partnership and made an attempt to buy those 25%, plus the fact that, according to the Law, we as managers and workers possessed a small share of about 5% (the remaining 3% were for restitution claims). The fact that we are having this interview now means that we failed. It did not happen.

- What do you think was your main success and your main failure during your directorship?

This is a difficult question. As far as the plant is concerned, I think our key success was that we managed to preserve the company in sound economic state regardless of all the pitfalls of the political and economic transition – high inflation, disintegrated and even disappearing markets, etc. All former socialist enterprises that were our customers practically disappeared and were replaced by new customers. Preserving the company in good shape in this economic environment is our main success – many fellow state companies disappeared in that period, but we survived. You can still see some of them, a dead building with silent machines inside.

Considered from the present-day perspective, our main failure is that we allowed the company to be privatised in such a way that its situation worsened. If we had taken the necessary measures – even some not completely legal ones – and had privatized the firm for ourselves, its economic situation now would be much better! Putting it directly, if at that time I had transferred some of our resources to some private firms under

---

[20] According to the Law every person above 18 years of age was assigned bonuses at the value 25 000 Bulgarian leva, to be invested in mass privatization via "privatization funds" established by various physical persons, political and public organization, trade unions, even mafia-like groups. Each holder of bonuses could invest them in a privatisation fund of his choice.

my control and then these firms had participated in the tenders, I could have managed to preserve the plant in a good financial and economic state. Unfortunately, at that time I thought capitalism was coming and the mass privatisation would bring real owners. I thought they would be interested in the long-term development of the company and would appreciate what we had done – that they had a production company well-established on the market, that it worked efficiently, etc. It appeared that this was not the case – instead of real owners, there were figure-head owners, who actually began to plunder their enterprises, and who in turn ruined many of the newly privatized firms. They did not come to work hard and with a long term strategy. Their plans instead were, in a few years, to drain everything possible in the companies and to redirect the resources thus obtained to other companies, controlled by those behind these dummy persons.

In this sense, this is our failure – if we had judged in good time how the privatisation in Bulgaria was going to develop, that there would be no real owners coming, interested in the efficient management of the firms, it might have been better for us, the people from the plant, to take the resources and use them for the long-term benefit of the plant. What I am saying maybe sounds very unpleasant, but seen from today, it was clear that company resources were about to be stolen – those who stole these resources made things worse. If we had stolen the resources ourselves, probably things would have been better. (He is laughing). Only God knows! But that is how I think about this now.

It is difficult for me to say now why the privatisation process in Bulgaria happened this way. Maybe one reason was that after 1989 there was a mass widespread attitude to steal and plunder state property – no one says this now, every rich man now tells how he began with his two hands, how he sold his *Lada* or *Trabant* car, etc. But the overall attitude of those participating in the privatisation was to buy as cheap as possible, or to buy the way the privatization funds did it: their founder just took over the shares of thousands of ordinary people putting their vouchers in the privatisation funds – a few people from the funds' management now practically owned the shares of the other 100 000 members. There are still no laws in Bulgaria protecting the interests of the owners of minority shares – the management of these funds announced for example a meeting of their members would be held early in the morning in a distant village, and then they increased the capital and in fact dispossessed the small shares of thousands of ordinary members…

These privatisation funds in fact were a scheme enabling a [limited] group of people with certain resources at their disposal to acquire cheaply the assets of the state enterprises put on the privatisation list… I don't know of a single enterprise that did well after mass privatisation. Only at the later stage did real owners go to some of the enterprises, when the funds were re-sold to them and when the new owners finally became interested in their long-term development. But most of the others were ruined.

These are my general thoughts about these events. You see, what happened then in Bulgaria usually happens only once in two or three centuries – in no country does property change owners every 20-30 years, so that public assets fall into private hands. When after World War II they took the property from private hands into public (Communist state) hands, there were few possibilities of stealing anything – when a private company worth 500 000 levs became state-owned, people could steal some small items, but you could not steal the company. In the reverse process which took place after 1989, this was possible. Some people knew this takes place only once in a century, so there was this widespread attitude to take everything you could – they felt that in three or four years every property would be privatised and you would not be able to steal so easily anymore. The main reason for this attitude is that until the mid-1990s there were few people in the country who possessed enough resources to buy assets legally – most people attempted to use some [illegal or semi-legal] schemes to cheaply acquire some property. It appeared that according to the then existing laws they were not criminal but were doing something legal… (He is laughing)

- *What happened after the current owners bought G. Ltd?*

O-o! (Laughing) Now as far as I know a bank owns the plant! After the privatisation funds bought their shares, an investor appeared who in turn bought their shares and he became majority owner. Then he bought the remaining 25% and took the entire plant under his control. Unfortunately, as I said, they did not come with the idea of developing it and producing efficiently… Now I think that at that time a certain amount of money was given to some figure-heads to privatise some industrial assets – in my view it was between 15 and 20 million USD. What their plans were, what the agreement was I really don't know, but obviously they selected certain companies with good assets, good positions both on the market and in the local community, including the regional financial institutions. Becoming owners, they announced how hard they would work, how they would develop these enterprises, what investments they would make, etc. Then they set the company assets at stake to take large credits from the banks. Instead of investing this money into the plants, however, they stole the money and left the company as a stake to the bank – "Sorry, we had good ideas, but we failed. Here are the company assets as a financial security!" Everything in this scheme is completely legal…

> *G. Ltd* had the chance to be well managed till the last moment of its existence as a state-owned enterprise. Hence it was in a very good economic and financial state when the process of mass privatisation began in 1996. The merit for this was of the former director I. D. – he managed to preserve its core personnel and material assets, which provided a good base for further development as a private company. I am respectful for what he did. At the last stage of his directorship they attempted to buy the plant under the Manager-Workers Buy-out scheme, but unfortunately they did not managed to acquire 50% plus one share – it was done by three physical persons from Sofia. Their financial-industrial group *ARECOM* bought the plant on August 26, 1996. Becoming owners, these persons immediately took a bank loan staking the assets of the plan. It was with this money the company was operating with after that… *(From the interview with the current director of the plant, 2004)*

The only problem is, as I said, they came not to make the company work, but to make 'fast money'. The money this investor took from *G. Ltd* under normal conditions would take 15-20 years to accumulate – to develop the plant, to invest in it, and to rely on normal rates of return. But why should they bother for 15-20 years to take 20 million USD when there is a chance to get it in less than 5 years?! This was the scheme, applied to the company similar to *G. Ltd* – you get a well-positioned company that every bank would love to give credit to, and you just take as much credit as you can. If the company was in a miserable state none of the banks would give credit to it and hence the new owners had to work hard to create a market, to improve the production, etc. What they did was the easiest way…

As far as I know, First Investment Bank now owns the plant, because the former owners do not pay back their loans. Now the bank is trying to sell the plant and to get back its money. It is not the bank's aim to manage the plant; this is not typical bank activity. But in order to sell the plant at a reasonable price, they try to manage it better and hence continue to provide some financial support, not allowing its price to drop too much. That is why they appointed a director they trusted, with the task of stabilizing the plant. But otherwise the plant has been declared for sale …

6. *M. Co.*, a World Producer of Machinery for Advanced Composites

Interview with *BS* - the founder and owner of *M.* Company
Town of Prilep, Macedonia
Interview taken by Ivan Tchalakov and Dejan Pendev in october 2007

Short Introductory Note from Company Web Site

During the years of Yugoslavia, a modern composites production facility was located in the city of Prilep, Macedonia, the largest in the south-eastern European region producing advanced composite parts for civil and military applications. After the peaceful separation, as an independent nation, of the Republic of Macedonia from former Yugoslavia, the local industry was broken up and sold off. *M. Co* was formed at that time as one of the few private companies producing high-technology products and preventing the experienced brain drain out of the region. *The former chairman of the composites production facility gathered the top engineers, putting them to work together in an environment where engineering excellence and positive customer impact would be guides to success.*

M. Co, starting out with a handful of engineers and university professors, decided to enter the composites industry initially as consultants. They began working on design consulting, building electronic components and designing machines for production. The people at the company worked very hard at breaking through on the international market, proving their concept and their ability to meet technological challenges face-on. The initial bet paid off, and the company experienced success with its know-how and respect from its community. Through its success and expansion, it outgrew its design office in the city of Prilep and invested in a large production facility aimed at developing sophisticated, specialized machinery. This decision was made to allow it complete control in how a machine is built, from conception to the delivery, and the start of production at the customer's site.

Throughout the years, the success of *M. Co.* has not been used as a blinder, but rather as a leverage to facilitate local community developments. The company continues to value the place it has chosen as its main headquarters by investing in the educational aspects of its workers and the wider community members. Continual learning and improvement of the company's employees has been a key factor to reaching such high professional results and being regarded as a company that outranks many of its US and EU competitors in its technical proposals and customer service. The company has provided back to its community by organizing free and personal educational services for the past 3 years to a selected number of enthusiastic adults through the *M. Co.* Academy. The latest endeavour was to establish the first private Institute for Advanced Composites and Robotics with the vision to become a centre for practical research for the common good of its world-wide community.

As director of a successful high tech factory in the early 1990s, B.S. was offered to participate in its privatisation, but he refused. He left the factory and his first business as private entrepreneur was a video-tape shop selling movies for home video players. In the early 1990s this was a very successful business and he was one of the market leaders.

Then, somewhere in the mid-1990s, he was called by a German entrepreneur who was installing newly bought American machines for production of composite materials. The German company asked the American producer to send an expert for the initial adjustment of the machines in putting them into operation. The answer was to call Mr. B.S. from Macedonia, because he knows everything about these machines.

B.S. remembers: "When they called me from Germany, I said my price – 50 000 euro. They said it was too much for a Macedonian man. It's your decision, I said." At the second call the producer insisted to the German entrepreneur that he should ask B.S. for the expertise, otherwise it would be too expensive. When the German company called him again, B.S. doubled the price of his consultancy, but it was paid after his team successfully put the machines in operation. This event, however, convinced B.S. to start his own business in the field - at that time the video business was declining, but it had accumulated some start-up capital.

M., spokeswoman of the company:

M. Co. was founded in 1990. Its founder has a long experience behind him, sixteen years of manufacturing activities producing different kind of equipment for Yugoslavian composite industry and more than 30 years of experience in composite industry in general. The business model of our company since its establishment in 1999 has always been manufacturing. Our vision is to be one of the leading companies, one of the best companies in the world in the production of composite materials processing machines. And of course we are achieving that through our core technologies – motion control, process control, and our deep knowledge of composite materials.

All activities in our company can be divided in two groups. The *first group* consists in designing and manufacturing machines for the composites industry. Those are filament winding machines, prototype fiber placement machine, and customized composites machining centres, and auxiliary equipment and software. The *other group* of activities are machines and computer controlled machines for processing different kinds of materials like marble, steel, aluminum and other materials, and, of course, laser, plasma and water-jet cutting machines that we are also developing in manufacturing in our company.

It is an interesting fact that in 2003 EU launched a "Plants for the Future" platform for increasing the competitiveness of the EU. The principles of the European manufacturing platform are compatible with or similar to our business model launched four years earlier. And we are especially proud of this.

We have a lot of achievements as a company, developing 50 different kinds of machines in a period of only 6 years. This is quite an impressive number, because it's very difficult to develop and manufacture such a number of different types of machines in such a short period of time. And, of course, we have our own software solutions - we are developing related software in-house, we offer it together with the machines we sell to the customers. We are developing also the concept of "virtual plant", where the knowledge for realization of system solutions according to our costumers' requirements is placed at the highest possible level.

Our first goals are, first, to increase both the economic and technological competitiveness of our Macedonian society. And also, to assist EU in providing an altruistic contribution to the above mentioned "Plants for Future" platform, being an active member of it.

Our employment profile consists of 20 engineers, 5 doctors of science, and about 10 manual workers. This proportion demonstrates that the entire production process is completely automated.

BS: You see from the structure of the staff that there are only 10 manual workers. And we are not living on public R&D funding programs - we are living by selling our machines. But the added value of the machines is so high that we don't need to keep too many workers in the production plant.

M: The characteristic of our personnel is that all knowledge they possess is acquired through the regular training that our company constantly provides for its employees. In that way in *M. Co.* we created something that is called 'general specialist'.

BS: The concept of 'general specialist' is a contradiction in terms, but we believe it is the future of our industrial profile. In the future, everybody should be a 'general specialist', because technology is developing so fast, that it is not possible, like it was in the beginning of the last century, when, in finishing your education, you were ready for work until your retirement, because basically nothing or little changed for years. Now technological achievements are changing every five years, and you have to develop the capability of building your knowledge in different fields and forgetting about your past investment in your knowledge. So you just need go on in your knowledge and to follow the new technology mainstream, you must always build up your knowledge, becoming a *general specialist*. This means you know a lot of things and you are ready to focus on a special competitive field and eventually master it. So our goal is to produce such a profile of engineers.

I defined this profile of general specialist some 16 years ago when nobody believed in such technological change, but now it seems that everybody should have it - if you want to be competitive against the Far East, with their very low prices of production. We have to forget about economy of scale, about cheap mass products, etc. – all this will move to the Far East. We have to think about creativity, innovations, providing added value to knowledge, assisting new products.

- It is easy to say this in theory, but it is much more difficult to make it a reality.

BS: We are achieving that. Practically all our engineers are young people. We have achieved that in 5 years. We have produced machines, we built up the knowledge of these people, and in 5 years we can do anything in our market, in our field of technology.

- What is the level of hiring and firing of employees, the turnover of the staff?

BS: Well, that was at the time when a lot of people would come to our company and then they would leave, because not many of them were able stand the high pressure of continuous updating of knowledge, of continuous improvement. Whoever could not stand that pressure, he and we separated, but we continue to hire people… Still it is a very young company – the average age is between 30 and 35 years, except a couple of guys like me [B.S. is approaching his 60s]. And also we are hiring through internship and looking for new talents – this month we are opening *M. Co. Academy of Knowledge*, which will give free-of-charge courses in software, machine design and so on for the interested young people. The goal is to find talented people. It doesn't matter how much we have invested in the training. They will receive a formal diploma; they have built up their knowledge for sure. They will probably be able to make money for having visited our seminars or courses, but that's not our goal. Our goal is to find the most talented among them.

- Where does the main pool of young people come from – from the region of Bitola, including Prilep, or from Skopje?

BS: No, no, from Prilep. All the staff is from Prilep.

- So you are a kind of community-based company…

BS: Yes. But to this *M. Co. Academy of Knowledge*, students come from Bitola, Ohrid, etc. We will announce our offer of courses in informatics, in programming, in design, free-of-charge for everybody in this region who would like to come and attend the courses. We are targeting in this region [the Bitola region, the ancient *Pelagonia* – I.Tch.] We are not targeting the eastern part [of Macedonia] or Skopje. It's not in our plans for the future.

M: And all the characteristics Mr. B.S. mentioned help our personnel to readjust, to be able to readjust and rebuild their skills rapidly so as to respond to the requirements. This is very important, because in that way we enable our customers to start as soon as possible with their own production process. On the slides you see some of the machines in our production portfolio in the area of composite materials - filament winding machines, fiber placement machine, etc., for different kinds of industrial applications.

BS: Our machines are used [in areas ranging] from basic research to aerospace applications. The customers are research institutes and the companies working in space research. But we are producing also low-level machines, adjusting ourselves according to the market requirement.

M: I'd like to add the fact that *every machine we produce is completely unique.* That means we don't have standard products, they are all designed for a specific customer.

BS: We never say to our customers: "Look, we have these machines; you can buy any of them". No, we say to him: "Tell us what you like to do, what your business model is". And he makes specifications. Then we often say to him: "Look, this is not good. We know this is not good or this is better than what you propose". And at the end we make a technical specification and, according to the technical specification, each of our machines is started from scratch - nothing before that had already been designed or built. But that means we also have a special concept for building machines with 'off-the-shelf' components. None of our competitors in the field had ever done this before us. We introduce this model, because we say: We are not interested in just selling the machines and making a profit. We are interested in making all customers be competitive on the market, and to build their market, to help them lower their costs, and then our customers will be able to buy new machines – again and again and again. It is not our aim to make money in an "after sale" market. We are improving… The concept is to build machines with off-the-shelf components from the most prestigious and best known companies in the world. We had to overcome specific hardships when going on the market, where everybody says: "Oh, you from Macedonia, you can't make a good machine; it's not a developed country". But we say: "No, all the components are from the best-known companies in the world. So you are not getting a machine from Macedonia".

- *Only the design?*

BS: Only the design. When we get together at fairs, normally everybody is trying to draw advantage from the others, that is, to say: "These are German-made machines!" which means, because Germany is a brand-name in machine production. And we answered in a different way: "Well, these are machines with German parts and Macedonian mind!" This is a little bit higher! So, they are very angry after that… (Laughing)

Anyway, we declared a new concept in controlling all these machines, the so-called PC-based control, in 2001. At that time all our competitors were laughing about that, but customers were satisfied. In the beginning we had a lot of difficulties convincing them. Everybody was asking: "Why are companies that have existed for 50 years not introducing your concept?" And we explain to them that it is because they don't have enough engineers to develop this new technology (laughing). Five years later we are selling PC-based machine control; all our customers are satisfied and have no problem with it. Last year in Paris our competitors declared they would introduce a new technology for PC-based control. Which means 5 years after us, after they laughed at us, now they say: "OK, this is the mainstream!"

Now we are developing the next step - we are planning, in three years, to introduce this approach in technology. We must always fight, because our brand name Macedonia, the name of the country, is lower than our name as a company… We must fight for the brand name of the country - because it always puts you in a disadvantage on the world market. If you are in the Macedonian market, that doesn't mean a thing. *But on the world market the country brand name is always very important.* Bulgaria will have the same problem. So you must fight not only for the quality and the brand name of your products, but for the brand name of your country. If the brand name of the country is not good, it matters less how good your product is. It must be good enough to go beyond the bad brand name of the country. Bulgaria, Romania – they will have the same problem. Same with Russia – they have, for example, the highest level of technological knowledge in some areas, coming from Russia it's goes down because of the bad brand name as a country…

This machine you see on the slide, for example, is delivered to the Norwegian government, for their submarine program - it is a six-axes filament winding machine.

- Actually you are designing unique pieces of machines. I just want to understand it, because I'm a sociologist and not an engineer. What I see below this picture is the shape of the composite product which they want to manufacture.

BS: Yes.

- And how is the shape designed? Your machines are...

BS: No, no. The shape is designed by our customers… For example this shape is designed by the Research Institute for Rocket Science; it is a booster motor. They designed that and they would like it to be made with composite materials.

- So, you supply those machines? And you put the form, the shape they wanted ...

BS: Yes. That's called a mandrel. They wind over the mandrel. These machines are winding on symmetrical and axis-symmetrical parts. Depending on whether it is axis-symmetrical you need at least six axes, sometimes more. We have produced nine-axes machine, they demanded only six axes of freedom, but the three extra ones are for technological reasons. For example this machine (points to another slide) is going to one of the biggest shaft producers for big tankers. We developed technology… Sometimes we developed a technology as well for our customers.

- So you are providing not just machines, but also services, consulting?

BS: Yes, yes. We are also giving lectures; we invite sometimes from some universities to give lectures on some specific aspects. For example we are very proud that the first university text book in the field in China has on the front page a picture of our machine. This is a big reference for the students! Everybody will open the book and will see the company *M. Co*. This is the brand name - we are the only brand name from Macedonia that is recognized worldwide in our field, of course, we are not in a field like Coca-Cola. But in our field of composite materials everybody knows about *M.Co.* So, I laugh when they talk on TV about building a brand name [for Macedonia]. We built that brand name 7 years ago. Everybody knows about us in this field.

- When I listen to you... Does this mean that public authorities should build the name of the country based on your brand name, and on the brand names of other Macedonian entrepreneurs, and not exactly the opposite?! If they are clever enough...

BS: Yes! You know, the first time we went to Paris, in the year 2000, and the Paris fair is the best known one in the field of composite materials – all the defense industries, aerospace industries, the biggest companies are there. We are one of the most respected companies – probably the smallest one that goes there. We were very lucky last year when an engineer from one of the biggest world companies, which works only for NASA, it is based in Cincinnati, the highest name in this field. The engineer came to us and asked for some technical advice. They have about 30 000 employers and they only work for NASA, they have the best machines. And I said: "How come you are asking us? We are so small…" He said: "No, no – you are not small. We know you were there last year; you were there in 2000". He knew our position at these fairs each year. He stood at our place for 4 hours, discussing with our engineers about technical problems, preferring to hear a different opinion – how it would be solved. Normally we like to help them, because that was not publicity, but that was just a discussion between the engineers. We also ask this type of question at times... We must sell something free-of-charge in order to receive something free-of-charge - that is common. But the way he treated us, a company with 30 000 employers, one of the highest levels of technical achievement in this field, was enough for us to…

- As recognition...

BS: Yes.

(M is showing another type of winding machine – "probably the best laboratory filament winding machine ever produced").

- Is this for research institutes?

BS: Yes. A six-axes machine. We have sold a few to the universities, to Fraunhofer University in Germany, to China, to the biggest carbon fibers institute in Europe, even though one of our competitors is located 50 km from that Institute. They didn't buy from him, they bought from us. And Professor Babkoff from Bradford College said when we introduced these machines, "With these machines you made when everybody was laughing at you as a competitor!"

- What is the advantage of these machines?

M: The advantage is the way of programming six axes, because this is a six-axes machine that possesses probably one of the best human interfaces in this field; also, the capabilities of the machines - so you can do any type of symmetrical and axis-symmetrical parts; control of the tension system - behind you can see a special electronic control of the tensioning, which is very expensive and it is part of the machine. I don't know how familiar you are with this technology, but it is a unique system where we provide continuous control from the beginning of the taking of the fiber, through the winding, all the time! Our competitors divide this process in two parts: first part is before the bath [with epoxy resin or some other substances that strengthen the material – I.Tch.], and the second part is after the bath. But we provide during the whole time. We do not break the chain of the tension control system. And especially for research – this is very important.

M: This is also a machine for composites industry, a high-tech five-ax machine. And we offer to our customers to come and get complete solutions. All made in-house.

- How did you move from the previous brand of machines for fiber winding to these other fields like cutting marble, wood, etc.? Was it because of your knowledge in motion control?

M: Yes, the control is the same, it is core technology. In some of them you have process control and motion control together. In other machines you have only motion control. In still others you have only process control. And combined with the knowledge on composite materials – in our three core technologies we are masters. All three technologies are part of the vision of some Japanese scientists who made the list of technologies that would be most important in this century. The first three are: motion control, process control, and composite materials. We have knowledge of all three of them and, based on that knowledge, we can do anything. The problem is whether our customers believe us or not, or whether we have money to find this in the beginning. But there is no problem to develop any machine based on these three technologies.

That is why our model of knowledge-based company is successful: because we chose the best technologies which are the industrial future… We did not choose to fund something that would not be valid in 10 years. But these technologies all through this century will be the main technologies, together with some others - such as biotechnology, nanotechnologies, etc. These three technologies: motion control, process control, and composite materials will remain among the first 10 technologies. You can consider these 3 technologies as primary 'Lego' components, as three primitives. To build any machine we need just these 3 primitives. These are flexible primitives and combining them you can build anything. That's our philosophy. That's why we don't care. One of my colleagues from Skopje said: "You are the only company that sells prototypes!", because all of our machines are prototypes. We never made a prototype and after that the new machine… No – we say to our customers: "Tell us what you like, we will produce it!"

- You are exploding the old notion of manufacturing... But to what extent is this concept of new knowledge base feasible without all these flexible tools you are using – robots, computer aided machines, etc. Is it the new production technology that makes your approach possible, where every machine is designed in a unique way?

BS: Not at all. You can see, we do not have first class production machines. All these are…

- Still, they are computer guided...

M: No, we build that. All these computers that you have seen were built in-house. We do not have such production machines. The machines you have seen in the production shop were bought in Bulgaria second hand on a 'kilogram'-based price. So, we bought it from Bulgaria for a very small amount of money.

- From some of the former socialist factories...

M: Yes. All of them are old, they are not new. But we don't need new machines! For the key parts of our machines come from producers known worldwide, these are the most effective. We cannot compete with them. If we need a motor, or we need a gear, or we need the gliders, or we need the bearings - there are producers in the world.

- You find them simply through Internet?

M: Yes. That's why Milena says we are a virtual plant. Eight years ago a professor from Skopje came here to see how we were able to produce such high-level machines. He was amazed, because at that time we were working in one workshop that was rented from us, a very bad one. "Where are your machine tools and everything?" he asked. And I said "We have one company in Germany, we have one company in France, one in Japan, one in Taiwan…" He said: "How? Are they yours?" No, they are not ours. But they are producing for the market. They have been producing 100 years for the market, I cannot compete with them! Why should I make my production based on that? I have to think and to use rationally the best products around the world. There is always someone in the world, who is producing something cheaper. I can't always go for them. These are just parts: machine parts, electronic parts and whatever. What I have to do is to take all of them and make a system. The creativity is the most important thing, not the parts. These machines in the production shop here are just to help us a little bit to make some surfaces, some adjustments and not to have to go anywhere else and to spend more money. But they are not important technologically. Everybody was amazed: we have the newest building, the highest level engineers AND the oldest production machines! – Yes, because that is not our philosophy, our philosophy is creativity and innovation.

- I see, but it is not so easy...

BS: But we do succeed. Nobody believed me 8 years ago. When I was speaking about that at the conferences and so on…

- At first it was an idea?

BS: Yes, sure. Since I'm the owner, I can introduce my idea into the company normally. I do not need much agreement (laughing).

- I would like to ask you: what was it before this idea came to you? I am positive this idea is based on the experience you accumulated from your previous activities?

BS: Yes. I was general manager of the most successful company in Macedonia before 1990, which produced many different things from composite materials. I was a very well-known engineer in composite materials. And I left the company at the time of privatization because I didn't like being part of a criminal privatization. I didn't like putting a stain on my name. Maybe I would have made easy money but I'm not interested in that way [of making money]. After that (after 1991) I worked as consultant for many different companies in the world.

- What happened to this plant for producing composite materials? Is it still producing composite materials?

BS: No, it was destroyed... They are producing something, but not at the level that I was producing at the time I left the company. At that time it was the richest company in the region: 600 DM (Deutsche Marks) average salary, it was 15 years ago. And they were getting their salary each first day of the month and 15th day of the month. They did not have to wait 6 months for their salaries as is usual today. And the company had 2000 workers, a lot of real estate – we had a hotel, many other facilities. I opened the first joint venture company, 20 km from here - it was between an American company and us. At the time when Yugoslavia was destroyed in 1991 nobody believed that the American government would give export guarantees to a company to export to Macedonia. I said, no problem - if you have a sound business, everybody will accept, nobody cares about this 'bla-bla-bla'. So, Bank of America financed at that time the highest level printed circuit boards in Europe!

- You are producing integrated circuits boards?

BS: The highest level - with 18 levels of integrity leans, 18 layers, multi-layers of integrity! That was a satellite technology at that time. I managed to transfer technology to that company because that was a joint venture company. Since 1993, when I left it, they destroyed that company, about 20 km from here – it is completely destroyed. That was the best company in Europe for printer circuit boards. They destroyed other companies, selling….

- We have the same story in Bulgaria, for example our DZU plant in Stara Zagora...

BS: Bulgaria was well known in the field of robotics, computer science.

- They destroyed the electronics industry in almost the same way.

BS: And also in machine-building – the Kazanlak military factory, they had a beautiful production site… At that time Bulgaria was responsible in COMECOM for certain types of arms production and Kazanlak was the center for that. They had top-level machine production with the highest level of economy of scale in this field. And we know it – when we became private [entrepreneurs], we bought from them some good second-hand machines for nothing… So somehow somebody was destroying us, especially our sophisticated industry…

- Do you have people you are indebted to somehow - from the university, then from business? People whom you will remember, from whom you learned a lot?

BS: I was always by myself… I finished university in Belgrade, which is a great university. I made my PhD there as well, at Belgrade University's Mechanical Faculty. But the concept of continuous education is one of our main advantages here. Each Saturday we have brainstorming, where one of our engineers presents some ideas that he has learned. Or he presents something interesting that he found in literature, which he read about in some book, and makes some presentation for his colleagues. Or, if we are not specialists in that field, we invite some university professors to give lectures here. They are trying in that way to provide education themselves and also to bring education from the universities.

- A kind of ongoing seminars?

M: Yes. New ideas, new technologies, and new achievements in the world - whoever finds something interesting on Internet or in the technical papers sends me the information and says: "I think this is very interesting for us." Then I say: OK, in this field there is a specialist – Dimitar for example, and I send a message to him to explore this – to find the books, to find all the information and present it before your colleagues. Milena makes a schedule for everybody and almost every Saturday we have brainstorming here and someone presenting…

- It's not only the continuous education of a person, but a circulation of these ideas!

M: Yes. We have the biggest digital library. Because on Internet there are a couple of projects where there are free books and you have to download them and you must use the appropriate research engines. Because there are many in pdf-format and then pdf-format it's not so easy to search it. For example, to start with that, we called a young guy who has a lot of ideas in library managing, who works in USA. We invited him for one day to explain to us… He is Macedonian but he was educated in USA. We invited him to explain to all of us: what is the best way to organize our digital library and how to search in our digital library – which instruments and so on. After that we installed it in our servers and everybody can look at the servers - more then 30 000 books. All are technical books…

[M continues with a presentation showing a marble cutting machine…]

BS: How did we create that machine? – The marble company is situated 1 km from here. They came to us and said: "Look, we are in a very big hurry for production. We do not have time to buy machines from Italy. We will show you the pictures and we would like to make that type of machine." We asked them to make a specification, they came here and they got the machine in 2 months. We had never before that produced a similar machine.

- *And it worked?*

BS: It works – no [need for] maintenance in one year and a half, three shifts per day! They had 4 Italian machines, but they are transferring all production to our machine, because it has never failed…

M: These are machines for processing wood…

- *Wait, you said you are buying all components for these machines from top companies? And what is yours - only the concept, the design?*

BS: Yes, this is the only thing we produce (laughing).

- *Which means you have a kind of computer-aided design?*

BS: Yes. We work *SolidWorks* and *Catia* CAD CAM . It is the highest level.

M: We are selling similar machines to schools in England, for educational purposes.

BS: These are for education - England formed seven CNC technologies centers, only for high schools, and they wanted them delivered in 3 months...

M: These are also CNC machines for cutting and engraving on marble, machines for steel industry - CNC laser machines, for glass. We produce also machines with a combination of plasma and oxygen, cutting machines…

BS: That means the laser etches the material like the inkjet prints on paper, the laser prints on granite, but not printing – etching on granite. All these CNC machines are aimed for the local market, to help small workshops or family companies develop their business. Why? - Because otherwise they would go to Italy or to Germany to buy such machines and experience language barriers, financial barriers, etc. So here they are closer to us, we educate them technologically and provide maintenance. *That's our duty – to help them*! And all these machines are successfully sold on a local market, and we are very proud. So you see many different technologies, based on these three core types of knowledge, three primitives I was talking above - whatever you like. There is no limit in creativity!

- So you have motion control, process control in-built in the machines, and just at the final stage you add different tools? Although for the latter you need to know some details...

BS: Yes, but that's why we have 'general specialists'.

- Very interesting... So, they are able to learn to go to the oxygen, to plasma cutting tools?

BS: Yes. No problem. They take a book and in a couple of days look in the book - *because they have general knowledge*. But they have to find a specific detail – what would be the size of the tool and so on. They are able to solve the problem in one weekend or so. Or if they can't, then we call for a brainstorming, for everybody to share experience and ideas.

- It comes to me that your ideology, as a company - maybe you indeed have a rather specific demand regarding the type of engineers you hire. Or you have the idea how to train engineers - because it's completely different from the way engineers are trained nowadays.

BS – Yes, absolutely

- But this means, if the relevant changes are made in the curriculum, at the technical university...

BS: Yes, but universities do not change their curricula. They accept what you offer without thinking our needs. I would like to speak about the *Bologna declaration,* about university reform in EU. It is a crazy thing for the Balkans area simply because the basic principle of the Bologna declaration was to make education cheaper for European countries, not to waste money on everything. But this model works only if you have jobs to offer, when the third year student knows what kind of job he will be looking for after two years, so he will adjust his education, his curriculum, choosing elective courses. For this relatively stable job market this curriculum is OK. But when you have such a high-level of unemployment as we have in the region, and nobody knows where he will work in two years, what can you achieve with this Bologna declaration and the rationalization of education it calls for? – Nothing! You will destroy the education – because, being a professor, you have one or two students who choose [to study] your subject by just playing bingo [at random], nothing else. Because the student does not know what he needs, and where he will work. So the students are scattered into small groups in different subjects and none of the professors has enough students. We have a lot of subjects for fewer students and we are wasting their time simply because, due to the Bologna process, we are introducing so many elective courses. While in fact we need *a general education, to prepare better generally educated engineers,* as well as in other fields, and to make them specialists inside the companies through a special training based on market requirements. When the student doesn't know where he will work, how could he choose the subject?

The Bologna declaration is for developed countries, it is good, but it is a big disadvantage for countries that are still developing and for countries like Bulgaria, Macedonia, and others, where the human capital must be more flexible… Western countries do not like their human capital to be flexible – they like to put less money into education and to control the pupils. We do not need that! We have yet to achieve that level of living. That is why we first need highly educated "general people" and they have to be trained to learn, not to be skilled – skill they will get latter. But first they have to be able to learn anything – from engineering to medical science, the same guy! The human being is the only flexible machine in the world that can do that. But you have to train him to learn, and not just skills. While the Bologna declaration is about making skilled people, not flexible… So we do not need to follow it blindly…

I believe what I am saying will be valuable one day for the Western countries too. EU has to change its production philosophy because of China, India, and other production monsters… We need to move to creativity, where added value will be based on human knowledge, on the human capital, and not on the machines. In China and other Far East countries added value is not based on human capital, but on vertical state integration - their economies are vertically integrated but inside the state, not inside one company. If you do not look upon China as a state but as a corporation, you have a vertically integrated company which is producing everything inside, but nobody knows what is profitable and what is not. In the end the state is profitable, but you don't know which part of it. We cannot compete with this type of economy – they will start destroying their vertical integration in fifty years, but not now. And we have time to adjust ourselves for fifty years to a new production philosophy.

- Very interesting indeed... I think it was not easy for you - although it's a clever idea to organize, to produce all these different machines in-house. Maybe you have some problems to cope with in your environment? I mean the political, economic environment in the country...

M: No, that's not a problem. Macedonia doesn't have inflation, but even if Macedonia had inflation, we hedge that because we are an export company. Inflation is bad if your company is on the domestic market. We suggest that if we had inflation we might have been in a better position. In exporting all our production, we don't pay customs, VAT tax is returned… So we had no problem with the environment. We did have a problem depending on which party is in power – like everywhere [in the region – I.Tch.]. When SDS, the former Communist Party is in power, they like to control every part of life, even if you are successful, they would like to control you… If they cannot control you, they try to destroy you. That is the problem. But like now, when VMRO party is in power, they have a kind of liberal capitalism philosophy. So they are taking care of their job, trying to make your life simple, and they are not interfering in your business.

- So you had to think about some defensive strategy before, while now it is easier...

BS: Yes. In the first case you should not open yourself too much to political weaknesses…In the other case you are relatively free

- Referring to Bulgaria, I call people like you 'authentic entrepreneurs' - because there you have another group of entrepreneurs, related to the old Communist nomenclature, and they are a different type... You, the authentic entrepreneurs, rely on your own ideas and knowledge, and often you have more difficulties.

BS: Oh, yes! But let M. finish the presentation. I apologize, M., we are interrupting you so much…

M: This is a process of CNC machine plasma cutting - it's a completely simplified process and there is nothing that cannot be done with these machines, not only with the plasma machines but also with the previous cutting machines for marble and so on. Everything depends on our customers' imagination and creativity. And everything can be achieved with our machines. These are the final products of a plasma cutting machine. And as I previously mentioned, the complete process…

BS: Thank you M. For example a customer came to us 6-7 years ago with a patent from MERK. He said: Look, this patent of MERK expired in 1953. But we would like to have a laboratory machine based on that patent. Can you produce that? - No problem, because this is a process control. We look at the patent…

- Was that a Macedonian customer or from abroad?

M: No, no. These are expensive things which no Macedonian customer is able to pay. So we developed the process control of a complete system for that patent. That is why we now have technology for any industrial production; we can make computer control of any of these processes.

Why? - What is the process? In any process the crucial thing is that you are able to control: the speed, the temperature, the heat, the flow. But these are basic physical quantities. Then you just have to measure them and the customer says: OK, this flow or this temperature or this heat… I like these correlations. And these correlations will be done with the motors, with opening, with valves, and so one. We just take control of everything, bring it together, and put the function to bring it together. That is process control – very simple. If you have a basic knowledge of physics and you have a broad mind…

We have been working for Spain now, a big project in Spain. We are the only Macedonian company that has ever been invited to participate in a big project developing new technologies for bridges. There is a consortium of 10 companies. And we have to develop the machines for them. They are financing us just for the machines. The young engineers from Madrid asked "Can you do this? Can you do that?" Finally, one of them said: "Mr B.S., you say 'yes' to everything, but can it really be done?" – "Yes, really! Would you like to go to the moon?" And they just laughed: "Why, you will make a rocket?" And I answered – "Yes, do you have enough money to pay me for that? If you have enough money to have a rocket and satellite made, we will make it!"

- When I am listening to you, you strangely remind me of the US entrepreneur Elon Musk and his company SpaceX. He is trying to develop a rocket 10 times cheaper than the existing ones….

BS: Why not? If you have knowledge and if you have a customer who has the money, you will make one. If I do not have enough knowledge myself, there are people who work for NASA, I will go and I will ask them to work for me if I have money to pay them. That is what I explained to this guy from Madrid: "If you have enough money for a space shuttle, bring it to me and I will produce it." The point is that the USA has the money to do it. How do they work – they bring people from all over the world, they bring them together, if they need some parts, they buy from everywhere, put them together, and you have a space shuttle… Maybe it is not quite so simple, but that is the model. It works, but they have the money to do it. If the customer has money to do something, we can help them do it.

- Maybe you will just increase the staff with a few more people...

M: Yes, but we are also cooperating with some engineers from abroad. When we are not specialists in some parts of a given machine, we find a database of people who are good engineers in this area and we approach them and ask: "How much do you ask for this project?" And we will finance, that's not a problem. If we cannot find someone here, we will find someone in India, in China. And if we don't find someone in India or in China, we will in the West. I say India and China not because they are the lowest level, but because they are cheaper.

[M is describing some final machinery form the slides, which like others is completely automated and has a different kind of software]

BS: This is an interface for process control where we control 250 points: temperature, pressure, speeds, and so on.

- The entire interface is designed by your engineers… with touch screens?

BS: Yes, yes. We need only specifications, nothing else.

- That's why you are selling so much to institutes, to schools and universities - because people can learn a lot using your machines…

BS: Yes, and it is connected with finite element analysis. So whatever you achieve as a construction of the part of this program, you can export it to *SolidWorks* and *Catia* CAD CAM software for finite element analysis and check whether your construction is OK. We are doing just that. First of all we make a construction – how many leans, what the angles are. And after that we export it for finite element analysis to *ANSI, NISA*, *Catia,* it does not matter, depending on what type of software the customer prefers – we make a post-processor for that type. And you check it and return it back. If *Catia* says 'OK!' you can make it, if it says 'No!', then using simulation you can make another construction. We are doing just that with these lighting bowls that we are developing – for Russia, a company in Saint Petersburg.

M: We offer full support to our customers. That means the representative of our company goes to our customer's plant and there we transfer our knowledge about how to manage the machine and to start their own production process as soon as possible. Everything is coordinated from here. Everything is so simple that our customers don't have to worry about starting their own production as soon as possible. Usually the time period for starting production is only one week. After one week you can start production immediately.

All the achievements of our company are always presented at the fairs all over the world, like in Hanover, Paris, this is the Brussels conference – one of the most famous conferences in the world for composites industry. And everywhere else in the world we represent our innovations. I'm very glad to mention that representatives of our company are invited everywhere in the world - this picture for example is in China, where our employees are to transfer the knowledge to the young students there.

- *It's your machine in Shanghai?*

BS: Yes.

M: For everyone who can't visit our company, we have a website and everybody can be informed very well about who we are, what we are doing and first information. And after that everybody is invited to visit our company. I would like to thank you once again.

(end of presentation)

- *I will continue in English. One question: obviously you are already well in this mode of production. Which are the biggest challenges for you in the nearest future?*

BS: Only the policy of the European Union - because if it continues to put borders around us, this will be the biggest challenge.

- *You mean once you are open and your country enters the Union, it would be much easier?*

BS: First of all I suggested at my public appearances that Macedonia should be as long as possible a candidate country, because it is a much better position for Macedonia rather than to be a member of the European community. While, as a candidate country, you solve the visa issues – after that you enter Schengen, we as a country have to try to stay as long as possible as a candidate, not a member - because the candidate status is a much more preferable status for clever guys. You have all the benefits of exporting and you are not pressured to open your market to the European community, even though we are not so important, being a small economy. But anyway it's a good benefit. And we have to remain a candidate.

The only problem is if you are good, I'm not speaking on the basis of the state, because that's not my responsibility. We never had any public funding for the company and we manage to survive. So if you have a good knowledge, a good product…, if you make a right choice, you don't have to make decision about big things. You cannot be IBM, you cannot be Coca-Cola. Small country, small economy – there is always a market niche for that. And economy on a niche market is much more flexible than any other economy. Because you are not on a mainstream of the business, which means you are not in the influence of the cycles in the business. The niche markets are not attacked by these cycles. You are always paid. So, the problem is to find these niche markets - they are not free and open to everybody. That is the creativity and the knowledge. But if you think on a global level with the small country – forget about your success. Macedonia is not an important country, doesn't have to get in trouble with the big guys, should avoid that and stay out of that, and benefits from all the funds that are allotted to this type of countries.

- *And in house, inside of company?*

BS: Inside the company we have no problem.

- *You believe there will be people coming and staying...*

BS: I always say: I built the company that doesn't depend on any individual except me, if I sell the company (laughing)… But there were times here with the very important engineers who tried to show they were the axis of power inside the company - because of their knowledge, or whatever. But I always fire this type of people.

- *Why?*

BS: Yes, because they should be following the philosophy of the company, not their own philosophy, their own power. The company must be indispensable, otherwise I, as the owner, will be employed by my employees - which is a ridiculous thing. If the employees or engineers get too much power, then they will think that the company depends on them. Hence I will depend on these people and we will miss all our strategic goals. We can discuss the strategies but the decision maker is me! They can have some power - I can give them part of the process of decision making, but the process of decision making requires a financial contribution and financial risk. You cannot make a proper strategic decision without taking any risk. So if they take power based only on the thinking that means they have excess power, and that the company will depend on them... That will not be rational. That was the socialistic system, a kind of worker Soviet we had in Yugoslavia!

I think about this technology like that and that. He is not contributing financially, does not have knowledge, but he makes a decision. I don't like to make my company that way. I do not suffer as a company when I fire some educated guys. But the philosophy inside the company must not depend on individual ambitions. Individual ambitions have to pass through making some achievement in the world. They have to be creative, to make good products, and at the end of the year I look at the achievements and say: OK, you deserve such a bonus, or such a bonus. Because my concept of salary is: the salary should be for bread and salt, and at the end of the year the bonus is what shows the difference between people and the value of their system.

- You have a system for monitoring and calculating the contribution of each of your employees?

M: Yes, sure. And also by organizing some internal interviews – we call them and ask them their opinion about one another, who is the best one among them, who deserves the biggest bonus. And we get knowledge about how to compare these results. If you say this is like in a song competition, like Eurovision, and you see that Finland gave 10 points to Norway, and Norway gave 10 points to Finland, then we know there is a corruption in the process. So we invite them to be not corrupted by this measurement, to make a judgment: who is the guy who has contributed most to the profit of the company. And they make a list. So we compare all the lists, see what's happening that we don't know about, and, based on that, we later on correct some of our actions.

- The young people you hire – most of them are always individualists. Did you find young people who were willing and moving in this direction – to work collectively?

M: Yes. If they do not like it, they can always leave the company. These are the rules. I'm the owner, who carries most of the risk, and I frankly say it to them. My sister's son is here, but he has the same rights as anybody. He was ready to leave the company two years ago because I was giving them a lot of pressure. But I said to him: Look, you leave the company; you can be good in any place, but not good enough if you leave this company without the proper training from me. That is to say that not anybody can make a Mike Jordan. Trainers who can make a good basketball player out of Mike Jordan. I have trained people putting very high pressure on them to make them good engineers as employees. Whoever can sustain that training, he will be good everywhere. Because anybody who leaves the company, when he looks for a job elsewhere and provides references he worked in *M.Co.,* everybody [says]: Oh, good, come here. Even though we fired him.

- Thank you very much for the interview.

(The conversation continued informally and then we decided to put on the recorder again)

- I have interviewed many entrepreneurs in Bulgaria, though they are of a smaller scale. And they say that at one point, once they became stable enough on the market, they found a niche, as you said. For example three years ago I interviewed entrepreneurs in the field of perfumery and cosmetics - our former socialist industrial giants were destroyed and we have a number of companies created by former managers or specialists, most of which are now in the Plovdiv region. They are middle or small size firms. And one of them said: "We are not ready to compete with the European market. So we have to find a way to survive in the process of EU unification". There was another who said: "It's too early, we love our company like a mother loves her child. And we are not at the level to sell shares, to buy shares, to build bigger companies and to think in longer terms." So my question is: how do you see the long-term stability of these niche companies? Should our small countries remain forever with small companies living on certain niches?

BS: No, no. The strategies of the small companies must be to make a brand name, to be valuable companies, and then to sell it to big companies and start a new business.

- I see...

BS: Because the idea is to make a business model, to achieve the recognition of the name and technology, and to sell it to someone who is interested. I have been approached many times but I'm still not sure about the right price. When the right price comes, I will sell the company and start a new business, and a new model. (Smiles) Because that's the key moment, you can make lot of the money.

- It's completely different from our Orthodox Christian idea about 'eternity': to try to stay as long as possible, to withstand...

M: No, no. Let me explain you. A couple of years ago I was introduced to a guy who was studying for a Master's [degree] in London. My son introduced him to me because they were roommates there. The guy has a very good idea about trading schemes for rights [for pollution]. This is a duty tax… [and it was] one of the subjects in his Master studies. The professor said to him that a global agreement would be made, where everybody would have the right to a certain amount of CO2. Something like the Kyoto agreement, and they would start trading those rights. Someone will have more rights, someone less. And they must trade these rights among themselves. So, the professor said, let's make a company based on that idea. And the guy made a company with some of his colleagues. And then a guy who had seen a high potential and who liked to develop much more, because it was a small company, not even a company, just an experiment, and this other guy bought that company for 8 million dollars! The idea of a small company is to make a model that is valuable for… Because no big guy would be interested in a niche company remaining a niche company!

A niche company that doesn't have potential in it, nobody is interested in it. But if someone sees the potential of a niche company to grow, then he will come and buy it, because he is buying a future market, not the actual value! Everybody in the world is buying the future. On the stock market you are not buying actual value, you are buying future value. Depending on what you think the future value will be - there is a difference between actual and future, book value, and the future value. If you want to make yourself rich you have to think of creativity, of the business model of a niche company, to show that business has a potential, to sell it and start a new one.

- What you are saying is not the Balkan way of doing business; it is rather the American style of thinking. How do your people respond when you say this stuff? You teach at the university...

M: I say that, not teaching - because this is not in the curriculum. I have a different approach in teaching. I do not like to teach from the books because they can learn the books [by themselves]. In the beginning I say: This is the book which is in the curriculum, read it, and ask me questions. And now tell me about what you'd like me to speak about in the next hour. If they are not interested, I say: I'm not interested either, because I already have an education, you don't have an education. You'd like to be educated like me. If they do not ask me, I won't talk about the book. The book is available to them, they can open it. I'm not an interpreter of books; I'm not going to read it for them. They have to read it. And ask me what they don't understand: so on page 114, you saw something you do not understand, so please, explain to me what that means. OK, I will open it and explain how it works. But to start giving lectures from the book – it would make them lazy. If they like to be lazy – OK. But I'm available to them to teach them, I'm not available just to interpret some books. Students usually like to avoid questions, but if you avoid questions, you are cutting off the students from creativity and thinking, just like by a surgical operation. You have to ask a question - they must learn about it, read.

7. Two Interviews with the Director of N-Techno A/S - 181

The First Interview

March 27th, 2001 - Karksi-Nuia, Estonia,
Interviewer: Jouko Nikula, interpreter: Helvi Pöder

- Shall we start with your personal history, your education and work history.

I was born in Viljandi area, in Viiratsi municipality. I studied till eighth grade and then I finished and went to Olustvere Polytechnical School, where I studied and graduated in agronomy and after that I studied at the Agricultural University in Tartu, graduated in 1972, married, and my wife was sent here, Karksi-Nuia, and I followed her. From July 15, 1972 I have lived and worked here at the same company. In the beginning I worked as a brigade leader in the branch of land amelioration machinery, and then I was an engineer and then 15 years as the manager of the repair shop. We had 236 employees then, we fixed cars, trucks and we also constructed lorries for the Tarto experimental-repair factory, which later went to the Soviet Union. We repaired more than 1000 lorries and we built some 1000 copies of those diagnostics cars. In addition to that we had the land amelioration department and "automajand", a special transporting department, which transported ash, gravel, and peat. That department had some 70-80 lorries. We also had a department of hydraulics, which repaired equipment and parts of excavators, pumps, motors, cylinders, and all others. The reason for this was that we had a lot of excavators for land amelioration and since there was no place to repair them, we took the job here. Finally the department became so big that it operated for all excavators in Estonia.

- *How many employees did you have in your peak years?*

In the peak year we had 836 persons, if I remember correctly. Currently there are 57 remaining in the company. At that time we transported people with two buses from neighboring villages to work here, every morning the bus brought them here and in the evening it took them back. In addition there were persons who traveled here themselves. In the other village there was more available labor, they were driven over here. When this de-collectivization began, our board started then.. I was production manager at the time, during those difficult years of transition. The former production manager resigned and went to Tallinn and I took his post and another guy replaced me as the manager of the repair shop.

All these buildings here belonged to Nuia EPT. We had our own heating center, our own kindergarten, and we built a lot of housing; we have more than 30 blocks of houses and detached houses in Nuia. There were hundreds of flats in these houses. During the transition we took PMT as a renter, we rented the operating capital.

- *What was the body that rented you PMT?*

The state, the Ministry of Agriculture

- *What does the PMT stand for as a name?*

It was changed at some point, earlier it was Estonian Agricultural Technology (Eesti Põllumajandustehnika - EPT), but when we established the joint stock company, it was renamed Agricultural Technology (Põllumajandustehnika - PMT). Since you cannot have two names, a long one and a short one, we chose the short one. But it is probably not the best of names, because there is not much left of agricultural technology in this company. We do not construct agricultural machines, we may install some parts in them, but we do not make any of them. We don't repairing cars either anymore. The land amelioration department was transformed into a private company and it got loose from us. Those were very confusing times and that department was the easiest to spin off from the main firm, since it had been an economically independent department already before and it had its own branch of operation. And there were very skilled guys to take care of that privatization.

- *Which year was it when they left you?*

The privatization began…our company was established on 15th May 1991, but I do not remember when the buildings were privatized. If there was any extra profit, it was not distributed but was paid to people as shares. And that led to a very big group of shareholders, which currently is an obstacle for us to some extent. Then we had about 300 shareholders and all of them with 1-2 shares. Such was the situation then. Now there are 230 left, some of them have sold their shares. At that time it was considered the right thing to do, but probably it was not completely fair and right. Then privatization began and we wanted and thought we would continue with transport and hydraulics and also make metal constructions. We prepared all sorts of metal goods, cars, "cockpits" for cars and everything that was ordered. We also made boilers in collaboration with another entrepreneur; he had no rooms for that, so he gave us the designs and we made what he needed and he sold the products. At that time he wanted very much to have that production line, but he did not have capital and then he assembled a very obscure group of businessmen and embellished them with a bright future. When the privatization began we gave up the kindergarten, heating center and other things to the municipality free of charge, because we did not need them in our production. This man got his group together and there in the privatization office was a competition of bids.. and we thought.. I was not there then.. our director thought that the price was going too high and if we were going to have it, we would need a bank loan and it would be the end of the firm. So, they gave up bidding. There were many buildings on sale then and we wanted only one building, where the production took place, but then we got an empty building, we bought it and bought all the machinery and later cars – that was very exciting then.

- *What happened to that other man?*

What happened to that man was that those guys were carrying guns – what happened to them, I do not know, but that group broke up soon, and the building, which they bought, the furniture, equipment and machines were sold and they told the privatisation office that they were not able to pay their shares in time and so the office put the building on sale again for a completely different price and its value was also different since it had been empty for a couple of years. There was a lot of valuable equipment, for example for hydraulics, all that had been sold. Later a local wood production company bought it in order to turn it into a production facility. They had it for many years and we moved our hydraulics production here, prepared production facilities in that hall over there. All the machines which were necessary for repairing cylinders, they remained in the old building and we had to find a solution. The solution was a company in Tönismäki that produced pipes, and we started buying from them and made new cylinders. All the equipment that was not registered there in Tönismäki – i.e. that was outside the book keeping, we collected and transported here.

In the beginning it was difficult, in the morning we came to work and figured out what kind of work we should give to the men that day – we even made wooden baskets and everything imaginable. Then I had an argument with the managing director and he wanted to get rid of me and so I told him, O.K., I shall leave no need to fight about it. Then I was unemployed for one and half years. But meanwhile the managing director tried to pinch something from the company and he did not quite succeed and was forced to leave. Then he started his own company and now he is doing fine. Then the general director invited me for a visit and told me that he needed a department manager. That was in 1994. And so I came here again.

- *Do you pay dividends to your shareholders?*

In principle we have tried to do so, but since there are so many of them, and a couple of times we tried to propose that we make investments instead of paying dividends, but there is always the question about paying the shareholders. And since there is a majority supporting that, what can you do? We have paid 5 %, it is almost the same as the interest rate for a bank account – so it is more a question of principle than anything else.

- *Has there been a process where a group of people starts to buy the shares of others?*

The procedure is such that if somebody wants to sell, then the one who is in front of him can choose first. I bought most and then there are a couple of persons who also bought something. However, I have only some 17 % of the shares; some have 2-3 % or 5 %.

- *So, one-fifth is owned by certain people, the rest is dispersed all over.*

Yes, you can say that. We are trying to go in that direction (that a majority be owned by a small number of people), in last year's general assembly we proposed that we issue new stocks in order to collect more capital, but there was not enough interest in that. But gradually we have to try to go in that direction, so that there will be something to lean on, because we have many pensioners who expect some dividend. And many of them have sold or their children. All are expecting dividends.

- There are obviously many persons in the company who have worked here all their lives, aren't there?

Yes, it is true. They have spent their lives here and want to participate in the life of the company in some way. They are not just random passers-by, but our workers, they are the shareholders.

- It was a well-known and successful company in the past was it not?

Yes, our economic figures were not bad at all, when the Soviet system still existed many schools and other buildings were built with our money. It was not allowed, but we did it, because our own children went to that school. At that time the system was different.

- What was the number of employees when you started work in 1991?

I am not sure, maybe 40-41, when we bought that house there.

- And how many are there now?

At the moment 57, for a long time we had 50, last year we made a great leap in production and hired more workers

- What was the leap?

We tried to improve the production of cylinders and obviously the production has grown here in Estonia, we produce cylinders for 7-8 companies now, which are making different kinds of machines and equipment to be sold abroad. For the domestic markets we produce very little and also directly for foreign markets our production is small, to some extent we produce for Finland, Sweden, and Germany. But most of the products go to Estonian companies – which then use our products for their own machines and equipment. We have very good relations with metal industry enterprises in Viljandi, they have very big orders now and they are incapable of producing all by themselves and therefore they give a part of the orders to us. This fact has boosted our development and we have participated in fairs and have increased advertisement.

- *What were the major investments that you completed in recent years?*

Purchasing that building is naturally the most important. In the beginning we produced cars and special trucks here and gradually we started to make constructs for metal industry and that hall was just too small for that production. And since that building was empty and Textuur had bought it but was not using it for anything, they sold it to us, likewise the other building that we had initially tried to buy. Since it was in such a bad condition after years of neglect, we have not yet repaired it completely, but we do it step by step. There was no roof, nor any sanitation facilities, we constructed them, we also built sauna and showers and also the heating center, which provides heating for the building. Soon it will be two years that we have been renovating – now it has big doors and there is a lot of space for completing bigger works. We have been developing constantly. We have naturally bought programmable lathes and now we are trying to buy a washing machine, which is very expensive, over 600 000 Crowns. That is to raise the quality of production. Currently we are moving into ISO-system in order to keep our position on the markets. Our estimation is that 50-60 % of the cylinder markets are in our hands, the rest is divided among 3-4 other producers. The share of cylinders of our total production is 50 %.

- *And what is the rest?*

We do subcontracting for metal industry in Viljandi and we also take some orders – for example we made the metal shades for the Rocca al Mare School and also for Kadaka market place, for some car dealers. In Tarto we built a pedestrian bridge over the river, the shades of the building in Tarto market place, and metal constructs for Biomeedikum. We produced metal stairs for some Finnish companies, and we use about 30-40 tons of metal each month. When we started we used maybe 2-3 tons.

When we were repairing cars, we had our own deposit of spare parts and there was also metal, it did not go anywhere when the car repair shop was shut down. There remained a deposit of metal and later we added to it building materials and electricity materials. And recently we built a shop there, its price was 0,5 million Crowns. When you enter this town, you see the Cultural Center; it is just behind that fence. Soon we must reach an agreement with the municipal administration that we want to make the entrance directly here… hmm..this year we began making hydraulic hoses and we bought machines for that. When I came to work as manager of the repair shop, the car repairs was developing well and that building was already old then and required renovation and we wanted to build a new building. We were offered a possibility to repair the old building and start car production in that building. But planning and all other things took so long, more than 10 years and by then it was already the time of confusion and changes. That cultural house, it was supposed to be the headquarters of this enterprise, a house for engineers, and it also had class rooms for teaching school children how to do car repairs and car mechanics. It was supposed to include also a bank and many other things. But the construction took so long and then came those times of changes. We built it with our own money and finally a commission came and it was decided that we should keep the production facilities and house, and the cultural house was transferred to the state and the state gave it to the municipality free of charge. Also, that old main building was transferred to the municipality, now there is a police and other offices. So, it went this or that way with the building and now there is the shop and still some 3000 square meters empty, without any use. We have advertised it and tried to sell it, but thus far nobody has shown interest in it. Our problem is that we are far away from Tallinn, we have no port or railway close to us. All that plays a role...

- *But how do you transport those big constructions?*

With trucks.

- *How much of your production goes abroad?*

Approximately 2-3 % is exported directly and I assume that 70-80 % of our cylinder production also goes abroad, through other companies. We are subcontractors for them.

- *How about the labor, is there enough labor available?*

Our labor dates back to old times, those who remained here, and, also, a smaller part we trained, but those that we have, they are good workers, because we cannot use men who cannot cope with their work.

- *So the major part of employees is from the times of EPT?*

Yes, those who remained, and there are a very few of those who had left. Now we hire new workers constantly and then we select the best ones. We always apply the test period, to see whether the worker remains with us or not. We hired a couple of sons of fathers who work here and then the fathers have trained their sons. I should say that our wages standards are at a normal level, people want to come here and work in this firm. Now we are… when I started, it was the year before last, the annual production was 13,5 million, last year it was 18,6 million and that means there was an annual growth of 5 million, which is a lot. And I guess that this year we will surpass 20 million. There are enough orders, no question about that. We are constantly thinking how to get more job openings, because the current labor is not able to do all that is necessary and ordered. We need more workers.

We have also sent workers to learn IT at special courses and to learn team work; we have trained bookkeepers, sales personnel, welders, now they all got certificates, because, as I said, we want to move into the ISO-system. Before we had only one welder, and when the production started growing, we hired one more welder, and when we were looking for one, 5-6 persons declared themselves willing to start here. We chose only one of them and trained him well - so we do not take just anybody who wants to come here.

- *So, in conclusion, you may say that there are no problems with labor?*

Yes, I would say there aren't, they do not revolt, not like in earlier times, when we had a trade union.

- *You don't have such an organization here?*

I don't know, there was some group, but it is not our duty to organize it and they themselves obviously wanted to resign from it, because it was mainly just collecting membership fees. They probably might have stayed in that organization, if somebody else had collected and accounted fees for them, but if you have to do it yourself, then it does not interest them. I know that a couple of years ago there were some 5-6 persons who were paying membership fee, but they also wanted to resign. There is a representative of employees who signs the collective agreement, so it is not that biased. They have elected their own representative.

- *Our interest in asking this question stems from the experience where we interviewed a number of entrepreneurs and they complained that the workers suffer from motivational problems, they do not work the way they should, and there are shortcomings in the quality of work. So, obviously you don't have that kind of problems in this firm?*

My principle is that a person should work 8 hours, not more than that, because the productivity declines clearly after that and the worker is not capable of working more and then he will get sick and all that. Naturally there are situations when an extra effort is needed, but it does not need to be systematic.

- You have been here a long time, since 1972, so almost 30 years. Can you say, if you take into account also that old EPT, where you worked as a brigade leader, and the current company, what are the main differences in terms of labor and workers' attitudes?

Sure there are differences. In the past the situation was that if I raised my voice too much, the worker would say "well, I'll quit here and go to another place to work". But nowadays they can't do that. In those days there was greater need for workers than today, I don't know why. Another fact was that the border with Russia was open then and more than 50 percent of our production went there. That was also the reason for the very steep drop when the borders were closed – there were not enough markets in Estonia and we had no access to Western markets. Those who at that time were producing for Western markets and did not have many contacts with Russian markets survived much better in those difficult times.

- How have you financed the development projects in this firm, with your own capital, with incomes from production, or have you also used bank loans?

All of that, if you want quick development, then your own resources are definitely not enough for that. We have not taken too much loans, let's say 200 000 – 300 000 Crowns. We have tried to manage with our own resources, but if we need to purchase something rapidly, then we take loans. Lately we have used leasing, when we bought that building, then we took a loan for the renovation, and also for buying equipment and machines. We usually collect resources for half a year and then take a loan and buy what we need. You must get the machine installed soon and it will start to earn money for paying back the loan.

- What are your plans for the future – is there a choice between specialization and continued diversification?

At the moment I do not see any… the main emphasis is still on hydraulic cylinders, it is the most profitable direction in our firm, and investments give quick results. There are markets for that production and there is enough demand for that, we just need to improve our quality. We must develop the painting process and we are aiming to already solve that problem during this year. Then we take a huge step forward. In production of metal products, we probably need some more machines, but that is not bringing rapid returns at the moment. Naturally we will not reject that production either. We are not putting any effort into transport services, because it serves only the transport of peat and wood nowadays. They do not have too many orders now and therefore there are no investment needs, because it would be an unproductive investment. We have four trucks now and these can take care of all transport services. At some point we even planned to shut down the transport, but since there was nobody wanting to buy it, it remained. It is not making big profits, but not any big losses either. It exists and people have work. The renovation of the hydraulic department will cost one million Crowns. We visited the Sampo factory in Finland, the washing machine will be ordered from them.

- *All this requires quite a lot of resources?*

On Saturday there is the board meeting where decisions are made what we will buy, but on paper there is already estimation that we need some 3 million.

- *Did I understand correctly that you are not in any specific hurry with this program?*

Our principle is that there is no point in taking too big loans, because it may happen, just like to our milk industry, that if something goes down, you are dead.

- *True, but what would you say are the main problems in this?*

I can't say, one day there is this problem, tomorrow another. Maybe the development of hydraulics is the key, we have been thinking about it a lot and during my sleepless nights I often think how to improve it.

- *Yes, that is related to development, but how about routine, everyday issues?*

There are all sorts of problems, sometimes personnel management problems, but that is not a constant problem, they are solved and then we go on. Our management has academic training for the most part.

- *How many of you have those IT- abilities or skills?*

All the managerial staff, 14 altogether. In this office there are me, managing director, development manager, personnel manager, and head accountant – four persons. In departments there are department chiefs, a master and a technician, plus one bookkeeper and a person who takes care of car inspection.

- How about client relations, some entrepreneurs have told us that their worst experiences and greatest losses of money are related to customers, especially those who are engaged in export. Companies order goods or services and do not pay their bills.

Naturally there are such problems and they are there constantly. Luckily those are not very big sums, but there are such cases. Last year we lost 15 000, it is not a big deal for us. Some of the companies go bankrupt, take a new name and continue as they did before bankruptcy, "forgetting" to pay. What we have done at times is that, if they are our old partners, we give them time to pay, but if it is a complete stranger, there are two options, either they pay cash or we give them a bill and as soon as the bill is paid, the goods are delivered. There are all sorts of firms, both Estonian and Finnish companies.

- How would you evaluate the relations between public authorities and entrepreneurs, what kinds of things would you hope to get from the municipality, county, and the state?

With the municipality our relations are O.K, we know their financial situation, there is not much to boast about. Now we are cooperating with the municipality in the construction of the shop yard, they have promised to help us as much as they possibly can.

The Second Interview 3 Years Later

July 9th, 2004 - Karksi, Estonia
Interviewer: Jouko Nikula, interpreter: Helvi Pöder

- What kind of developments have there been in the last three years?

We have had positive development. Our net production was 18 million Crowns three years ago, but last year it was 32 million. Same thing with the profit. The number of employees has remained the same; we have 2 or 3 people more than we had then. Those who came here have stayed here. Some people have retired or moved away, but nobody has left this building because of their work. I have tried to keep the wage higher than the Estonian average. The average wage we pay is around 7000 Crowns or more. Three years ago we didn't have the ISO certificate. Hydraulics department has also received the Logistics quality certificate. We have thought all our things through. We have improved the quality of products and working culture. We have built new painting and washing facilities, now it is more economic, less hazardous for the environment and health. There are new testing schemes for hydraulics. We have tried to improve the working conditions of workers and we have built and renovated the sauna and shower rooms. There is too little spare room for the hydraulics department and we have to think about a new building in the near future. We have already bought some land and a detailed plan is on its way. We need more ground for production and for workers' rest rooms in case we suddenly need to increase production and hire additional engineers. We have formed a repair department, which would take care of maintenance of technical equipment. Until now the repairs were done when something broke down, but now we'll have regular inspections carried out, which would save us a lot of working time. In brief, this is all. Then we purchased new computers and a technical drawing programme for the metalwork department.

- *Did you take a loan for these investments?*

We took bank loans in 2 000, but last year we tried to manage without. Our profit was a little under 3 million and we invested it all. We did not pay much for dividends, maybe some 100 000. This was paid from the profit of the previous year. This year's net profit will be invested into the building.

- *How many owners do you now have?*

The number of owners has been decreasing each year. Today we have 41 shareholders, but three years ago we had 100 shareholders. We have made offers to smaller holders to buy up their shares. Small shareholders are selling their shares. When this enterprise was reorganized in 1991, every employee received a share, and we had 300 shareholders in the beginning.

- *You have quite a stable labour force.*

Yes, there have not been many changes.

- *What is the average age of your workers?*

I can't say exactly, but 2 years ago the average age of workers was 51 and of constructors 50. Some older workers retired and we hired some younger workers so that now the average age should be somewhere between 45 and 50.

- *Where do you find these young men?*

From here and there. We just advertised in yesterday's newspaper that we are looking for a welder. It is easier to find unskilled workers. I have trouble finding a good welder; they are actually one of the hardest specialists to find. We desperately need good engineering-technical specialists; we don't have enough of them. Last year it took us 6 months to find a technical specialist and the same thing for a chief operator. They have to know metalwork and have to be able to do technical drawing and use a computer for that. We can manage with locksmiths and unskilled workers and we even have lathe-operators coming from Viljandi and Mõisaküla. Locksmiths, welders and lathe-operators come from a 50 km radius from here. Usually when someone starts working here, then sooner or later some of their friends will come along.

- *To whom do you sell your production? Have there been any changes?*

There have not been major changes. Maybe there have been some changes in metalwork, because we have developed good relations with Finns and we manufacture wood choppers and shovel and that kind of tools for them. Because of this we have had a growth on our industrial side. In the winter there is not so much construction and it is good for workers when you have work for them all the time. In the summer you have to work too hard, because there is so much construction going on that it is hard to manage all this work.

- *What are the other big problems? Workers, lack of work?*

I wouldn't say that we don't have enough work. We relocated and expanded our painting facility and we have some free space there. We want to hire a few welders to increase the volume of production. We could produce more if we had more space and more people to do it. We don't have any lack of work here right now. I just looked and saw that we had a growth of 17,9% last year. This year we will probably not have so big an increase in the volume of production.

- Where will you be in 5 years' time? Would you keep your current course?

Our course will mostly remain the same. We are the biggest manufacturers in Estonia in the field of hydraulics. We have laid a solid foundation and we'll develop it further to increase the production speed and quality. The metal works department needs modern workbenches and equipment. When the new building is finished, we will have to start to complement future works.

- What kind of relations do you have with local government?

I would say that we have good and normal relations. We get along with them very well and the mayor is actually a shareholder of ours. Some of our former employees work there and we get along.

We sponsored sporting events in Nuia. The municipality organised this Midsummer event and we paid for the prizes. Then we sponsored motor races in Abja and volleyball and football, mainly youth sports.

- Do you have any kind of cooperation with schools?

Practically none. Two years ago we tried to organise one event where local enterprises went to school and introduced themselves and what they do and later students had a chance to visit those enterprises. Four girls came here. The boys said that the monthly salary of 7000 is too small for them to work here.

- What do you, as a local resident, think about how this municipality is governed?

I don't know. I am not very involved in what is going on here. I know that they are doing some things and trying to develop some things. It was a big step forward that they undertook to finish this cultural centre. The library near the town square stayed empty for years and from time to time they did something to the library, but constantly ran out of money for that. Now the municipality puts finances into that. I think that life is certainly getting better here and the municipality has more financial resources. Two or three years ago the municipality was constantly broke, but after the municipality and town merged, it has a bigger purse and can make better use of it. What we need are more high-profile entrepreneurs, because then workers are paid higher wages and when they earn more, then the municipality will get more money.

- *How important are you in Nuia as an employment provider?*

Tekstuur is the most important employer, it has almost 200 workers. We are in second place. The municipality itself is a big employer; it has schools, teachers, kindergartens and maybe 150 employees altogether. The municipality has 82 workers; there are this Iivakivi and Karksi Puit, which employ dozens of men.

- *What about the municipality's financial support?*

They don't give it to metal works. They support tourism and catering and they give their attention to that. Also, new enterprises receive some financial support for starting their business.

- *When you had to apply for something, then did you ever use the service of having projects written for you?*

So far I haven't, but I have studied those opportunities that you can order a project. There is that kind of measure that you can have this written for you. There is this possibility, that you prepare those projects and you can ask money for this. You can receive 50% of the money.

- *What do you think about the state's policy? What can the state do to support enterprises?*

There are all those measures related to what financial support is paid, and they organise all kinds of seminars to introduce them. I have taken part in some of these, because I thought that maybe we too could get some support. But it turns out that while everybody else around us gets support, we don't receive anything. We are inevitably that kind of enterprise that gets left out. You can apply for export support. Then when you are involved in tourism, you receive support. You can get support if you build waste-water pipelines and power cables. We did, but its cost did not exceed 100 000 Crowns, it was 70 000 and so we were left without. We have received some support for training and some for fairs a couple of times. It was 8 000 Crowns or so.

- *Could you (as a company) have gone in some other direction?*

I can't say that because I got involved with this in 1999. Before that other men ran this business and they had very different views, because the council wanted one thing and the board another and also there was disagreement among the board [members] and those people were released from their duties.

- *Do you have a workers' union?*

We have a workers' trustee. We have signed a collective contract, where the terms of wages, vacation time, and bonuses are written down.

- *What do you think about unions in Estonia in these days?*

I don't know. I guess the trustee knows more. There is not much need for a union in our enterprise, because we signed collective contracts anyway. Before you sign it you can just go to the workers, let them read it and you can discuss it. If you need to make some changes, then change it. Life changes all the time and there are always some amendments that have to be made. I don't see the need for a union in our enterprise.

- *But do you see it as your enemy?*

No. I think that in places where the wages are really small, like in textile industry and fishing industry, where they are paid 2 000 or 3 000 a month, the union can help the workers get a raise.

- *Work here is for qualified workers, isn't it?*

In principle, yes. Samples of our work are sent for inspection and it is X-rayed and if it is below the standard, then we don't get the certificate and this is the way it is. Then we are not allowed to do welding on construction, because the building might fall down. We very carefully choose our welders, because we have been fined. Some men who try to get a job here come here and we test them and they just try and try, but nothing comes out of it, and we just let them go right away. We have seen men who remember from kolkhoz times how well they earned, but their skills actually don't match up. They have to know how to use the equipment. Our equipment itself is good.

- *What about boys from vocational schools?*

I say bad things about them. Maybe there are one or two capable ones out of ten. We have seen those boys from vocational schools and they have left such a bad impression on me that I don't even want to talk about it. They can't read the technical drawing; they can't tell what the material is. They just say that it is iron, but when I ask what kind of iron, then they don't know. We had two or three who tried to do the welding. The boys who don't want to study go to vocational schools after 9th grade. The more students the school has, the more money it receives from the state. So schools are interested in keeping their students and they let them pass and they drag them through the school even though the boy does not bother to study. The school gets its money and nothing good comes out of it. Maybe they can weld some things together at home, but they can do nothing else.

- *So the level of vocational training is poor?*

Yes, I went to talk about it in parliament. It is pretty hopeless. We haven't found younger lathe-operators; they are probably in the towns. We don't have a desperate need for them and we have managed so far.

- *Haven't you taken apprentices from vocational school?*

We don't have good jobs for apprentices, because trainees have to do simpler work, but here he could do maybe some calculations or help some welder. This kind of work that we do here, we can't give to an apprentice.

- *Is the cooperation between vocational schools and enterprises important?*

They have practical trainings and welding itself could be taught in a few months. But the thing is that they need to be supervised and trained and their work has to be inspected, X-rayed so that they would know what the quality of their work is. I can't do anything about that. Viljandi Metallurgical Industry employs more welders and they a have bigger need for welders, so they built a room for trainees, where they can learn simpler work. But at the same time there are some kinds of work where they can't take the risk of letting trainees do it.

- *The same problem exists with university education. Industrial enterprises cannot take the risk of producing something of inferior quality.*

If your work does not have quality, you won't get orders anymore. There are three factors: quality, deadline, and price. If the first two are in place, you can negotiate over the price. But if they are not, you can do nothing about the third one. We had Finnish customers who used to order from Tartu, but were not satisfied with the quality of their work and so they turned to us. This is the way things are.

- *Do you belong to any organisations?*

Only to the Chamber of Commerce and Industry.

- *And how has being a member influenced your development?*

We took part in a trip to a fair in Sweden, which they had organised and partly financed. Then they organise trainings and send out information. This is very useful for those who want to buy or sell something. They offer information on cooperation possibilities and we are interested in that, but so far we haven't found suitable partners yet. A lot of them are too small for such a big enterprise as ours.

- *What do you think about keeping this size or does you enterprise have to grow bigger?*

I guess we are trying to expand. As I said we have to plan a new building and maybe expand our metal works. I cannot say yet when we will do this. We still have to think whether we should buy a new building. It is a possibility and we have to look around for suitable industrial buildings. There are not many possibilities for expansion in Nuia. Then there is always this problem with labour or qualified workers. EPT had a lot of skilled workers, but when the hard times arrived everybody had to get by somehow. Many workers left for Tallinn and a lot of workers retired. Three of our present workers are pensioners and one will retire in autumn. Young people who graduate from university go to [work in] university or become entrepreneurs; they don't want to become a bench operator. Here is the divide, because those who don't go to high school after 9th grade, they don't want to learn or they have other problems such as not having money to go to school.

- *What do you think about sales?*

The thing with sales is that we manufacture what we have received orders for.

- *What about demand?*

It is constantly growing. In the case of hydraulics the demand has doubled in the last three years. We manufacture cylinders and we have 1300 drawings in the computer right now and every day new ones are added so that by the end of the year we will probably have 1600 or 1700 drafts. In the old days you constructed a machine and tried to fit some cylinder in afterwards, but now you manufacture the exact cylinder you need. If you have 1300 drafts, then you depend on the computer. We also do repair works for Estonia. Around 10% of the work that the hydraulics department does is repair work. In the beginning we took this attitude that we won't do repair work, but we had a constant flow of people coming here asking for it. When superiors turned their back, then they asked the workers to do those repairs and we just saw that we couldn't carry on like that. So we decided that one worker would take care of big lots and another worker takes care of single orders. Those repair works don't bring us profit, but we just want to help and those people have to turn somewhere.

- *Comparing your salaries with salaries paid in this area, how do you fare?*

The salaries in the trade are much smaller; people are being paid 2 000 or 2 500 a month. In Polli there not many young people, residents are mostly pensioners or people who will retire soon. If we pay wages that are at the national average, you just can't complain about that. Workers who work on a regular bench get 8 000, automatic bench operators get 10 000 and engineers 12 000 a month and more, when they earn profit. Engineers can get 20 000 a month.

- *For a rural area this is a very high salary. Did you take part in drafting this development plan?*

We were there two or three times, when the general outline was set. The enterprise took part in drawing the plan, where the residential areas, the industrial areas and the roads will be.

- *Are you satisfied with the end result?*

We actually haven't received the final map. It does not affect us very much, but it is for the overall development to plan ahead where you build those things. Our main problem is that we don't have much space for expansion and all this land around here is used. We have space for one hangar here, but not more. We have a building here, then we have a big hanger, then we have a building there, and one down there, and the building of technical inspection of vehicles is even outside of Nuia. Tekstuur has bought all the buildings around here.

New innovative Entrepreneurs

These are mainly entrepreneurs who started their careers during last years of socialism and early years of post-socialism. The key elements in their strategy for future success are clear: success requires technological renewal, product development from more simple to more processed products and understanding the worth of immaterial factors, like skills and know-how. The basis for all these is careful and long-term planning of financial and human resources. For them management has nothing to do with paternalism of socialist type, but only a matter-of –fact type of relation between employer and employee, entrepreneur and public bodies, like municipality or the state.

8. "E. Cosmetics and Sons" Ltd.

Interview with the the owner and executive director of the company
Stara Zagora Region, Bulgaria
Interviewer: Vladimir Nedev. March 30, 2004.
Selection of the firms, questionnaire design; and supervision by Ivan Tchalakov; under project "Eastern Europe Economic Transition Policy Revisited: The Neo-Schumpeterian Model", Centre for Policy Studies – CEU, Budapest, Hungary

- *When was the company created?*

In March 1990. In my view this is the first private firm for perfumery and cosmetics in the new economic history of Bulgaria, after 1989.

- *What were you material assets in the beginning?*

Very poor, we had few items - no land, no buildings, no production halls. We began in a simple family house or rather part of one. It was a nice big basement room, where we launched our production. The employees were not very qualified, just ordinary workers. As far as the money was concerned, it was our own money, some loans from friends, a very small capital. In terms of know-how we got support from some Western firms; they were selling ingredients [for cosmetics] in Bulgaria. They were interested in having those ingredients put into finished products. Since we did not know how to produce it, they helped us with reference books, recipes, etc. In terms of market – the Russian market in the beginning was not bad. We exported a lot, through intermediary firms of course – as far as I remember, to Chechnya before the war, and some similar regions. We sold on the Bulgarian market too. In terms of packaging – we were buying it from Bulgarian producers of polymer bottles, boxes and other packaging, the labels from printing companies, etc.

- *How many employees did you begin with?*

It was our family! I mean three or four people – those who were able to contribute. Then we gradually increased the number of employees - first we hired one, then two, three… Their number went up and down - we reached ten people, and then again fell to three-four people…

In the first ten years or so our development was pretty uneven – maybe depending on the state of the country – in 1994 there was some decline, but the currency was devaluated strongly, the US dollar exchange rate increased by 100%.... 1996 was also a huge problem, 1997, then in 1998 things went better. 1999 was not so good, at least for our firm. We are too small firm to pretend that we are influencing the big, macro level economy or the market as such. Rather I think the falls in production were due among other things to our ignorance and the meager experience we had regarding economics – in terms of marketing, knowledge of the market, and in general our limited experience as producers: there was no one to tell you how to produce! The old industrial structures built during the time of socialism probably had some advantages, but they could not be applied... There was sort of a slight chaos... there was no narrow specialization at all, specific requirements for each position. Only in recent years have things become stable, things gradually came to a situation where one person deals only with laboratory work, another with administration, a third with distribution, a fourth only with storage, a fifth only with production…

It was hard to pay the narrow specialists before. But if one wants to do a serious job, a well-organized job, one should attract such people, better educated ones, more stable, aged 30-35. They are more responsible, they think realistically, they have good expectations from the firm, but are also more cautious, think about their future. And that is exactly what we are trying to do: to reassure people that the trend in Bulgaria is toward private enterprises. A thing like that can't be done in one or two years. After 1990 a big problem was the workers' way of thinking. Nowadays it doesn't seem to be so big a problem, now they somehow accept things more naturally - they understand they must work, must be persevering; that the firm has to survive, that it pays their salaries; that they must be responsible for the production, for the end product; that they must always think about the client. Yes, now the workers themselves are far more responsible, in other words; we, as owners and managers, we grew up in these 14 years, but the workers also grew up with us.

I am not saying that now we know everything, but the fact is that we are developing constantly… I often travel abroad and I must say that we are far ahead as an organization, as a way of thinking... Frankly speaking, we looked at how things were, including things in the West, in 1995, 1996, until about 2001/2002, but we did not begin to see. There is a situation, where a person looks but does not begin to see, to see what his basic problems really are. I mean in terms of the staff, the equipment, the market...

- Could you give some more details about the initial period – about the first products, how they were created and produced?

Our first products were shampoos – hair and body shampoos produced in simple plastic packaging, with simple caps and labels. However, among them were the first pearl shampoos produced in Bulgaria, and at that time this was a rare item on the market. So these items of work pulled us ahead. Later we designed our first hair and hand balms, which are still in production. Then we produced toilet milks, lotions, anti-dandruff shampoos, hand peeling cream, hair mask… We produced and began selling eye anti-wrinkle oils such as almond oil, then bleaching powder for hair, oxidizer, and when we later combined the bleaching power with the oxidizer and stabilized it, a finished product appeared. We produced and started selling also powder hair dye. So we began with cosmetics, it is in the last three-four years that perfumery has become the main pillar in our production list, before that, cosmetics dominated. Now our perfumes *Aglaya* and *Evterpa* (the company perfume) are well known.

Recently a new item entered production, a very complex one and difficult to master – an oxidant hair dye. It cost us a lot of efforts, because this complex product requires a lot of machinery, very good equipment. I had to go abroad to buy some piece of equipment that unfortunately I had not managed to find in Bulgaria. Otherwise I prefer in principle to buy local equipment – not only because of the price or simple maintenance, but, as a Bulgarian producer I would like to promote other Bulgarian firms. It is better for us to spend our money buying each other's' products. This makes us stronger, which is not the case when our investment money leaks abroad.

- How would you outline the main stages of your company's development?

It was the general Bulgarian politics and economy that shaped it. If the currency had been stable then, say, in the early 1990s... If there had been order, laws, like there are now – but it was not possible for such to exist then – things would not have happened as they did. I think things would have been worse, frankly speaking. Inflation helped us, because it supported the export. As strange as it may sound, the wild inflation of '93, '94 and the even wilder one of '96, '97 aided our development to some degree... In the present situation, when the market is stagnating, when the Bulgarian currency becomes stronger due to the Currency Board, it would have been much harder for us to develop production in those years, when things weren't so 'fiscal' yet, so strict financially. Since 1997 the Currency Board has fixed the exchange rate of the Bulgarian Lev to the Deutsche Mark, and since 2001 to the Euro. So the initial years were years of storm, of explosion, years of chaos… But in one way or another, we were doing things and we were developing. So I would distinguish two stages in it – a stage of initial accumulation and a second stage that includes raising the qualification of our employees, entering new markets, improvement of our packaging, etc. The second stage concerns the 'upper', the intellectual part of our work, the 'superstructure' so to speak, our know-how. But the 'groundwork' was completed 4-5 years ago.

- *What about technological development in your firms? Are you investing in new products? The sector of cosmetics is rapidly developing worldwide...*

Investing in technologies is my key priority. I adore science. I am a medical doctor who re-qualified in perfumery and cosmetics and I often travel abroad, see fellow enterprises. So one of the first things we created in our enterprise was the laboratory! Many of my colleagues produce lots of products without having a lab. Me – I first created our lab and then create a product. There is no know-how without science – it does not come from reading a book, or by following a ready-made prescription. The know-how comes by experimenting, thinking, researching, reading a lot, searching in literature, etc.

- *Do you invest in your personnel, in human resources?*

Yes, that is a continuous process. We invest in people and I am very glad that – especially during the last several years, our people are taking us seriously as a company. For we are not something short-lived, for a year or two, they see us as serious owners, who are responsible towards them and they continue to respect us as their employers. It is important for us that our employees should feel better and work better; when we invest in our people, they see a long-term perspective in their job, to work for us even until their retirement. So that one day their children will work in our company too – just like in some Western companies, I saw this in many towns and cities when travelling abroad.

As far as education is concerned, we are at a pretty good level. We have five university graduates working in the firm: two chemical engineers, one with bio technology, two economists, and one textile engineer. The latter came here by chance, but he strives to develop since he obviously did not find a vocation in textiles. He will grow into a good sales manager, looking after our customers, our presence in the country and abroad, our distribution network, etc.

- *Do you have experts in marketing, in advertising?*

I personally deal with marketing and advertising, although I had limited experience. Yet I feel I am getting better, maybe because of the many mistakes I made (laugh).

- *What about your suppliers? Which are you key business partners?*

We have many suppliers and have the possibility of choosing among them. We are using raw materials and ingredients from different European companies, but I can't say we have a 'strategic partner'. Everything is a matter of price, so when a company offers us a cheaper ingredients without compromising the quality, we are ready to change our supplier. The more expensive the raw materials, the more expensive the end product – when the quality is compatible, it is natural to look for cheaper raw materials since it is the price of the end product that matters most.

- *Do you have partners in research and innovation?*

Frankly speaking, I am planning some more sophisticated products… I am thinking about synthesizing some ingredients to be used in our products and to be sold to other firms. But I am still not ready for that – I have no relevant specialists and technical facilities. I am considering getting help from some scientists, especially those having experience in applied research, in real production, and eventually developing some prototypes together [with them]. I always think about the equipment, this is the first step when you are seeking new production. If we intend some synthesis, this means you need a corresponding column, if you need a more complex cycle, you need other equipment. Initially it has to be on a smaller scale, to test the process and to optimize the technology, so at a later stage bigger machinery can be introduced. That is how I have been proceeding till now – first I buy a small machine, and only after it has proven itself in one or two years of operation, I move to larger equipment. In case of a mistake, it costs me less. But when the process proves efficient enough, we buy the bigger items in order to increase the economy of scale.

- Do you have specific contacts with some scientists?

We have been collaborating recently with a researcher from Agricultural University in Plovdiv on an agent that has nothing to do with cosmetics – a substance for treating parasitic fungi in some fruit trees. We collaborate also with some (now retired) applied researchers from former big state-owned cosmetics plants; they share their experience in the mastering of different technologies...

- What about your financial partners? Do you have any bank credits?

No, I don't think we need credits; the business is developing normally, at least at this stage. However, we are buying some machinery, including cars, on leasing, a kind of credit too.

- Could you describe the main difficulties you have experienced since the start of your company and until now? Also about the decisions that have been made...

Trade unionism was a big problem! Especially when you have a big order and five workers decide at that moment to unite and demand a bigger salary. They ask for 20 BGN more, for example, and when I agree, they change their mind and ask for 40 BGN… I call this arm-twisting; this is a very unpleasant situation. Sometimes you really don't know what to do… especially when these are people you have been investing in for years. Usually our most experienced employees do not act this way, but when some people with 3-4 years of service unite in the so-called 'syndicalism', I really get troubled. You cannot increase the salaries chaotically, under pressure! But on the other hand you have invested in these people, so it is not so simple to fire them – they know so much, you cannot just hire some novice and put him in the workshop, they need to be trained first… So this arm-twisting is a big problem.

Also, some worker suddenly decides to leave temporarily and to travel abroad – to Greece, or to Spain, etc., to see his relatives there [between 1991 and 2007 large communities of Bulgarian immigrant workers were formed in these two countries – I.Tch.]. This is also a problem; since it is very difficult to replace such people. When this happens, you just see the firm going backwards… So it was not always possible to apply a subtle personnel policy – to keep your employees, to qualify them, to satisfy their requirements in advance. We are lagging behind to some extent in our human resources policy. In general, our production problems are related mainly and almost entirely to the employees, all other problems can be solved easily enough.

- Do you have difficulties in launching new products, when for example people need to acquire new skills?

No, there are no such difficulties. It is normal to make mistakes – you may have to throw away initially some production – once, twice, five times. But this is a normal process, this is not a problem.

- What do you do when it is necessary for some employees to be (re)trained?

This is the know-how I mentioned. The best is to take your employees from college or university. It helps that most of our employees live in the town and nearby villages, they love their houses – most of them have beautiful big houses, with big courtyards. They possess everything. What they need is a good income. And those willing to learn are promoted… Currently I have announced two university scholarships for chemists. They will study five years, then there will be a specialization, some retraining, depending on the exact nature of the work - you need to appoint two persons, to see who the better one is. Then we will invest in economic specialties. We also have a lot of computers here and we need qualified people to work on them.

- Do you cooperate with your colleagues - in branch associations, or in some other forms?

Yes, it is necessary, but there is no cooperation in fact… Formally there is – when at the end of the years you need to approve the Annual Report of our branch association Board of Managers, to approve its budget, etc. But these are rather formal activities. The real cooperation will emerge on the basis of common interests – for all the 100 or more companies in the sector. However, at the present stage, our interests diverge! That is why real cohesion is missing – we all compete with one another, but on the other hand there are possible common, 'higher' interests. Similarly to the consensus about Bulgaria entering NATO – you remember that all political parties voted for it, both left and right. So when you have common interests, it is possible to unite.

To this end, however, one needs a kind of thrust, motivation. I am motivated to participate in our Branch Association on Essential Oils, Perfumery and Cosmetics, and I am ready to contribute to its development provided it is useful for me. If it does not help, I don't need it! But if it proves itself necessary, I would be motivated to support it. So we need a kind of 'positive thrust' to keep our association alive. It exists now as it is, but I mean some other, serious issues, that could be dealt with. We need discussions – I participated in many discussions inside the association, but we rarely touch upon the core issues. Those are the fundamental issues, related to the big economy, to the general business perspectives in Bulgaria – not only in the field of cosmetics. These are the issues relevant for entrepreneurs in other sectors as well - shoes and textile, etc… In order for there to be an association, *I have somehow to come to like my competitor*. And this is possible if based on a common interest.

- *How would you describe the competition in your sector?*

Well, I think the future is clear enough – private business. In Bulgaria I think small and medium entrepreneurship is particularly relevant. The average medium-sized company here is between 50 and 150 employees. A company having a staff of over 150 people is something rather big in our branch - it has to be known worldwide in order to be able to hire so many employees. Considered from the point of view of cadres, of production teams, I think we in southern Bulgaria are better positioned than our colleagues in northern Bulgaria – we have better communications, especially the highway, the economic centres are stronger… As far the final products – there is incredible variety here – in terms of prices, of packaging, quality. Most of the firms here are at a similar industrial level, neither too advanced, nor too backward.

- *In what areas is the competition stronger – for example, in tenders, in hiring the best specialists?*

No, we have never taken part in tenders, especially state tenders. Generally, I don't feel we have any strong competitors…

- *Do you collaborate with other firms in the sector, beyond the branch associations?*

Well, sometimes we borrow some materials from one another, but it has never happened that some other company's specialists came to help with the machinery, or that our specialists go to other firms. However, we have many distribution partners, maybe because we specialize in production rather than in trade. There are traders, and we don't want to enter their sphere, especially in export. We have a good distribution network in Bulgaria, these are serious partners, and we have lasting and well-defined relationships.

- *Could you mention some names?*

I think it would be better not to mention any names.

- *Then what is the share of export in your turnover?*

About 20% of the turnover. There were periods in the last 14 years, when the annual export was 60%, mostly to former URSS. But now we sell mostly on the local market.

- *What are the tendencies?*

We are developing rapidly. I believe we are one of the serious producers in Bulgaria – that's certain. Every year we move forwards, there are no steps backward – this means we are going in the right direction. Maybe it is possible to grow faster, but such are our resources. As far as our presence on the European market is concerned – we'll see when we become a member of the EU. There are lots of requirements to be fulfilled and I expect some changes will take place, some rearrangements in the sector.

- *How many are the 'serious cosmetics producers' in this country? How many of them will survive on the EU market?*

Well, there are always leaders in the branch. In my view in Bulgaria there will be 5-6 companies of about 100-150 people staff, another 5-6 firms of about 40-50 people staff, 10-15 firms of about 10 employees, and the rest will be 'family' firms, less than 5 people. But the companies that are developing real perfumery and cosmetics will be about 10-15 firms.

- *You started with a few employees, where are you now? Have you ever experienced the so-called 'head hunting', i.e. attempts of other firms to attract some of your best employees?*

Now I have 46 employees. There were cases of head hunting, but you know – one is learning constantly. That is why I travel so often to the West; this is also a kind of countermeasure to head hunting. But in general this is not a serious problem, since we are conveniently located in a very good production zone – at some distance from big industrial centres (Plovdiv, Stara Zagora, Kazanlak), but not too far from them. Looking at the investments made in Plovdiv in the last few years, the city will be a kind of 'Bulgarian Milano', the most powerful industrial centre in the country.

- *Are there foreign investments in Bulgarian perfumery and cosmetics?*

I don't know of any foreign cosmetics company investing in Bulgaria…

- *What about the legislative basis of the business, and about government economic policy?*

I am satisfied with the government policy. Many people don't like it, but I see that a real economy, real market is taking over. It smells more of capitalism now than before, and it does not smell of socialism so much…

- *You mean that state intervention in the economy decreases?*

Yes, and I feel it somehow – we have less problems with bureaucracy. It seems to me that now the attitudes of bureaucracy have changed – they say "Go! Produce more!", they also feel that when you are producing and selling more, they are getting richer too. There is an element of this – finally there is a kind of understanding, even a kind of 'joy', that we private entrepreneurs are moving forward and doing something in the economy. My experience with public authorities is limited predominantly to our relatively small town, of course. I don't know the situation in other regions, but I have no problems with the local administration.

- *I would be happy if you could tell us more about your investments in technologies?*

It's simple - full speed ahead! We still have to catch up with the West technologically. But the gap is not so big. Prior to my visits in Germany and other countries in Western Europe I thought they were very advanced in terms of production facilities, equipment, technologies, and specialists. But in fact they are not! I personally verified this and in my view in 10-15 years we will be able to compete with them.

- *Could you mention the name of some firms here able to fill the gap?*

It is rather a matter of policy. I can't say that Bulgarian companies will become exporters of perfumery and cosmetics in the EU. Things depend on government policy. I am not saying that Bulgarian companies will be exporting cosmetics to the European Union – that would be too difficult. But I mean the Bulgarian market at least – there will be Bulgarian cosmetics companies here, I am absolutely positive.

- Do you feel the government supports the export oriented firms? Are there relevant legal and institutional frameworks in this respect?

If you are asking about subsidising the export, this is definitely not the case. There are no subsidies. But our branch association could be very useful here, and I think these issues should be the association's main field of activity – to find potential markets and to promote our business there. Here, however, the internal competition surfaces. Who will benefit from these markets – the top 20 companies or all members of associations (100 or more)? You see that here the common interest is not evident. Still when the 'big policy' is being designed in Brussels, when we are adopting the EU legislation, I don't know what the Bulgarian economic priorities are. They say it would be tourism, agriculture, light industries… But nobody is giving any details – would there be some quotas, export rules, restrictions in terms of quantity or type of goods, etc. This is not clear. I've subscribed to some bulletins, I read State Gazette, but there is no specific information about these issues. And when I talk with my colleagues – not only those in perfumery and cosmetics, but also in other sectors – they express the same fears. They don't know what to expect… They say our entering EU is neither good nor bad, because it is not clear what will happen. If they expect opening new markets, more income – they say 'It's OK', but if they expect having to close down their firms because of competition and new requirements, they are less positive.

- Did you experience political interventions in your business during these years?

Not at all, at least not in our firm.

- What is the list of your products now?

We are producing about 85-96, almost 90 different positions.

- How do you get informed about the market, about new products and technologies?

I search the Internet regularly on these matters, the State Gazette, other sources… We also buy a lot of literature. When I travel abroad I regularly buy specialized literature – like during my last trip to Germany. But the literature quickly gets outdated and needs constantly to be updated, in order not to miss something important…

- *Is the know-how of the most advanced firms accessible?*

I am not convinced they will share it with us without a fight (laugh)… It is their strength, their treasure; it is the source of their income. However, I am positive we Bulgarians are clever enough; we are able to do lots of things. I am very serious – we started our company a bit for the fun of it, but you see where we are now…

When we started from nothing but a basement and one shampoo, we hardly expected that one day we would make a factory and that it would grow, would determine the lives and way of thinking of the staff, their life prospects: even the birth of their children and the growth of their families. It takes courage, that's all; we are intelligent people, healthy – we're a bit lagging behind, but we will advance...

- *What are the most successful points in the history of your firm?*

The discovery of the know-how. Once we implement some know-how, the firm starts growing by the hour... It's not even always a matter of new products: there is know-how in the very organization of production, which brings in money. A restructuring of things brings money and we feel we had been making a mistake for years and we hadn't changed a given sector, hadn't invested, and hadn't paid attention to it... We took a few steps and things started to pick up instantly. Also, the know-how in managing the company and in structuring your activities is at least as important as that in technologies.

As far as the chemistry is concerned, when we bring off a new product, especially when its parameters are closer to those of the world-level products, we are extremely happy and you see immediately how the market responds positively, the orders increase, and we are getting praises at the fairs and exhibitions. This is very important for us. In fact, this is the company; it creates its perspective – when someone sees a product of ours in the shop and says 'Yeah, this company is not bad!' This is truly important. We get feedback without interruption – a few hours ago I had a call – a merchant who is short of money at the moment is buying less stock and asking for maximum abatement. I agreed – the present moment is a bit stagnant, you can't expect a big turnover, and we should be attuned to the state of the economy. But when the market is growing and they continue to ask for high abatement for minor stock, then we behave differently. But in this specific case I agreed – the sales are low now, it is still rather could, people are not yet in the streets, the consumption is limited, but the man strives to sell, he asks for abatement because he wishes to make profits at least as much as [he made] last month and he got our support.

- How did you choose the location of our company? Simply because you personally come from this region [a small town, approximately the same distance between two big cities – I.Tch.]?

First, because my roots are here. But also, I always pay attention to the words of my grandfather, God rest his soul. He used to say: "You should be where there are rails!" Now the highways are even more important. It was an important choice where to invest – around Sofia, around Varna, or around Plovdiv (the three biggest cities in Bulgaria). This is a fundamental issue and it defines your future. When we started in 1990, Plovdiv was a fading city. It had big industry before, but I was not sure if it would be so active in the future. However, when I see how the foreigners are investing in this city, I realize they single it out as a key industrial zone in Bulgaria. I am pleased with this development – to have a big industrial centre in your proximity means a lot! We are located about 50 kilometres from the city of Plovdiv and its technologies – printing houses, packaging, raw materials, everything… More foreign investors are coming, the prices are going down, the market is getting better and easier in terms of contacts, etc. You could find everything there. Imagine we were located at a distant place with difficult communications… Sometimes you need a simple detail which is possible to find only in big cities and if it is not within your reach, this is a real problem. Now we just have to call the firms and their office boys are instantly here with our orders! So my grandfather was right – having railways, a highway, and a big city around is a great advantage. Please note that it is not coincidental that the big cosmetic industry in the country is located around Plovdiv - I am positive the city will remain its core. This is not only because of the tradition, but also because of the current investments there.

- For a medium–sized company like yours, what is the optimal level of investment – in technologies and equipment, in distribution, etc?

It depends. An investment is never one-sided; it is a multiple-aspect process. You can't invest in technologies alone – build big columns, large production facilities and only then think about sales. You should invest also in the market itself – be presented at fairs, exhibitions, and conventions, visit your partners and contractors, create your distribution network, representative offices, etc. This is a serious job that requires relevant investments too. For example to establish a distribution network abroad for selling my products, I need 10 million euro! I am not ready for that. So maybe these investments are even more important than technologies. In my visits to West Europe I have seen small companies but fully automated and with millions of turnover – they have a turnover of 10 or 15 million, produced with a staff of 10 people, and they work round-the-clock.

- So you have a network of offices in the country?

No, I have no offices; we work with a network of merchants and distributors. These are independent firms; they sell as they please. This is determined by the market itself. If the market says one day: "This isn't possible anymore!", I should think about something different. But now things are going well this way. There is growth and that is what we are aiming at – an annual growth rate of 6-7-8, even 10% is something serious. This means you are in the right direction. Last year our growth was 30%. This year, I believe, it will be over 50%... That means things are getting better. When the macro economy is well structured, there is growth. I have fellow entrepreneurs in the shoes industry, who grow by 200%; they grow in hours, can you imagine that? - This is in the town of Peshtera, which is the centre of this industry, it is also near Plovdiv. In our branch of cosmetics we are lagging behind. What spectacular growth, what sales, and what motivation they have! I believe the small companies have a bright future here…

- I think we covered the planned topics. Thank you for the interview. Do you think there is something we omitted in our talk?

I think this is the historical moment – when one looks and begins to see [to distinguish things, to discriminate – I.Tch.]… This is very important! The other thing is that, in order for Bulgaria to exist, an economy is needed. Bulgarian goods must be produced and sold on the market…

9. The Rose Oil Producer "R" Ltd

Interview with one of the owners and executive director of the company
Karlovo district, Plovdiv region, Bulgaria, November 19th, 2003
Interviewer: Tzveta Dimitrova
Selection of the firms, questionnaire design, and supervision by Ivan Tchalakov under the Project "Eastern Europe Economic Transition Policy Revisited: The Neo-Schumpeterian Model", Centre for Policy Studies – CEU, Budapest, Hungary

- *Would you describe the founding of your company?*

Our company was established because of the land restitution process that took place in Bulgaria starting from 1992. Me and my wife, we got back the land inherited from our parents and grandparents, which was taken into the former cooperative farms after WW II. We had about 20 hectares of inherited land in Boitsa and other villages in the Vidin region (the north-western corner of Bulgaria). So when they passed the Restitution Law in 1992, I checked the details and realized that I could exchange this land for an equivalent amount of land around the town where my wife and I were living, Plovdiv region in central-south Bulgaria. Because it was too far away, I had just retired and we decided that it would be better if we had land closer to us, since our children were also living in the region. So I took the necessary steps at the Ministry of Agriculture, they agreed, and then I began going through all the bureaucratic procedures – first the authorities in Vidin had to agree to take my land into the regional State Land Fund, then find state-owned land in the Plovdiv region, for which the local authorities had to agree to transfer it to my ownership... It was a long and slow process. Nevertheless I found about 50 hectares of state land in the village of Chernozem, Karlovo district, 40 kilometres north of Plovdiv, which was equivalent to my land in Vidin (being in a fertile plane area, it was of a higher category than the land in the semi-mountainous region of Karlovo). The village authorities gave me a letter that I could acquire this land provided I had the respective permission from the Ministry of Agriculture. Similarly, people in Vidin also agreed to accept my land and issued the corresponding documents. So that is how the process started. But in Chernozem the village major told me that they would agree to give me these 50 hectares of state-owned land if I did something for the good of the village. I asked them – 'What do you want?' And he told me – they had a mill which was closed down. They had a dairy – it was closed down too. They had a sunflower oil factory which was also closed down, and finally they had a rose oil distillery which had also ceased to work. So, they said, it is your choice what to do... And suddenly I decided – I will set up a rose oil factory! It came to me as if out of nowhere...

- Had you ever before dealt with perfumery and cosmetics, or with cultivation of roses?

Never! In north-east Bulgaria where I'm from, there are no rose plantations, it is too cold there. We grew crops – maize, wheat, sunflower, etc. But I said – I will establish a rose factory. OK, they said – please write a demand. So I wrote one and they allocated me 1.5 hectares near the river Stryama, a beautiful place. And I began with this place, long before I managed to exchange my land. I paid for this place and it became my property, then I ordered the design of the factory, it took about 6 months. I paid for it and in July 1992 we began the construction of the new factory. It took almost a year and we opened it in May 1993, just on the eve of the rose harvest, so that we managed to boil and to distil rose oil.

- So you established the firm precisely for dealing in rose oil extraction, and not in any other business?

Yes, my idea was to make use of the land I had inherited. And then these people from Chernozem came with their demand... So I succeeded with the exchange of my land only few years later, maybe by 1995. But I stuck to my promise, established the rose oil factory, and already in the first year I brewed some oil, while the following year I brewed 167 kilograms of rose oil! So the business started very well and every year we increased the yield. We were four partners in the firm – me, my son, and two of his friends - each having an equal share, and me being the 'first among equals'...

- What are the resources you had in the beginning? Where did they come from?

Mostly bank loans, but also some money of our own that we got from trading with fuel...

- I have seen, in the Rose Oil Museum in the town of Kazanlak, such a copper distiller for brewing rose flowers ...

Well, these are old small utensils, very primitive... Ours are huge distillers of 9-10 tons

- *And the principle of oil extraction?*

The principle is the same – you distil the oil the way you distil brandy – you boil the rose flowers, then the vapour goes through a tube to the cooler with cold water and at the end you have rose water. [http://en.wikipedia.org/wiki/Rose_oil] The rose water goes through other tubes into so-called Florentine vessels, a kind of tank. Through these tanks the rose water is pumped into a kind of refinery, narrow elevated containers with so-called rushing rings where the filtering takes place – the oil is separated from the water and then collected and put into the safe. We have a security safe[21].

- *How did you find the staff for this specific production?*

We immediately found the necessary employees; there are well-trained people in Karlovo, from the state-owned Bulgarian Rose distilleries. In the beginning I was rather ignorant about technology, but we hired good specialists, who knew the craft. I hired first a retired expert, my age, and then a young engineer replaced him, also a very good technologist.

- *You produce rose oil only?*

Rose oil, lavender oil, rose concrete, and lavender concrete [in the concrete the oil is obtained by solvent extraction and not by distillation].

- *These are your products. Do you manufacture cosmetics too?*

We produce also salvia oil and salvia concrete. These essential oils are input material for cosmetics. We produced some cosmetics based on these materials, but when you use the proper ingredients it is quite costly. Since there are lots of false products on the market, produced in garages and similar make-up factories, our products were not competitive. So we decided to specialize in producing essential oils only, that which comes from the soil, sun, and air, and to export it. We began producing rose seedlings – to supply the rose fields we were planting. Now we have a 130-hectares rose plantation, another 200 just planted and we intend to plant another 50-60 hectares. So we solved the problem of supplying raw materials. Later we also expanded our factory, adding an installation for

[21] The wholesale price of rose oil is about 4000 Euro per kilogram, and the retail price is much higher (see for example http://www.bulgarianroseotto.com/?gclid=CPWkq-SKk6ICFQmA3godIFEljg).

solvent extraction based on hexane and other petrol derivatives. It is the biggest installation in the country. And you should bear in mind that roses for oil are cultivated only in Bulgaria, Turkey, and Moldova.

- How did you find your first customers? Are there still any state-owned firms or state structures controlling the market?

Yes, there is such a state structure; it is called "Laboratory No. 5", at the Bulgarian Perfumery and Cosmetics Agency. It's not an agency but rather a kind of department that controls the export of essential oils. Initially they did not allow us to export – "You never asked us for permission to produce when you established your factory!", they said. So this lab did not provide us with a certificate. And you can't export without a certificate. Slowly they allowed us some export of 10-15 kilograms per year, just enough not to die of hunger...

- So how did you survive?

Well, we also had another business, fuel trade and that is why we survived and did not give up. We were also dealing with import and export of petrol derivatives.

- You mean derivatives for solvent extraction of essential oils?

No, we were importing ordinary petrol and diesel fuel for cars. This is where our money came from to build this rose oil factory and the rose plantations. Now we are the biggest factory and one of the biggest rose oil manufactures, with one of the best plantations – we have 85 hectares of 8-year-old gardens, another 30 hectares of 4-year-old roses, etc. They are all planted by us.

- I do not understand this business too much, but obviously you got your customers through this agency in Sofia?

No, my contacts came from some conferences and symposia in the town of Kazanlak, here in Bulgaria, as well as in neighbouring Turkey... Because I was one of the first private companies, a kind of white crow, so they remembered me. At that time the market was dominated by state structures – the Bulgarian Rose Plants in Kazanlak, in Karlovo, Plovdiv, etc. There was a big conference in Kazanlak on the 330th anniversary of rose oil production in Bulgaria and there were many foreign firms – from US, France, India, etc. So they found me and came to us. While the other Bulgarian firms were blackmailing us – *"These are newcomers, they have no experience, they are not producing quality oil, etc.".* But it is precisely this blackmailing campaign that impressed the foreigners!

- A kind of negative publicity?

Yes, sometimes this helps. So there was a mister Roque, who was buying rose oil for France. He came directly to us from Turkey: *"Your colleagues are smearing you too much, that you produce bad oil, and that you are not a professional company... I would like to see your oil first hand".* So he took a sample for study and after a while we got a call – "How much oil do you have?" "160 kilograms", I replied. They bought it all up... Since then they have been buying most of our oil, directly for France. We are selling only 15-20 kilograms in US and about 50 kilograms to Japan, for Toshiba... For some years we also sold small amounts to Taiwan and India. Mr Roque likes our oil very much – precisely because we produce a simple natural product, without any chemical interventions in it. Recently he told me: "Your oil is the same quality as it was the first year I bought it from you!" He said he did not need a certificate from a laboratory in Sofia, he bought directly from our factory. So we won his trust...

- What about the domestic market?

There is no domestic market for this product. You can't sell even a kilogram here... Our oil is exported mostly to France, which dictates the fashion in perfumery – it is packed in special 5-litre vessels that go to France and then to Nina Ricci, Chanel, Paco Rabanne. And then they sell us back their perfumes.

- Has the fact that you only export somehow influenced your business?

Our National Association for Perfumery, Cosmetics and Essential Oils insisted that all export go through it and the laboratory in Sofia. We tried a few times, but once an Indian partner wrote us a letter – "your oil was not the same as what you sent me last time", he wrote. And this was the oil we passed through the Sofia lab, so we lost trust in them. We never gave them our oil anymore; it is exported directly from our company. Thanks to the people in France, this year we sold the entire produce.

- And what about the other products?

The rose concrete was sold too, also in France.

- What is the difference between the two products?

Well, as I said, the concrete is produced by solvent extraction, not by boiling the flowers. There is our new factory – you put about 300 kilograms of rose flowers in the tanks and they are filled with petrol ester or hexane, this is a kind of high octane petrol. The hexane extracts all the ingredients – oils, waxes, etc. The final product is a thick mass like marmalade and it is used in perfumery. But it is cheaper than rose oil – its price is $ 650 per kilogram, while the rose oil is $ 4500 – because you produce one kilogram of oil out of 3 tons of flowers, while a kilogram of concrete is produced from 300 kilograms of flowers. In a sense the concrete is more profitable, because 3000 kilograms of roses give you 10 kilograms of concrete priced $ 6500, instead of 1 kilogram oil priced $ 4500. In perfumery production they use not only oils, but also waxes and other ingredients, so the concrete is profitable for them too.

- Could you briefly describe the main stages in the development of your firm?

Initially we worked mainly with village cooperatives, about 7-8 villages in the Karlovo region. We bought the rose flowers from them, but gradually it turned into a real fight to buy flowers. Since we were one of the new firms, they blamed us for the shortages, and often we ran out of flowers... So we decided to create our own plantations. It seems that we were among the pioneers in this too. In the mid-1990s, with the gradual decline of cooperative farms, the rose plantations in Kazanlak and Karlovo were dying. This made our competitors in Plovdiv preserve their gardens too. At a period of time when the cooperatives were simply abandoning the gardens, we were planting gardens at that time, which was rather unusual... So we caught the upsurge, in a way we were one of the engines of this revival. So we built our factory in a period when rose production was in decline and we planted our gardens when the other gardens were dying... But a few years later the others followed us, now many private owners are planting roses too. However, I already have an 8-year-old plantation. Because the yield from rose plantations comes after the third year and it lasts about 15 to 20 years depending on how they are cultivated. The bushes have to be rejuvenated regularly, to have strong roots, and to be cut properly; this is the most important thing.

- *So you built the factory, bought up flowers, and when the production grew you planted your own gardens?*

We planted the gardens as early as in the third year of business, I saw there were not enough flowers...

- *So your plantations supply enough flowers?*

No, they cover about 40% of our needs. The rest we buy. We have a rather big capacity – about 100 tons, while we process about 35-40 tons.

- *When did the market revive?*

About the forth year after we entered this business, we became a factor on the market and others took us into consideration... Now we are among the biggest producers.

- *Where you bought your machinery?*

We bought our equipment from a production plant in Karlovo. It had been prepared to be exported to Cuba or Mexico, but the export failed because of the political changes. The same person who recommended me the village of Chernozem (the mayor there was his friend), he told me: "There is a ready-made installation for rose oil distillation! Come and see it." So I when to the plant and saw it lying there unsold... I asked for the price and they said it cost 1,9 million BG levs, but it was not possible to buy it directly, they needed to announce a tender. However, I arranged not to buy it, but to lease it, and bought it later. That's an old story.

- *And your second factory?*

When the mass privatization began in 1996, we decided to bid for the distilleries in Plovdiv or in Karlovo. The one in Karlovo was valued at $ 3 million, but we were all economists – me, my son, and the other two partners. So we checked its balance sheets and realized its value was about 1,2 million. So we took part in the bidding, but it went almost to $ 3 million – its director decided to privatize it as a management buyout and he offered this money. We withdrew from the tender and that is why we built our new factory in 1999, its cost was about $ 500 000.

- *What about the lavender?*

We buy part of it, the rest is produced in our plantations – we have about 50 hectares of lavender in the town of Strelcha, and another 30 hectares in Bregovo.

- *How did your petrol business develop?*

We were among the first in Bulgaria to buy a gas station, early in 1991. My son told me – "There is a gas station for sale in Pazardzhik[22] for about 800 000 BG levs, we could buy it. Please help find money!" I told him that my apartment cost about 60 000, but the rest... My son was chief accountant in the state tourist organisation *Balkantourist.* So I asked him – do you have a friend in some bank? – He said 'yes'. So my advice was to put a mortgage on the gas station, I did this many times as state official in railways and transport companies, it is called 'advance mortgaging'. My son did not know about this means. So he went to his friend in the bank and he supplied the money. We bought the gas station and mortgaged it the next day.

Now we needed fuel. My son went to Sofia to look for fuel. At that time the only supplier was the state-owned *Petrol* combine. They kicked him out, because we were 'outside the plan'. Fortunately, there was a young person in Petrol, who told him there was a newly established private firm importing fuel from the US, or at least somehow connected with the US. So he managed to sign a contract for 3000 tons of fuel. I said to him: "This is too little, we need more. Go and sign a contract for 50 000!" Fortunately, he agreed and a few days later we had a contract for 50 000 tons. How we can sell all this fuel, my son asked. I told him, "I'll take care of that..."

As I told you, I had retired in 1990 as economist in a state transport company, and all my friends were still well-positioned. So I went to regional transport companies in the big towns of southern Bulgaria and offered fuel. This was a period of great fuel shortage[23] – for many of them my offer came as a salvation! So at one moment we were supplying about 10 auto-tanks weekly, each of 20 tons and more. However, in the spring of 1991 there was a Government decree forbidding the private import of fuel – fortunately, we anticipated it by two weeks – we signed our last contract on May 30, and the decree came out two week later! There was a special

[22] Regional town 40 kilometres west from Plovdiv.

[23] In the turbulent year 1990, when the government stopped payment of the country's foreign debt, there was a severe shortage of petrol for a few months.

article in the decree stipulating that export continues until the contracted volumes are exhausted. The Prime Minister Dimiter Popov was my classmate in the Vidin high school, so later some speculated that it is because of me this article appeared in the decree. Bu this is not true – this is normal commercial practice. Since we had this 50 000 tons contract signed, till the end of the year we sold fuel all over the country – I sold about 30 000 tons to my friends in transport companies, my son supplied more than 10 000 to the *Petrol* branches in northern Bulgaria, we managed to sell everything. We made a profit of about 1000-1100 BG levs per ton... We bought other gas stations, the business grew. However, soon after that came those boys with the thick necks (the emerging Bulgarian mafia) and pushed us out of the business – they started illegally supplying fuel to Yugoslavia, etc.

And then I said to my partners: here is a goose that lays golden eggs – and told them my idea about a rose oil factory. So we decided to withdraw and to invest our money in the rose oil business. We preserved only four gas stations - two in Sofia and two in Pazardzhik. As I told you, at one point these gas stations saved us from bankruptcy.

- Are you investing in research and development activities?

We maintain contacts with professors in food technology from Plovdiv University and with Plovdiv Agricultural University. They are professor Georgiev and professor Tsachev on roses, professor Dimitrov on essential oils. They help us with our production and especially with cultivation of new plantations of roses, lavender, salvia, etc. By growing our own seedlings, we closed the production cycle, especially after we mastered concrete production, which was something new for us.

- Do you have any partners that contributed to your development?

Yes, our French partner *Bioland Perfumery* helped us a lot. It is a company that supplies all big perfumery firms with essential oils and other products. We trust each other, we even became friends – their representative comes here, we go to France. They are our main partner.

- What do you think about the Association of the firms in the sector? What is the role of the Association of Perfumery, Cosmetics, and Essential Oils?

I am rather sceptical about it. The perfumery and cosmetics firms in Bulgaria don't use natural essential oils but some cheaper surrogates. So our oils are exported abroad, and come back mixed with some chemistry, or as derived components. We found this situation on the market and there have been no changes – no one cares to put our own oils into his products... And those who are processing our oils are selling ingredients.

- *You mean what?*

I mean the Western firms, especially the German, Swiss and French companies.

- *What are the specificities of the competition in your branch?*

In the last few years there has been a huge demand for rose and other flowers for processing. Many private distilleries were established in the last ten years, and I could say that not all of them are sound. One could say that some of them are laundering money – they have no factories, but come and buy flowers at a high price and I don't know what they do with these flowers. You can't pay more than 60 cents per kilo, and they are paying almost 90 cents. There is something wrong about this. I think they are legalizing some money this way. This also adds instability to the market, but we do not care too much, because we have our own plantations. There is no competition for the specialists, because there are enough highly qualified people in the region, if you pay them well, they stay with the firm.

- *So there are no 'turning points' in the development of your company?*

We have a constant progress. It was difficult in the beginning, when we were stockpiling our oil for several years, but then after the breakthrough to the French market, we have had no problems. Since 1995 it has gone up.

- *Were you affected by the mass bankruptcy of the Bulgarian banks in 1996?*

Not at all, because we had our money from the petrol business, which was well invested. We don't care about political changes. I am right-wing in my political affiliations and I support the Democratic Union. However, in the mid-1990s, when the former Communists were in power, it turned out that the father of the Prime Minister Videnov[24] knows me – maybe because my transport enterprise was one of the most successful in the region. So he sent people to me – they offered me $ 5 million to invest them in agriculture, but I refused. Yet it is remarkable that I was offered

[24] Videnov and his family are from Plovdiv.

this money, although they knew that I was not a Communist! I stay away from politics, although I think the policy of the Democrats is better for business.

- How do you invest your profit?

My latest idea is about biotechnologies – I decided to expand our business on neighbouring fields, to produce bio-food – vegetables, fruits, for which the Plovdiv region provides excellent conditions. We bought 10 hectares of land and now we are building facilities for all-season production of vegetables using green houses, refrigerators, evaporators, small electric power stations on natural gas, etc. So we will close the production cycle again. We are now designing all this, including the 5 MW power plant on natural gas. We will need about 500 kW, the rest we will sell to the national electricity company. My son and his friends they invested also in several hotels at the Black Sea and winter resorts. Money must turn ...

I could say that most people in Bulgaria are waiting for someone else to come and arrange things for us. This is our worst feature, because those who have no brains, they have no money either. And in business you need three things – brains, to know from A to Z about what you want to do; money – if there is no money you should look for credit; and finally – trust. That is the secret.

10. K-tree A/S

Interview with the director of the company
Viljandi county, southern Estonia
Date: March 26th, 2001
Interviewer: Jouko Nikula
Interpreter: Helvi Põder

- Could you tell me about yourself?

I graduated from the Nuia high school, and then I was in the army. After the army I did practical training. Four times, three months each time, I did practical training at a Swedish farm and then we started farming. But the situation being what it was at that time, I had to look for paid work. One and a half years I worked in Võrumaa, at Tohta Ltd sawmill, thanks to my knowledge of the Swedish language and my connections. For a year I worked as a consultant at a Swedish sawmill which operates in Latvia – I sorted out timber there. Four years ago I started my own company here as a side-business to bookkeeping.

- How were you "found" to this business?

Because I had worked at Tohta sawmill, when I worked there, there was a Swedish manager and his job was to construct sawmill, to dismantle it in Sweden and reconstruct it here in Estonia and launch it. After he had done that, he was offered another job in Latvia and he took me with him to work there and our cooperation was smooth and effective.

- So, the development of the firm was good?

Yes, in 1994-95 it really was.

- How did the establishment of this firm occur – was it necessary to ponder the issue a long time?

Yes, in the sense that I was drawn into these timber business circles and I already had some experience from that branch. That particular project started thanks to one Dutch agent; it was his idea to make planed timber here for the Dutch markets and even now about 70 % of our production goes to Holland.

- How many owners were there when you started, or were you alone?

There were two of us; he was my schoolmate.

- How did you divide the shares; fifty-fifty or in some other way?

Fifty-fifty

- How many employees do you have at the moment?

About twenty five.

K: How about the financing, loans and such things?

I took a loan from that Swedish family to buy these buildings, they helped me.

- *Was that a cheaper and easier solution than to go to the bank and take a loan here in Estonia?*

It is not possible; the biggest problem for Estonia, at least related to banks, is that it is impossible to get any loan for setting up a firm. We took our first loan about a year and a half ago.

- *In which year did you actually start the firm?*

In 1997.

- *What is the most difficult part of taking the loan – the collaterals or something else?*

The Estonian banks are only interested in turnover; that is the main thing. If you don't own an acting firm, they may listen to you, but it is difficult to prove that your idea is good and in addition your collateral has to cover the sum double. For firms that are just starting, it is… it is not possible. Someone who already has that much money, he does not have any problems with starting a firm. When a firm is founded, it means that when you put your apartment or house as collateral, what is it worth? Maybe 60 000 Crowns but some 30 000 Crowns in business is no money at all. This is the big problem. Of course we are living in transition, banks have resources to lend, but there is also those who take the loan and the markets are not yet complete. Maybe the problem is that they (banks) make things as simple as possible for themselves. So that there are almost no risks for them. If you did not know somebody personally and you did not have the right kind of relatives at hand, then it was almost impossible to get a loan in those years.

- *How about the state-run systems? Some years ago there was the Eesti regionaalarengu program (Estonian Regional Development Program), was there any possibility of getting help?*

Yes, but there was the same problem in general – you had to have at least some degree of entrepreneurial activity. Of course, it depends on what kind of activity you have, but since we chose the timber business and some 80 % of our total turnover is timber or raw material, it is very expensive and to cope with such a business – even though I haven't personally asked them – I guess, it is almost impossible. If we had established a textile factory, you had to purchase sewing machines and other such things, it would have been different. But with us the biggest problem was the operational capital and financial resources for raw material. For those purposes we would have needed a loan and we still need one. We got some support from Development Fund for Rural Life – there too you had to have some funding of your own – i.e. some collateral. In the beginning you get the money, but the 25 % which is required as your own funding share for buying something necessary, it is too much for a small company. They should have made two parallel systems, where you could lease your own share (the property) and you could also get the money (the loan), then it would have solved the financing problem. For us it came just at the right time and we got it. No, actually they financed only those 25 % and we had to fund the remaining 75 % and so they gave us 100 000 out of 400 000.

- Were there any other conditions, other than your own share?

Yes, there were clear branches, where they gave money, for example there was funding for alternative employment in rural areas. And we got the money because we created jobs here.

- When you were establishing this firm, did you get assistance for the business plan or other kinds of advisory service?

Well, I can say that we managed by ourselves. I am very good in practical matters; I'm not a bit interested in paperwork. We have managed so far through my experience and instinct alone.

- Well, without your experience there would probably not be any firm, would there?

No, not this kind of firm, because it is a logical continuation of those ideas that were born in 1996. In those days Estonia was still a rather closed country and especially the rural areas. In Tallinn information was circulating, but rural areas were closed and thanks to those contacts I acquired at Tohta sawmill; those were the things that created the basis for this firm. If I had not had those contacts, I would have done something else.

- Like what?

Well, it is hard to say right now, but most likely I would have developed that farm. I am quite frank by nature and if I get an idea, I will carry it through to the very end.

- O.K, let us return to this firm. How did you make the investments, did you buy the machines second hand or were they new investments?

All of them are used, only the computers were bought new, the rest is second-hand stuff from Sweden. Thanks to my contacts there and language skills in Swedish.

- Are those machines still in use, i.e. you have not refurbished them?

No, no, we change them all the time, not for completely new ones, but for used, second-hand machines. Because we started with such big difficulties and without any funds, and due to conflicts in the beginning…hmm, when, in the beginning, there were two of us, we got so-called negative profit (loss). In all the subsequent stages of development we have tried to improve using our own resources; naturally we have a goal and we know what we are trying to achieve, but at the same time we proceed gradually by revamping the old machines into new ones. We do not want to get too much in debt, which most certainly would ruin us. Our aim is to operate in such a way that we will not be indebted to anybody, even if something were to happen.

- There are still two of you?

No, not anymore.

- How long did it last?

Only six months

- And now you own the firm by yourself?

Yes, I do.

- How did you get the premises and buildings?

We bought them, after the kolkhoz was closed down, there were two firms and after the second went bankrupt, we bought them.

- So, there was a firm, which went bankrupt and then came another firm, which also went bankrupt, is that it?

Well, I don't have any information about the first firm, or actually I do have, the first one went bankrupt and the other firm bought it, but the buyer was a share-holder in that first firm as well and he bought it just to get his money out of it. Then he sold it at the price which was equal to his share of the original investment.

- So, it was not very expensive, was it?

Well, it depends – nowadays it does not amount to very much, but then it was quite expensive, 100 000 Finnish markka.

- After you paid the price to the seller, you were no longer indebted to them?

No, I am not.

- The first loan you took, was for buying these buildings?

Yes, we took a loan from Sweden.

- Do you have any debts now?

We pay 26 000 Crowns every month for leasing. Then we have credit, the last agreement was signed six months ago, for 1 200 000 Crowns. We took it mainly to cover the income tax, because we export most of our production and therefore the return of income tax is delayed. So, we buy materials and equipment with tax but we export without and that we have to get back from the tax office; between the tax report and return 1,5 – 2 months pass, and in order to cover expenses during that period we took the loan.

- You told me that you now had 25 employees, how many did you have in the beginning?

Only four.

- Has your production profile remained the same during all this time?

To some extent yes, in the sense that the company was founded as a planer firm, it was the objective we have tried to achieve since the beginning. In the first year most of our work consisted in just planing, there is a sawmill nearby here, which we have no longer been using in the last three years, and the second factor is that we bought our raw material, we sorted it and re-sold it. Because the plane that existed in this building was in very bad shape and therefore we did not start any production and it took six months to create the first load of production.

- And you are mainly doing plane work now?

Yes, we do some birch, it is only some 1 % of the turnover, so that we buy and sort, but mainly we do planing.

- You said that 70 % of production goes to the Netherlands, how about the other 30 %, is that for domestic markets?

The rest goes to England, Sweden, and here in Estonia.

- How much have the amounts grown during the years?

Well, I could answer in a descriptive way. Here is our history from 1997-1998, here are the bills of purchases, and here is 1999, it was a slightly thicker file, and then in 2000 we had three files, and in the year 2001, until now we already have one file full in the first quarter. So the turnover has grown more than three times in a year. During the first year turnover was one million Crowns and last year it was thirty (30) million Crowns.

- Impressive figures. So you do not have your own system for obtaining timber, but you buy all the timber you need?

Yes, we do not cut timber ourselves but buy it, and this is more convenient for us, because the technology is very expensive and the period of sale is quite long and if you cut yourself, you will never get what you need and it is a hundred times easier to buy everything you need from a sawmill. And our biggest problem still is the lack of operational capital, if I were to change the production cycle for so long it would be impossible, it would be a huge step back and we would be starting from zero again, like we did three years ago. Currently we buy from the largest sawmill in Estonia, the Imavere sawmill – we buy the whole monthly produce of that sawmill, for us it means the whole annual production. In that respect it is quite a big percentage and for those services and goods that we produce for markets, for us to do cutting by ourselves is out of the question.

- O.K, let's move to the issue of labor, are they local people and have you had any problems with the labor?

I guess the problems are similar all over the world; I can say that we do not have problems and those that we have, are eternal and constant ones between employee and employer. We have no problem with alcohol; we have no problem with work discipline or with what we demand from them.

Sometimes they forget, but in principle I can say that no, we do not have any problems with labor.

- That's interesting, because many entrepreneurs complain that they have many problems with their labor, why not you?

Quite a lot because that I am..well it is the employer's own problem in the sense that a lot depends on the employer and I believe that a lot depends on the fact that I observe things continuously and I try to keep an eye on what is going on. Another factor is that our employees are well-paid, they don't just go to work, they want to work. We have piece-rate wages and there is probably also some fear of losing a good job.

- Well, you are clearly an exception among the firms that we have studied thus far in Estonia. All others are complaining that the workers are lazy, incompetent, and prone to excessive use of alcohol. And the reason is the kolkhoz mentality that the people have.

They pay their workers too little; obviously because that.. well, I cannot say for sure, but I have seen and heard the same things. In principle our workers have never had a problem like not having anything to do, there is always something and there is more work than we could ever do, and, as I said, our wages are 15-20 % higher than the average Estonian wage, which was presented in the newspaper Äripäev just recently. Especially here in rural areas the average wage is very, very average. There has never been any delay in paying the wages, the thing that is quite common elsewhere in this region. Our people know that they get their salary on the 5th of every month and if it happens to be Saturday, it will be paid a day before and if it is a Sunday, it will be paid a day later.

- So, you mean that the people who talk about kolkhoz mentality are the ones who themselves are not capable of taking care of things properly?

Yes, I believe that's true. For an employee the most important things is, and also for me, is that the worker gets pay for his work and gets it on time. In that regard one should not deceive people. The fact that we pay higher wages than the average in Estonia does not mean that our workers live well, what they get after taxes is not quite enough for coping. Usually people have plans ready for how they'll use their money, so, there is not much to save and if the payment is delayed a week for example it causes extra stress for them. If I keep my promises regarding payments, I can and will also demand more from my employees. Naturally there are problems, but I do not consider them in that way – for me it is clear that there are and will be problems between employees and employers. If I use robots, there will also be problems, not to mention that we work with human beings, problems will always be there – somebody will fall sick or somebody has problems with the children and those problems are mediated here too, and it affects their work.

- Well, probably we are talking about trust here, trust between you and your employees – that you pay enough wages, on time, and that there is enough work to be done and they as employees do their work as expected. But how about clients, are there some kinds of problems? I am asking this because some Estonian and also Latvian entrepreneurs said their greatest disappointments were with their foreign clients, they promised to buy something or do something but eventually they did not buy or do anything or, what's worse, they did not pay for the services or goods they had received.

Well, that is normal. It's always like that, we too have come across such swindlers, but they are related to the so-called growth problems, which will be overcome. And one thing, which is our philosophy, is that it is better not to do anything, but if we do, we do it with all precautions. We will not cooperate with just anybody, but we must select very carefully, and most of our contacts come from personal networking – acquaintances and other contacts have recommended us. And that has saved us from major backlashes. Our philosophy is that we are not interested in high price, but in the possibility to work hard. The basis of success is that we try to produce as cheap as possible, as much as possible, and as efficiently as possible. We want to develop ourselves and earn money.

- What is the situation with competition in this branch?

Yes, there are a lot of competitors in this branch and the toughest competition comes from the Nordic countries, because I have visited a number of sawmills where they do the same things as we do and they have such powerful machines that if we calculate by running meter this machine costs me as much as one employee, but it produces 20 times more than my employee. In that sense there is competition everywhere, but they are foreign firms. On the Estonian domestic market there is no other company based 100 % on Estonian capital. There is AS Raitar, their history is clearly much longer than ours. I guess then there is no other at my level, there are those that have foreign owners or those that are owned by some sawmill and they are at a different level in relation to distribution of capital and productivity. Naturally there is some on the sales side and especially here on the domestic markets, but I cannot say definitely, because there is competition in everything, starting with pins and ending with tractors. And it is most welcome. But there is not the kind of competition that could force us to close down anything. In some places they respect us because we have done a good job, we have never cheated our customers, and we are very universal and helpful. So we are trusted and therefore I do not see any serious competition on the domestic markets, but on the foreign markets, yes, there is competition.

- So, you have your own regular clientele?

Yes, independently of weather conditions, we have never remained without work. And the markets are good enough, those who have bought something from us once, usually want more. Last year we prepared 24 000 cubic meters, and there was a reclamation demand for only 50 cubic meters. And even that was not our fault; there was a misunderstanding in the discussion over the phone. We made a product slightly differently from what the customer wanted.

- How does the future look? What shall you invest in and what are the means for development?

It looks gloomy.

- Why is that?

Because two years ago I said gloomy and I also said gloomy last year. Well, I cannot predict like that, for the simple reason that there is technology involved – to produce things at the same level as the Nordic firms are doing, it is almost impossible here in Estonia. There will be problems with raw material. Now and then I find myself thinking that at this moment I am 32 and there is still 33 years to go before pension age, what shall I do after the next 15 years? But for some reason my thoughts are not directly linked to this. Time will show. I cannot say. Now it seems that if I have the chance of continuing in the same manner, I would need somebody, a major investor or sawmill or somebody, who would cover the financial needs. With our own resources we cannot go very far. In the future for each cubic meter the profit will be reduced per unit. And one day it will be zero. To go further on from there is impossible; we would need more operational capital for the next step. The next step will be so expensive that one cannot take it through one's own resources.

- Have you been thinking of getting a foreign partner who would invest; a Swede, a Dutchman or a Finn?

Well, that would be a stone to mulki's[25] cabbage field. And on the other hand they say that if something is divided into two, the thing that exists today would be multiplied by four. And to have four times higher growth in this region, it makes no sense at all. Because at the moment there is only a harbor in Tallinn and the other one in Pärnu. The biggest sawmills are in central Estonia, in Pärnu, and in Võrumaa, where this Tohta is. Tohtan is already twice smaller than Paikus and four times smaller than Imavere. In that sense this location is strategically wrong and there is no railway here for any import from Russia. From the point of view of logistics we are in a completely wrong location to make any bigger investment profitable. First of all, there will be the family of products that we have undertaken – valuable wood, furniture parts from birch, and production of those parts. That idea is in my pocket now; we are gradually starting to move in that direction. Now we have proven to ourselves and to banks and potential investors too, and we have a kind of balance sheet on what we have done and which proves my company's potentials. Maybe something will come out of that, I am not sure yet.

- If you are planning to move in this direction, would that mean new technologies or equipment or would you manage with what you have now?

Yes, but in principle we have, those buildings that we built – the strategy, we watch out that what we have made we don't have to rebuild anything, and another thing is that we have to invest in such technology and get machines that are needed for this small-scale production. They are so expensive that small (firms) would never be able to get them. There would not be the amounts and turnover that we now have. So to get such strategic capital for large scale production we need to have some kind of production that can be developed and that gives enough money on which to live.

- What would that mean for this firm, in terms of number of employees, would you reduce the number of workers or?

No, I don't think that the number of employees will diminish, because the things we do now will remain the same for at least the next 5-10 years and it probably means more work for women, because if we start with

[25] Mulki is a name for both the area and the people in the Viljandi area, who are regarded as entrepreneurial and active.

birch, the turnover would be so small in the beginning that it would be impossible to feed more than 20 people. 22-23 loads of products every month and from there on there is the problem that it is too expensive to do, in terms of raw materials and in terms of labor. Well, I cannot say for sure, but I do not see the need to reduce labor, even if I wanted to do so.

- O.K, let us now talk about the relations between entrepreneurs and public authorities, have you had all the support that you needed and what kind of support have you asked for?

Well, I have not; I have not asked them for anything. Certainly I would have received if I had asked. My sister's husband was the director of that beer factory here, and when it was sold, he was the privatizer there, there were some problems with banks and all those taxes and other destroyed that company. Their sales were so small that it could not compete with those big firms like Saku or Tartu Beer.

Some time ago there was also the German support program in Öisu technical school, where they trained beer makers and they were driving together with that German group and the municipal leader passed by. The Germans asked who that fellow was and my sister's husband said that he was our municipal leader. Don't you say hello to him?, asked the Germans. Why should I, said my sister's husband; if a director of a firm with 120 employees in Germany passed by the municipal leader, the municipal leader would not only greet him, but he would have taken his hat off and bowed. This anecdote describes the development and relations in the whole of Estonia, I would say. You probably know how people treat some PhD or researcher, if there is no response in the whole world that you have such a good researcher, and then the government also does not notice him at all. This is how things are in the Estonian republic.

- O.K, let's approach the question from another angle, what are the biggest problems in an entrepreneur's life. We have been told about unpredictable legislation, high taxation, and the big amount of bureaucracy. Do you share these views?

I would say that legislation is developing in a logical direction, how well or how bad, that only time will show, and maybe our children will see that, because Estonia is following her own path and it takes time. Naturally there are laws that just look after their own interest and so, but that is the case in every country and I am quite sure of that. If the situation in Finland had been similar to ours, there the legislation would have been exactly the same; it is simply the logical route of development. Bureaucracy, well I have seen bigger bureaucracy outside Estonia..and taxes, there are no taxes, firms do not pay income tax, tax on wages is lower in Estonia than it is in Sweden or in Finland. And now there is talk about tax on turnover, what they will do with it, something was done, and it is beneficial for us, then they want to reduce taxation for employees in hope of getting more money. That is the right attitude. I do not know, but I am happy to be in Estonia, even though at times, the thing that disturbs our work is a state within the state of Estonia and that state is the customs office. Such inflexibility!

But with flowers and cakes we have succeeded in establishing good relations even with them; we try to remember their birthdays and other annual celebrations and therefore they listen to us and they meet us well and we are expected. It depends a lot on the way you take care of your things and issues. If you are friendly, you are treated in a friendly way. I would not say that there is too much bureaucracy in Estonia. The only thing that is transparent is the private life, and the state official, their relations, the state official does not always understand who is paying his salary, but I believe that the same problem exists in Finland as well and elsewhere. That is an issue that one can see every day. It is a logical path of development and to create a state in ten years is impossible when there are 50 years missing. My attitude stems from the fact that I am very much a practical guy, I do not study anything, all [my] knowledge and experience comes from practice, and maybe that's why they do not look upon me as… well, all those laws and amendments, naturally there are amendments and rapid ones. Sometimes we joke about the amendment to the law concerning the amendment of the amended law. And that bureaucracy, it is even necessary at some point, because there is still quite a lot of cheating and speculation. In Soviet times we had very strong control over legislation and so-called order, but in fact there was nothing, I think that from the legal point of view there was only chaos, if you were in good terms with your boss, you could do anything, and the main thing was for the Party organizer not to find out about anything, he was the only person that everybody was afraid of. Now they try to put all that within some frame, so that it is forbidden to smuggle cigarettes or export them, they try to limit all that, and therefore the customs make such laws and take such stands. They are trying to make their job easier. Everybody is testing and trying to innovate the right formula, to get control over things. It takes a lot of Swedish and Finnish money to strengthen the Estonian borders. In that sense everything is logical and one cannot do it in one day or two, it takes years. I have no complaints about that.

- Is there anything that you would like to get more of from the state; research results, support in marketing, product development, training – in Finland we have a state-owned institution for developing forestry and forest industry; they try to find new ways for using wood in construction, in small-scale industry, etc.

I cannot say, we also have such programs. Many of them are private, like the Eesti Tootjate Liit (Union of Estonian Producers), who organizes many such things. In this respect I am stupid, I cannot answer [your question], and I do not want anything just because it is nice to get gifts, but if I had the chance to choose, then I would not take any, because our own view does not usually fit those trainings. I have participated in many courses that were meant for middle managers, and also many extension trainings. Most of the participants thought they were good, but I did not like them too much. I found many details about which I subconsciously already knew why I did not use them and in that sense the information remained, but the practice is changing so rapidly and constantly and they are so important. At the same time I admit that if I had to finance that training for my employees, then I would prefer to take them to another, competitor company or a similar company to this one. I visit Sweden regularly and I take some of them with me and show them what the future looks like. I do it so they can update their knowledge, but it usually remains only in the framework of everyday production issues or training, so I think it is too early for me today. Because I do not know yet how far we will go. Another issue is the changes in equipment and machines and in that sense it is not worthwhile to make changes now. What the municipality could do to assist me, is the financial issues, like those Phare programs and such. To find that particular information, mediation and apply it to concrete firms. The mayor should know, at least in principle, what we are doing here, even if in reality he does not know. And I guess that he does not know exactly how many employees we have. Our firm is small, in the office there are two of us, me and the accountant, plus those 23 persons outside, who do the daily work, which we have to handle, make preparations, check, make legal, all the issues, just two of us, we have a lot of work, but I have no chance to employ a special person for that work. Even if there is a person in the municipality for this work, he could propose that this particular program would be perfect for this and this firm, this and that entrepreneur, and ask - "hi, entrepreneur, there is such a thing coming, are you interested?" It could be semi-private, all jobs have to be paid, of course, and with the taxpayers' money we should not pay private work for a private enterprise, but in a way it gives returns, because it is precisely that work that creates local entrepreneurship and development. It would be one of the actions. The mayor is like a state within a state, in fact. But I cannot say for sure. Some years ago there were people in Tohtan and in Luua from the newspaper Äripäev who wrote a story and they put these words in my mouth, that I do not get any training, that [I think] it is not important at all. But they misunderstood me, or I explained it in a bad way. My point was that they tried to pressure us to say what training should be begun for that enterprise, but the enterprise was not running yet and we were just building it, and therefore I asked, who should we train and in what, when I don't know the employees or their skills and abilities. Why should I send somebody to school and waste the money of the state or the entrepreneur, if he [the worker] comes back after a month and he still does not know anything, maybe he cannot even read. I have to find a person and test him how he copes in his work in practice and only after that can I start to develop him. That is my attitude. Maybe I am being too thrifty, but I cannot see any need for us to take a person from the street, train him and only then test whether he is capable of anything. Nowadays the information is within everybody's reach and success depends on how much you can receive and process information, but at the same time the firms like ours cannot go too deep into all that, in the sense that you search in that thick pile of papers a sheet or two that might fit your needs. That's the point concerning local government, strategically thinking, it is very logical for the municipal administration to be interested in whether there are firms in the municipality or not. That kind of lobbying and preliminary work could be done by the municipal administration. That would be a great help. It is logical in all respects and practical too. If we had 20 firms here and if you got some new information every day, then one person could go through that information and distribute it to those 20 enterprises, this [information] would fit this firm, and that, another firm. Why should those 20 firms waste their time for such work if it can be taken care of by one person?

- O.K, fine. Then some questions about cooperation among entrepreneurs, is there a joint organization for entrepreneurs in this branch or some other kind of cooperation?

Yes, there is.

- Are you a member in it?

No, not yet, there are so many unions. Now I could join, this year we joined the Estonian Chamber of Commerce and Industry and most likely we will be offered membership in the Union of Forest Processors, because we are already known in this branch.

- *What are the main benefits of membership?*

For example, in disputes with the government, and when preparing proposals for laws that would promote the development of Estonian forest industry and not hamper it. All such issues, and the possibility to voice one's opinion and influence things. Then there are some practical experiences, exchange of information between entrepreneurs, for example, about firms that are in debt to other firms.

- *If we say that to start a firm and be an entrepreneur is a kind of a learning process, then what was the most important thing that you learned and what was the most difficult?*

I answer in one word and the word is honesty – honesty is the basis of success.

- *You said in the beginning that if you were not an entrepreneur, you most likely would be a farmer. Does anybody take care of the farm now?*

Not at the moment, no. Until last year we did both, but then we thought that it is not possible to do both, the workload grew so big. So, I did nothing for one year and now I might start to work the land again. I am starting to work with the weeding and I try to keep the land in good shape for the children. At the moment it is not profitable, but Swedes formulated it so nicely: the land is a thing that cannot be produced any more, but what you have, that you should try to maintain.

11. Two Interviews at T- wood A/S – 239

The First Interview

Interview with the Chief Executive Director (CEO) of T-wood A/S
Viljandi county, Southern Estonia
Date: March 27th, 2001
Interviewer: Jouko Nikula
Translator: Helvi Pöder

I started with wood-processing, because I was not interested in agriculture - I liked industry more, the big industry. I graduated Estonian Agricultural University after studying there as a distance student and I studied machine installation and maintenance, to be a machinist, as they say. That was years ago. Currently there are 170 employees in our company and the turnover last year was 43 million Crowns. So we are relatively small, but in the next couple of years we should start growing significantly. The amount of workers should stay the same. The productivity will grow and also wages, so that the good workers might remain with us and not go to Finland, for example.

- Are you a local person – born and studied here?

No, I am from Läänemaa, I studied in Olustvere and after that I came here to work, I was a supervisor at Körgemaa sovkhoz.

- So, you started 15 years ago, in 1985 and with what did you start?

In the beginning the situation was such that one had to work, there was a work duty[26] , meantime I was a teacher at Nuia school, two days there, and on other days I was an entrepreneur. We started with greenhouses, and at that time it was not possible to have any industrial facilities. Then we constructed the greenhouses, grew cucumbers and tomatoes. As soon as it became possible, I switched to industry – I sold all the greenhouses and got money for establishing an industrial enterprise.

- Was it here that you started?

Yes, in this area, here I established the enterprise; also that house was constructed at that time. The greenhouse was not a single-man enterprise;

[26] Obligation to work at a determined place for a certain period of time, typical for the graduates in socialist times.

there were other partners too. The basic and the main share was mine, others had smaller shares in the company.

- When you started the industrial enterprise, were you the sole owner or were there others as well?

There were others too, there were about 15-16 persons, some of them were small owners, who had 1-2 shares.

- But you had the majority?

Yes, I did

- How did you choose to become a wood-processing entrepreneur; did you have earlier experience in the branch or education for it?

The raw material is local, it was a decisive thing, wood was well available.

- But you did not have the training for the business?

No, not directly, but we learned while working.

- How big was this firm in the beginning in terms of number of workers, and what was your main product?

We had only one employee; we cut down trees, constructed something, and so on.

- When did you start to expand the company?

It was the era of cooperatives and in 1990 we began to enlarge, from 1995 there was another wave of expansion, our stock capital grew, and then two years later, in 1997, we grew again. Now (2001) too we are expanding. We want to buy machines from Finland, we are currently negotiating with Finns and by autumn we want to have a sawmill here.
We shall invest some 30 million Crowns in this in autumn.

- With what kinds of capital did you..well, you began with your own resources and where did you get more capital?

The same capital that we had and then mainly loans. Loans are getting cheaper all the time, because we are doing well, the capital has grown –

and from 1995 there was a new company with a capital of 6 million Crowns.

- You also acquired new shareholders?

Yes we did.

- The bank loan, however, has been the most important means of funding, has it?

Yes, we take loans and we pay them back constantly, most of them are already paid for. Now begins the construction of a new company, and it takes money, which we get from loans.

- You are one of the rare entrepreneurs to have taken a bank loan, because almost everyone says that it is too difficult and risky even to try. They say it is difficult to get, because collaterals are insufficient and the risks for banks are too big. What is your opinion is it too risky or difficult?

The bank loan is the only possible way to get money in a situation where there is no money; what to do, you need to buy a new machine, which starts to bring in money. One has to economize, and then it is not too expensive to get a loan. Naturally, our own savings go for keeping up the production, but also the bank loans. The first loan which we take we keep on paying back and in the end of the year there is some 40 % to be paid still. Now we will get a new loan and the company will grow three times bigger than it is now. And it will start to make three times more money.

- Can you tell me, how big the first loan was?

It was 2 million Crowns, now it is paid, the next one was 13 million in all, we want to make a new project, so it is probably more productive and we can start to pay back that new loan. Our idea is that there will be 50 percent own capital and 50 percent bank loans, with that combination we will manage well.

- So, you have not had any problems with the banks so far?

No, by now we have a relatively good reputation, so we have no problems with banks. In the beginning it was more difficult, but now we are coping fine. Nobody knows about the future. Now we want to move to Merita (nowadays Nordea) bank.

- What are the differences between the Finnish banks and Estonian banks in relation to loans are the interest rates similar or higher in other banks? And in which bank are your accounts and loans at present?

We were in Yhispank, but we hope to get better conditions from Merita bank. Or if not, we will keep in both banks.

- Some questions about the staff. You said that you began with one employee and it certainly has developed from there – nowadays you have more than 100 employees, do you?

Yes, currently we have 170 employees. But it will not grow too much anymore, we are introducing new machines to replace some of the workers and this will increase productivity. In 1995 when our company started, we had some 40 employees, I am not quite sure about that.

- Are the workers local people?

Yes, they are.

- Are all of them skilled workers or are there also other groups?

The more simple work is learned very quickly, there is nothing too complicated or difficult. Metal work requires longer-term training, but wood work is quicker, two-three months is enough to reach the status of a skilled worker. We have men and women equally, maybe men somewhat more.

- How about production, what was your original product and how has that developed and changed during the years?

In the beginning we produced this and that, cutting boards just to test. We cut down trees and sold them for paper production. Now we have glue-laminated timber as the main product. We make a kind of board from pieces by gluing them together – you can see some examples there on the roof. Now we produce these boards for furniture factories.

- So, you do not produce furniture yourselves, but act as a subcontractor for furniture producers?

Yes, we do not produce any furniture. The process of making those boards is as follows: the planks are sawn, dried, and processed – we cut them into definite measures according to the order; glue them together, and that's it. Even if it is a relatively simple process, it is also a relatively expensive process, the machines in furniture production are cheaper than ours, we have two sides, a saw and board production together, they are both expensive.

- *So, the price of the product makes your production profitable?*

Yes, that is true.

- *Is there a lot of competition in this branch in Estonia?*

We have a lot of orders; the demand is greater than what we are able to produce. There are competitors, but thus far there are enough markets. Our boards are evaluated as high-quality products, we have not asked ourselves, but the banks have made some inquiries among our clients.

- *Could you briefly describe the whole process, do you have your own resources for raw material or do you buy planks from some sawmill?*

We buy logs and that is the beginning of the process. First we cut them and then the timber is taken to the drier, then it is cut into pieces, and then glued. It is a simple process, there is nothing too complicated in that.

- *From whom do you buy timber?*

In Estonia half of the forests are owned by the state and the other half by private owners. So, we have an agreement with both sides, with the state and also with private owners. We transport the timber by ourselves.

- *Who are the most important clients; domestic or foreign?*

Both, and the largest share of production goes to domestic producers.

- *Who are your biggest clients?*

That is the kind of information that we do not share.

- *O.K, what does the future look like then?*

It is the same, a new saw, and with the saw we increase the production of boards - 50 % of incomes from saw and 50 % from board production.

- So, the saw will also start to produce?

Yes, the problem is the rapid aging of the technology, it is necessary to develop constantly.

- Do you have some target as to how far you plan to grow, in terms of number of workers, markets, sales, turnover, etc.?

No, we do not have any exact plans, we will continue as long as we feel that we are able. When we feel that that's enough, we will stop. But at the moment we have no choice, we must go on, after 3 years we will be lost if we do not make reforms and invest.

- What could be the obstacles that might prevent your plans for development, could it be location funding, labor, or markets?

Location is perfect, the main issue is the money – if there is money available, we can make investments, if not, then.. Another issue is our own economy, how well it is maintained, whether expenses are kept under control. Sales follow the market; what they pay, we cannot ask more than that.

- So, there are no problems with the workforce?

No, there is enough labor available, to some extent the problem is state-related, and the quality of labor is somewhat low. But for us, there is no problem, we are very happy with the current labor.

- Does this mean that you are not experiencing - in Estonia, they complain that the labor is not motivated and does not have any idea about the importance of the quality, and the work morale has more or less been lost?

No, I say that this problem stems from the entrepreneur himself, how well he can solve it. Naturally if things are in disorder in the company or in the management, this reflects on the labor as well. One can, of course, say that the labor is no good, but it all starts from above, with the kind of discipline there is. The fault is in the managerial style.

- In concrete terms, what do you think, is it a question of wages, work conditions, or what?

All of that. All that is necessary, cost-effectiveness, the vision of the future, what it takes to get there, and on that the wages too will depend in the future. The worker is not there for the sake of charity, no, he is there for the sake of the wages and since no better [job] is available, he has to be there. But as soon as there is a chance to get a better one somewhere, he leaves immediately. Considering all that together, at the end of the day we can pay what is possible, but we cannot pay too much. We must go on, because the money is the thing that buys new technologies. And because it is the thing that saves labor, we buy technology. Our wages are low, but in Sweden and in Finland the productivity is 5-6 higher, because here most of the work is done manually. The price level is roughly the same, when we sell our own production. Technology is the thing that must be invested in.

- How do your wages compete with those in other firms in the area?

The trained labor, the people who do more complicated work with machines, get some 4 000 – 10 000 Crowns. Which is the average wage in Estonia. But another part of labor, they are low paid, but in the autumn when we put this new technology into use, the situation will change completely. The people who are now doing that cheap work will not be needed anymore and will be transferred to higher paid work. The wages in Finland are higher than in Sweden, aren't they?

- I think they are at quite the same levels.

Since we have a 2-3 times lower level of living than you have in Finland, the salary that your workers get in Finland should be divided by 2,5 and only then can we obtain the appropriate level for us and it is about 6 000 Crowns after taxes, then it is almost equal to the Finnish standard, since living costs are higher in Finland. In the near future they should earn this much. And we get 10-15 % less from production than your workers in Finland. If we get to the level where they (the workers) should be paid the same salary (as in Finland), it means we should also get the same price as in Finland. It also means that only those who can smarten up and modernize their production will be able to survive, and those who are not able to do that will have to terminate it.

- That obviously means that your main strategy will be heavy investments in new technologies?

Yes, since taxation is currently at zero-level, and since one can expect it will rise up to 20 % in the near future, it would be utterly stupid to waste that money after 2-3 years. All the money that comes must be invested now.

- I guess that the tax exemption is most useful for such investments that you are planning to do, is it not?

Yes, indeed it is.

- They tax the dividends, do they?

Yes, immediately. They are not tax-free. But the profit that is invested is given tax exemption.

- I have heard rather contradictory opinions about this tax exemption decision. In Kehra I had a talk with local small entrepreneurs and very few of them found it at all sensible. Most of them thought it does not benefit the large enterprises, because those enterprises did not pay taxes before this or they have created off-shore companies, which are "tax-free", but small entrepreneurs have always paid their taxes and in that sense the decision does not change things to any extent in any direction.

Yes, all that is true if you are a swindler, but if you conduct your business honestly, there are a lot of benefits to be drawn.

- I have met different kinds of entrepreneurs, some of them say that the most important thing for them as entrepreneurs is that they can offer employment and livelihood for people, and then there are those entrepreneurs who see entrepreneurship only as a means for quick profit, i.e. for personal benefit. What is your philosophy of entrepreneurship?

I have no philosophy, just an internal urge to do this and get some money too.

- O.K., these last questions deal with the issue of relations between public authorities and entrepreneurs. What is your view about this: has the local municipality anything to offer you and have you received any sort of advice or support from the county or the state?

Until now we had very bad relations, but now, since the power changed in the municipality, we have very good relations.

- What was the main reason for bad relations with the former municipal leadership?

Because it did not matter at all for them what happened in the municipality, they were there just for the sake of the office. But now the situation is different, we have a new municipal government. Before, politics were mixed into the peaceful life of the country, and if you were not a member of their group, you were completely ignored.

- Would you like to get something more from the municipality – financial support, information or something else?

Cooperation and a wish to promote things here, there is much you can do as long as the municipality wants to promote things. For years we had the goal of creating an area of cheap municipal services, so that people would move here to live, so that they would not move out, there would be enough labor and young people. But no, they were not interested; on the contrary, they raised the price of services. Now, with the new leadership, we managed to reduce the prices, and we aim to keep people here, so they will not move to Tallinn.

To sum it up, one could say that the local administration is there to create the infrastructure. But thus far, nothing has been done to create it.

- How about the state – would you need some help or support in marketing, in research and development, in exporting, etc.?

We hope there will be a good government someday, but now, when we see what they are doing there, I am ashamed that we have such a government. If ministers in Finland did the sort of things that they do here, they would not be able to live in Finland but would be forced to move to Africa or somewhere, where nobody knows them.

- Are there some party organizations in this municipality?

Yes, there are.

- When there are elections, is it the political program that determines the election results, or is it personalities, or some other issues?

Well, here the results of the last elections were very interesting, because those parties that have very hostile mutual relations in Tallinn are all in the same coalition

- What do you think, how will the coming membership in the EU affect your enterprise, is the "European quality" and competition a serious threat or an opportunity for you?

Well, we are not afraid of anything, we must work in any case, and we also need money. Maybe the impact is that there is no need to go through separate gates at Helsinki airport, as we have done until now, but we can all go through the same gate.

- Well, I must say that you have a very well and relatively quickly developed enterprise – can you tell me what the main ingredients are in the recipe for an entrepreneur's success?

Secret, there is no secret; you only have to save money, nothing else. Many entrepreneurs use too much for their own consumption. One must invest constantly; we don't go on holidays to Caribbean islands.

The Second Interview Three Years Later

Date: July 9th, 2004
Viljandi county, southern Estonia
Interviewer: Jouko Nikula
Interpreter: Helvi Põder

- Last time we were here in 2001 you mentioned that the enterprise plans to take a loan and make some reorganization. So what has happened in the last three years?

Everything we said happened. We took a loan and it has already been spent on production by now. Not a single cent has been paid back, but we hope to pay some of our debt back in the autumn. We have been working hard and we are doing fine right now. We have managed to follow our investment program. We made investments this year and we will pay back our debt next year, and then our enterprise as a whole should be complete and should be able to compete and stay in the market along with the big enterprises.

- How much were your net sales last year?

Around 70 million Crowns last year. We plan to have net sales of around 80 million this year. It has been growing year by year.

- How many employees do you have?

We have around 180 employees. When our net sales reach 150 million, then our enterprise should be completed and ready to compete in our economic sector. When we reach this level of financing, the number of employees should decrease to 140-150 employees. Then the average salary will probably rise to around 10 000 - 12 000 Crowns in three years. By this time money will be drawn out of the enterprise and invested into other areas whether the enterprise is completed as a whole or not, as the owners should sell the enterprise in order to receive their gain from this enterprise and invest it further into something else. The enterprise will manage fine in the future as long as there is enough wood to process. Big enterprises put a pressure on [purchase of] wood as they buy it up before us, and in order to survive, little enterprises must be able to meet this price pressure.

- *Are you doing sawing works and plywood?*

Yes, we buy the timber and saw it and process it and sell sawn timber. According to the list of top enterprises of Viljandi County in 2003, we were the most successful enterprise in the county outside the town of Viljandi. The year before, we were 5th in the county.

- *You talked about your average monthly wage reaching 12 000 Crowns?*

It will take around three years, by that time we will have paid back our loan and we will have financial means that will be used to raise workers' salaries.

- *How much do they receive now?*

Around 7 000, but there are major differences, as the most valuable workers receive around 9 000 -10 000 a month. But there are around 30 to 40 unskilled workers who are doing work that should actually be done by machines and they receive around 3 000 to 4 000 Crowns a month. Their major benefit is actually having a job and their wages are paid at the expense of those machines. Right now we can produce cheaply and we use our profit to pay bank interests. In three years' time those additional financial means will go to raising wages. So we have some resources for paying wages. We count on middle-aged employees; we cannot count on young workers, because they leave for Finland and Germany. Those who are not able to or do not want to leave, can meanwhile work here. We do not have to pay higher wages as there is cheap labour on the labour market, and certainly this money cannot come at the expense of the owners. But as we make investments, we should also invest in our labour in order to survive the economic hardships.

- *How many of your labour force are women and how many are men?*

Around half and half. The men work on machines, for that requires greater physical strength. The most important factor in our development is the availability of wood. What we need are contracts with the state, we receive some financial help from state resources, but automation of production is very expensive.

- *What is the price you pay for a cubic meter of timber?*

We do not buy spruce, but pine log is about 800 Crowns per cubic meter when it is thicker, the thinner kind is cheaper.

- *At what price does the private sector sell thinner logs?*

We do not get much of the thinner log from the private sector, most of it is bought from the state, but state prices have risen considerably recently because of the big enterprises. The tactics of big enterprises are to raise the prices until small enterprises go out of business, and then they can dictate the prices. Forest owners are cheering because of the high prices they are now getting paid for their timber. But those big enterprises artificially raise the price, then they will import the major part of timber, and in 4 or 5 years' time those prices will drop drastically. The price will be manipulated, but this is market economy, and nothing can be done about it.

- *Do you sell your fibreboard to furniture manufacturers and abroad?*

We sell it everywhere, mostly to furniture manufacturers, who export their products. So, thanks to us and the furniture manufacturers, those forests are 100% utilised and additional value is added as timber is not exported in the form of logs or sawn material, but as furniture. But without support from the state, sooner or later there will be only one big enterprise left in Estonia, which will employ only 100 persons and will probably export timber without processing it.

- *How many owners does the enterprise have?*

There are two owners: a Dane and an Estonian company. 67% belong to the Estonian company, 33% to the Dane.

- *You were one of those who established this enterprise?*

A long time ago, when I wanted to get rich, but it is out of reach.

- The enterprise is doing fine for now, but do you ever worry about its future?

I'm constantly worried, because you must constantly think how to get by, what is happening in every field, what is happening in Estonia, what is happening on the labour market and which direction should be taken, how much should be invested. Last year we used our own resources and invested over 10 million, but this year we are afraid of investing so much from our own resources, as we have taken long-term obligations. For example, last year a new boiler house was built and we have new expenses for wood processing. You cannot rush to put your ideas into practice, and you have to consider your ideas very carefully. It used to be easier, but the sums of money are far bigger and you have to be very cautious all the time. You must count every penny and keep in mind the amount of work that has been put into this, because if you do not consider those things you could easily end up going bankrupt.

- How satisfied are you with your employees and what is the situation on the labour market?

You can generally be satisfied with unskilled workers. But it is very hard to find skilled workers like electricians, electronic engineers. And this sets limits to our development, for example to manufacturing of furniture. If you start with that, you would need fully automatic machines, which are based on electronics and computers. Unskilled workers are settled, they receive sometimes a higher, sometimes a lower salary, maybe around 10 000. But try to find a skilled chief operator - it is almost impossible. We have been looking for those specialists for years. We have found some specialists, but if one of them leaves, then we have major problems. Due to lack of skilled workers, we are not able to develop furniture manufacturing. This is all caused by educational politics, which should be reformed in the same way that agriculture was reformed. Agricultural reforms had a very high cost for many people, but if they had not carried them out, the situation could have been far worse. When I make a mistake, I can correct it, but if a farmer makes a mistake, it is hard to make up for it and he will go straight bankrupt. What kind of people took up farming? Some tractor operators who had no knowledge of agriculture, and since they failed now they blame it on the government. Nobody admits his own mistakes, and maybe the function of government is to be blamed when anything goes wrong.

- *You worked as a teacher?*

Yes, by force of circumstances.

- *It was a long time ago, but what reforms would you conduct in the school system?*

What is our school system: we have high schools in Mõisaküla, in Abja, in Nuia and in Tõrva, but what comes out of it? Physics and maths are being taught in high schools, but if you ask something on those subjects, such as some laws of physics, almost nobody knows. How are they ever going to serve this country and with what kind of work are they going to earn money? Investments in education have been so stupidly placed and there is this constant public discussion in the society, but nothing has come out of it. People should be educated and taught how to work, and this is all it takes. We would immediately hire 3 or 4 persons and we would pay them 10 000-15 000 Crowns a month if only we could find those skilled workers we desperately need. Those who have talent should not go to high school after the 9th grade, but should be trained to become electricians, technicians in vocational schools. Only maybe 10% of all students should continue in high school and that would be enough. But the others should be taught in vocational schools or high schools with special programs so that they can obtain a profession. But here high schools let students pass those grades and this is a total waste of money. When they graduate, they have no skills and they can do nothing and the state gets nothing in return. And they go abroad and they do the odd jobs and unskilled work there and our state gets nothing in return. Something should be done about that immediately and people should be trained to become skilled workmen. We need welders and we could pay them a monthly salary of 10 000 Crowns. One of our welders left for abroad, but we have nobody to replace him, because the education system does not train them anymore. People should be taught how to work and this is the most important form of education, the state's money should be directed to that and the state will soon see return on those investments in the form of taxes. Teachers complain about how small their salaries are, and of course they are, when there are so many teachers. Find teachers who can teach practical skills and train workers, they could be paid 10 000 and the state will receive 4 000 from this pay as taxes and the states revenues from social tax will increase. You will see its benefits very soon. There has been much talk that there will be an educational reform soon, but I do not have much faith in it. The answer is very simple - people should be trained to be qualified workers.

- *If you had an opportunity to do this, where would you teach them?*

Here I can do nothing about it, but a group of experts should be formed to organize how those teachers should be retrained. It cannot be done in a year or two, but some agreements should be reached and money should be immediately invested in this retraining of teachers. If necessary, foreign specialists should be hired. There is a lack of skilled workers for the necessary jobs. We could pay good wages, but we do not have those workers who have skills to work with machines. We could pay them 10 000 -12 000 a month and the state would receive more tax money from it. But we pay 3 000 - 4 000 and have to keep 2 or 3 of them in every position. Constantly one of them comes and says that he is not able to work, he has been drinking, and we have to hire a next one. Around 10%-15% of our labour force has that kind of problems. We feel such a pity to pay them such small wages, but what can we do about it. We could pay them more, but we need money for that.

- *The sum of taxes received from it will be pretty big.*

Of course it would be. There is not much need of those teachers who teach physics and maths, as almost nobody gains anything from this. When the state employs some of those teachers even with minimum wages in other fields, it would gain more by this as concerns taxes. It does not have to pay money from the state budget, but it would see money coming in. This should be the work of an expert group, how those things should be done. But here there are 4 or 5 high schools in such a small area and after three years that these students spend there, the state has produced only unemployment. The state has spent a lot of money on it, but is it even necessary?

- *Do you cooperate with the local government of your municipality?*

There is some cooperation; we are all in the same municipality. We built a new boiler house, and we are responsible for the heating of the school, and we cooperate with the local municipality on building the heating system for a new cultural centre, which will be completed soon. Of course there is cooperation, but there is not much that the local government can actually do, because most of its budget goes for teachers' and government officials' salaries and not very much is left over after that. Every enterprise has to manage its affairs by itself; the local municipality will not do that for them. Estonia cannot offer the kind of support to its enterprises that Finland does. Local municipalities do not have that kind of money, so it is useless to ask financial support from them. They are more likely to be asking for support than to be giving it.

- *How much does your enterprise support the local municipality?*

It is not like we support the local municipality, but most importantly we provide them with energy, which is around 50% cheaper than anywhere else. This is our contribution, for example, heating the school would cost around 20 000 a month, but we can do it for 12 000 and the local government saves 7 000 or 8 000 Crowns and this is already something. We provide locals with cheap fuel energy, our central heating systems and collectors are beneficial for local residents in those multi-storeyed block buildings, and this contributes to people not moving out of this area. Keeping an apartment here is cheap and their prices are also lower, so they are all occupied.

- *So the apartment market is functioning?*

Yes, apartments are bought and sold; they are not very expensive, although I heard that some of them were sold at 70 000 Crowns. Our central heating policy is certainly one reason why the cost of communal services here is low and this is why apartments are bought here and there are also job opportunities here. You can move to Tallinn, but you must pay several thousand a month for your apartment, whereas here keeping an apartment would cost a few hundred a month.

- *What do you think about the state's policy towards enterprises?*

It has been favourable and the economic situation of our enterprise has actually improved in the last few years. In 1993, when the currency exchange took place, neither the state nor the enterprises had money. The exemption of income tax for enterprises helped us a lot, for without this we would not have survived. This is one of the most fundamental things the government has done. Certainly the state would have received more income, but there would not have been so many investments, enterprises would have been so much weaker, and wages lower. Enterprises should be exempt from income tax for another ten years, and then with state subsidies, Estonia would be built up. It would be bad if the state tried to redistribute those finances. You can redistribute only what you have earned. We have not paid dividends and all that money has been invested in our enterprise. If we had paid dividends, we would have gone bankrupt. It is the same thing with the state, when it starts to redistribute too early, it hardly ever reaches the goal it has set. You feel compassion for the people who are caught in the middle of this economic hardship and who must manage on 2 000 Crowns a month, but what can you do?

- Do you have a workers' union here?

Yes, some people came here to establish a union. We had a conversation with them. They came here with social policy, did not ask any permission, gathered the workers and talked to them. They said that it is their mission to come and establish a union.

- Where did they come from? Tallinn?

Anywhere else and they visited all the larger enterprises. There are only around 10 enterprises in Estonia that could be considered large by European standards; the other enterprises are medium-sized. We are among the medium-sized enterprises. Estonia has around 33 000 enterprises and the average number of employees is 5 or 6 or even less. We have 180 employees, so we are pretty big. But you have to have at least 250 employees and net sales over 500 million to be counted as a large enterprise. We could never achieve this, so we will remain among the medium-sized enterprises, and we work out our policy according to that. Sooner or later this union movement will reach here. There is no way we can stop this. You can ban smaller groups from forming a union, but if you have over 100 employees, they would establish it anyway and there is nothing you can do about that. Unions will appear, but you cannot establish them at somebody's order. Our enterprise has taken a direction where we try to pay our employees a little bit higher wages than other enterprises in our field do, because then employees will be more satisfied and we have no reason to be much afraid of unions. Establishing workers' unions starts from large enterprises that belong to the state, like Estonian Railway, and spreads from there to smaller ones. In Western countries too this does not involve very small enterprises, but large ones, like the airline industry, where there is more money. An enterprise with 4 or 5 employees is a family enterprise; it has not much to do with unions.

- What do you think about nepotism?

It makes you angry when you hear that some tens of thousands of state money were paid for counselling through off-shore companies, but why should I get upset about it, I have enough troubles. I have paid my share that I had to pay, and you can put this money where you like. People have elected the parliament and when they have elected scamps, then what can I do about it. I have only one vote and I always vote for those who do not come to power. Money disappears and every nation deserves its leaders, they put aside 40 million. My condition would be that they buy pine timber furniture. It is bad when this money stays in a bank account. It should circulate and I would be satisfied if some of it would end up in furniture stores. Why should I worry where it is put aside? That's life and it's the same everywhere, for example in America. The sums that disappear here are so much smaller. The sums that disappear there are enormous by our standard.

12. A-Heat A/S

Interview with three directors of the company
Karksi-Nuia, Estonia
Date: March 27, 2001
Interviewer: Jouko Nikula;
Interpreter: Helvi Pöder

- *Please, tell me about yourself, your education and work history.*

In this firm I act also as director of one daughter company, we actually have three daughter companies, one in Pärnu, one in Aravete, and this third one here in Karksi-Nuia. Here I am project leader. I graduated from the Agricultural University in Tartu, where I studied mechanization of agriculture some 7-8 years ago, in 1991-1992. Then I worked in a company which imported and installed heating equipment. I was office manager in Viljandi.

- *So you still live in Viljandi?*

Yes, I live in Viljandi, but the daughter company is in Aravete.

- *And the headquarters are here in Karksi-Nuia?*

Yes, in this very room.

- *Where did you import that heating equipment from?*

That company still operates and the ownership is partly Finnish and there are two managing directors, it is a joint-venture type of company, with Finns. And the equipment, it came from all over the world. The contacts came from there (Finland) and now it has developed in another direction, it has spread to Latvia and Lithuania too. Actually it is quite a big company.

- *And you worked in that company as well, but not anymore?*

Yes.

- *And then you quitted and came to this company?*

Yes, I did – I came here.

- *Why, may I ask, did you leave the previous company?*

Well, I was office manager, but I wanted to do something by myself. I got very good experience in that company and I felt that my price was higher than what I was being paid. I had already been there for five years and I had an urge to do things differently. We still have very good cooperation with them, no hard feelings.

- *What year did you start this company?*

It has been working for 4 years now – since April 1997. I have been here for 1,5 years.

- *What kind of team started this company?*

By two men in 1997, two men, the other was working then as director of a municipal company and he also got such experience and skills, which it was impossible for him to use in that municipal firm. The other man was working in some electrical company and they started working together.

- *And what kind of work or services did they begin with?*

With the same they are doing now; currently the main operations include production of heating, construction of heating centers, equipment; everything that is related to heating – servicing, not very simple work, but such as requires knowledge and skills. That is something which is lacking here.

- *Production and selling of heating, or?*

Yes.

- *So you produce and install the equipment?*

We buy the equipment, but we assemble the electrical boards, so you can say that we produce something.

- *So, you plan, buy, and construct heating systems?*

Yes, as well.

- *The customer comes and orders a complete heating center from you, does he/she?*

Yes, exactly.

- *What is the structure of ownership in your company nowadays, do those two directors still own this company?*

Currently there are 5 shareholders and 4 of them are involved in the everyday running of the company?

- *And you have some employees too?*

Naturally, yes, together with those daughter companies.. practically, I am director of one of those companies, one shareholder is a director of another firm, and a third is the actual director, who decides everything – or coordinates, actually we do everything together. So in these daughter companies we have altogether approximately 20 employees.

- *All these enterprises do the same services, do they?*

In those daughter companies there is not such a skilled labor force as in the main company, there we have employees who have received special training and can help in the more demanding jobs. If you want a skilled and trained worker, you must be ready to pay him well, and in order to be able to pay well, there must be enough work for him. Each company helps the other in these matters.

- *Where did you get your employees, are they from the same business or?*

In the daughter companies the heating centers are the basis, we produce heat and we all came from that same company that once existed. Usually production of heat ended at some point and managers were not able to cope with that matter, and then maybe some 10 persons, and then maybe one or two of them were found and employed (by our firm) and then with time.. we usually find our employees by somebody recommending somebody to us and so on. The training takes place through work; usually they have learned the work by working.

- So, you train your workers?

Yes, we do

- Who are your main customers - municipalities or private persons or both? And how did you acquire your clientele?

If the question is about heating, it's clear; the heating center is in the middle of the village and those who are at the other end of the pipe are our customers. That is one thing, but then there is also construction - there our customers are firms, local administrations, and the share of private persons is very small.

About that construction business, I and the director of one daughter company, we used to work for a short period of time in another firm. Because this place (town) is so small and this business is so special, we do not need to spend money on advertising ourselves, the work itself makes the advertisement and those customers that employees bring with them or if people in previous firms were satisfied, they also follow. I studied in that sad time when distance learning was coming to an end, we were the last course, and it was not possible to do it later on; life changed so rapidly then that (my studies) remained unfinished – I studied three years altogether (in Agricultural University).

The municipal firm went down and there was no work anymore and therefore we had to establish this firm. This company is 4 years old and it was created entirely from scratch. There were no premises and no workers either. And no idea what to do.

Or in the beginning there was some idea – I and two other men, we put our money together, all the equipment and other stuff together, and started working. We rented an office from the municipality building of Karksi, repaired it, and started there.

- How big was your starting capital?

It was around 40 000 Crowns (approximately 2500 euro). Currently the capital stock is 800 000 crowns. And we have two daughter companies. Each year the revenue has grown 2,5 – 3 times; in the first year it was almost 800 000, in the following year it grew to more than 1,8 million Crowns, last year it was 4,2 million, and this year we shall get over 10 million Crowns.

- When you were founding this company, did you discuss whether there are any markets for you and where, or was it just your skills that you based it on, a conviction that you know how to do the work and so "let's start working"?

We knew that there were very few who could do that job in Estonia, but since I had a long experience with heating centers, I've been in this business for 16 years, here in Nuia too at some point of [my] history. And it was precisely what we started to work. We did not advertise at all, and it was not possible, because then there would have been a different situation, where we would have had too many offers, which we would not have been able to handle properly. Then we took fewer jobs but tried to do them as well as possible.

We have been expanding constantly and when we found skilled men, like Toomas, who was in the same business, and then Tarmo, who is the director of another daughter company. He graduated from Tallinn technical high-school. The sphere of skilled persons is rather limited, and this fact has actually been the most serious obstacle in our development – finding the necessary people who can do this work.

- So, you could expand immediately as soon as you find the skilled labor force?

Yes, if we could only find people with technical or engineering training, for there is a lack of engineers. That's because engineers are not valued nowadays, even if we look forward into the future: Now everybody wants to study economics and… If somebody happens to study, it will sooner or later become evident that they are needed, because there are so few engineers now. It is a question of those markets, I was here then, but it gives us security, because we can see what kind of people we have here around us and they give us security regarding the markets. Because the basic capital of our firm is the people who work for us. If those four men decided to leave now, we would very soon go back to zero, where we started. A lot depends on labor – all the agreements would of course remain, so that we would not go completely back to zero. But we would not have those persons who can organize our work.

- You said that there are not enough educated and skilled persons, but what is the reason for this; there is education but it does not correspond to your needs – in other words, is it the wrong kind of education or what?

The basic mistake in educational policies in Estonia after independence was that the emphasis was put on humanities and social sciences. And also on economics, legal studies, psychology, and such. But there is very little training in engineering. I can't say about the technical university but in the Agricultural University we can clearly see that state orders stopped coming at the technical faculty. I could mention, about energy economics, that if we think on a larger scale, then we have a lot of problems, because politicians want to sell the energy economics of Estonia to Americans. It makes me really wonder: are there no engineers in Estonia, who could revive the basis of the energy economy, because it is pure physics and everything can be calculated; how much energy we can get from this or that material. Do we really need to import experts from abroad who buy this and that and then start producing here? I think that we had education in energy economics in our universities; do these experts not know how to promote this business and fill the markets in Estonia? One can't help feeling that Estonia is being sold piece by piece to foreign buyers and investors. Occupational training is very inadequate; it is very difficult to find employees and we have to train them ourselves, they learn by doing, through practice. And if such a worker leaves and you take somebody else to replace him, we have to train him all over again from the start, because there are no skilled workers available.

- Let me put it the other way around; if you hire somebody who has received some training, is his education the right kind, appropriate for you? And for example, are electricians still being trained somewhere, in vocational schools, for example?

Yes, they are being trained, in Viljandi and in Vana-Võidu too. But the quality is really poor.

- So their level of training is not enough for you?

No, it is not.

- You need persons with college level training, do you?

Yes, he/she must know what he/she is combining and what he/she is doing, he/she must be able to read drawings and understand why one thing works and another doesn't.

- So you think that current education gives too low a level of skills and you have to re-train them, and you need better education, do you?

Yes, we set them a task and they must be able to do it, and if all the necessary information and tools are given to them, then he or she should be able to cope with the task. But, because we have electrical and heat energy economy combined, they must know more than an ordinary electrician knows.

- So, the deficiencies in training is an obstacle to your development, but how are you improving the situation?

Our workers do the work and learn, there is always somebody monitoring their performance and giving information and advice. They are supported for a long time until they can manage independently.

It does not matter whether you are a manager or not, if the people cannot cope with their duties, then the managers must show them how to do it. And only when the worker can work independently can the manager concentrate on his own duties. In the beginning the situation was such that we worked together with the workers – the workers watched us, what we did, and learned to do it. If there were any problems, they asked. It was the only way to acquire experience.

- What are your future plans, shall you keep the same line of development or are there still some expectations for growth, and if so, is it possible to realize them through your own resources or do you need external financing, and where do you get it?

Sure, we want to slow down the rate of growth a bit, because it is not possible to continue growing at the same rate for many years. Therefore we are looking for factors of stability – revenues are at the level where we can start creating stability and plan a normal rate of growth in the future – whether we choose or aim at 30% or 40% or 50% will depend a great deal on the capacity (amount and magnitude) of the jobs we will have and also on the tasks of work and naturally on whether we can manage those jobs. Our idea is that, currently, growth is not our primary goal, because we have a small enterprise and it is not our goal to make it too big, what is decisive – for the kind of profit we will have – is that we maintain the stability that we have already achieved here in Estonia.

- *So, you want to strengthen your market position, or?*

Usually it happens that when something grows too big and powerful, the quality will eventually suffer. That's why we do not create a big company, but are flexible, monitor changes and, if necessary, move into new systems. Big enterprises are rigid and if you want to change something in a big company, it turns into a catastrophe. We try to do things that big companies are not doing.

- *How about the obstacles to development, do you have enough resources for that?*

I could say that the biggest obstacle here in Estonia is envy, envy towards others, and if you visit foreign countries you notice that there people have the habit of trying to do better than your neighbor, but they do not prevent the neighbor. But here in Estonia if a person is doing well, they do not try to do better, but use all that is in their power to put all sorts of obstacles to your success. If we could get rid of this Soviet tradition, I believe that business life in Estonia could advance significantly.

One of the obstacles here is the relations with the local administration, the too narrow circles of administration, where everybody knows everybody, it is just too introverted.

Now, when the reform of the local administration is being planned, I think that it should be done more thoroughly and they should be merged more mercilessly in order to get rid of this kind of things. All those games continue, but they do not concern every small detail. The municipal council here consists of those people from the same environment; the municipal leader is from here, and nobody wishes anybody any harm, and in the municipal council they play their games in the sandbox – "I want this and this and you get that and that. But if the whole county was just one municipality, then the council members would come from different villages and it would prevent playing games with the details and everybody would think highly of the whole local administration (municipality).

But now the thing is that people are thinking of ways to get something for themselves personally out of the municipal council, and not how all may benefit and life could improve here. That radicalism that they pursue now in the municipalities is very fragile and dispersed. We felt, when working with the local administration, that the different parties had good relations with one another, in general there were no problems. We have tried to play with all the cards on the table as far as possible, to discuss problems with them. But a typical comment coming from the mouth of the municipal or state administrator is "what can I get out of the offer" that will save money, let's say 100 000 Crowns every year, and there should not be anything unclear. Our line in these cases has been that we declare to the person who is asking, that "no, you really don't get anything out of this" and usually things stop just there. And that is the local administrator. But if we manage to get to a higher level, where there are higher wages for administrators and where there is interest in saving money, things get started immediately and without any obstacles. But if you cannot pass that lower-level administrator, then there is no hope. It is the smallness of that local administration that causes this interest in personal benefit. This implies that, if some improvements need to happen in the local administration, they should benefit that official as well, who makes the necessary decisions. Regrettably, officials are not held responsible for anything in Estonia. They might give you wrong advice, this might cause millions of Crowns of losses, but this official keeps his position and is not held responsible for anything in any way. But if an entrepreneur makes some mistake and causes losses, he will go bankrupt and is responsible for everything with his own property. So, we (administrators and entrepreneurs) are in different position as concerns responsibility and this is probably an obstacle to development. Administrators should also be responsible, so that if they have done something wrong, they should admit it and be held responsible for it.

- Thank you, but I am still interested in this envy, does it mainly come from the administration or from other entrepreneurs?

Personally I have not been bothered by envy, but if we talk about problems, then most of them are related to local administration. Naturally there is envy but. I mean that I shall not let it disturb me, but if there were less of it, then the resources of the Estonian would grow significantly. A very big amount of resources lies behind envy. Nowadays it is a peculiar phenomenon that when you meet somebody you know in the street and ask how he is doing, if he says "I'm doing fine", the person who asked the question becomes sour and gloomy, but if you say you are not doing too well, he is happy that everybody else is also going through bad times. Naturally it is a question of the living standard, you can't be happy if you have to worry all the time about how to feed your family, this too causes it. Here in the rural areas people do not have much money. And, of course, Estonia has taken a giant leap in the last ten years; none of us imagined that we could get clear out of the Soviet system in this time and reach the level where we are now.

- O.K. You are living in Nuia now, are you?

I live in the forest, in a detached house, in Veskimäki village. For some time I lived in Nuia, but I wanted to have my own home.

I was born in Tartu and came here when I married some 18 years ago.

- I have an impression that – of course I could be wrong – that Viljandi is a larger town, Pärnu even bigger, but Nuia is a small place and the smaller the place, the more present and visible envy is, in the sense that in a bigger place you are more anonymous. And envy is not that visible. Does your experience correspond to this?

Yes it does. The same idea that those local administrations should be larger, because we have currently the Möisakyla Municipality, where the biggest employers are the school, the municipal administration, and perhaps the local museum. It is like a joke. It is exactly the fact that a lot of money is spent that prevents development. Everybody knows how big share the administrative costs are of the municipality's budget. Indicative of this fact is that when a local administration is short of money, what do they economize on? The first thing is to turn off the street lights. If the administration does not have money, they will not reduce the number of administration officials or decrease their wages, because that would cause a big problem, somebody might protest. But if you turn off the lights, somebody might complain about dark streets, but then we can say that there is not enough money and that's all; it is the easiest way to economize. But it also means that when the streets are dark, criminals have more possibilities to act, and then they say that we have so much crime. Why are we paying taxes? – In order to keep the street lights on, have good roads, a clean environment, with the taxpayer's money, not to have a lot of officials.

There are so many local administrations that there are not enough good administrators for all of them. And the cities are really dark. One other thing, about education. When we were talking about deficient education as an obstacle, this can also be a benefit for the enterprise, because we have learned these things by ourselves, they are not taught anywhere, because there simply is no education for it, that can be a true competitive edge for us. If we can find that correct curve or point and study and learn it, you also have the point why the enterprise cannot grow too big, because then all other matters follow. And we have found our own niche in all that. Another thing which prevents enterprise from growing too big is the administrative costs, the bigger the enterprise, the bigger the administrative costs as well. And we can do all those things, but if we just sat behind the table, then we would lose that competitive edge, and therefore we cannot grow too big. The situation is such that all those four men that we talked about are now in this room; this situation has been possible for a couple of weeks this spring – it is very rare that we can all be here at the same time. Usually there is only an accountant [here] and we, the others, are somewhere else.

- *Selling your know-how?*

Exactly, we use it in our work and sell it out.

We in our own circle, we will not tell things to outsiders, how we deal with our customers. We know what to say and we can control what we promise and all such things. The idea is that those workers we have, for example if they cause something to explode in the heating centre, they must be able to justify it to the customer; why it was necessary. It means that our worker must also be completely skilled and capable of dealing with issues that concern his work. We have had quite a few special situations and had to manage them, now things are calmer, when it's springtime, we calculate finances and so on. But in autumn we would not have met with you and given interviews; then we have a very hectic time.

Maybe the skill to keep the form of enterprise and to understand that you use your skills through or in that type of enterprise. There are a lot of skilled people in different areas, but they lack the skill of enterprise. It means that they cannot sell their skills properly. We have our own experience in this, when they expanded operations in Aravete and we got a person in our company who completely lacked the ability to sell his so-called golden hands; he can do anything he wants, a really skilled guy. He just sat at home, went sometimes to heat the central boiler, but could not sell his skills. But now he has a good salary and we can see how his eyes shine and he likes what he is doing now. If people only understood that what they can do, or learn that, if they can sell it to the employer, or if his/her circle becomes too small, then the best thing to do is to set up an enterprise through which to sell skills and knowledge. That is a basic skill, that people must be implanted among people.

- *We have interviewed many entrepreneurs, but you are a special case, since you really sell the training and skills that you've received. And you know how to do it.*

In principle, yes. As I said, there are many who have knowledge, but not so many of them can use it as an entrepreneur. Knowledge is knowledge only when it is used in practice.

- There must also be an entrepreneurial spirit, so that nobody else benefits from that knowledge except you? But how you do it in practice; you are from Viljandi, another person from Pärnu and a third from here?

I stay mainly here and visit daughter companies and coordinate. It is interesting because Avo is the director, but at the same time he has the most practical experience. In principle it is also the case that if the three of us get in trouble, one person can save us and the company.

- I must say that you are very wise men; the person who knows most and is most experienced is also the director. Just imagine if it were the other way round; if the person who was least skilled should be the director, then you would have all sorts of internal conflicts and so on.

That was our practice in the Soviet times and this fact was the one that was especially repugnant to me then. When you went to see the director and you had a good idea, which was also very useful, the director would say it was not correct. You leave the room and you must do just as he says, because there is no alternative. That same mentality has also remained here in independent Estonia and you still meet such directors from that period in some places. Let's take for example that director of E-firm, a director from the Soviet period, he is still there in the other company. But he is no good as a director, his skills are already lost and he was reared to carry out orders, nothing else. He waits for orders from above, but a director must also give workers a chance to decide – where a joint decision determines things.

- Have you had conflicts within the company?

Yes, of course, there must be conflicts, they make things advance. But we must be able to reach compromises. Until now there have not been any, because we've existed for too short a time for conflicts to appear, but maybe they will come. But it would also be abnormal if there were no conflicts at all.

I was working for a short period of time in another company, there was talk about deciding yourself and we also made very good offer for the scale of Viljandi. But after being there for three weeks and in the beginning they expected me to be an expert and therefore they bought me out of the former enterprise, but then it became evident that I would not have access to the group of decision makers, and that was enough for me. Then I came here. Before this enterprise there were those two things [job offers] to estimate, they made me a very good offer at that previous job, with guarantees for the future and a lucrative offer. Then I had an offer from this enterprise, we had been cooperated previously, I was there and after only 10 days it was clear that I had made the wrong decision. I decided to quit there very soon and find out whether the offer from this enterprise was still valid – and it was.

- We have been talking a lot about the role of the municipality and you did not draw too rosy a picture of it. However, can you imagine some issues about which you could get help and support from the municipality?

I think that there are deficiencies in the education of the municipal administration – a municipality is in reality a kind of enterprise, it has to "sell" proper services to residents of the municipality, but at the same time they must be able to see where their money comes from, what is the basis of their incomes. It is [the money comes from] an enterprise again. In reality life starts from entrepreneurship and returns back to entrepreneurship – and so it goes. The more it (the municipality) promotes entrepreneurship, the bigger become the incomes for the municipality and the better life becomes for the people in the municipality. And the municipality gets more and more new residents and more enterprises are born. It is a rolling snowball – if local leaders finally understood that this is precisely the way they should do their business, and then things would be fine between the municipality and entrepreneurs. And life would develop in a normal way. It is very common for municipality officials to say "what are you complaining about, you are an entrepreneur". It appears that if you're an entrepreneur, then you have a lot of money and everything, while he (the municipal official) is a poor fellow. For example my wife is the financial director of Abja municipality and she has often been told that "you have nothing to worry about, because your husband is an entrepreneur". In reality the day of an entrepreneur is much longer than just 8 hours, often it is 16 hours or even longer during peak seasons. But the municipal official never works longer than 8 hours and during that time they take care of their personal matters. But such is the prevailing attitude. And from that begins the same thing, which municipal councils appear, lots of them, and they decide matters, but ordinary people are elected into them, who as a rule do not know what they are supposed to do. There is nothing wrong with the system but we lack people who can wield power correctly, and their education is deficient.

- So you mean that municipal officials have an attitudinal deficiency – I have seen this problem here and there, in many municipalities the officials respond when asked about the role of entrepreneurs for the municipality that, well, they give some employment for residents and pay some taxes, but nothing much otherwise.

If an entrepreneur gives employment to even one person, then the municipality receives taxes from him/her, and on the other hand the municipality does not have to pay subventions or support this person, which means that the municipality saves that much – and gets taxes. It means that when one person gets work, the municipal income grows threefold. This is something that they do not understand. Therefore they could support the entrepreneur in some issues so that the entrepreneur could keep those people employed, because the municipality would have more benefit this way than if the enterprise went bankrupt and was compelled to lay off the workers. This would be an additional burden to the municipality, they would get fewer taxes and they would have to pay relief to the workers. It means that roads, streets, education, and other things would necessarily suffer. Entrepreneurs are tightly connected to the municipality and therefore the administrative reform must be very radical. And it must be done in everything at once; there is no sense in cutting the dog's tail piece by piece. Then the development would go faster and then we might be able to train the municipal leadership. Then there would also be competition for the leadership and for the places in the municipal council. And only the best would be selected. If we had a larger municipality we could pay competitive wages and a good expert could organize county matters as well. At local level only lower-level functionaries are needed to receive and handle papers, but the real expert would operate at the level of the county. Then it is possible to hire good experts and the quality of administration would improve significantly, together with the quality of life.

Let's take one good example, we started to take care of the heating of a local school, I don't remember exactly the prices, but the magnitude was such that our price was 400 Crowns per megawatt (around 25 euros) but they could not get along with each other, there were some problems. We made the deal, the mayor was a young man and the process started to move on. And then talk started in the municipal council that strangers are heating our schools, this is here in the Viljandi county – we, "strangers"? Before it used to be our own - now they had to give notice to one man, but then we told them that, see what was the price before and it became clear that it used to be 700-900 Crowns per megawatt (45 – 55 euros) and it means that for a single winter month there was a difference of 20 000 Crowns (1200 euro).

We told them that we, the strangers, are heating your school but please pay those 20 000 Crowns as a welfare benefit to that person who was dismissed and after February-March and December-November you are still making a profit and 10 000 Crowns are left. But strangers!!??

- How about the state, what would you like to get from there?

If one follows the current changes, then the planned changes should be made as planned, then the state will develop positively. I personally believe in right-wing forces, not in leftist forces, because during my youth I had quite enough experience with those. Then I had to push against a wall and still nothing changed.

- As an entrepreneur, do you expect something from the state?

We've gotten used to getting by without any help from the state. I support the idea that the legislation should be much simpler, even though the state does not get all the revenues, but the matter should be much simpler. And I feel that we are moving towards simpler legislation; laws have to be as clear as possible. Also the prohibitions, the fewer the prohibitions, the more society will be able to develop. Because prohibitions only lead to what exists in Estonia now.. one example is alcohol; many municipalities and cities ban the sale of alcohol. A ban creates immediately a market for illegal alcohol. There cannot be a void in a society; bans should not ban things that exist in a society. If we ban the night-time sale of alcohol, then immediately we will have the so-called taxi alcohol, illegal liquor. Then the police will be more occupied with such things, but I guess they have enough work without that. All those bans, they do not help, it only gives somebody a chance of making money out of it, because each ban gives somebody a possibility to earn. That is the specific thing about that matter. I strongly believe that the government should try to simplify these matters, like they exempted enterprises from income tax and I would say that this was a very welcome reform, because it made it possible to bring all the incomes of many enterprises out into the bright light of day. And the state has a chance to make reliable statistics. Naturally all tax exemptions are beneficial for us; the smaller the taxes, the more transparent everything becomes and the fewer swindlers can benefit from them. Then everybody is equal to everybody else.

- So, taxation is not too heavy and there is not too much bureaucracy, right?

The system of taxes must be so simple that even ordinary people could understand it. And if it is simple, it is easy for the state to check it. Filling out a tax declaration is such a task that I do not even want to deal with it. But if we remove income tax from the enterprises, then business revenues will be invested freely or we could save part of it and divide investments over many years, so that we do not have to invest everything at once. But if you do not invest, then you will be taxed and then you probably will not have that money to invest it in the operation of the enterprise. And if incomes are paid as dividends or as incentives (options), then it all comes back to the state as taxes – why should they be taxed twice?

- What is your opinion about the statement that I heard here in Estonia that the state's economic policy predominantly favors the big enterprises, not small and medium-sized enterprises? And if the state wants to support and promote the SME sector, then there is a need for more state interventions through the educational and other systems, but in this strategy all enterprises are competing at the same level or line, even though they are very different in terms of economic strength and such things?

I think it is not a problem, of course big enterprises have more advantages and therefore they cope more easily, but the state has no means to dictate money in that manner. We as entrepreneurs, we know how money moves and functions, we know that banks are banks and their main goal is to sell money and all sales and purchases follow fluctuations in demand and supply. If banks have a shortage of money, it is sold less and at higher interest rates, and if there is more money, its supply grows and interest rates go down.

Business is such a strange curve; there is much work and little income. If you have strived for a long time, then the curve rises faster and you are getting more income. But many quit just during that first or second third.. they think that the work is not getting less and incomes are not rising and they leave everything, they give up. We have a lot of such cases in Estonia when people give up and miss the chance of enjoying the fruits of their work. People should be more confident about their goals, if one wants something a lot, then it is possible to get money from the bank. Because the bank also monitors whether the entrepreneur is determined enough. But every society needs big firms and small firms, because the small firms fill those gaps that the big firms cannot fill. But at the same time it is self-evident that not a single firm is able to produce cheap products for the mass market.

Some words about the state policy; I think that Estonia has been a relatively enterprise-friendly country, I do not know about other legislation except through the newspapers, but until now there is a little bit..in relation to social policy, not too much has been done or emphasized, even if it is a very "juicy" topic, they have succeeded in keeping it under control, so that all sorts of support programs,,, I understand that they are necessary in some places and situations, but they are very difficult to manage, one should not exaggerate with these subventions and supports. It is very difficult to distribute them in a just way, there are always single mothers and… they must be supported, but those unemployment benefits and rises in pensions that are not covered by the revenues in the state budget, we should avoid such a government coming to power.

It is also a problem that distributing money requires money and if the tax payer's money goes to government and it is redistributed again, then how much money is spent on maintaining all those bureaucrats who distribute the money? All that support that came from the West, where did it all go? It went to market places, to be resold to customers. We all know that Russia is being assisted a lot right now, but we also know that some groups get rich on that assistance. But naturally there are those who really need that help and we should make sure that the help goes to the right people. But here, with us, it is often so that those who really need help represent only 10-20 % of the population, the rest do not really need it, but they have got a hold on it through social networks.

13. A&B Software

Interview with Mr.S- Information technology director.
Moscow, February 9th, 2004
Interviewer: Raimo Blom, interpreter: Michael Chernish

- I'd like to ask how you came to your position. What are your educational background and other kinds of experience you had for the present job?

I graduated the Telecommunication Institute, with the specialty of space communication. It is a kind of specialty that requires a lot of programming, a lot of programming skills, and a lot of computing, and that's how I became good in programming and started my career in the business. I continued my education at Moscow University (...). I worked and I studied at the same time. Those were the years of the fastest development of computer technology. My specialty was automation programming for nuclear reactors. There was a special boost for years after the Chernobyl catastrophe. So, I was not involved with the problems of the Chernobyl reactor, I was more closely involved in making software programs for other kind of reactors, like water and steam reactors (WWER). Like the one which is located in the Finnish town of Loviisa. After that I had a job at the Academy of Sciences.

The Soviet Union was developing the flexible automated production line program. Hence it was one of those Academy of Sciences jobs that suffered most when the systemic crises of the Soviet Union became evident. So in 1991 the laboratory was almost paralyzed. After that I tried to find employment for my employees and after that I got an invitation to work in Germany. I was an intern in the company, which is called DEC - Digital Equipment Corporation, it does not exist anymore. Prior to the visit to Germany I was just a good engineer but only when working in Germany did I acquire my first knowledge about how to run projects. There was no project management in the Soviet Union - it was the normal process management that existed here. It means the process of managing the research programs, but there was no project management as such in those days in the Soviet Union. When the Soviet Union disintegrated it became Russia. It was now Russia, but I did not find application for my skills there. So, I sent an application to go to China and later for half a year I worked in China. After returning to Russia I started to focus on the geographic information system. From the start I was not only an engineer but also co-owner of the business. It was a very interesting project for investigating possible material resources with no direct applications. There were geographic maps, then space photographs, and other background maps that we use to forecast the natural resources. However, once again money was lacking for running the project, so I had to close down this business and dismiss my employees. Afterwards I started to work as consultant and I got an invitation to work with the *Siemens Nixdorf* company. That was the computer division of Siemens in those days. Now it is the business services department of the Siemens Corporation. I worked in the company for 4 years and there I began my career as consultant for systems integration and later I became the business process consultant. All those 4 years I had to study. I realized that a consultant is like a colonel who teaches others to perform operations but does not perform any operations himself. But I also realized that, as a real manager, I needed to have a functioning company. I was made a proposal to work for a Russian construction company, which has affiliations in all regions of the Russia. After this project was completed I got an invitation to work in their office and currently this is my second year in the company. Now the technical bases of the company have been completed and currently the company is also completing its new facilities. Information technologies are supplemented and there use is measured. And failure to do so is a failure of management.

- *Can you say little bit more about your current responsibilities and main tasks?*

The Company operates in 6 countries: Russia, Germany, Ukraine, USA, Sweden, and Cyprus. Currently I am responsible for the technical management of the company. It means the technical bases of functioning of the business processes in the company. So, there are several functions for the department - administrative functions, the basic side of administrative duties and economic duties of the company, basic logistics, right? So, not long ago I was also entrusted with the human resources services. Thus, life is full of unexpected things. It's not a boring life at all.

- *It seems you have very different tasks... how are they related inside the company in the management? What are the relations within the management?*

It is a special kind of company: a software production company. So, its tasks are not very complicated. They are production of software, testing of software, and selling and marketing of software. But basically the personnel in the company are very specific so it is reasonable, optimal that all the tasks which might cause friction within the company should be concentrated in one department so that programs might not create tension in the company. So, it's the 8th part, the HR functions of the company, that is the most valuable asset, it is what the company cares a lot about, the election process is very peculiar and very specific. First of all you take 220 candidates and out of them you find and select 50 persons. And out of them you choose 4 candidates for the job of a programmer. And out of 4 candidates you hire just one person.

- *As the company works in 6 countries, how is co-ordination achieved between the national units?*

No programming job is done outside of Ukraine. So, only intermediary processes are dealt with by the others. Mostly it is a financial and cost effectiveness management. The most difficult sites to manage are Russia and Ukraine, because these are the locations where software is produced. So, in the other countries there is just sale of the products but in Russia and Ukraine the whole process of producing software is done. That requires strict technological discipline.

- Then about the company. You have specialized products. What about the customers, are there any more important types of the customers?

Most of the products of the company are based on linguistic technologies. The first product is the electronic dictionary, a dictionary which can run in any kind of environment or units. The second product is the optical scanning software program and system text recognition program. The dictionaries are mostly home-based and system text recognition and scanning programs can be either home-based or corporate ones. For instance, the corporate kind is a system of collecting text forms. The second kind is objective program software for the processing of the results of the unified state exams for school. So, the programs of the company can process hundreds of thousands of forms which are filled out in schools, offices, and in state departments. Banks are also possible [customers] and not only in Russia but also in the USA, Germany and maybe in Finland also. The company sells its products directly.

- What about the competition? Who are your main competitors in the field?

There is one competitor, an American company. Our company is advancing and putting pressure on the market. So, this is not the case only in Russia but also in Europe, in Asia, and other parts of the world.

- Now, a little bit more about managers in general... if you had to define what is a good manager in Russia? What does it take to make a good manager?

The same things as in any other country – confidence and honesty; confidence can be described broadly as an ability to study all the time, learning from colleagues in other companies. That's why a professional association is organized. Thus, there is a national club of IT-managers of which I am a co-founder. This is a non-commercial organization and all the managers working in IT companies get together in their free time. So, IT companies themselves ...not the only IT companies, but also all retail, cultural... firms too. All the IT directors have the same problems. The main problem is shortage of funds, as always. So, there is no IT director in the field who has enough funding to cover all possible costs. So, what is done is a kind of probability management of the budget and you take money from some areas that are not so important and put the money into some vital strategies, important for the company. The main problem is that the information system should be created for the companies that are quickly changing. These companies also meet the challenges of the market. So, the system of management should be created to meet the needs of the developing companies. The system of management should be arranged to be at the same level as the company itself. But then the company might run faster than the system of management. And that is the problem.

- I notice that there is a close relation along professional lines and inside IT companies. What other social relations are important for business?

So, ours is a special kind of personnel. You need... these are highly motivated information professionals. And it requires a different kind of motivation; it's not only the money, although the money is [important] at the market level. It is good money that the company pays. But it is more important that there is the possibility to communicate with the personnel in the company in a constructive way. Hence the company relies on the matrix kind of management which stipulates that any employee of the company can contact any other employee regardless of his/hers status. Therefore I can talk with anyone in the company, and even an ordinary programmer can come up to me with his problems and I respond to them. We are human and there is a private part of life that may create problems and get integrated into the production. Therefore the manager must take care of that. If a programmer comes to the manager and talks about his personal problems, the manager will take care of them as far as he can. Help him to be more productive. The manager should build up a system of priorities for himself. First, what to do, with whom to do it, and under what conditions it should be done, and what should be the payment, the funds for the job. And probably most employees of the company have the same set of priorities.

- What about the future? Are there long-term development strategies in the company or the plans?

Yes there are; the board of directors has built the strategy and this strategy – long-term strategy - must receive the endorsement of the shareholders of the company. He is responsible for the information of the company so that the company should not have any shortage of information in the future either. And also it should be remembered that this department of the company does not make profit and therefore the number of people in the department should not exceed the number of the people who are directing and producing commercial products.

- Now the final question is what comes in the future? Do you see some special line of products that will be the strong points of the company in the future, and what are the main problems?

Now we are in an open society and from that viewpoint the prospects of the company are great. There are more and more people who need these products, the linguistically oriented software. But the main problem that arises here is that it is increasingly difficult to find people with the necessary skills. The quality of education is low in Russia and in many other countries too. There is also the problem of the generation gap; there is a big difference between generations with respect to skill levels. This is also true for Germany and this is also true for Russia. In China the starting point is too low.

14. Killey, Bulgarian Cable TV Entrepreneur from Tanzania[27]

Veliki Preslav, Bulgaria
July-September 2004
Interviewers: Boyan Tzonev, Peter Aladzhov, and Todor Kolev

Foreword

Let us assume that cable TV is a *game*, and that, as in every game, there are players (cable TV operators, public regulatory bodies), rules of the game (laws and licensing regimes), an audience (cable TV clients), tools, technologies, and strategies that the players follow. So how did that stage of the game emerge in Bulgaria in the 1990s, and how was the game played at that stage?

Short Outline of the Development of Cable TV in Bulgaria

After the dismantling of the totalitarian regime in the country, the social and economic space for new ventures appeared. In the mid-1990s dozens and, later, hundreds of cable TV networks appeared and spread. They first appeared in the big cities, but only a few years later cable TV penetrated into smaller towns, defacing the apartment buildings with their

[27] An essay for the 'Sociology of Entrepreneurship' Summer Practice, 2004, organized for third-year B.A. students in sociology by Ivan Tchalakov, associate professor, University of Plovdiv, Bulgaria.

webs of cables. The new cable TVs illegally broadcasted foreign TV programs and even attempted to produce Bulgarian clones of the popular international film channels. The separate networks even exchanged among themselves their pirate programs; their customers paid charges that, though not very high, provided significant revenue for the cable TV entrepreneurs. During those first years cable TV was indeed a very profitable business, since the entrepreneurs practically had no payments to make for licenses and copyrights.

In the late 1990s the newly established government institutions, such as the Telecommunications Commission and the National Council for Radio and Television, tightened control over the media market. By the late 1990s and the beginning of this century it became increasingly difficult for the cable TV providers to broadcast pirate programs. Gradually, the so-called 'retransmission rights' became one of the key assets the new entrepreneurs had to buy. Many smaller cable TV networks lost a significant part of their clients, as their owners were unable to pay the copyrights for the most popular programs.

Yet this process was slow and inconsistent – those who did not comply with the rules were given a term in which to improve their programs and buy the necessary rights and licences. During the prolonged process of normalization (or rather 'legalization') of the cable TV business, the bigger players strengthened their positions, being able to negotiate larger concessions from the public bodies and copyrights owners (or their representatives). Producing also their own programs, these networks squeezed smaller providers out by attracting their clients and imposing higher charges for retransmission. In a few years many of the small providers were swallowed up.

Killey's Path to the Cable TV Business

Killey, a young entrepreneurially minded foreigner, took part in these processes. He grew up in a well-to-do family in Tanzania, which was able to finance his study abroad. He came to Bulgaria, a country unknown to him, impelled by his desire to study radio and TV technology. In the interview he said: "The country did not matter for me, I was mainly interested in my favourite speciality". In the summer of 1989 he arrived in the Bulgarian city of Varna and enrolled in 'Radio and TV technology' at the local technical university. During his studies he married a Bulgarian girl, a student at the nearby Varna University of Economics. She came from the small town of Veliki Preslav, located about one hundred kilometres west of Varna. As evident from the text below, this event seriously influenced his business decisions.

Killey graduated in 1994 and, due to the harsh economic situation in Bulgaria at that time, he decided to look for a job in the United Kingdom. A few months later he was appointed TV engineer in the London area winning this position in fair competition between candidates: “I began working for CHANNEL 5, owned by Rupert Murdock, while my family remained in Bulgaria. My position was that of a technical expert in building a cable TV network – we built first the studio, the ‘themes’ galleries, transmission lines, etc. I spent three years in UK and came back to Bulgaria because of the strenuous life there and nostalgia for my family. We settled with my wife and the children in her home town of Veliki Preslav”.

During the times of Communism Veliki Preslav was a small but well-developed industrial town with about 25 000 residents. In the late 1990s, however, most of the industrial enterprises collapsed and the town’s population decreased by more than a third. The prolonged economic crises dramatically reduced the incomes of those remaining in the town. When in 1997 Killey came back to his family in Veliki Preslav, there was already a cable TV provider called ‘ROSAT’. It was the only provider in the town, having limited coverage of the central areas and a few hundred clients. The high charges for users made the cable TV services inaccessible for the majority of the population. According to Killey the signal of the ROSAT networks was of low quality due to their outdated equipment. Subscribing for their services, he soon realized that ROSAT were, in addition, very negligent towards their clients.

Having accumulated the relevant expertise in UK, and taking into account the situation on the cable TV market in the town, Killey decided to build his own cable TV network: “I had enough courage with my knowledge, experience and the money I had brought from UK. My work for CHANNEL 5 in London was a great schooling for me. But I needed partners and local support and that is how I turned to my former colleagues from the Technical University in Varna. I also needed employees qualified enough and I hired some people from ROSAT, paying them better salaries. They also provided important information about the town topography, relevant for the building of the cable network, as well as about some of the weaknesses of my competitor. However, I had to teach these people to work in a different way, both from a technical point of view and how to serve our clients - they had to learn to care about clients and to satisfy their needs. I told them this was the only way the clients would stay with us, so my people had to learn how to communicate with 10, 20, 30, 50, and 70-year old clients so that everyone should be satisfied. We cannot provide everything the clients demand, but we can't give them negative answers. If necessary you should cheat a bit, offering something slightly different, always searching for a balance.

When building a cable TV network, people usually start with the city centre where the high paying clients are. It is also cheaper and much easier from a technical point of view. However, I built my network in the opposite way, starting from the periphery – there were more people living there, so that during the first months I concentrated my efforts on that area. Then the demand for our services rocketed – there were people from all over town willing to subscribe. You know, the town is small and the word spread "This is a cable TV that creates no worries!""

Building and Spreading its Own Cable TV Network

Killey's strategy was to make a massive invasion on the cable TV market in the town, aimed at attracting most of the potential clients. He offered lower rates, providing some reductions in the price for retired people and some other groups. To meet the initial rise in demands, he chose a more expensive and difficult technical scheme, which, however, allowed faster spreading of the network and preserving a good-quality signal. Killey designed the technical scheme and its components together with his colleagues and friends from Varna Technical University – some of them already owned or serviced similar cable TV networks in the big city of Varna, others were producing or supplying equipment: "I used my connections with the Technical University. When I bought some equipment, I tested it at the university laboratories so that I was able to select the optimal configuration for my network."

To guarantee the good quality of the signal, Killey bought the latest generation digital equipment and he spared no expense for that – "One such receiver cost USD 680 and we had ten of them. With this money you could build an entire TV station of the older model." He explained to us how he had built his network and gave us a lot of technical details: "The main station is the 'heart' of every cable TV network. Its positioning is determined by the topography of the town. The station consists of satellite antennas that provide the input signal – these are with different diameters depending on the intensity and frequency of the received signal. Then the signal arrives in the receivers, which at the time were both digital and analogue. The digital receivers provide better quality and they gradually replaced the analogue ones. Every receiver is connected to a channel having a converter and amplifier in it. For every single program you need a separate receiver and channel. At the entry point the signal comes with a low frequency of 1-2 db/mv, while at the exit point its level reaches 80db/mv, which is still not enough for cable transmission. Passing through the amplifier, the level increases to 100-106db/mv which is now suitable for transmission. However, the cable (type RG11) attenuates the signal with about 10 db/mv per 100 meters, hence you need another amplifier at every 200-250 meter to bring back the signal to the necessary level of 100-106 db/mv. Then the signal is sent to a distribution box through another type of cable (RG6) whose attenuation is 15-18 db/mv per 100 meters. The box consists of tap and splitter, with attenuation elements that reduce the signal level to 60 db/mv - the standard for a TV set. In building this network, the key technological solution was to put 'smart' amplifiers between every two simple ones, so that the former regulated the work of the other two amplifiers and kept the entire network in harmony. This configuration guarantees the high quality of the signal to the clients."

Managing the Cable TV Business

The management of the new business was simple enough – Killey and his wife shared it. He assumed the technical management and development of the network, while his wife was responsible for the finances. Hence, the main decisions were made within the family, which controlled all key resources. His wife headed the "Finances and Administration" Department, while the rest of the personnel was organized into several other departments – "Station" Department dealing with main station, "Technicians" Department serving the clients, "Maintenance" Department responsible for repairing damages and breakdowns in the network. Last was the "Studio" Department, the aim of which was to design and produce their own TV programs for transmission in the network and possibly for sale to other cable TV providers.

'Control' is the key term describing how Killey managed to keep in order the expanding business. To maintain control, he kept in touch with his clients, both meeting them personally and opening a 'hot' telephone line. He was able constantly to monitor the system and to take necessary measures in case of emergency, to correct the work of the technicians, etc. In this process his 'smart' amplifiers helped him a lot, compensating for the errors and providing immediate response when deviations went beyond a tolerable limit. He decided also to use a *black* cable in his network, which made it easily distinguishable from the network of his competitor and facilitated keeping its integrity. Killey soon won a place for himself as the dominant cable TV provider in the town. His business entered a period of stability. The steady flow of money made him think of expanding the business.

He decided to establish his own TV channel with home produced programs, i.e. from being a simple distributor of TV programs, to become a producer of such programs. He invested a significant amount of money in the new venture, buying studio equipment, hiring additional personnel, buying copyrights for popular movies, etc. In 1999 he launched his own TV program, which existed for about a year – it soon became clear that the program was not paying and he was losing money. In the interview he said he did not evaluate correctly the potential market of the new program; that there were no significant revenues from advertisement; that the program staff was not good enough (there were few people in the town qualified for TV programming), etc.

The Former Monopolist Strikes Back

Imposing his company as the main provider on the local cable TV market, Killey broke the monopoly of the ROSAT cable TV network and put it in a situation unknown before – they had to compete. They soon began to lose clients because of the better technical quality and lower prices Killey offered. Being unable to respond in the same way, ROSAT owners turned to their 'social capital'. Being in close relationships with local political and administrative circles, they pushed the local police to confiscate key components of the Killey network under the pretext that he had broken certain rules of the local administration. For several months some expensive pieces of his equipment were kept at the local police station for the purposes of the investigation.

To solve the problem Killey turned to the regional authorities, but in vain. Then he approached the local Member of Bulgarian Parliament, but the latter did not intervene either. Later he was told the MP was also connected with the ROSAT owners. Finally Killey turned to the media and wrote a letter to the Minister of the Interior, describing to him the arbitrary acts of the minister's subordinates. This time he got a positive response and, after the personal intervention of the Minister, the problem was solved favourably for Killey.

However, the hostile action of the ROSAT owners continued. Now they attacked him by pushing some providers of popular TV programs to stop their transmission on Killey's network. At the time one of the popular channels was SCAT TV, transmitting from the city of Burgas. Being schoolmates and close friends with the SCAT TV owner, the ROSAT boss convinced him to sell the rights for retransmission exclusively to their network. Killey travelled to Sofia and submitted a complaint with the Telecommunications Commission, but they did not intervene. However, the Ministry of Transport and Telecommunication said this agreement violated the rules, and this allowed Killey to continue retransmission of SCAT TV. Next year he finally reached an agreement with SCAT TV.

It was Killey's courage and implacability that won him his victory over the illegal action of ROSAT against his business. We should keep in mind, however, that these events happened during the Democratic Union Government (1997-2001), the anti-communist political party which carried out the privatization in Bulgaria and took decisive steps to integrate the country into the European Union. Respect for the law and support for entrepreneurs was one of the Government's officially declared goals, and by making his case public Killey forced the central Government agencies to intervene.

The U-turn of the Game. Killey Selling his Business

During the first years of his cable TV business, Killey, similarly to other entrepreneurs in the sector, worked under the conditions of an unregulated market, where copyrights and other forms of intellectual property, fiscal duties, etc., were barely respected. This allowed an excessively high rate of return for all cable TV providers. In the beginning of this century, however, the relaxed fiscal situation in the sector changed. The Government initiated the process of licensing, which was obligatory for all cable TV providers, and the regulatory bodies mentioned above (Telecommunications Commission, National Council for Radio and Television, Electronic Media Council) began to closely monitor the business of providers. Killey also applied for a license as cable provider in Veliki Preslav. Unlike many of his fellow entrepreneurs, he managed to pay the required high charge and get a licence. Those who were unable to pay the charge or did not meet the requirements were swallowed up by the bigger cable TV providers. The analysts called this process 'the first mergers and acquisition wave' in the cable TV business in Bulgaria.

The remaining large networks with national or inter-regional coverage imposed new requirements on their smaller competitors – for example, they usually possessed the copyrights for the most attractive TV programs and imposed high charges for the retransmission of these programs by smaller networks. Killey appeared to be in the latter group and saw his operational costs gradually increasing. He soon found his company was working at the margin of profitability: "Most of the televisions channels imposed onerous requirements – for example DIEMA TV said; "If you want to retransmit us, you should also buy the right for retransmitting the channels DIEMA 2 and ALEXANDRA, they all go in a package. But I know that while my clients like DIEMA, they rarely watch the other two programs. So I am obliged to buy something that few of my clients need.

In addition to that, the biggest providers appeared to know practically everything about my business – when I called with a proposal to buy their programs, they said "Yeah, you have 10 000 potential clients in Veliki Preslav, you should pay such and such an amount of money for the retransmission!" They did not ask at all how many clients I had, they set the prices against the potential viewers of the program. And I barely had a choice, because your clients demand these programs. So I was paying more than I got in return. The only way to survive in these conditions was to become a bigger provider, to have a large cable network – when you have a large network with tens of thousands of clients, you are able to negotiate the price."

Killey soon found his company was in a vicious circle – in order to survive he needed to expand his network, which required large investments while at the same time his revenues were shrinking steadily. At one point his balance became negative. The same happened with his competitor – the ROSAT owners sold their business to the Varna-based cable TV giant M-SAT. Ironically, Killey fell into the same trap he had previously set for ROSAT - coming to the cable TV market in the town; M-SAT demonstrated technological supremacy coupled with a richer portfolio of TV channels. M-SAT offered Killey to buy his business. He did not accept the initial proposal, but after a series of negotiations mediated by the local MP, who obviously had personal interest in the deal, he reached an agreement with M-SAT and they bought his company: "There was no other solution since my expenses rocketed while my revenues were going down. Besides, I had almost reached the limits of my expansion and there were fewer new clients. At one point you suddenly realize how small you are and how limited your business is, as if you have reached the peak and see there is nowhere to climb. Most of the entrepreneurs don't like such downturns, yet you have to sense the moment has come when you should free yourself from the stagnating business. This is very important; you have to be able to look for other opportunities, in other areas."

So Killey became a victim of the 'second mergers and acquisition wave' – the cable TV business in Bulgaria also became a world inhabited almost exclusively by big players.

Why was Killey Such an Interesting Case for us?

A foreigner came to Bulgaria in the turbulent time of post-socialist transitions and took part in the establishment of a new, previously unknown market in Bulgaria, the cable TV. This man established his own 'cable TV kingdom' in a town that was once the medieval Bulgarian capital, a provider comprising people and technical artefacts, and managed to rule it for several years. He built his 'kingdom' (in fact a socio-technical network) applying courage, knowledge, skills, and money. But this did not help him to remain on top for long – his own creation, the cable TV network, built according to the highest standards for that time, soon surpassed him and 'freed itself' from his power. It required more investments both in technology and content (TV programs and channels), which he was unable to provide. So the day came when he had to transfer it to others and was pushed out.

Postscript

What next for Killey? The entrepreneurial spirit is still alive in him. Today, more than two years after he sold his company, he is venturing in new fields – he is creating a small TV network in Veliki Preslav's neighbouring villages, spreading his cables. He spends more time with his family and leads a calmer life. At least for the time being…

Surviving Firms

The entrepreneurs in this group are former managers of larger socialist industrial enterprises and new entrepreneurs, who exploit the business opportunities that they were given or that they seized during or after privatisation. Common for them has been a gradual decline of their businesses, due to political (losing the eastern market) or technical reasons. The declining business means shrinking revenues, inability to renew technology or develop new and competitive products for export. Therefore for them cost-efficiency is the key issue: they produce cheap products and utilize low-skilled labour and do not seek new markets for their products or try to improve their products, not to mention innovating new ones. The managerial strategy of the third group is the most traditional patriarchal ways of control without any care: the entrepreneurs try to keep their work force loyal with threats; low wages, no or very weak security of employment and constant threatening of replacing current labour with new.

15. The *A- Service* Company

Interview with the owner and executive director of the forklift truck company.
December 20, 2005.
Interviewer: Desislava Boykova.
Selection of the firms, questionnaire design, and supervision by Ivan Tchalakov under Project “Policy Lacunas in Promoting Innovative SME in Bulgaria”, Centre for Policy Studies – CEU, Budapest, Hungary

A Short Introductory Note

The *A- Service* Company produces and repairs diesel and electric forklift trucks. It is located in Plovdiv region, one of the centers of forklift truck industry in Bulgaria. This industry was one of the country’s specializations in the framework of the former COMECOM, and was managed by the socialist industrial combine BALKANCAR. One of its main plants was Record Machine Works in Plovdiv, which produced tens of thousands of diesel trucks annually for export to COMECOM countries and other. A few years after 1989 the BALKANCAR combine collapsed and it no longer exists. The former giant factories that employed thousands of workers have been closed down. Yet during the 1990s many engineers, managers, and other specialists in the field of forklift trucks industry established their own companies and resumed production and services in the field, even though on a much smaller scale.

The interview presents one of these companies. The interviewed owner, who is also its manager, was sincerely astonished by the topic of our study – the problems of innovative firms, especially those in the sector of machine-building. He said “*I do not see future of this sector in Bulgaria, because no one is interested in it and it is at the bottom of public priorities.*” He personally was not directly involved in the BALKANCAR combine, but after establishing the firm in 1990, he hired some of its former employees, especially blue-collar workers. At the time of the interview, there were about 130 people working in the firm.

***

- You said your company deals mostly with delivery of spare parts, forklifts and warehouse equipment. You also represent in Bulgaria the Japanese company TCM and some other companies. Do you produce your own forklift trucks?

Yes, we do.

- Do you have employees coming from the former BALKANCAR combine and its plants?

We do have such people, mostly machinists and fitters, but very few design and R&D engineers. As yet we don't really need them, since our machines are almost entirely based on the *RECORD 2* model forklift truck, produced for more than 20 years at the Record Plant in Plovdiv. During this period the machine was tested thoroughly and any bugs (design and technical imperfections) were eliminated.

- Which means that you are not designing new models?

That's right. I believe it is a long process to design, develop, produce, and debug a new machine – it takes so long that today it is not necessary, given our decades-long experience accumulated in the former BALKANCAR. My desire is to produce a machine that is tested, cleared of all construction problems, and accessible in terms of price, as cheap as possible.

- How was your company established?

We started by hiring a small workshop in the village of Kaloyanovo near Plovdiv. Now, after more than 15 years of hard work, we are building our own industrial facilities. We bought more than 2 hectares of land in Plovdiv's new industrial zone near the highway at the exit to Sofia. We will put there all out activities – offices, show-room, 2000-square-meters depot for spare parts, and production facilities of the same size. A few years after we established our Kaloyanovo base, we rented another warehouse from the factory "Success", owned by the Union of Blind People in Bulgaria.

- Who were your first customers?

We started with recycling BALKANCAR machines sold previously to their clients. We repaired and upgraded these machines upon demand or we sold them. When recycled, the forklift trucks are very cheap yet still very reliable machines. Our first customers were from Turkey, then from

Russia and the countries of the former Soviet Union. We also supplied spare parts there, as well as to countries like Romania, Czech Republic, and Slovakia. Even today all the customers are from the countries where BALKANCAR previously sold its machines – we realize about 90% of our turnover there, and only 10% in Bulgaria.

- *How has your company developed during these years? What were its main stages of development – in term of technology, human development, etc.?*

It is difficult to distinguish any clear-cut periods. Our development was slow, step by step – one customer, then another, later a third, fourth, etc. It was a constant struggle with suppliers of spare parts, in order to keep the prices as low as possible – we sell with very low margins, aiming at bigger turnover rather than big profit from a single sale. Because the higher our turnover, the lower the prices we could obtain from the suppliers. So it was an evolutionary development, without 'big jumps' – we slowly increased the number of employees, hired new offices, etc. During all those years our policy was to produce good-quality trucks, to guarantee the quality of these products, and if there were any problems, to help customers solve them. Now these customers are seeking our support and services by themselves, they know they can count on us. This is the result of our straightforward approach and years of working hard for them. In our business the honest and correct approach to customers is crucial – when they have a problem, you go and solve it! We try to keep 99% of the work for solving the problems within the company rather than make customers look for other companies... Although rarely, there are customers whose pretensions are so difficult to meet, that I prefer they had never approach us. But we have an equal approach to all of them.

- *Does it mean you have been trying to provide full service to your customers since the very beginning?*

Yes. The novelty is that one year ago we launched the production of a new machine, a diesel forklift truck – an entirely new machine, 100% newly completed. However, it is based on the *"RECORD 2"* truck I mentioned in the beginning – the good old thoroughly tested machine. Another new point is that our company became regional representative of the Japanese company TCM – maybe one of the best forklift truck producers in the world. They made the first such truck in the world in 1905! The quality of their machines is perfect, very reliable machines. TCM trucks are much more expensive than Bulgarian trucks, but they are suitable for companies with a high work load, needing machines able to work non-stop in one, two, and even three shifts daily. To the companies with limited resources and which work their trucks for 1-2-3 hours daily, we recommend the cheaper Bulgarian machines, and we provide 1 year or 18 months guarantee.

- What kind of investment did you make in this new machine, in recycling the old trucks, etc.?

Well, we are buying new equipment to produce some details and spare parts. The main reason is to be able to control its quality. Because in the beginning we had some problems with the quality of spare parts supplied by other companies – some of the Bulgarian factories deteriorated the quality of their products. This creates problems for our customers, and spoils the quality of trucks we are producing. One example is the *WAMO* diesel engines plant in Varna – they have made no improvement of their *D 3900* diesel engines during the last 15 years. And they are not servicing these engines at all – neither in Bulgaria, not abroad. So when a customer gets a truck from us, he is not interested whose is the engine, gearbox, etc. He rightly says: "You sold me this truck, and you have to solve my problems!" So during the years it got difficult for us to use Bulgarian-produced parts in our products. This is a sad fact, because I do like to sell Bulgarian machines, machines produced here – sometimes we sell these machines almost at cost price, hoping in one or two years to be able to sell the same customer spare parts, etc. The life of Bulgarian trucks is very long, and they are easy to repair. They are able to work for 20 and more years, then you recycle these machines and they continue to work… It is practically an 'eternal' machine; you only need to maintain its engine.

- So when you sell at cost price, this is a kind of investment in the future?

You could say that. The profit comes not from the trucks sold, but later, from servicing these trucks, and from spare parts.

As far as the investments are concerned, we also buy new computers, new computer-guided machine tools, so as to be able to produce some details and to supply the customers with our own spare parts – steering axles, power trains, as well as any standard items produced in large series and sold in large quantities. By producing them in-house we reduce the cost price of these items and we win against our competitors. There are some funny competitors – two people in a room with a fax machine, sending price-lists in all directions. If you ask them for a specification, they need a month… This spoils the market, but that's the real situation.

Otherwise it is not possible to introduce new technologies in truck recycling – we have limited resources, and no help comes from anywhere… the state gives no preferences to us. Instead, the state is choking companies like ours with its taxation policy. The tax offices regularly issue various indictments; we contest them in court and we usually win. The tax officer smiles at me – "While you are suing us, for one year this money will remain in our hands!" he says… Their impertinence is boundless! At the same time I am investing in the infrastructure of our new industrial facility, paying for drains, telephone and electricity lines with our own money. I am creating new jobs, but the result is silly indictments by the state agencies, which wastes our time and money. The Bulgarian state is the biggest oppressor of private firms like ours.

- *So you don't see any hope?*

No hope. All [government institutions] are oppressors: they see you are doing something and say –"Yes, there is money to be gotten here!" And they come asking for money. One of the worst manners of doing it is VAT. We pay VAT for all our local supplies, but when we have to recuperate the VAT we paid, the tax office usually refuses it – they say someone in the chain did something wrong. But why should I pay for someone else's faults? Instead of punishing the violators of VAT, the state punishes the accurate companies… Because they are unable or don't want to catch them. For me this is pornography [shamelessness]! The only bright thing in this picture is that there are other people like me who also seek to develop, to build and create instead of to destroy. But we pay the price…

- *Could you summarize the main difficulties you are faced with?*

Machine-building is a difficult, ungrateful branch, also difficult financially. You need warehouses, rents, transportation; you need a lot of additional staff, which in turns means salaries, social security, etc. I am used to it by now, but if a newcomer comes and faces all these problems, he will be surprised. To get your money from the customers is also difficult, because they usually do not pay in advance. Rather we first supply them our goods and services, and then we wait for the money to come. The customers are used to this type of business relationships – partly due to the competition between us, suppliers.

Finally, there is not sufficiently qualified personnel – I am looking to hire machinists, offering as much as 400 Euro salary [well above the average for the Plovdiv region – I.Tch.], but there are no people. They don't want to work. We are also trying to hire dyers – no candidates…

- *What is the reason?*

The Bulgarians are lazy. This is definitely true! But the worst thing is that most of the people have no impulse for a better life – they tacitly agree to live with 1.5 Euro a day and do nothing. Just bleating all day long for a piece of bread, a worm's life…

- *Officially there is still quite high unemployment here…*

The unemployed in their majority are lazy people. Now in Bulgaria there is an abundance of workplaces. A few months ago I met an unemployed man in the street; he was asking for 30 cents for bread. I told him: "Come to my company, there is work for you in the depot, 5 euro per day as a non-qualified worker". "I will come", he said, and I am still waiting… He prefers begging instead of regular work – a young, healthy man! I have no words about such cases. The people in the villages around are the same – they still live with their parents, waiting to slaughter the pig for meat on Christmas…. That is their life, miserable people.

- *You think the reason is the laziness rather than lack of education and professional skills?*

Certainly! Everyone could be qualified provided he is motivated. He will come to work and with time… When I started this company, I would take apart on Saturdays and Sundays, I would disassemble the trucks myself, then I would clean the parts with a water gun. When the mechanics came on Monday to start repairing, everything was ready for them, no time was wasted. When they reassembled the truck, we cleaned it again and painted it. In establishing this company, I haven't been manager all my life! I also personally visited the customers' plants and factories with my car and trailer hitched to it… So if you have the wish, you will learn what to do, you will qualify yourself. It is not so complicated; you only need to wish it. In one year you can pass through all the stages and you will become a mechanic - it is so simple!

- *Do your people stay in the company? Do they leave abroad or go to your competitors?*

I have not seen anyone leaving. Some moved to other professions inside the firm. But in general the people we started with some 10-15 years ago, they are still here. I fired a few thieves, but maybe 99% of the people remain. They get their salaries regularly on the 5th day of the month, and on the 20th day they receive advance payment. This is our law – not a single man should leave because his salary was not paid or something in his contract not fulfilled. No such people.

- *As far as I understand, you prefer to hire unskilled people, whom you later train in the company, to develop them as they work inside the company?*

It is always better to hire a specialist. There are some in the company – I hired them with a high salary. But when there are no such specialists, you have to be ready to train the less qualified. It is difficult to find well-trained professional, but it is more difficult to train a new one, because most of the less qualified are lazy.

- *What have been your main achievements during these years?*

The increased number of our customers is an achievement. We became representatives for Bulgaria of several foreign firms, supplying some strategic spare parts – *Magneton* starters, *Mefin* fuel pumps and nozzles, gearbox discs from the German company *Helbeger*, a Turkish firm producing crankshafts, etc. We also represent a German truck equipment company that has a plant in Turkey. Above all is that we are representatives of the Japanese company TCM, as I mentioned above.

Unfortunately, most of our customers prefer foreign equipment. The reason is that they have built good factories and warehouses – new, clean, spacious premises. There` you supply a Bulgarian machine. In a few months it is leaking oil, spilling it all around, and the owner throws it out and asks for a Western one at any price. And we have to respond to these demands. That is why we now sell these Japanese trucks.

Yet I instructed my traders whenever possible to sell Bulgarian machines, and not the Japanese. Because when you sell the latter, you have some profit, but it ends at that – it is reliable and does not require any maintenance, no repairs, so there is no more business in it.

- *This means the quality of Bulgarian forklift trucks is much lower?*

Yes, but it correspond to the price, which is much lower than the Japanese.

- That is why Bulgarian trucks are still produced, because of the lower price?

Yes, plus the specific design of our machines – simplicity of maintenance, cheap service and repair…. Our trucks are, as the Russians say, 'idiot-resistant' (durakoustoichiv'ie). Our trucks are made for the simple-minded drivers, a bit stupid and irresponsible. While Western trucks are packed with electronics, they require special servicing, computer testing, etc. However, our machines have their [market] niche too.

- Do you have partners that contributed to the development of the company – suppliers, customers, financial institutions, R&D organisations, etc.?

I can mention a number of people and plants in Bulgaria that have been our good partners for many years – *Balkan* Lovetch, *Dynamic* Sofia, *Garant* Byala Slatina, *Hydraulica* Yambol, *Ruen* Assenovgrad, *Iska* Sofia, *Budeshtnost* Chirpan, *Kaproni* Kazanluk, etc. Our business implies many suppliers and many customers. When both sides are in agreement, that is, paying on time and fulfilling their obligations, the relationships are good. The large majority of our suppliers are very good. And we have about 50 regular customers.

Unlike the industrial partners, there are no financial institutions that helped us when we needed it. The banks here are ready to help when you, in fact, don't need them – they come when they see that your business is doing well, then they offer you money. When you are in trouble, there is no bank to come and say – "we know you have problems, we are ready to help!" Now, with the economic stabilisation, the banks are giving money even to Gipsy families who rummage in the garbage and most of them are totally unemployed. But when my company asks for credit – the bankers set thousands of conditions... It is true there has been some recent development; it is easier now to get credit. It is more important, however, that I always try to put my money where it works most.

Government institutions are the same – in the fifteen years since our establishment no single government institution ever helped us. But when there's a chance for them to take something from us, they are ready. So we have no help from the banks, or from the public institutions.

We have much better relationships with foreign industrial firms – those from Lithuania and Latvia are very honest; the Czech, Slovakian, Hungarian companies too. We also work well with Romanian forms. We have problems only with some Russian firms.

- *What about research organisations?*

There are no such relationships. As I said, at this stage we do not need them.

- *Are there any forms of collaboration between forklift trucks companies in the Plovdiv region and in the country as a whole?*

Practically not – it is not possible at this stage, because some companies in the branch aren't upright; I mean their owners and managers. You sit down with someone, reach an agreement about something, but then he covertly goes and does something very different! How can you team up with such people?

We really have very good collaboration with *Record* Machine Works in Plovdiv, although now, after the privatization, it is a much smaller plant [instead of twenty and more thousands trucks annually, they now produce a few hundred – I.Tch.]. We are their customers, and they are ours - a real partnership. "V&R" Ltd. is another good partner. But most of the remaining companies in the branch are. Recently there have been attempts at teaming up among some forklift truck producing companies, but it is still at the stage of 'wishing', a little dummy. We had two meetings lately where we discussed the possibilities to apply for EU money in support of machine-building. Maybe this was the main reason to establish the association, to take some public money.

- *In what areas in your branch is competition strongest?*

We don't compete for the market shares – each company has its share, bigger or smaller. All are producing various kinds of machines that differ mostly in their design. I don't think there is serious competition as far as forklift trucks are concerned. However, we have serious competition on the spare parts market. I like competition – it keeps you awake and fit, and helps you stay down to earth - because when megalomania comes in, that is the beginning of ruin.

The competition in our branch, however, is of the Bulgarian type. It helps only the able, and destroys the unable, and who can't face it. Some companies such as *R.*, *A. 11* and some others are not upright – they produce absolutely poor-quality machines, using recycled parts, and they sell these machines as brand new…. Sometimes they manage to find customers willing to pay for such machines higher than the price of a new truck, uninformed customers with little experience. But they soon realize they were cheated, so they fight their supplier, go to court, etc. That is why

I call this home-type competition a 'Bulgarian' one. With time, the customers learn which companies are reliable and which are not. You know, time is the best judge if a company is good or bad. When the sales go down, it is clear enough where such a company is going…

- *Where do you sell your products and services?*

As for forklift trucks – equal shares in Bulgaria and abroad. Spare parts – 90% abroad and 10% in Bulgaria. Working abroad has it particularities – you collect specifications, you load the cargo truck and it leaves. Then you wait for the payment to come – sometimes you wait quite long, 2-3-4 months, even one year. While in Bulgaria the clients come to our shops, they choose, and pay. It is difficult to work abroad, but the turnover is much bigger.

- *Now we are going to enter the EU – how does this influence your business?*

We need to pass ISO standardization – it is not obligatory for everyone, but still, standardization improves your organisation of work, increases your prestige, as well as the quality of your products. We are doing this, although it costs money.

- *What has ultimately been most important for you?*

I think I told you the most important stuff. It bothers me that our state is confused at its very core. You know the proverb "It is one thing to eat the halva [a kind of sweets], and another to lick the paper it was wrapped in". I mean few people control most of the resources, the rest have to struggle for what amounts to almost nothing… The Government does not support and encourage real business, those who create something, who provide employment, etc. It seems to me that the best strategy for this country is to do nothing… On the other hand, however, life passes and you have to leave something behind you after you are gone... That is why I am in the business. But I don't see changes, because the governing people from the changing governments are practically the same – they try to rob those who work hard and waste money on lazy and thieving people, on the parasites that live better than the hard-working ones.

It's quite simple: a man has to create something by himself – a machine of one's own, a small state of one's own, so to say. I don't mean 'state', but some [organizational] unit, to work in it and establish good rules, so the people there will be responsible, work well and be rewarded for this. In my life I have asked help from no one – neither from parties, nor from people. That is why I don't care which party is in power. All I need is peace, no wars, and to be able to work. Nothing beyond that is interesting for me – neither banks, nor states, or any other nonsense.

- *Have there been any political interventions in your business?*

Not in my business. Although I have heard colleagues complain that some people came asking money for some political parties. In the time of Ivan Kostov's government [*Union of Democratic Forces* anti-communist government (!) which ruled between 1997 and 2001 – I.Tch.] there were quite a few attempts at interference in business – especially if some company was making big money, the economic police would come, or by using some other tools, they asked for their share.

- *How do you see the future of your company?*

I see it going up and ahead – this is my nature as a person. If there is something wrong, I can't sleep until I fix it: correct something, pay money I owe, find a good specialist I need, invest something… The company can't stand in the same place, it has to develop – a company either develops or declines, there is no third way. And we keep developing, this is our destiny.

What I want to do? – To start production of electric trucks, to expand the production of diesel trucks. And most of all – to manage one day to make the Japanese come here and invest their money in a new forklift truck plant. This will be great – to produce Japanese machines for Europe and Russia. That is my dream. But it is too early for that, and maybe too beautiful to think seriously about it now.

The electrical forklift truck is a closer goal – we already produce some electric trucks based on the old BALKANCAR models, designed in the *6th September* Plant in Sofia, which no longer exists. And we recycled a lot more. The Bulgarian electric forklift trucks beat all competitors on the world market in terms of price, having at the same time pretty good quality. So we too consider expanding production. This is a more promising business than the diesel trucks. We have about 50 customers for electric trucks spare parts, and they are potential customers for new machines.

- *But then why did you say in the beginning of the interview you saw no future for forklift trucks?*

Well, for me the truck business is part of a large business, it goes together with selling entire warehouses, Japanese trucks, etc. In this context one day I could also sell specialized cars. There is always room for growth.

- So you are not afraid to change or modify your portfolio?

Absolutely not – we will sell and produce trucks and spare parts until it is necessary, until there is demand. But if the big international consortiums push us out – Japanese, Chinese, etc, because they work with billions of dollars - we would have to change business! We are a 'small fighting unit' and we can't perform miracles. If they decide, they can afford to sell one year on our market without profit and even below their cost price. What shall we do then? The big fish always eat the smaller ones, if they like[28].

- Why are they still not here?

A: Simply because this is a funny market here – 200-300 trucks annually. The big markets are in the biggest countries…

16. J-sewing S/A

Interview with the director of J-sewing A/S
Harju county, northern Estonia
Date: September 8, 1999
Interviewer: Jouko Nikula
Interpreter: Helvi Pöder

- Let us start with your training and work history

O.K, my training is from University of Tartu and I studied to be a lawyer. I used to be a lawyer in that large state construction company EMV, which built this factory. Only men were working in production, there were no jobs for women. Then we had a joint project with Baltika (a tailoring firm in Estonia). And since I had prepared all the legal documents, the managing director of Baltika asked me whether I would like to become a manager in this sewing company. I told him that I knew as much about sewing as I did about Chinese. My condition was that they would provide me with a technician who had knowledge about textiles. So in the beginning we had 30 workers, now there are 50.

[28] Yet by 2012 the *A. Service* company is still working and on the market.

- *In this same place?*

Yes, here.

- *How long have you been operating?*

We started in 1991: for 5,5 years we were a subsidiary to Baltika Company, but now we are independent. For more than 3 years now.

- *Can you tell me how this director chose you to be manager in this firm?*

It happened that there was a competition and then the owners, the construction firm, Baltika and some private persons, they liked me. And that's how it was decided.

- *Who are the owners of this company now?*

There are two owners now, me and my wife.

- *What are your main products?*

Trousers and skirts. Both for men and women, and for children too.

- *Is your production mainly meant for domestic markets or do you export some of it?*

5 % of our production is for domestic markets, the rest is exported. The Estonian customer is Ivo Nikkolo, he is a designer and he takes some 5-7 %, the rest is subcontracting for Swedish and Finnish companies.

- *What are those Finnish companies you work for?*

There are PTA-Group, Terinit, Turku Tailor and Punkamo Oy, a company which produces suits for ladies. PTA-Group is the largest company for us; about 35 % of our capacity goes to them.

- *Let's go back to the year 1991, when you came here. You were a paid manager, but you didn't own any shares then, did you?*

Yes, I did own some shares, after that I bought shares both from the construction company EMV and Baltika.

- *Did you pay with a loan or in some other way?*

I paid them gradually, in smaller instalments.

- And how many owners were there besides Baltika?

Three private persons and EMV.

- How has this branch developed during the past years, has competition become tougher or has it remained as it already was in 1991?

Sure there is competition, but on the other hand, trousers and trouser for suits are not being made so widely anymore. There is Baltika, and another company in Haapsalu, and in Viljandi there is a subsidiary of Baltika. It was sold to Turku Tailor (a Finnish company). So there are producers and there is competition, but not too tough.

- How has your production profile changed – have you expanded the assortment or changed from one product to another?

The models change and now there is a tendency for women's trousers to be ordered in large quantities. We have a new customer who orders a lot from us. So, the product is the same, only the models change. In the end of 1991 we bought machinery and other necessary things from a small Swedish factory that had gone bankrupt. Or, as a matter of fact, the Baltika company bought it and we bought it from Baltika.

- You were able to get the necessary machinery and equipment at a good price at that time, were you?

Yes, especially if you compare it with nowadays. A bankrupt company is not very expensive. When we started, there was a company in Finland originated from Sweden and with the name Lapidus. Then the owner of the firm died and later it went bankrupt. We got some currency and we changed it into roubles, which had quite a good exchange rate at that time. In general, if you have only one customer, it might come about that something happens to the customer and then you are in deep trouble. But luckily we already had 5-6 customers by that time and plans were made according to season – depending on whether it was the spring or winter season.

- Have you made additional purchases since you bought that first machinery from that bankrupt company?

Yes, we have, for example, an automatic sewing device for making pockets and something else, but our running capital is just not enough. That is because we recently bought another building for production and it was a very expensive building and now we are paying it, month by month, about 2-3 months still remain. But it takes all our free capital, but on the other hand, we had to do it, because if you work in rented premises, it means that you are just throwing your money away.

- Let me ask you about the production process. Is the designing done in the customer company, and they send you the patterns (models), and you then cut according to patterns?

The patterns come here and we cut the clothes: each lady has her part in the process; nobody makes it from start to final product.

- How about the labour, do you get your workers from this area or do they come from farther away?

10 persons of our staff come here every day from Tallinn, from Arukylä – 5, and also 5 from Harju municipality, and the rest are local – approximately 40 % of the total. After the local kolkhoz was closed down all the women came here and declared that they could sew, "take us for work". But it is one thing to sew at home and another to sew here; we have electronic sewing machines and other high tech. A lot of women were here to be tested how they would manage – we have a test period of 4 months, we see quite soon who is able to sew and who is not.

- How stable is your staff – has the turnover been reasonable enough?

At the moment only some 2-3 % of the labour changes annually. That is not much, I would say.

- What are their age categories; are your employees mainly older ladies or young ones too?

There are both young and old, there is even one 60-year-old. It is the case in clothing industry that when your employees are over 30 and have two children, these are the most stable workers. Young people come and rather soon they take maternity leave. For a sewer it is not a big problem, but if you are some specialist, a technician for example, within 3 years you will lose your professional skills. The pace of development is so high.

- What occupational groups do you have in this firm?

There is a technician, supervisor, on the upper floor, where the sewing is done, there we have two supervisors, and downstairs, where we cut and finalize the product, and there we have one supervisor. Then we naturally have a mechanic and a driver. My wife is the production manager.

- How about marketing and customer relations?

Those matters are my responsibility – I look for new customers and our accountant does the same.

- What kind of plans do you have for future development?

We won't expand, because now we are of optimal size – some 3-4 years ago we had a large series, about 3 000 – 4 000 was one big order, but now orders are about 500-1000 and that is also considered a big order. Models are changing and the customers are looking for firms that can produce just-in-time. If it is a large series, then it is either Klement or Baltika, no others, especially not small firms, like ours.

- What is your assessment of the situation of textile industries here in Estonia? Are there too many firms and what are the market prospects?

If we talk about textiles in general, then everything comes from Europe, in Estonia the Kreenholm factory produces some textiles, but they are not of very high quality. You get material for making pockets. I cannot say whether there are too many firms or too few, but firms like ours, small ones, we call "cellar firms", there were huge numbers of them in Estonia right after Independence. Those included entrepreneurs who came from Finland and who paid black wages, in envelopes, without taxes. Also, a couple of ladies left us and went to Tallinn to earn more, but soon they came back. Those entrepreneurs told them "you will be paid well", then the ladies worked for a whole week, including Saturdays and Sundays, then there comes a break. The break may last two weeks or even a month, and the ladies sit at home, waiting for the next job. But a person wants to work every day. Nowadays the number of such entrepreneurs has decreased somewhat. Such entrepreneurs came both from Germany and from Finland and they mainly produced sports clothes, cheap and of low quality. Our customers and partners are well-known firms with a good reputation.

- So, stable and serious firms are now becoming a majority and those who seek quick profits are leaving the market?

Yes, there are fewer and fewer of them.

- *What kind of system of work agreements do you have – concerning wages and work hours and other things?*

We have had work contracts with every employee for the past 4-5 years now.

- *Is there a trade union in the company?*

No, there is no trade-union here! That is something we do not need here. It is, how should I say, those unions, they take us back to socialism. I know that in Finland and in Sweden there are unions and that is a big problem for owners. For the time being we do not have them. In the past I was in the trade union, I was even chairman of one union, so I know what it is, but that was in Soviet times.

At the moment, as far as I know, there are no unions in any textile firms. Obviously there is a worker's representative, based on law, in those firms that have more than 50 employees. For example, in Baltika they have a workers' representative and they make a collective agreement, but not in small companies. Each person sees things from his/her own perspective. Naturally, an employee wants higher wages and that one should not work so much, and our social policy is such that if you have 1-2 small children and you stay at home with one child for 10 days, you get 100 % compensation, and then you stay with another child and you get full compensation for the whole month. But nobody wants such an employee. With us, luckily, there are no such persons who are sick a lot, usually they are not sick, but the children are. In our firm the sickness rate is not high, because people need to earn money and those who are satisfied with 80 % compensation, we have also some, but there is this one group of people who use this social policy. Currently the social policy and sickness insurance affects these things. Because the doctor gets something from each visit and each paper he writes, he can claim them from this sickness insurance. Doctors like to grant sickness leave for flu, for example. At the Klement factory there was the case when the flu epidemic was circulating, they said on the radio that doctors did not have time to visit each home, but people phoned the doctor and said, hey, I have a fever and I cough, I need sick leave for a week. That was a mass phenomenon there: luckily it was not that bad here. If the normal rate of sickness is around 10 %, at our factory it is 2-3 %.

- Fine. Are there any other specific problems hampering the development of entrepreneurship?

The problem of a producer is that if the customer does not pay the bills on time, he has to collect the payments, but on the other hand the debtor is the one who makes orders for the producer. And the producer does not want to spoil his business relations with his customers, but some customers are always late on their payments. That is one problem. Another problem is high taxation, for example if the worker gets 100 Crowns, I pay 33 Crowns more for social expenses and from those 100 Crowns, and the worker pays 26 % income tax.

- How does the governments' decision to lower corporate taxation influence this problem?

Well, there are no definite answers as to what it means, what those investments are and all that. Here it happened that when the government approved this law, all municipalities, except Tallinn and two other municipalities in Harju County that were richer, got tax exemption for income taxes, if they invested in buildings. But if one bought a machine or equipment, that was not considered to be an investment. One who starts to build something huge here and there, that is..well, politics. If all investments were given tax exemptions, that's fine and clear, but if they start to divide that this is an investment, this isn't, then it's just politics. For example, if I create a new job, it should be considered an investment. We can only hope that this law becomes more concrete and that it says what should be exempted. But that is more of a problem for big enterprises. Small companies try to transfer as much as possible into expenses in order to minimize the support for Toompea (the Estonian government is on Toompea hill in Tallinn).

- But do you think that this decision to lower corporate taxation is a decision in the right direction?

Well, I personally think that the government should completely remove the income tax from private persons, so that he or she gets the whole wage that he or she earns, without taxes. With this salary people go and buy things and it makes the economy develop. But that idea is naturally being opposed. Then people would not hide their wages and other things. I just read in the newspaper that dairies and all other firms are buying, through off-shore companies, boats that cost 15 million Crowns and at the same time they are not able to pay money for the milk they collect from producers. That is ridiculous. But this government is better than the previous one or than those who say that all should be equal, that all should have the same amount of everything. Maybe it is said that the one who does not earn that much, he has all sorts of grants and subventions, well they are not that high, but in any case they say, look, in Finland and in Sweden there are all sorts of supports, grants, and all that, and maybe it is a perfect model of socialism. Where they help those as well who cannot cope by themselves, which is mainly a political matter.

- O.K, thank you. Let us go back to your personal history a bit. When did you graduate and when did you start to work?

I graduated in 1981 and now I have been working for 20 years.

- Of those 20 years you were for 10 years a normal hired worker and from 1990 you became an owner. If you think back on that time, what was easy for you then and what was quite difficult?

Well, it is quite evident that when you were an employed worker in a firm in the time of Socialism, it was a completely different world then. And as a lawyer it was easy to see what was wrong and what should be different. However, I think that if I were a lawyer in some company now, I probably would act differently from how I acted then. At that time I worked in economic enterprises, I did not have any ambitions to go to a prosecutor's office or be a lawyer, because only a minority of law-school graduates could aspire for that position. The directors at that time had this attitude, that I am the Director and others are just subordinates to me. It started from the Party and all organisations around it, but also at that time the lawyer was appreciated according to his ability to defend the interests of the firm. At the moment the situation is the same, just the methods are different. Even though I was not a Party member, I was summoned to the Party committee to explain why things were this way and not the other way. There were such cases now and then. That experience has obviously given me knowledge about management, and I have read books about management theories, and I have participated in some seminars about the matter, but a seminar serves the interests of the organizer more than those of the participants. Naturally I cannot say that about all seminars, but about quite a few, yes. For example they ask to be paid a lot of money, and materials are distributed, there are coffee breaks, but there is no efficiency. The decision to undertake entrepreneurship means also that you must calculate each and every penny, what to do, where to put your money, and how the money circulates. The difference is even bigger than compared with when I was a shareholder and a paid manager. When there were two big companies, who owned the firm, things were so organised that neither of them could get a majority ownership – i.e. majority of votes – that was my goal when I made rules for the company, that the Baltika Company should not be able to impose its will on us. There is an example about that, a factory behind the city of Keila in Harju County, this factory went bankrupt, because Baltika made them do cheap work. We had various contacts and we acquired some orders independently. In that situation they could not pressure us very much. Results were such that we did not make any profits, but we were not making losses either. Naturally, if the other partner wanted to give cheap labour (low-priced orders) and the other owner took a large sum for rent, there was nothing much to ask, and my principle at that time was that it is not my job to earn profits for anybody, just to keep the company floating. Now things have changed. In that regard it is much easier to plan in a family business or as a sole owner, financial strategies and all that, because you yourself are making the decisions, not having 5-6 persons around the table talking nonsense without any results. You are responsible for everything.

Back then there was no profit, no losses, but I made it clear to those owners that if you demand a lot of money as rent and you give us work with low value – cheap mass production of low-quality sports clothing, there is no reason to expect anything from us. Naturally, when a paid manager turns into a real owner, you have to .. as they say, you should understand your workers. In our company the attitude of the workers is, however, that "I don't give a damn how the company is doing, we just work here from 8 am to 4.30 pm." Luckily the firm is not that big, I can talk with everybody individually. Part of the workers are of different nationality, they are used to mostly being given orders and then they understand. In that respect the owner of a small enterprise cannot just sit behind his desk and think up strategies. That you can do at home late in the evening and alone, but here you must take care of five jobs or duties. My wife works in the same company, so that during the holidays, on vacations, at home..we work together. On the other hand it is good that you can trust at least one person. So that if something is done badly, it is very easy to say that my working day has just finished, it is not my responsibility. That's that. This has changed to some extent. Especially the attitude towards work, but being the owner makes you take into account many things in a much broader and deeper way than ever before, ponder and calculate. In the past those things were not your concern, but only the concrete tasks that were set to you.

- Well, that was a good account about your personal changes and challenges. How about your workers, I have been travelling around Estonia and interviewed many entrepreneurs and other people and quite a few have said that there is still this attitudinal problem with workers, that there is this kolkhoz mentality or socialist mentality, attitude towards work. Do you think that this statement is still valid and have you noticed any changes in this regard?

Yes, it has changed. Especially the work habits of Russians have changed – because if you wish to live in this state, then you have to. For example in Tartu there is a sewing company and they do not hire anybody who does not speak Estonian. But in this business it is not so important whether somebody speaks Estonian or not. It is clear that if a person is between 30-40 years and has never spoken a word of Estonian in her/his life, it is a sign of development if he/she greets you in Estonian or starts to understand something. Very many Russians have understood that they can do that work and don't go anywhere else to look for a job. If she has all the time done the same job and is a local resident. Those who are from Tallinn, those workers are all Russians. They come every morning by bus here and go back in the evening by bus. They have monthly bus tickets. It shows that these Russians are starting to integrate into this society. As I already said, the best kind of sewer is 30-40 years old with two children, maybe even divorced. Then she has nobody to rely on and she has to manage by herself. But the youths, they come from school, and when you look at their papers, you realize that they have not been taught anything at the school. And often they do not even want to do this work. So, what sense is there in hiring such persons? Naturally there are different kinds of cases too, for example a 17-year-old girl and she has already been working here 6 years (?!), she is very good at ironing the clothes.

- Then I would like to ask about the wage system, is it based on piece-rate or is it an hourly or monthly wage?

Yes, we do piece-rate, a price for a standard minute. The system comes from the UK and Baltika was the first to apply it in Estonia. Each stage in the work process has a price and we pay accordingly, the one who has a more demanding job will be paid more – he/she has a higher coefficient. Wages vary between 2 000 and 5 000 Crowns (130-300 Euro) per month and the one who gets 2 000 is simply...there are ladies here who cannot do anything complicated and do just simple tasks. They cannot be trusted with anything more demanding and naturally the wage is also lower.

- But still, she has the chance to work and get those 2 000 Crowns, is that not fair enough?

Yes, sure. In our company 1/3 are skilled sewers, a bit more than 1/3 are ordinary level sewers, and about 1/3 are such that if there were any chance of getting better ones, then..For the time being we have not fired anybody, there are enough machines, but who knows what may happen in the future, maybe we will have to select whom to keep and whom to let go, because productivity is so low and the result is just an abuse of the machines. Those who are very poor performers, we are not giving any machines to them at all. In the sewing industry the trend lately has been such that since the level of vocational schools is so poor and since big textile producers have made proposals that they should have their own teaching premises and classes, they could train the necessary sewers by themselves if they would get support from the state, but so far they cannot have it. Anyhow, the current training in vocational schools is simply lousy. It is the same in many branches in Estonia: the level of education is so low that there is no use for it in working life. They use 10-year-old machines to teach students to use modern sewing technologies. The state should do something about that. Now when the light industry technical school got new machines it was boasted of as something big, but in fact it was only 10-12 machines. But from the point of view of Tallinn it is such a small amount of machines that it's not worth mentioning. In that sense the state does not give support in any way. For example, last Monday our main compressor broke down and there's such an awful noise when we use the reserve compressor. It should be repaired and changed, but our capital is not enough, and to get a loan from the bank, the interest rates are so high, and in any case they do not give loans to small companies like ours, you must have a super idea, then you might perhaps get something. Some years ago it was easier, but now banks do not credit small businesses. Now I cannot get any loan, because my house is mortgaged and before I finish paying it back there is no possibility of even thinking about any loan. Everywhere they demand real estate as a guarantee - machines, or equipment does not interest them at all.

- It seems difficult indeed. But, is there any leisure for the entrepreneur, have you time to participate in associational activities, and are there any associations for entrepreneurs?

This Turo Tailoring inspected our factory and then the Viljandi-factory, but obviously Baltika owned 90 % of that Viljandi-factory and told Turo Tailor that if you do not buy that Viljandi-factory, Baltika will stop buying any Turo Tailor work – Baltika was subcontracting to Turo Tailor some 60-70 % of their (Baltika) production. I am not sure, because I was not there, but eventually Turo Tailor bought the Viljandi-factory. Of course it is an old building and they have rather cramped rooms there, they employ some 10 people less than we do, but now they completed a major repair with Turo Tailor's resources. Turo is a good company, naturally, since it is a Finnish company, their models are changing, but they produce one single product all the time and it is no problem for them if the models change: whether there are two pockets in the back or one, it is just a small detail. But if you have 6-7 clients and 6-7 products in process at the same time, it makes things a bit messy and difficult and affects productivity negatively. So if somebody from Finland came and offered to buy, then why not sell.

- *Would you sell?*

Certainly I would.

- *How about this leisure issue – are you a member of some association?*

I am a member of the Lions club and I play tennis. I have to take time for myself, our child is now 5 and soon will be going to school, and then we will have different kinds of problems.

- *Are there other enterprises in this town that are of same size?*

No, there are no similar firms here.

- *Well, I meant the size mainly, not the branch of economy or such things.*

There was one firm, an heir of the kolkhoz, they have some 20 persons. They have milk-cows and fields and other such activities. Then there are repair shops, with 5-6 people working, but there is no big employer besides EMV. They have a production site here, they sold part of it, the wood-processing, but they still have the machine workshop, employing maybe 100 persons. I had a talk with the mayor [who said] that EMV is the biggest tax-payer here, because the income tax comes to the municipality.

- EMV used to be one of the biggest construction companies, but recently the news was that they tried to merge EMV with somebody else. Do you know about that?

Yes, it was Merko who tried to capture EMV, it happened in the end of last year.

- It did not succeed, due to some legal problems?

Yes, there was this Mr. H, the one who bought a lot of shares, and then there was the board of EMV. Those two parts played in different baskets or goals.

- Merko is building all around Estonia, is it not?

Yes, it is. It has won all the bids, such as the renovation of the airport in Tallinn, how it wins them is another matter. For example, the director of the airport, he shot himself last year, so who knows what happened there. Construction business is a story in itself. Before the collapse of the stock exchange and bankruptcies of banks, they did well, they had big orders, they built tall glass towers and a building for a bank that went immediately bankrupt. There was a lot of talk about Phare programs and support for small businesses, but the actual practice was a different thing. They are stuck somewhere at the ministries and by administrative obstacles. The Finnish government should take a closer look at who to support and cooperate with.

17. K- Radio Plant

Interview with the director of the plant
Tukums region, Latvia
Date: May 5th, 2000
Interviewer: Jouko Nikula
Translator: Sandra Sumane

- Can you tell us something about your personal background?

I began studies at the University of Latvia, the Department of Physics and Mathematics, but I did not graduate from it. In 1977 I began to work at Riga Radio Plant (RRP). I had worked there for two years and then I was recruited in the army. I was in military service for two years. In 1979 I went to the Institute of Polytechnics and studied at the Department of Radiotechnology as an external student. I worked in RRP till 1982 when I moved to Kandava. My whole my life has been connected with this firm. I began my career here as a technologist. Then I was foreman of a machine-shop, after that I was the head of that department, then director of the production department. Since 1993 I am the director of the enterprise. For about the last two years I have been both the director of KRP and of Kandava Fish Plant.

- *Was KRP a part of RRP?*

No. There was a production association that included four enterprises – KRP, RRP, Riga Electro-mechanic Plant and the Development Team "Orbita". They were united in the association, but they were, in a way, rather independent of one another. In 1991 the KRP was privatised.

- *When and why was KRP established? What is the history of the plant?*

It was established in 1963. And the reason was that at that time the employment of women in the countryside was rather low. Initially KRP was one of RRP's workshops. Different blocks, pulleys were produced here, but not complete products. In 1975 KRP was formed as an independent plant. Initially it produced record players here – "Akords", "Melodiya". Since 1982, 1983 the plant has specialised in the production of Bantam radios – like "Selga 405", "Selga 309". And for now, it is still continuing to produce them.

-From 1963 till 1975 it produced only parts?

Yes.

- And from 1975 - sets?

Yes.

- How did the production structure develop? Were the decisions made here at the plant or "at the top"?

I cannot say about the period before the 1980s because I was not here then. But later usually it was like this: there was the Development Team "Orbita" in our production association that designed the new models; the developed models were assessed within the association and each enterprise made the decision whether it was able to produce them. For example, "Abava" was one of the developed models and it was possible to produce it in RRP or KRP. The final decision about who would be the producer was taken in the association. And since usually the construction of models was not done completely, after the decision about the producer, the model would still be improved in the enterprise that was going to produce, according to its possibilities.

- This means that you had some research and development department in the plant?

Yes, we had a technological bureau, a development team with three or four employees. They worked both here in the plant and on the adaptation of the models already elaborated for local production. The development Team "Orbita" did not deliver technologies, it only elaborated models. And our constructors adjusted them for production on our fixings. If there were some specific parts that we were unable to produce in our plant due to some technical or other reasons, then we would look for some other plant where it was possible. Sometimes we had to look for such opportunities even outside our association – in Latvia or even in the Soviet Union. However, at that time the standpoint of the plant's administration was that we should produce here everything to the utmost. Today we have the opposite standpoint: we are looking whether we can buy cheaper parts somewhere, and many parts we do not produce here anymore, because we can't produce them so cheaply. Many parts that we had produced before – antennas etc. - today we buy from Taiwan or Hong Kong or some other place.

- Were there some production plans?

Yes, there were such plans. We agreed on them both among the enterprises in the association and in Moscow in the 4th central board. But those plans more or less fitted the real possibilities of the plant.

- What was the amount of production?

We produced around half a million sets per year, around 40 000 sets per month. Usually we produced two models at the same time. Besides the ready-made sets we also complemented around 15 000 sets with details for Cuba where they were tuned and fitted up.

- Which were the main market areas?

The whole Soviet Union. Also Cuba, Bulgaria, Romania, Czechoslovakia. We also produced main condensers for all the radio sets produced in the Soviet Union – about several million per year. In small amounts this ware was also exported to capitalist countries. In such cases we received currency and bought some equipment.

- *Could you use that currency for your own plant or did it remain in Moscow?*

Maybe some part of it remained in Moscow, because all that trade with foreign countries was organised through "Sovexport" in Moscow. The enterprise could not make a direct contract with a foreign enterprise. After the deal was done, we would be informed that there was some money in our bank account and we could buy what we needed.

- *Did you get some bonuses from the produce sold abroad?*

Yes, we got something. But at that time I was not yet so close to the administration of the plant. For some time there was the following system – for example, if I had sold goods for USD 100, I could get USD 30 and the other USD 70 for a gainful currency rate in roubles. Not all the money that we received from this foreign trade could we spend.

- *How many employees do you have? How has the number changed?*

I do not know about the first years. There was a time when there were 1000 employees. It may have been in the 1980s, when the enterprise was most stable, from around 1985 till 1990. But not all of them worked here in Kandava. We had several branches in Kemeri, Stende – in Tukums and Talsi districts. The kolhoz in Allazi helped us with spool winding. Thus, some of the operations were done outside the plant.

- *What was the employee structure?*

There were around 300 workers here in the plant. The administration was around 100 people, including also the operating personnel and mechanics department that ensured the operation of the fixings.

- *What was the structure of wages?*

Wages depended on the qualification, but for workers they depended on their qualification plus the work done. The basis for the wage was the gains. It depended on qualification and quality. And from around 1985 to 1990 the wages were from 200 to 300 roubles. And it was more than the average wage. It was among the best paid work in our district.

- *What kind of organisation of production did you have then?*

Problems there have always been, at that time too. Every brigadier and worker knew how many sets must be produced during a month. We also had work in shifts in some places. Of course, there were people who drank and who might not come to work someday. There were some narrow professions in our plant, for example, tuners, an occupation for which there was always a shortage of employees. Because the appropriate education was necessary. Of course, there were people, but not enough. If such a specialist did not come to work, then the administration would go to his home to look for him and to learn why he had not come to work. If somebody did not come to work, other employees worked overtime – not 8, but 9 or 10 hours. Of course, they received money for this. There were even cases when some employees had to work two days at a stretch.

- *Did the company administration have any means to make the floor level workers work more effectively?*

Maybe it was due to the plan economy. If you have to produce 50 000 sets per month, then at the end of the month the workers were tired and perhaps they did not care too much about the quality. Therefore people even looked to see when the sets had been produced – in the beginning or in the end of the month. But there were also other problems. Our enterprise was connected to different providers of parts from the whole Soviet Union, also in Samarkand, Irkutsk. We had such a problem – our plant in Latvia worked all year round. But in Samarkand, when the harvesting of cotton began, there was nobody at the plant: everybody was working in the fields. Hence our plant also had to stop production. But we had to fulfil the plan. Then we would send workers from our plant to Samarkand and they worked there to produce the needed parts. It was similar in Ukraine, Kirovgrad, we sent our workers there to produce blowers for our sets.

- *What were the principle means of maintaining work discipline when there were problems?*

The workers that were incorrigible were dismissed. But usually it was regulated by payment – ordinary workers had a basic wage and premiums around 40%. While the premiums for engineers and technicians depended more on the quality, fulfilling the plan, etc., for ordinary workers it was simpler – if he came to work, did not drink, and did the minimum, then he earned his 40% automatically. Thus, the workers' 40% depended more on their work discipline. If somebody did not work well we could also shorten his vacation.

- Were there some recreation services?

There were social services. Employees travelled – the whole association had resort homes in Jurmala, near the Black and Azov seas. There was no problem for the plant's employees to go there during their vacations. The plant also supported amateur art activities– a chorus, etc. For example, it allocated the bus for their trips.

- What kind of other social services, benefits?

All the apartment houses here are built mainly by KRP. Only some of them belong to the agricultural technical school. KRP also renovated the cultural centre, the post office building, and many infrastructure sites, treatment plants.

- Were there any difficulties in recruiting qualified workers?

Yes. We have had problems here getting highly-qualified employees. Also today. All the production techniques and technologies have developed rapidly and specialists also have to constantly acquire that new knowledge.

- Could you explain why there were such problems with the work discipline?

There were not many cases here of workers drinking during working hours in the plant. Maybe there were some cases when there had been some party on the previous evening and then it was difficult to come to work next morning. But drinking at work was not common. The problem at that time was rather that the specialists with rare skills demanded extra money, because they were aware, of course, that the fulfilment of the plans depended mostly on them, because there was nobody else who could do that specific operation. If it was some assembler that was not working, it was easy to find a better worker.

- If those hopeless cases of workers were dismissed, did they also lose their apartments?

At that time it was not easy to get an apartment. There was a deficit of apartments and usually they were allocated to those employees who had already worked in the plant for 15-20 years. The majority of workers lived not in apartments but in hostel-type houses. Thus, retirement did not impact much on the apartment policy. However, there could be a situation where the apartment is allocated for a family where the wife [also] works in the plant. After a while the husband retired, but the wife stayed on at the plant. Then, of course, the apartment was not taken away.

- What was the "coming-leaving" proportion for workers?

It is difficult to say. It was not so big; it could have been around 10%. They were not the engineers. There was some rotation within the plant when employees changed the departments they worked in. Usually they were ordinary workers and service personnel. In the transport department the rotation was higher, among drivers, loaders.

- What was the role and relations of trade union, administration and Communist Party?

I think that the previous director of the radio plant had been a rather big dictator. The Communist Party did not have a big impact in the enterprise. The trade union was responsible for culture, the cultural centre, the chorus, allocation of the vouchers for resort homes, allocation of apartments. The trade union also elaborated collective labour contracts about the obligations and rights.

- Then was the trade union functioning in the field of social and leisure organisation?

Yes. It also elaborated the schema for production premiums for specialists and workers, also the regulations about extra holidays for those working under unhealthy conditions. For example, press machine operator was not an unhealthy profession according to the standards of that time. But since nobody liked to work as a press machine operator, because it was not pleasant work, in order to attract people, after it was submitted to the trade unions for approval, about 12 or 6 extra vacation days were allocated for those employees.

- Were there any conflicts between workers and managers? What was the trade union's position?

There were no serious conflicts. Maybe during the transition period in 1992, in 1993 there was a problem with respect to payment of salaries. It was not possible to lay off somebody without the agreement of the trade union. I was head of the department and, for example, I saw that a given man would never be a good worker. But it was difficult for me to retire him; I needed the trade union's acquiescence. But its representative said: "He has three little children. What will he do?"

- How did the privatisation process happen?

The first shake-up began as early as 1989. It was still the USSR, but the first wind of changes appeared. A co-operative was established on the basis of the plant.

- Was there some plan? Who made the decision?

The decision was made by the plant's administration. The USSR legislation allowed the possibility of establishing co-operatives. Taking into account that the expenses in state enterprises were very strictly defined – so much for salaries, so much for culture, so much for social expenses, etc., and there were also price restrictions for state enterprises. Taking into account this situation, the co-operative was established. Around 100 people participated in its establishment – both engineers and some ordinary workers. Every one contributed 1000 roubles – it was big money at that time. Maybe the number of charter members would have been higher if the money had been less. There were very few people who were ready to risk 1000 roubles. When the co-operative was founded, everything was rented here and KRP as a state enterprise stopped working. We could not buy it yet at that time, but we rented everything here from the state. In 1991, when Latvia was an independent state, a joint-stock company KRP was founded. There were around 400 charter members – workers in the plant.

- Are they shareholders?

Yes. At that time 25% of the enterprise belonged to the state.

- How did production develop during the time of the co-operative and share company?

It was still increasing a bit till the end of 1992. Then the production decreased. The enterprise was oriented mainly towards the USSR market. After the USSR collapsed, it split into independent countries each with its own currency, and there were problems with customs. This resulted in the decrease of the volume of production in 1993.

- *Were there any efforts to create new models or to conquer the Western market?*

With respect to models – they were replaced from 1993 till 1996. But as concerns the Western market – even now it is impossible for such a product to enter the Western market. During this period we substituted our Russian parts for completing with Japanese ones, also with Philips. There were several projects for production of several products for Western countries. A serious one was in 1993. At that time there were still many enough workers here. The people came to the plant and they were interested because there were skilled people here, who would be able to do that work. But the Latvian government was not interested in this. We got together, but the taxation system did not satisfy them and this project was not carried out. There have been some smaller commissions.

- *Do foreign companies get any tax relief?*

There was an income tax relief for joint ventures. But foreign companies compared [the situations in] Latvia, Lithuania, Estonia, Bulgaria, and Czech Republic. One of the issues that was a serious barrier at that time, but which is solved for now, was about value added tax – you had to pay it already when the completing parts were brought into the country. This means that your money stayed blocked for a long period of from 3 to 6 months, from import to sale. It was too long a period for their production volumes. They were not willing to invest any extra money, and 18% is a big amount of money. Now this problem is solved and it is possible to get tax relief if you import some parts for processing. But at that time this problem was not solved and that company opened its plant in the Czech Republic.

- *What is the situation today? How many shareholders do you have?*

290.

- *Is the ownership concentrated?*

Yes.

- *What part belongs to high level managers?*

Around 35%.

- *What is the amount of production?*

Since 1993 the production volume has decreased 10 times.

- *Did this decreasing process happen step by step or was it changing?*

There was a decrease in 1996. Since 1997 the production volume has stayed at the same level. For now there is even a tendency that it might go up. The situation is changing. There have even been some periods of increase, but we hardly begin to get into it when something happens and we are back down again. We lost our money deposited in Bank Baltia. We had fulfilled a big order but we did not receive our money. It took more than a year to recuperate. The next blow was the crisis in Russia last year. All those years we had collaborated with Russia, we had sold our production there.

- *It seems that, for now, you are rather optimistic.*

Yes.

- *Have you changed your machinery, bought something?*

Very little. Of course, there is need for this. We have not bought any basic machinery. But we should. New technologies are coming in, also with respect to the assembly of surfaces.

- *It seems that the core of economic problems is not inside your firm but in the general unstable economic situation in the country?*

Both. There are enough problems inside the enterprise as well. But problems in the country as a whole have impacted also on the situation in our enterprise. Some issues that are not solved at state level block the development of the enterprise.

- *How many workers do you have for now?*

There around 40 workers employed in radio production. The numbers change a bit. We also offer some transportation services that are not related to radio production. And so, there are 14 workers working in this service sector – transportation, turnery, metal working.

- *What are the salaries now?*

Between 50 and 120 lats.

- *What happens in the rest of those buildings?*

They belong to the plant, but they are rented to other enterprises.

- *What is the main market for your production?*

Mainly Latvia, Lithuania. We still have small barter deals with Russia. We do not sell there anymore, but receive from them the needed materials – metal or speakers, like in the previous times. But our market in Russia is very marginal – only 2 or 3 %.

- *In Latvia, especially in Riga, there was one of the best traditions of electronic industry. Could you explain why this industry has gone into bankruptcy?*

One of the explanations is the unsuccessful state policy during the period when there were still enough workers in those plants. Another one was the fact that until 1991 the access to Western technologies was denied to engineers and technical managers. Many of our products were not bad with respect to their design or application, but their price was high. Enterprises were not able to shift to Western technologies. Also – when Western electronic companies were allowed to enter our market freely, this process had to be organised through local electronic enterprises. For example, Philips imported ready-made irons but there was no duty for entry. But maybe some completing of their irons should be organized in our plants. Our enterprises and foreign companies were not in the same situation. They could practice dumping.

- *There are many specialists in Eastern countries. And some Western companies make use of this. Nokia has a branch in Hungary.*

We have discussed this issue. The salaries are low in Latvia and the competence of our specialists is high, but when you add up all production expenses, then in the end Latvia seems rather expensive – energy, taxes, heating. In Latvia the expenses for one working day are such that you should have to pay 5 lats to a worker and 2 lats for social tax and the other taxes. While in Czech Republic they can afford to pay 6 lats to workers because the rest of expenses are not that high. And, of course, the producer looks to see where the end product will be cheaper.

Institutional entrepreneurs

The interviews in this group represent another specific type entrepreneurship during the post-socialist economic transition. It was indigenous response of the difficult situation public research and educational institutions felt into during the early years after 1989. These were characterized by sharp decline of public funding of the research establishments and lack of demand for R&D services and innovation form industry and agriculture due to the severe economic crises in the region. As we pointed in the introduction, the early years of transition have been characterized also with lack of financial and institutional framework in support of start-up small and medium enterprises, as well as the relevant legal and business consultancy. All this was to come more than ten years later as part of the EU accession process and the relevant EU funding programs. In this situation the entrepreneurially minded academics had several options to choose, the two main being

1) Creation of specific institutional arrangements inside their research organizations that allowed such entrepreneurial activities while shielding to certain extent the entrepreneurs from the uncertainties and risk related with the commercial activities. These arrangements also provided some initial support of academic entrepreneurs in terms of research and production facilities, accounting services, legal consultancy, etc. The positive attitudes of research organization's management, including their Scientific Councils and Ruling Boards was key condition for realisation this option. When this was not the case,
2) Leaving parent organisations and establishing of researchers' own spin-off companies or other forms of commercial activities *outside* the institutes and universities was the obvious solution. In this case the academic entrepreneurs had to bear the entire risk and had to rely on their own social capital (family and friendship networks), and on the contacts with industry and with foreign partners they possibly accumulated during the socialist period.

The interviews in this group illustrate the feasibility of the two options and conditions that made them possible. They provide rich empirical evidences about the advantages and shortcomings of both and allow now, almost twenty years after the events, to critically assess the strategies the early post-socialist academic entrepreneurs have chosen.

18. Academic Entrepreneurship in Bulgaria – Two Stories

Two university professors at Technical University
Bourgas, Bulgaria
Interviewer: Ivan Tchalakov under Project *PROKNOW*, VI Framework Program of EC

Short Introductory Note

The two stories below present the entrepreneurial efforts of applied scientists in a leading technological university, that in Burgas, a city on the Bulgarian Black Sea coast. Established in the early 1960s with the task of preparing chemical and mechanical engineers for the industries located in the region, the university's academic personnel was also engaged in providing R&D services and solving technological and production problems of the local industrial enterprises. When its first graduates entered industry, they became an additional bridge to these enterprises and often turned to their former professors for consultancy and advice. So unlike many 'pure science' research establishments, this university was closely linked to industry from the very start; this pattern still persists today.

The relationships between this university and industrial enterprises display many of the defects of the socialist administrative economy (see Tchalakov, Mitev, Petrov 2010) – such as using research expertise mostly in design and construction of new industrial facilities, and a lack of real interest in innovations in the daily management of production. This, in turn, impelled some applied scientists to undertake the task of seeking application of their inventions. Yet at least for some socialist enterprises, especially those working in high-tech sectors and under the COCOM embargo, collaboration with the academic sciences proved crucial – researchers have been often invited to be members of the boards of directors, the enterprises provided research equipment for the university labs, and at some of these labs and departments there emerged unique research units closely serving the production program of fellow enterprises (in electronic industry, in petrochemical industry, etc.). After 1989 most of these units collapsed together with the collapse of the industrial enterprises they served. Yet other units survived and, relying on their previous achievements and excellence in research, they redirected their industrial relationships to Western research institutes and multinational companies. They not only survived but pushed the development of Bulgarian university science in new directions.

Some of the stories in the book in fact describe spin-off companies of former researchers, or what is traditionally called 'academic entrepreneurship'. Their experience is remarkable enough, because in the early years of transition they had to cope not only with market uncertainties, financial crisis, etc., but also with the hostile attitude of the scientific community, of the management of the Bulgarian Academy of Science, and of most universities, who *officially banned commercial activities of scientists* and controlled any contacts they might have with industry. (for more on this, see: Tchalakov, Mitev, Petrov 2010, pp. 203-209, as well as other stories in the volume - Risk Engineering, PROEL).

However, the stories presented below reveal another specific form of entrepreneurship that we have called *'institutional entrepreneurship'*. It emerged in the conditions of radically reduced public funding for research; thanks to their operational autonomy (inherited from the socialist period or newly acquired from the higher level research organizations), some directors of institutes or heads of university departments organized their research on an entrepreneurial basis. They were able to enter into contractual relationships with private and public entities, selling services to industrial companies, other research establishments, government agencies, etc., using the received income to deal with the shortfalls of the transition – to compensate for low wages, to upgrade research equipment, maintain communications, etc.

Here the socialist legacy played an important role – the late-socialist reforms allowed public research institutions to run commercial activities and to generate additional income from small-scale manufacturing, leasing of research facilities, etc. This was legally provided for when the academic organizations were granted the status of legal entities under the trade law. These arrangements have lasted during the entire period of transition and were even expanded with the aggravation of crisis and cuts of state research funding. The results of these activities were mixed – in our study we recorded sad stories about stripping of public assets that such arrangements made possible.[29] Yet in other cases such income-generated

---

[29] In one of the studied cases a small-scale integrated circuits manufacturing line worth 2,5 million of USD became a spin-off in the early 1990s, the research institute preserving a 75% controlling share. The firm worked more than a decade, but for this whole period the institute received a total income of only 10 000 BGN (about 8000 USD)! For fear of further abuse of its property rights, in 2006 the institute management discontinued its participation in the firm, receiving a compensation of 50 USD (!) for its initial investments! Of course, the firm was paying salaries and taxes, but it did not declare any profit until the complete amortization of equipment.

activities provided for many years more than half the organizations' annual research budget. As these activities were carried, the research organizations preserved entirely the ownership of their valuable small-scale production assets. So ultimately it was not the hidden privatization and divestment of public research assets, but precisely the *academic spin-offs* and *institutional entrepreneurship* that became a basis for maintaining and developing sustainable science-industry relations during the transitional and post-transitional period.

Story 1: This is my Situation – I am doing science, I am running production and if you ask me where I am, I really don't know which part is more important…

This is the story of a university scientist, an extraordinary woman that is simultaneously at the top of three different activities – she teaches, she does research, and she runs a small production laboratory that commercially applies some of her scientific achievements. Our interviews took place at the biochemical lab in the university – among tables and desks covered with glassware and apparatuses, and we were often interrupted by her younger graduate students and assistants. She was busy enough all the while, but during our talk she never tried to shorten the interview – it was clear enough she loved what she was doing, and her work was exactly what I was asking her about…The text that follows is arranged as a single talk about her life as an applied scientist, and my questions and some auxiliary details have been cut out.

I graduated this university and immediately after that was appointed on a temporary contract as chemist in our Central Research Laboratory (SRL). A year later I was reappointed at our Department for Applied Research (DAR*)*, later I became a research fellow there… Then I moved to the University as assistant professor and completed my PhD thesis. Professor Aristotle Dimov was my supervisor.

My research field is 'immobilized enzymes and micro-organisms'. We are trying to immobilize them on hard surfaces, mainly on polymers, but also on some inorganic surfaces. These enzymes are manufactured industrially, but the field is very interesting. And when you take an interest, your work progresses rapidly. When I went there between 1986 and 1989, this was a very modern field, and especially during the last decade the intensity of research has increased worldwide.

My background is that of a polymer chemist (she used the Russian word 'polymerchik'). When I entered DAR, I was doing mostly analytical work and in a few years I mastered practically all analytical methods – spectrophotometry, volume analysis, infra-red chromatography, gas-chromatography, liquid-chromatography, etc. Knowing these methods helps a lot in studying immobilized systems; hence my stay at SRL and DAR was very useful for me. While in DAR, I worked with polymer membranes that are very suitable for immobilizing enzymes. That is how I entered the field.

Then in 1991 we established a new Department of Biotechnology. It was founded by Associate Professor Shopova. I was one of the first people appointed in the department and after Prof. Shopova's retirement I succeeded her as head. I managed to form a group of young PhD students; most of them had already defended their theses. Two of the girls that graduated are already my assistant professors. One of them specialized in immobilization of enzymes, the other, in micro-organisms.

We entered this field alone – struggling on research papers, because there was nobody around to show you in practice how to do this type of research. Most papers were in English – initially there were few Bulgarian authors in this field. Later we established contacts with other colleagues from the Bulgarian Academy of Sciences, its institutes of polymers and of microbiology, with colleagues at the University of Food Technology in Plovdiv, with Italian colleagues, etc. Since 2006 we have been working with Prof. Mitar from Naples, Italy, in the framework of a large consortium, consisting of 24 universities…

We designed our own polymer membranes (ultrafiltration and microfiltration membranes). This came from DAR as well – there was a membrane department and that is how I learned how to synthesize such membranes and to modify them. The method is called 'chemical modification' – after modification the membranes are very suitable for immobilization of biological agents. The membranes are biological polymers formed in very thin layers that are able to fix the enzymes and micro-organisms on their surface using so-called covalent bonds. These immobilized enzymes and micro-organisms are widely used in industrial biology and medicine; this is an applied field of research.

Our main application is the production of diagnostic test strips for quick analysis of biological liquids (blood, urine, etc.). The strips are of our own design and are produced in a laboratory affiliated to the university. We established it in 1991. We signed a contract with the Ministry of Health to supply the test strips for diabetes patients in Bulgaria. The contract lasted almost twenty years, although soon after that some foreign companies also entered this business.

The other applied result was the immobilization of two micro-organisms (trihosporum boutaneum and aspergillus awamori) on polymeric granules – these are the core of an excellent system for biodegradation of phenols. The micro-organisms transform it into non-toxic compounds. The large petrochemical plant near Burgas was producing phenols and they were very interested in our work in order to deal with their environmental pollution. Unfortunately after the privatization of the plant in 1999 the phenol installation was closed down, there is no such pollution anymore and they lost interest in our work.

So the lab producing diagnostic test strip remained our main industrial activity. We have been selling since 1991 but we never get rich, always remaining at the margins - the initial contract with the Ministry of Health was very good, but in 1997, with the establishment of the National Health Insurance Fund, the contract was transferred to it on a much lower scale. They now cover only clinical labs in the hospitals, and the diabetes patients have to buy the test strips themselves… Still we have this regular, though small, source of revenues.

Advertisement of the lab's diagnostic test strips

Source: www.btu.bg/bg/Strukture/NIS/BULURI**TEST**.doc

We run the lab as a branch of DAR. As I said, it is not easy to establish and manage such a small enterprise on a private basis – that is why I sought shelter at the university - we do not pay rent for the facilities and this helps a lot. Maybe I could have taken the risk of running it privately if we had larger revenues. If we had such, maybe I would run it myself. But the situation has always been rather uncertain…

Otherwise we designed a rather sophisticated product – based on the quantitative results of the test, you can determine certain diseases – not only diabetes, but also hepatitis, inflammation processes, etc. Almost everything done in a clinical laboratory could be done out with our test strips. Our products are registered but are not protected by a patent or other form of industrial property – it's too expensive [to patent it], and I am consciously postponing this. Because when you patent something, you reveal to the competitors what you are doing. For we have a lot of original stuff in the process of stabilisation - we did not discovered America, other companies are also able to stabilize their products, but I believe we found a specific approach to stabilisation of the bio-components and I do not want to reveal it to others.

Since the early 1990s we have been facing very strong competition from the foreign companies that entered Bulgaria, such *as Boehringer Ingelheim* (Germany), the Czech company *Lachema*, etc., which are large, well-established companies. Nevertheless we manage to gain and defend our market positions, maybe because of our lower prices combined with the good quality of the products. There are a number of hospitals that are buying our tests strips, which are indeed compatible with those of the foreign companies.

You should keep in mind that our competitors are running large research institutes; they have large production facilities and decades of industrial experience. However, we also managed to achieve stability of our products, so the different series of them provide the same results – we achieved 100% reproduction of the results of the tests, although this costs us a lot of efforts. We check thoroughly every series of the product; we monitor the behaviour of our test strips under different conditions, etc. Moreover, we are constantly improving and developing our test strips, making them more stable and sensitive. This is because we are the designer, we can always 'go into the product' and change something in it.

Still, running a production is a very difficult endeavour. There were 10 employees in the lab - my assistants at the university don't work there. Recently we reduced the stuff and now there are only four, because the demand for our strip diminished. Mainly because of the new provisions of the National Health Insurance. But interestingly enough, all the clinical labs that we began to supply in 1991 – they are all still our customers! The problem is that we are unable to expand their number. We need more advertising, a real distribution network… But all this costs a lot of money, which we lack. *Boehrigner* and other competitors have distribution networks in the large cities, they give the directors of the labs and hospitals large bonuses – we can't afford this, being a university-run enterprise.

Sadly enough, I see only growing difficulties in our business. There are very high requirements when producing medical items - you have to guarantee a sterile environment, which means air and water control, special equipment for the workers, etc. According to the requirements of good production practices the production line has to be divided in separate rooms, with a special storage room, special room for quality control, etc. These are Europe-wide requirements and we have to comply with them. This means lots of investments. Last year we completely renewed our faculties to cope with the requirements of the control agencies.

Yet I am still afraid about the future - the best solution will be to have separate facilities (special building) for our lab only. Unfortunately the university is not able to invest in such facilities so we continue to work in the main DAR building together with the other labs. And since 1991 there have been no external investors willing to put money in our lab – neither from Bulgaria, nor from abroad. A few years ago a German company specialized in technology transfer came to our university. They introduced themselves, collected information about our resources, but nothing followed from that. I wrote a special message to their representatives in Bulgaria, but no response… Frankly speaking, till now I too have not searched actively for investors to expand the production, to improve the advertising, to build distribution network, etc. Maybe because I believed the only thing we could offer to foreign partners was cheap labour, plus our experience in this biotechnology, which is very difficult to master. But our competitors also have such experience, plus the fact that neither do we have autonomous production facilities, nor can the land owned by the university be legally shared in a joint venture. It would be sad to close the lab down and to lose everything we have done in it so far. It costs us so much efforts and tears! It was very difficult indeed to run this production during all these years - I am also engaged in research work, in teaching students, in supervising PhD students, etc.

Yet so far I have always managed to devote some time to the production lab, it is working slowly, but it's working. In a way it was worth the efforts, because we were able to pay all our needs with the revenues from the production laboratory – electricity, consumables, salaries for the employees, I and my assistants, we also receive some additional income from it, which compensates for the low wages in the university. Besides, it is not only a question of money – you have created something, and you are producing it and you are receiving many letters of thanks from diabetes patients, which sometimes breaks your heart. These letters are very useful, very necessary, we keep all of them. Sometimes we send our test strips free-of-charge to people who wrote they needed them but had no money. Eventually we feel great satisfaction that your product is really valuable and much needed.

During all these years we were also able to finance our research activities with the revenues from the production lab – some mission trips, some consumables – both for research and teaching. For example, all enzymes for laboratory seminars with students come from the production lab, because these are very expensive (200 euro per gram). Few biotech departments in Bulgarian universities can afford these consumables; the universities are still too poor. We are one of the exceptions.

Based on the applied research we do for the production lab, we also have publications, since the diagnostic tests are in fact immobilized enzymes. Hence there is a direct link between my scientific publications and the applied industrial research. These papers are the results of my work in improving the diagnostic test strips, although not always. When you are improving your products in the market, you are not aiming at a new publication, this is a by-product.

So this is my work – I do science, I run a production lab and if you ask me where I am, I really don't know - maybe simultaneously in both fields. There is satisfaction from both activities, as well as from my PhD students who successfully defended their theses. All these different engagements made me more orderly and practical-minded. I mean I spend less time finding the right path of research and teaching, especially of research. The applied work changed my teaching – the students admit that my lectures are more oriented towards application of knowledge. When teaching a given subject I always tend to demonstrate where and how it could be applied, what the value of a given technology is, which way is more efficient. Maybe that is why the students like my lectures – I rarely boast about myself, but this is noticeable.

Otherwise there are few people in the university doing applied research and industrial production. I don't blame my colleagues - many of them also have a second job because of the low salary. But they prefer ordinary work in some company, often part-time work, that has nothing to do with applied research and the practical results based on it. Maybe I am too severe in my attitudes, but I do believe we should introduce the rules of Western universities, and every professor should be evaluated both on his teaching and (applied) scientific research. I had an Indian PhD student whose brother was a university professor in Finland. He said most of the professors there are on temporary contracts, not permanent like me and my colleagues. He said "the teaching is your duty, but you are also evaluated on the basis of your research projects". So if you have no projects supporting your teaching, maybe your contract will not be renewed. They have much bigger fluidity of labour force. I like this type of organisation; this should be our future too…

Story 2: From serving the giants of Socialist industry to serving multinational companies: the rise of *professional science* in Bulgaria

Here is the story of Prof. Ovanes Mekeyan, which reveals something that I, as a sociologist of science, have always dreamed of finding in Bulgaria. It appears that it had been there for many years – far away from the capital Sofia, with the noisy pretentiousness of its venerable scientists. It existed modestly and without much publicity; put in the context of the ongoing debates about the future of the Academy of Sciences and universities, it points to an interesting perspective. I hope there are those who will understand it.

Until recently every year there were millions of laboratory animals that died in tests of the toxicity of new chemical substances. In EC-15 alone about ten million died each year. Now the idea is for these mass experiments with animals to be replaced by the so-called QSAR (*qualitative structure-activity research*). They seek to find the links between the structure of molecules of the chemical substances and their effects – toxic or biological in general. So we try to link the structure of the molecule with the behaviour of these substances, its biological properties – mostly the properties of the functional groups in the structure. I should not go into greater details, it is a rather complex process – you could find out more on our website (http://oasis-lmc.org/).

Our development started from the initial academic (I also call it the "amateur") stage of development, which lasted from 1983 until 1991. Then there was an intermediary period from 1991 to 1994. In general, what we have in Bulgaria is either academic science or no science at all, but rather some practical applying of partial knowledge by professors. Today most scientists deal with producing plastic bags, trading with some specific materials, some minor production, etc. But the more important thing is that the academic science we have (oriented predominantly to teaching) *is not* professional science.

Box 1 Laboratory of Mathematical Chemistry

LMC was founded in 1983, in the Black Sea coast city of Burgas, Bulgaria, as a Laboratory for Structure Activity (property) Modeling. It was first headed by Prof. Danail Bonchev, member of the Bulgarian Academy of Sciences, who is presently working as a guest professor at Virginia Commonwealth University, Richmond. The present head of LMC has been running the Lab since 1989.

Nowadays, LMC has a research staff of 21 scientists and 1 technician, including 2 professors, 5 associate professors, 7 research associates (chemists, physicists, programmers, and mathematicians). The University has provided LMC with a large office area, including two conference rooms, and a total of 30 PCs. All computers are connected to the University LAN. For heavy computations, other university-owned UNIX workstations are used as well.

The major impact of LMC in Structure-Activity and Structure-Property modeling could be summarized as follows:

Building IT for structure complexity evaluation (conformer flexibility and metabolic transformations)

Assessing molecular reactivity and interaction mechanisms

Building probabilistic QSAR models

Evaluating model applicability domains

Selecting chemicals for strategic testing

3D databasing

LMC has bilateral cooperation and research contracts with major industrial companies in the World (Procter & Gamble, 3M, ExxonMobil, AstraZeneca, DuPont, BASF) and State Agencies (Canadian EPA, Health Canada, US EPA, Danish EPA, Japanese METI. JRC, European Chemicals Bureau, Italy).

LMC hosted and organized the IX International Conference, QSAR in Environmental Sciences, which was held in Bourgas, Bulgaria, on September 16-21, 2000 (QSAR'2000). (Source: http://oasis-lmc.org/, September 2011)

What are the *principles of* what I call 'professional science'?

1. Professional science is *market oriented.*
2. It is *goal-oriented science*. It proceeds from clear requirements and application frameworks, not just out of curiosity. The curiosity is subordinated to the goal, to the user requirements.
3. Professional science *presupposes market economy*. You couldn't have this type of science in the previous [that existed during the times of Socialism] conditions. At that time we had a good professional level *as scientists*, but you can't say we had professional *science* - because professional science presupposes clearly defined users of its results.
4. Professional science needs *market relationships in the field of education*. It should be clear that universities produce labour force for the market - every employee in my labs was selected on the basis of competitive examination. They are attracted by the high salaries compatible with those at any similar level in Bulgaria. The money my people get provides them with a living standard comparable to the standard they might have in Germany for a similar position. Hence it makes no difference whether they will stay here or work in some West European country, they are in similar conditions.
5. *Globalisation* is an important component of professional science. The way the economy is globalized today is applicable to science as well – you can't say there is no science in the lab X only because no one knows what the scientists there are doing there. That is why EC today sponsors big projects comprising many partners from different countries, with many institutions involved – this is a coordinated science, i.e. a *global science*.

I am sharing these thoughts because I should. But it is not my business to change the situation in the country. I simply can't do it – I have no such high pretensions, nor do I have time for it. I think I am just a good professional in my field and I am doing my job.

What are the *algorithms* for making professional science?

1. You need *large investments* in building a solid science base. Without it there is no professional science. This requires a lot of money – that is what we are doing in my lab today.

2. *Publishing and advertising* your research results – in the relevant journals or in your web site. Otherwise no one will know what you are doing.
3. The *application of science* in practical instruments – software, design projects, technologies, etc.
4. The *application or sale of* your practical instruments – your product needs market realization!
5. Finally, with the money from your sales you pay your expenses from the previous four stages and the rest is reinvested in the lab into new research. Hence this is a circle, an evolutionary spiralling growth and improvements. This is a kind of self-financing science; where at every turn of the spiral you increase your scientific base, your product and its realization.

You can't do science today the way they did before 1989. I grew as a scientist in that epoch and have nothing against it – it was a useful stage of our development as researchers. During that period I got a good education and good personal development. Till 1989 we achieved a good professional level in science, but still we lacked *professional* science because, as I said, the latter presupposes a clearly established user. Many research institutes at Bulgarian Academy of Sciences (BAS) and colleagues in this and other universities were doing some kind of research, but practically no one was interested in their results. We had a generous state providing enough money for the development of academic science – and this still continues, although the funding now is on a much smaller scale. But in terms of organization and attitudes there is no big change.

Some colleagues often compare our situation with the Max Planck institutes in Germany. However, I would like to make a clear distinction – [unlike our institutes and labs], about half of the money for Max Planck institutes comes from industry, and the other half comes from the government. So these institutes could not exist if they were funded only by the government. Take, for example, the well-known company BASF, my lab has contracts with it – BASF provides 50% of the budget of many German research institutes working in polymer science. There is a kind of reciprocity and these public institutes have to do some work for the company. Hence there is a good combination between two sources of funding in Germany, which we lack in Bulgaria. Here too it should be this way, but obviously we have not reached that stage. Plus the fact that there are few people here doing professional science in a way that would make their voice heard loudly enough.

Twenty years after 1989 university education in Bulgaria is still not market oriented – it is entirely financed by the state and as a result the level of teaching is gradually decreasing. I claim that university education is near collapse although few are ready to acknowledge this. It is not in the interest of the current rectors, university professors, and state officials to acknowledge it. But as a user of the product of Bulgarian universities, because I am constantly searching and hiring good students, I see that the best students are going abroad and very few are left for us. You need market relationships in education, at least partial – then students in the universities would know what they are studying for, so they might become good professionals someday. Professional science needs such people.

How can we be sure, that a given research unit is doing professional science? The answer is simple enough – if the results are published, and what is published is realized in the market, this is professional science! It does not matter if this science is done at the university, at a public research institute, or in a spin-off private company. It is a matter of choice. I can easily spin-off the research out of the university into a private firm – what is important is to have this helix-like movement, to turn the circle.

How can we survive in the time of globalisation? – Simply you have to be part of it, there is no other way. Otherwise you are thrown out and your only hope is to wait for the government to provide some subsidies for your research, some meagre few hundred euros.

What does 'global' mean? One of its key components is *cooperation*. In professional science you cover the global market via cooperation, and cooperation is the only way to withstand the competition. I participate in projects and in each of these projects four-five key players cover the field. If a single research institute thinks it will compete with such a consortium alone, this means they have a rather naïve idea of how science works today. There is no money for such lonely labs – Europe is investing a lot of money in science, but the money goes only to the best labs that are working in cooperation with one another.

No laboratory can cover a given research field alone. I have about 30 research fellows in my lab, but we are not able to cover an area for which a tender for research applications is announced. Often the tenders are global and this provides some freedom for applicants to say: "I will consider the problem from this angle, from the second angle and a third angle!" This means there is a different way to realize the project that the reviewers are looking for, how the applicants approach the problem and do the job. They see for example that I, in Bulgaria, don't have nuclear magnetic resonance equipment (NMR) or researchers in synthetics. My lab is doing computer design, but I will contact partners in NMR, others in the synthetics business, and we will have a solid consortium. With such cooperation my chances of winning increase enormously. Unfortunately, many good public or industrial research units in Bulgaria ceased to exist and now we have to look for foreign partners. During the last two decades industrial science practically disappeared, while public labs in BAS and universities lead a meagre existence.

Because the socialist state was generous enough to subsidize science, it understood its importance. Nowadays this is not the case – they say the market decides. So we, as scientists, we have to be in the market. But it is very difficult – people had gotten used to state funding and when it stopped, they did not manage to reorient themselves. Most of the professors now are 15 years behind the front line of their science. They do not know what is going on in the world, how can they teach then? This is why education is breaking down – you ruin research science, this ruins university science (teaching), then the teachers in high schools are badly educated, so fewer good students come. It is a vicious circle, but at the Ministry of Science and Education they do not see it.

Going back to professional science, globalization is only one of its aspects. Another important aspect is *interdisciplinarity.* You see the staff of my lab – we have chemists, mathematicians, physicists, statisticians, software designers. Each of them has come here to contribute to a certain project and so my lab will have enough expertise in different areas. It is not possible for software designers to know biochemistry – to solve a biochemical problem, you first need the biochemists to define the tasks and then to transfer it to software engineers. The interdisciplinarity is related to the third key aspect of professional science - *the ability to diversify the products you offer to the research market*.

The awareness of so-called 'market instability' is crucial for those working in professional science. What does it mean? – You go to a company and they say "We need this very much!" Or they say we need that, and that, etc. You have to open your eyes and to listen very carefully to understand what they really need, so that when you come back to your lab, you will invest your money the right way. Next time you visit the company, you say –"We have this!" Because now the company is paying for a project at stage 'zero' and for the promises about what you will do in the next three-four years. The dynamics of companies' demand is high because the market is very dynamic; hence science has to be dynamic too.

The slow and clumsy projects today are financed only by the European Union – it plays the role that the Socialist state used to play in the past. They invest in research in many directions, they expect something, but it is not crucial to have a completed product at the end. Unlike the EU, the companies, even the big ones, they exist because they sell on the market. They need products they can offer on the market. So they usually buy from us professional scientists those products, which in turn are developed into marketable products. The subtle thing is *that you have to work on projects that are not in demand yet, but such a demand is expected and you have to be prepared...* That is why you need constantly to invest the money you have won, back into research and to know in advance where to invest it. These dynamics stem from scientific globalisation, and if you are not prepared, you are out of the game.

That is why international cooperation is so important – you see how many people throughout the world we are working with – companies like Unilever, Procter & Gamble, government agencies like US or Danish Environmental Protection Agencies (EPA), etc. This means that our consortium includes both industry and government agencies. When a government agency like EPA uses our software products to evaluate the chemical substances, then the industrial companies also buy it; in order to see what these agencies see in it (laughing). Hence, if you as a researcher take a position between government bodies, regulatory agencies and industry, then you are in a winning position.

I can easily organize my research so that some of us remain in the university, and the others work in the private (research) firm. However, continuing the research work both in a public university and in a private firm disturbs the 'infrastructure' of the system, and this is not the only inconvenience. Many of my research fellows also teach in the university: they go upstairs to the seminar rooms; give two hours of lectures and come back down to this floor to the laboratory. If they worked far away on the private firm's premises, they would have to travel to the university. This would be a problem even if the firm were situated closer to the university; you often have only minutes to react to the demands or inquiries of some customers and I cannot wait for my fellow to come from the other end of the city or to read his mail next morning. The dynamics of globalized professional science is such that you cannot afford to be late – if you are slow to react, others will fill the niche. On the other hand the teaching is important because we are able to pick up the best students.

Otherwise if you consider this issue from a personal aspect, my interest definitely will be to spin the laboratory out of the university as a private lab. My people will be better motivated too, because they also will own shares in it. But *in the long term it will be detrimental for the lab*. As I said, academic science is the first and basic component of professional science. There is no professional science without academic science (the only problem is that many researchers remain 'academic' and rely on the state for funding). So even if you decide to privatize you lab, it is crucial to keep your relationships with the university. Firstly, this means your fellows should keep their positions as university professors. Secondly, the university somehow has to be interested in the prosperity of your lab.

The classical model of a spin-off company presupposes that it leaves the university and does its business alone. What I propose is to make the university interested – it may own some shares of the company and receive part of the profit – for example 20%. Meanwhile this is exactly what we provide now to the university under the existing provisions. Usually the theory claims that establishing a spin-off company increases the personal motivation of the people. But what would actually change if my fellows changed their status from university employees to employees in my private firm? The autonomy of our university preserves these possibilities. Now we are autonomous as a private company and we provide 20% of our income to the university. Teaching and research is done practically at the same place, and we are able to select talented students. This is a very convenient arrangement and that is why I stay in my lab in the university.

There is another option – the research is carried out by the university, it owns the results as intellectual property and licences the results to a spin-off company which will commercialize them. This is a possible solution that exists in some countries, and can be easily applied here in Bulgaria too. In US universities this issue is managed by their Technology Transfer Offices (TTO). But our universities are still very poor, they are not interested in such long term (and with uncertain outcome) efforts – now they rely on government subsidy and that is why 98% of the university teachers are completely ignorant about what is going on in the world of science. This is an option for rich countries where academic science is funded sufficiently under the National Science Foundation or some other schema. There professors are well paid for teaching nine months of the year. During the rest of their time they do research on NSF sponsored projects or are hired by professional science. I have in my lab such an American chemist, a university professor who comes here every summer to work for me. We have a contract and he earns good money. So we have no brain drain in my lab – we have the reverse movement, US scientists are coming here to work for us… (Laughing)

19. R Electronics Ltd.

Interview with the owner, acting manager of the company,
Interviewer: Branko Ponomaryov in 1999[30].
(Introductory monologue of the owner of the company).

... The company was created in 1990. Till then I was head of department at the former Institute of Technical Cybernetics and Robotics (ITCR) at the Bulgarian Academy of Sciences (BAS). By the end of the 1980s this large institute was split into several smaller institutes, one of which became the Institute for Applied Cybernetics, also at BAS. There my department carried out R&D on industrial computers, and later on personal industrial computers. We worked closely with number of plants from the electronic industry like the computer plant in Pravetz, near Sofia, Memory Devices Plant at Veliko Turnovo, etc. I've worked a total of about 10 years at ITCR, plus the years I spent as a PhD student and some other employment.

So I was head of the Department of System Design and Computing Architectures when the political changes in November 1989 took place. Our task was to develop Bulgarian industrial controllers, there was a system called MIC-2000, and I was responsible for the hardware. They were produced under the commercial names of Pravetz 16B. We also developed some emulators helping the PC design, such as RISC 16F. The abbreviation 'RISC' actually means 'Research on Industrial Systems and Computers'. These were the first professional R&D systems in Bulgarian electronic industry, which have been used in designing various types of personal computers – for example 'RISC 16' means that it was for 16-bites processors, etc.

This is in the past now. After 1989 it soon became clear that there was no room anymore in our institute for serious work – it requires a serious investment, but with the collapse of the electronic industry, nobody was ready to pay for R&D. We entered the so-called period of transition. But you know – before 1989 they also called Socialism a period of transition to Communism. So I have been living and working in a period of transition ever since my childhood, maybe I will also die in a period of transition; we are still learning how to walk. (Laughing)

So in early 1990 it had already become clear that there would be no funding for R&D, the plants were (partly) closed down, and the situation

[30] Selection of the firms, questionnaire design, and supervision by Ivan Tchalakov under Project *TACTICS*, IV INCO-Copernicus Framework Program of EC.

changed for the worse not 100% but rather 1000%. So we simply had no work to do. Something had to be changed. There were two alternatives: the first was to stay at BAS on our meagre salaries of senior research fellows pretending we are doing science – but it was not possible to do science since there was neither funding nor demand for it. The second option was to lower the technological level of my department and to try a more market-type behaviour, possibly to become a company. And I chose the second option.

I established a company, which I would now say was a rather 'social-democratic' one. I am not an adherent of social democracy, but I did it unintentionally. The company was a kind of cooperative, like a 'kolkhoz' – there were few people who really did any work there, but the money was shared by all. I mean that the company was established as based on our department and it had many co-owners. Many of them were much unprepared for the change; they simply did not know how to behave. But this was my first company and I simply had no experience – my colleagues were good specialists, but to be co-owner of a company is not enough, one needs other qualities. I was the boss, but to be head of the department at a R&D institute is one thing, and to have your colleagues as partners in business is another thing. So I gave to all of my colleagues quite large shares in the new company and I did not preserve the controlling share for myself. This later proved to be a mistake.

By 1993 our company was already moving ahead, although in the beginning we still had some of our own designs, our own products. This was a kind of inertia continuing from the institute's work – these were rather advanced and expensive products which remained unpaid or were paid below their cost. For example, we designed a video-control system for Bulgarian TV which for the first time allowed graphic management of the content and was used for presenting the data from the first public opinion surveys, etc. But they barely paid us for it. We designed also a large video wall, where the image was divided into a number of screens simultaneously and you could see it from a distance. Nowadays this is widespread; in 1991-1992 it seemed that the market was not ready to buy this product either. So we gradually moved to simpler low-tech products that, however, yielded better financial results – we began to import components, to assemble PCs, etc.

The lack of capital was the first problem. In the early 1990s it was not possible for a normal company to take a loan from the banks in reasonable provisions. I asked many banks for loans. I lacked, so to say, economic and financial know-how and I still lack it even today. But even with my simple knowledge it was clear to me that to take a loan under conditions proposed then by the banks would ruin our company. I was so naïve that I never considered the option of taking a loan and not paying it back – which was a serious mistake, because there were a number of companies in the early 1990s that behaved that way. They took large loans under officially very severe provisions, but they never repaid them. Later it turned out that the high interest rates and other unfavourable provisions aimed only to repel companies like mine, while in fact there existed much better conditions, but only for a limited number of companies… Well, they repaid their loans, but much later, when the inflation had reduced them to nothing, etc. This is just one example.

I succeeded because of the contacts I had made abroad in the 1980s [he means his personal contacts with Taiwanese firms he made during his visits there before 1989 – I.Tch.). There were foreign companies that allowed me commodity loans – so they agreed to send me some computer equipment to be paid after it is sold. It was a lot of work, almost 24 hours a day… It was a period when good imported computer technology was still scarce and few companies had their depots. The still preserved old habits of the state-owned firms were also helpful for us – the state companies were used to paying in advance for the imported items. This was the practice of the former socialist Foreign Trade Organisations (FTO), they asked companies to pay in advance, sometimes months before they got their commodities. So in the beginning we too were collecting money from our clients, who trusted me personally. These advance payments, together with the commodity loans I got from abroad, allowed our company to establish one of the first consignation depots in the country. What the foreign companies were giving us were items they had difficulties selling on other markets, and which we assembled in-house.

For example, we imported entire cargo containers of printers, monitors, and other peripherals. So our company was able to carry out R&D, to introduce new items into electronics factories, but in the early 1990s this was not in demand. What was in demand was services, although indirectly – it was more precisely a specialized trade combined with customer support and some (highly qualified) services. This was what we chose, and it allowed us to survive, to stay on the market and win the trust of quite a number of customers. Today it is not possible for a company to behave this way, because the situation has changed.

Now I realize there was another reason for our success. Our institute ITCR was already known during the socialist period by a number of industrial customers. Because, unlike some other BAS institutes, we have never been a closed, isolated research institute doing pure science only – just the opposite, we have always been open to our customers thanks to the clever policy of our chiefs. Today the advantages of this policy are clearly evident. So this helped us a lot in the beginning. By 1993 we were already a serious computer company, offering on the local market brand-name computers of COMPAQ and related services, with a well-trained staff, although in general our qualification was higher than the actual work required. We were also assembling good PCs under our own brand name, and we continue to do so even today. Already as head of department I had an entire group working on computer networks, and we developed this line of activities too, although some of my colleagues left the company and others emigrated abroad. Only the video-systems division disappeared, since their work did not pay.

By 1993 we had accumulated some capital and were well positioned on the marked, when the internal quarrel started. This was typical for most of the successful companies in Bulgaria. My initial mistake in creating such a 'social-democratic company' [now] yielded its fruits, and after a series of partitioning of the ownership, when I lost almost everything, I managed to save only the name of the company and a small part of the capital. So eventually I remained together with only two partners, and the original company fell apart, as usually happens here. I and my partners, we went back economically for a few years, but we gradually re-emerged and you see now – six years after those events, we are a serious middle-sized company. The sales are up, we have good customer support, and our assembled computers under our own brand are selling well. You know, there are still some old notions, inherited from the socialist period, saying that commercial activities are something humiliating for a scientist or at least an R&D engineer, who is supposed to do research and more sophisticated stuff. I found this stupid, because everywhere in the world real business implies good knowledge of commerce – maybe not just simple trade, but everyone has to keep an account of his business. You can't tolerate R&D activity as an end in itself, a kind of meaningless R&D, as was often the case under socialism: "Let us do R&D, because someone has paid for it!" However, whether there would be some useful results out of it, whether it would be used by someone and implemented into the economy, whether it would bring some positive effects – no one thought about that.

Now our company carries out almost no R&D activities, and the reason is that there simply aren't favourable conditions for it. Who would pay for R&D nowadays in Bulgaria? – Nobody. For many years after 1989 there were no customers for original products. For example, we had at the beginning a serious software team. But to create software and to sell it was unthinkable. So this team emigrated long ago. We also had a solid hardware design team and for several years we still continued designing new computer hardware, just to loosen the reins, so to say… But we soon realized we had no customers for this original hardware! And even when we did occasionally find some, they paid a miserable price, far below the cost. Because R&D is something very expensive – a highly qualified staff, as we were, has to be paid well, you need expensive equipment, consumables, a lot of things. And a new private firm struggling to survive on the market finds it hard to provide all this.

Those first years we still worked under the umbrella of BAS. However, the BAS leadership displayed complete misunderstanding and hostility towards us. At that time together with my colleague Nikolay Iliev [founder of another successful computer company, DATEX] we tried with our firms to establish what in the West is known as a 'techno-park'. We wrote a strategy for the future techno-parks at BAS and, being members of the first democratically elected BAS General Assembly, we presented it there. But we met with no understanding – I can say that at that period BAS took a very conservative and vicious position. These people simply dislike changes – what they want is to receive their annual subsidy, to live well, and that some else should work instead of them, because they possessed the titles of scientists and were accountable to nobody!

At that time I was member of the BAS Budget Commission and attempted to introduce some changes. Our idea was very simple, even today it is a very logical one and should be accepted. However, ten years have passed and now the situation has changed. We proposed techno-parks to be established at BAS, comprising companies based on the departments of the institutes – at least BAS technical institutes, because it was clear that, with the collapse of industry, technical institutes have no bright future. So these techno-parks were to serve as a kind of shelter until the new companies learned how to survive in real market conditions. The idea was that this transition should take a more organized, civilized form and eventually more and viable companies should emerge. BAS could have facilitated this transition, because - by God! - it is very difficult in the beginning. Those who entered private business then and who today are more or less successful – we were maybe the stubborn heads in this field, most of the others were taken aback, they did not dare to establish their own firm and simply emigrated abroad. Eventually only old or mediocre people remained at BAS… We were blamed that we were pursuing selfish private interests and we were told: "If you want to continue, you have to leave BAS, and if you want to use our facilities, you should pay the highest possible market rent!" They even issued a special ordinance forbidding private activities of scientists. Their reasoning was "You were the bad guys, but since we're merciful, you may live." It was predicted our company would go bankrupt in 1994 at the latest… Now we are in 1999 and we are still alive. Well, there is always a risk that things might go wrong, but at least we will never go bankrupt at the order of BAS (laughing).

Now, ten years later now, in Bulgaria some people in the government are talking again about techno-parks, but the train departed long ago, as we said. Those people, who were able to run these techno-parks, are gone, and those remaining are a different kind of people. This is an irreversible trend, just like a chemical reaction… And it is not possible to create new people, capable of running the techno-parks, due to a number of reasons. Above all, I can't see who would finance these techno-parks. It seems to me that when they are selling this idea now, these people aim to get some government money that will allow them ten more years of happy life, until their stupidity becomes evident. Because now the situation has changed – the people have almost disappeared, the equipment is outdated and broken down, the money has been spent. In our case all the money left at the institutes after our departure was spent through the inefficient management of those remained. They spent them very successfully, but for themselves, creating nothing.

Our firm today is something very different. It is impossible for us to carry our R&D and it will be very difficult to resume it. Now we are providing services, highly qualified services – these are also almost unpaid, but they boost our sails. That's life. We sell COMPAQ computers, so we are their servants, in a way. So we have highly qualified staff trained by COMPAQ, we work for banks, other organizations… These are relatively big customers, they require reaction time, rapid intervention in critical situation, etc., and we are coping with all this.

We also assemble our own personal computer under our own trade mark. When some ten years ago my previous bosses at ITCR in BAS asked me to do this, I was very unhappy. I considered it humiliating – me, the great R&D expert, to assemble PCs, such a simple thing! Now it is not a humiliation anymore – we are doing it, and we are doing it well. Unlike many of our competitors, we carefully select our component suppliers and I believe we are selling the best on the market. We are certified in ISO 9001, following the world standards. We learned to do business. Looking backward, I realize now that in Bulgaria there have never been conditions for real fundamental research, especially in engineering sciences. Not during the time of socialism, even less so today. And now, ten years after 1989, they are talking again about applied research! However, the right time for this was then, years ago, in 1989, not now. But in 1989 they were talking about fundamental research. (Laughing) That is why I am not very optimistic about BAS, although it is not my concern anymore – when this generation dies out, BAS will simply be nonexistent, maybe even earlier.

It seems that our country is moving towards democracy and market economy, but at the same time we are such an amorphous fabric, and which is very difficult to define. There are many structures like BAS in our country. What is BAS? Where are its specialized economic structures? Where is science? Where is R&D? Where is production? – You can't say. Everything is mixed-up. That is why our society is not doing well. There is complete demoralisation, because those who pretend to be scientists, in fact they are not! When they refer to business, they see it as jobbery, speculation – just moving from here to there, and they don't possess any know-how. I think the main problem of our society is the lack of professional approach – dilettantism predominates everywhere. So we came to the situation in which we are now – not just in recent years, during socialism it was the same, and even before that… You have always changing governments, situations where everything changes when the people in political power change, and there is no professional approach. And this is not the case in the sound countries, because there, there are professional people that do their job and the entire state is based on their work. They do not take part in politics, although they are able to influence it, though indirectly.

- Could you tell us about some of your successful products and services?

What does 'successful' or 'unsuccessful' mean? At the dawn of our business we were very successful – in terms of sales – with our video controllers. It was an original product, very serious, and they are still used in our TV studios. Yet it was a success mostly in the ideal domain, and not in the material domain – because although successful, the sales never covered our costs. The same was with video splitters for screen-walls - it is only in the last few years that some Western companies have been selling such splitters, and their functions are the same that our splitters had in 1990-1991. But when we offered it to the market, there were very few buyers. Our market was limited and very poor. So these were successes, but mostly in the emotional sphere, to prove to ourselves that we are good specialists…

During the 1990s, in order to develop as a company, we had to do simpler things. Maybe it is not a big achievement to establish a serious service office for COMPAQ computers, but we did it and part of our money comes from that. After winning a tender, we also sold to our Parliament several hundred computers funded by the US government. In

1992 the Bulgarian Nuclear Power Plant at Kozloduy became one of our customers. The Kozloduy NPP possesses one of the biggest computer networks in the country, designed and built by our company. So these are the kind of achievements that brought us some profit. I will not say these are exceptional achievements, although they demonstrate our capabilities as a company.

The sad story is that today it is more difficult to have such achievements based on normal business practices alone. I mean that today, in order to win such tenders, especially state orders, the professional achievements of a company, its know-how, etc., are less significant than bribing some high-level official. In this sense during the last several years we have fewer 'achievements' of this kind, maybe because I am too conservative, old-fashioned, or I am getting stupid and unable to bribe, although I'm an old flint (Laughing). That is why one needs to carefully define what an 'achievement' means – if it is solely the money flow, then maybe the best thing to do is to organize a channel for illegal import (of computers). Unfortunately, we have no such achievements, but there are other companies who do it – officially or semi-officially.

- *What are the daily concerns in your business?*

We have always strived to approach the problems professionally and to benefit from the situation. The result is that we have no 'great hits', like for example a sudden enormous order from the state, etc. No, we usually get smaller orders, which are very difficult, because this requires a professional approach and lot of work. Hence the public administration is not among our customers, although it organizes the biggest tenders. To win there one has to pay some of the political parties, to sponsor someone, etc., which is not our business. On the other hand, we have as customers some very serious big companies that have an interest in the work being done well. For example, the biggest foreign investor in the Bulgarian media market – the media company Westdeutsche Allgemeine Zeitung (WAZ), Bulgaria's biggest mobile phone operator Mobil Tel, United Bulgarian Bank, etc. There are also some other foreign companies just entering the Bulgarian market. They still have limited presence there, but we expect they will grow – for example the Austrian Oil Company OMV, the Dutch company Unilever, Xerox, Heidelberg Cement, and some others. They are all our customers. As far as local industry is concerned, most of the sectors are still in a difficult situation, except for telecommunications, the wine industry, and some others. So we have some customers there. Most of them are private companies, with little or no public shares.

- Could you say a little bit more about competition in your sector?

The business environment we are working in is not just competitive, it is aggressive, and even unfair competition. Due to the specialisation of the country in the field of electronic industry during the socialist period, we have many computer companies and fewer customers. So there is tension on the market. Since the legal environment and law enforcement is rather weak, subjectively you feel this tension more sharply – there is a large share of illegal business in our field, which is officially supported by the state officials. The very fact that the illegal business survives the changing governments means that there is some sort of flirting with public power. Until recently this flirting took the form of not paying taxes and custom duties. Now, thanks to the efforts of our branch association (BAIT – Bulgarian Association of Information Technologies), the import duties have been sharply reduced and this channel for illegal business was closed. However, the misuse of VAT started – there is import of components declared at extremely low prices, and the market is flooded with cheap home PCs… We know these companies, the government knows them too, but there are no penalties. So the SOHO market (Small Office-Home Office) is practically closed to us. Because we pay all custom duties, issue receipts, etc… This is one of the reasons that you cannot buy a computer in METRO hypermarkets, like you can everywhere else in Europe – METRO cannot afford to sell without paying VAT, and this is 20% of the price. That is why I say our government is simply not fulfilling its duties to provide fair conditions for the market.

The government orders are the next big market, which is also closed to us – because of the bribery, corruption, etc. There one is facing, as I say, management games without computers – who is going to pay whom, who is going to be sponsored, etc. Here everything is under the control of political parties, politicians of all colours – red, blue, orange, green, etc. [the interviewee means the parties' banners]. We call this 'dalavera' (jobbery) and it is predominant. These are considered illegal practices everywhere in Europe and they are persecuted. In our society it is considered normal. And as I said, maybe I am too old-fashioned to play these games, and we almost get no government orders.

Now you realize that two of the largest segments of our market – government orders and the SO-HO market, are practically closed to us. What remains is the professional segment, the private companies. This is our market and this is our strength. We are well positioned and I hope we will stay there. Here the customers are very pretentious; they have higher requirements and are interested that the work be done well. They choose a company they consider reliable, and often we manage to convince them that this is our company.

- How are you managing your business – decision-making procedures, etc.?

I have never studied economics and I'm not familiar with management even in theory – what parameters to look after, procedures, etc. I manage the company more or less by intuition, and I apply a very simple scheme. I am following the major indicators such as turnover – both in the company as a whole and its branches. I set some marginal conditions, which guarantee some surplus from the sales. And I also follow the input, our purchases. We have to buy at prices 'not higher than…' and to sell 'not lower than…' This is not always so easy to achieve, because it is connected with turnover and we have to constantly calculate the margins. But as I said, there is no formal system of management, and that is why sometimes I have difficulties determining whether a given transaction is profitable or not… We also have a computerized depot system, everything is documented, and hence I am able to monitor the volume of sales, possibly the profitability margins, to keep the expenses under control… Eventually, the very fact that the company has existed and developed nine years now means that it is managed more or less reasonably.

- What is the structure of your company now?

It is very simple. We have a head office in Sofia and six more offices in the country. It is managed from Sofia by me and my partner Todor – together we are co-owners, presidents and managing directors. Because this is not a big company – it is rather a medium-sized company. In the head office we have a secretary plus several departments: trade, production, technical services, system services, and depot. The trade department manages all external contacts – they buy, sell, etc. The production department controls everything that passes through the company – components, PCs, servers, other equipment. These are configured there and supplied to the customers. Unlike most of the other companies in the branch, we have not one but two service departments. Technical services department, responsible for the hardware we sell, and system department, which is responsible for the installing and maintenance of the operational systems, computer networks, structural cabling, etc. They also design computer networks. Both the trade and system departments are closely connected with our customers, they provide the so-called system support and services. We have many such contracts. The system people do not work with prices, etc., but these are the people who diagnose the problems and what has to be done – for example, if it is a hardware problem, it is moved to the technical department. Additionally, we have a depot, which technically deals with storing components and equipment, import, customs, etc.

We also have another sister company under the same name, which is LTD, with foreign shares. It manages our duty-free storehouse, so that we are able to fulfil orders for customers with some preferences – some customers have the right to buy duty-free commodities, a kind of direct import. This is covered by the second company.

Finally, we have a third company called "Computer Products" dealing only with distribution - it buys from our duty-free storehouse and sells to other small companies.

- So how many people work in your company?

The main company has 50 employees, and the other two companies together have a staff of five people.

Postscript: By 2011 the firm R is still one of the important players on the Bulgarian computer market, and has the same president…

Declining firms

In this group are two firms, who have their roots in the socialist era and which then were esteemed as high-quality and high-skill firms, the Bulgarian company producing very complicated high-tech products in the sphere of information technology and the Estonian company produced high-quality consumer goods for "internal" (Soviet) and very guaranteed markets. With the entrance of market economy, the markets were lost and the entrepreneurs were not able to sell their know-how or develop their products. The two other cases represent new entrepreneurship, one from Russia and another from Lithuania. The underlying cause for their failure is very volatile and difficult business environment, where necessary institutional basis is underdeveloped or missing and normal business strategies are not functioning or produce unintended results.

20. L-apparel A/S

Interview with director of the company
Rapla county, Estonia. March 17th, 2000
Interviewer: Jouko Nikula, interpreter: Helvi Pöder

Short introductory note

The history of the company dates back to 1939, when the company was established. It produced mainly women's apparel, such as handbags, purses, etc. At its peak, the company gave employment to more than 1000 workers in 5 departments. Currently the L-apparel operates only in Viljandi and it is part of a larger company based on Estonian capital. The company's production profile is still concentrated on consumer goods made of leather and synthetic materials. In addition it does subcontracting for foreign companies.

- How long have you been working in this firm and what kind of positions have you held?

We were a department of the larger company. We made women's handbags. I was a manager in that unit. Then when the privatization began, then we set up a joint-stock company and I became the managing director. Then later I was the director of the board. In the beginning we had 80 employees, now only 3, a heating worker, a cleaner, they work part-time.

When we were still in Soviet times, our produce went to Moscow and Leningrad. And it was in such demand that our own people had no chance to buy them. We got permission from Tallinn and it had to be extra-plan production. Only in that case did we have permission to buy. So we lived that way a long time, and then came the joint-stock company, we bought the building. In the beginning we rented it, the company rented it from the state, and then the next step was when we bought the building and the machines. Then came the Estonian kroon, Estonia became independent and foreign goods arrived into Tallinn. This kind of stuff sold very well in Russia, naturally the most beautiful models were sold out, and these are the ones that are left. Then the Finns told us that the company would be closed down, because our main designer was trained in Moscow. And he could not design a single thing that would have sold on Western markets, and the technology for example, we have very complicated technology, all the glues and inside textiles.. it needs a lot of work. The modern technology, we have a Finnish company next door with modern technology and our production was diminishing constantly. Markets were full. For example we had an agreement with a department store in Tallinn, we kept our part of the agreement, but one day a container from Finland arrived in Tallinn, full of Finnish goods and our goods were not accepted anymore. They (the Finns) also had an agreement, but we were small producers and could not produce such big amounts and they terminated the agreement. We had our own shops in Pärnu and Tallinn and our goods did not sell, people wanted foreign-made bags, then goods came from Hong Kong, people bought [them] and came to us asking, please fix this, the zipper was broken, the lining was torn and I was supposed to repair those. I said; send them to Hong Kong to be repaired. That is the way the capitalist makes it, so that it will break down, he uses low-quality thread for sewing and then people have to buy a new one. I have been working here for 10 years, I got leather bags for my wife ten years ago and she is still using them today. Let's take the school bags for children, those foreign bags have to be changed every year, sometimes even twice a year, it brings money.

Another problem we had was the Soviet person, she/he did not want to work, but she/he wanted to get paid. The trade union demanded us to pay. I said that they must work. At that time there was less work and we made losses, in the beginning we made a profit and then we could buy this building, it cost more than one million (roubles)

- *When was it that you started to make losses?*

Hmm... let us say four years ago, maybe later. The Crown came in 1992 and 1993-1994 was relatively good.

- *When did you buy this building?*

It was in 1993.

- *It was already the time of Crowns?*

No, we bought it with roubles, in the beginning of 1992. Then I acted this way for two years, so that during the first year.. in 1994 we paid dividends. With that money I organized my son's weddings. It was the time when I took cash, but usually…we had the possibility that anybody who wanted could take cash, but those who did not want to, they invested. And in that way we got stock capital, about 180 000, and we were a joint-stock company in the beginning. But then came a new law demanding that the capital should be 400 000 Crowns. In the beginning we believed that this was possible for us, but then people did not want to invest anymore and the situation became hopeless, there were no markets. One could produce, but one should have to sell as well. Nowadays we are not a joint-stock company anymore, but a cooperative enterprise.

- Excuse me, but you keep saying 'we', who are' we'? In the beginning, when you established the company, who was in it, in addition to you?

In the beginning we had 30 shareholders

- They were your own employees, or?

Mainly yes, but also employees from the central factory, those who were in managing positions, the director general and others. They also had more money. A worker had so little money that we took the price of a share directly from his or her salary. The price was 100 Crowns for one share. We established the company back in Soviet times, and then the price was 1000 roubles.

- When did the management from Tallinn leave the company? Or are they still there?

Yes, sure they are. But they have not received any profit in many years, we are making losses, we removed 300 000 Crowns worth of production from the bookkeeping. There is still production in the warehouse.

- What do you still have?

Similar kinds of bags, different colors, ten different models.

- How many shareholders do you still have?

More than 40.

- Former employees, or?

Yes, former employees, they are currently employed in that Finnish company. And now they really have to work. I am alone here. Earlier they had a trade union, the chairman came here, he was a member of the board, and said that we couldn't go on anymore, the salary was too small. One person I had working... it was the time when social tax was paid on minimum wage, but that person she could not even earn the minimum wage in piece-rate work. I paid for state social taxes and sickness insurance more than she earned.

- *But she is now working still?*

Yes, but naturally it happens that one person gets 5 000 and the other 2 000. But in Soviet times the wages had to be equal. The sewers watched closely that nobody should earn more than anybody else. Then the trade union distributed the pieces which had to be sewn and everybody got the same amount of pieces. Some persons worked only for half a day, because they were ready with their work much earlier than the rest of the workers. Then we also had those who were slower, they were already at work at 6.00 in the morning. A big factory hall, all the lights on, and only one worker doing her work. But electricity is expensive. But in Soviet times wages had to be strictly equal.

- *You had wages according to the task, did you?*

No, we had piece-rate wages and no more was given; you had to accomplish the given amount of work on time, no more and no less.

- *But you certainly had different wage categories, according to skills?*

Yes, in the beginning we did, but later they paid equally, according to the amount of work. Later it was so that if one was doing a more complex job, it was paid better. Only the best workers could do any sort of work. The majority, however, were such that they had learned some individual operation and they just repeated that operation all day and every day, around the year. I did not sack many workers, wages were low, but then came new working places, new firms, which paid more, and people started moving to those. Some of those firms are already closed down, so I did not pay much compensation for firing [people].

- *So, it was a gradual reduction of the number of employees?*

Yes, it was.

- *I would like to ask an iterative question about the work motivation – if some worker is quicker and more productive, but gets just the same wage as the worse and less productive worker, how does it affect the overall atmosphere?*

Here we had ladies working, and a worker that was quicker had a shorter working day, she went home and did her house chores, while the slower worker sat here until evening, even till 10 pm.

- So, the motivation was elsewhere, not in money, but in free time.

Then we started to pay so-called envelope wage. In the beginning it was so during Soviet times that there was a list of wages on which all the information was written, the person did not look at her own wage but at what the others got. But when the envelope-wages appeared, everyone got a paper and in the envelope was the personal wage documentation and money, so nobody knew anymore how much others were getting. Naturally people were talking among themselves and heard what they got. But a person was so used to that Soviet system that she/he does not understand that things were different now. Then I rented out the 3rd floor to another company, it is a local firm, there had been a fire there and I emptied the whole 3rd floor, since it had been unused for 2-3 years already. And some of our workers moved to that firm. Then our production was constantly decreasing and we tried to do something else. We made bed sheets for Belgium; the sewing of bed sheets, well, we had a different kind of technology, slow machines, and they are unable to sew long seams, but bed sheets should be sewn quickly and made with long seams. People were not used to it; they did not learn it. We had a master and technological specialists and we showed them that it was possible to sew, but no, people did not learn it. Then many of them became unemployed when they left us and when they were unemployed for a couple of years, they started to understand that it was necessary to work. And they returned to work in that Finnish company.

- When did this Finnish company come here?

He has been here almost three years already, in the beginning another factory in our firm in Viljandi subcontracted for his firm, he was mediating for goods for Finland. And then, thanks to his relations – because we are closer to Tallinn, he came here. In the beginning he had only one room and then two, then one floor and now two floors. I act as a kind of labor office here, I recommended my workers to him. I had bag sewers here, who went to a regular sewing company to work, but it is a different thing to sew clothes than to sew bags.

- This Finnish entrepreneur, did he bring his own machines here?

Yes, some of the machines he owns and some of them are from our firm.

- How many employees moved from your firm to his firm?

Well, I don't know exactly, but I guess that in the two firms there are about 40-50 workers, the local firm and the Finnish firm. All of them are my former workers that are not retired. Everybody is satisfied, the building belongs to L-apparel and the work is the same as before. The owner is different.

- Do they visit you sometimes and chat with you?

Yes, they do. I have given them old machines and equipment, boxes, and they came to fetch their old chairs and coffee cups too.

- So, you have good relations with the Finnish firm and workers?

Yes, normal.

- O.K, let's return to your company, when did you stop production in this firm?

A little over two years ago we stopped our own production and produced only to order.

- Was it an abrupt termination of production or a gradual process?

It was reduced slowly, if there was a popular model, we made it, and we tested new ones, pockets for mobile phones, for example, but at that time the phone was a huge gadget, now it is small and measurements are constantly changing.

- Did you try to continue production with your own models or was it just production to order?

We designed them ourselves, in the beginning we ordered the models, the costs were about 2000 - 3000 and if it wasn't successful – well we did not have any marketing research then… if it was not profitable, then we tried to do it ourselves. It declined slowly. Now our company is on the safe side, we are not making any losses now.

- So, where does your income come from?

It is derived from rents; and we have our own boiler room, we also sell heat. And the electricity comes through us.

- *What about all this that you still have here?*

We are selling it gradually.

- *To whom, to your neighbor?*

Sometimes, and our former so-called colleagues, the former departments of the Linda company which are still operating, even though most of them have gone bankrupt and changed both their names and owners. The former headquarters of L-apparel Company in in Tallinn was sold at a much cheaper price than this house here. We paid 1 100 000, the headquarters was sold for one million – I mean in roubles. Later it was resold for 22 million Crowns. Now, this big building is ours, the storage is ours, and the other one that is within the fence is called 'real estate'. In legal terms we are the owners of this real estate.

- *I guess it is profitable.*

Yes it is, the rent that we get, we obviously have to raise it; thus far I have not done it, because we get along, but we have to start renovating the building. I shall wait so long as these firms are also getting along. That Finnish company ended in bankruptcy in Finland – then they came here, because it is cheaper to produce here. I plan to retire after three years, I have to manage until that time. I tried to buy our stocks, so that there would be fewer owners, but nobody was interested in giving them away.

- *So, this is a firm which makes profits?*

They hope that I will sell it someday and then they would get money.

- *At what price would you have bought stocks?*

The lowest selling price is 100 Crowns, but nobody sells at that price. Our stock capital is currently 180 000 Crowns, and the value of this building and the whole real estate is clearly much higher.

- *What is your estimate of the current value?*

Well, just for the sake of fun, I say that I will not sell below one million.

- In such a beautiful place, close to Tallinn, the value is growing all the time.

Yes, the value of money is decreasing but the real estate remains.

- Well, going back to Soviet times, you had quite a big complex then.

Yes, we had, there were about 1000 workers in L-apparel – in Tallinn we had the board, factory, and department and in Ulemiste there was a department, it also went bankrupt later. In Tallinn there was another department on Tartu Road, one in Tapa, in Tartu, in Viljandi and here in Kohila. A renovation was done in all these buildings during Soviet times and we were the last ones in line – then capitalism came and they did not find time to do repairs here. We were supposed to get a golf course, a tennis court, and a new heating station, and a new leisure building, a shop, and a block of flats. The flats were already distributed. The Tapa building is also rented out now; they made mainly sports bags and rucksacks there. Then they started to make rucksacks for the army, but that was a failure. The department in Tartu went bankrupt, but in Viljandi it is still operating. We made an offer for bags for general census workers, but it was considered too expensive – I proposed artificial leather bags. The Viljandi department got the job, worth a million Crowns, they ordered 6 000 bags. I had a talk with the director of that department and he admitted that they made it too cheap; they have had difficulties with that. But I am doing very well now.

- So, all those departments, they are independent companies now?

Yes, all of them are independent. In Tallinn there is nothing left anymore; I am independent, there is an annual meeting of shareholders once a year, nothing more.

- Are those other firms also called L-apparel or do they have different names?

Well, they are still L-apparel firms, but then there is some additional name too. The Tallinn factory was called Agro-L-apparel; their director went to work one day and at the office door there was a security officer who met him and told him that now there was a new man in your office – they had not told him that the majority of the shares had been bought.

My firm is a small one. Back then we were the first ones in the final years of the Soviet period to adopt the barcode. If there is no production, then it is not needed anymore. When the borders were opened, foreign goods flooded into Estonia, goods that were not accepted anywhere else. Now they sell that stuff in all market places, coming from Hong Kong.

The purchasing power of Estonians is low; they say that only the people in Tallinn have enough money to buy. Because leather goods, especially bags, are very expensive. Stockmann is also a Finnish company, I had very beautiful products, they took them also to Stockmann, but they were not put on sale, so when goods came and then they were sold at the same price and our products at a three times higher price compared to what I had asked for. The price was high, not much was bought, and I did not get any money before all was sold. And those were genuine leather. At the end of the Russian time, the money circulation was 18 days, it was good, profit was 40 000 in the early days of the Crown.

- How did the working and work organization change when you were transformed from a state company into a private joint-stock company? For example did you have your own designers during the Soviet time or were they in Tallinn, and also the sales department?

Yes, they were in Tallinn. Artists, designers, technologists, about twenty persons there at the central factory, they developed models and distributed them among the departments. Each department had their own line of production, we produced women's bags, Viljandi produced wallets and sports bags, Tapa produced children's bags and rucksacks. We produced briefcases; I still have 11 000 handles for briefcases in the store. The times were such that, no matter whether you had orders or not, something was being produced all the time. Those briefcases were very popular, they had wooden frames and, apart from that, they were made of artificial leather and the price was 5 roubles and 70 kopecks. But the factory that produced those frames burned down and there was no other firm to make them – they had special machines for them. And then came briefcases with plastic frames from abroad. Briefcases were produced on the 3rd floor; on the 1st floor we produced motorcycle helmets. The Salvo factory that produced them went bankrupt and I was left with 4 tons of plastic helmets. Salvo had prepared them; you just had to assemble them, and those I sold. I had 150 kilometers of ribbon, now there are still 100 kilometers left. It was meant for those helmets.

- What other very interesting things do you still have?

I have hundreds of thousands of rivets. Different sizes and the copper was, naturally, taken to metal traders. Also aluminum. I get some money to live on.

- *What happened in the time of this joint-stock company?*

The head designer of the Tallinn headquarters used to live here in Kohila

- *And he still designed things for you?*

Yes, he did, but he was already an old man, he did not learn new things anymore. He just did things the way he had learned to do them. I visited Finland many times, went to trade fairs and to the University of Turku in order to study capitalism, but it was clear that people were not capable of acting differently.

For example, I bought a fax machine and the foreman asked me, why did you buy such a machine, it isn't working. Then we had an order from Sweden, they could not do it, and the Swedes sent me a fax, they had scanned the picture, and when the picture came through the computer, my people stood and stared at it in astonishment. I asked them, do you understand now why I bought the fax, and they said that yes, now they understood. Or the mobile phones. Moving from one place to another was difficult, because people were old, the smart young ones, they went to Tallinn to work. Trains run every morning, about 100 persons go to Tallinn every day.

- *You have not recruited anybody lately and there has been nobody to hire, has there?*

No, there hasn't. And the reason why it ended is that there was no demand for our goods.

- *Well, what should have been changed so that there would be a demand? The Finnish firm is still producing, is it not?*

Why is he producing? He has large markets, Scandinavia, Norway, Sweden – he is a known trademark there already, it has a name. Our trademark nobody knows. Let us take Sony or Panasonic or Nokia, for example, the trademark sells. But his quality is significantly lower than ours. And now he has those people working for him, whom I did not appreciate at all, their work was not of good quality. We used to have our own quality control then, everything was inspected, each product had a tag saying who had made it, and if it was of bad quality, it was sent back. We never had complaints about the quality of our produce.

- How did you maintain the quality, what were the consequences if you were caught with bad quality?

If a product was of low quality, it was sent back to the worker that had done it and she had to make it again. She was not paid for doing it and naturally she lost the quality prize. There was a big book where it was all recorded who did how much, and what the quality was.

- Are there still any domestic producers in this branch?

In Tallinn there are a couple of small firms, but they have their own designers and their production has also changed, it is similar to Western production. But that Finn, he is also a designer, he designs his own products.

- Maybe this particular stage, when an old factory producing consumer goods is being transformed into a capitalist firm, is more difficult [for you] than for a company that produces machines or other capital goods, what do you think?

Yes, indeed, and an additional matter is that, previously, our markets were mainly in Russia, we produced some 30 000 bags every month. A truck came here, a container was loaded, it was taken to the railway station, and that was all that we saw of those bags later on. There were no such bags in Estonia. Goods were in high demand; it was by accident that something might remain in Estonia. All the bags that my wife has we got with a special permission from the director of the marketing department. There was no other way, such were the times. The Tallinn department store had their own quota, which they got, then the driver took the goods there and bought bags from the department store in order to bring them back here in Kohila.

- What was the main reason for the loss of the Russian markets, prices or something else?

No, Estonia became independent and double customs tariffs were set. Those who succeeded in importing via Finland to Russia, survived, because there are no customs tariffs for Finnish goods in Russia, but for Estonia there are double tariffs. In that case [the goods] were not allowed to carry the word "Estonia". We produced bed sheets for Belgium, but we were not allowed to have our name on those sheets. For the Finnish markets we produced car covers and many other things.

- Do you know of any firm that produces similar kinds of products and that might manage to survive successfully through the transition and to cope on the new markets?

Here, in the rural area, no, I do not know of any firm that would be successful. There is one that produces wooden toys, and I have a feeling that they will survive two more years. The price of electricity is rising, since the American firm that produces electricity is not managing at the current prices. A tobacco factory was sold and transported to Sweden. Or the Eesti Buss, it went bankrupt recently, it has a Danish owner. This has a big impact here in rural areas, because those buses drive between the villages.

- What do you think will happen here after 5 years, the Finnish company will continue or?

Well, I will be retired and perhaps I will have sold the buildings, but I will still be working here. The Finnish company continues, because he has already brought so many machines here and he occupies two floors and has enough labor. I guess he will continue. If not, then there will be a hotel or motel here.

- What are the progressing branches here, wood processing, or something else?

We are already too late, if there had not been the Soviet Union; we would already be ahead of Finland in development, because we are more to the south. If we had had the Winter War, but we did not. I was told in school that the Germans bombed Tallinn, but I asked the teacher why are you not honest, who really bombed Tallinn? He admitted that yes, it was the Russians who had bombed, but we should not talk about it. We never talked about the Winter War either, that the Soviet Union had been beaten by a small nation. What we have, information technology, genetic research, artificial insemination, all that is at a high level in Estonia. We have good physicians and astronomers too.

- But how many are making their living with gene technology or physics?

Yes, as long as they bring in cheap potatoes from abroad and American chicken legs...when there are still those frozen products dating from World War 2. There have been such cases recently, when there is no control at the borders. When I imported artificial leather from Lithuania, I needed permission from the veterinarian, because there it said leather on the sheet of paper.

21. Parallel Processors Company "P"

Interviews with Mr. Y, manager and co-owner of the company and his partner, who is a co-owner.
Interviewer: Ivan Tchalakov
May, 1999 under the TACTCIS project, INCO Copernicus IV Framework Program of EC.

Firm P. was established in the spring of 1991 as a high-tech firm, specialised in research and development (R&D) in the field of information technologies. It originated from the Department of Parallel Processors of the former *Institute of Microprocessor Systems* (IMS), a branch of the famous *Central Institute of Information Technology* (CIIT) at the former IZOT State Corporation. The entire staff of the department of around 40 people went to work for the new firm. The team has specialised in designing parallel processor systems assembled by specialized integrated circuits called *transputers* (see http://en.wikipedia.org/wiki/ Transputer). The latter were imported from Western countries (USA and UK). Designing new system architecture was a rather complicated task, as it involved the development of relevant algorithms, compilers and programs based on principles of parallel computing.

In the early 1980s when we entered the field, parallel computing was a new and underdeveloped field of study. An important additional problem was how to match and accommodate for work together the newly developed parallel computing software with a traditional computer program based on the classical principles of von Neuman. My team developed certain clever techniques and offered their customers parallel processors adapted to deal with ordinary, routine calculations. We always achieved some acceleration of the work done, even though far below the potential capacity of the new parallel processor. However, in each customer there have always been some software engineers that were fascinated by our processors and they soon began writing applications for them. This was the shortest way to enlarge the number of your customers – you can't make your customer throw away his available technology and accumulated experience and start from scratch…

In the 1980s and early 1990s the main customers of the Department of Parallel Processors at IMS were the military and some research laboratories in nuclear physics, meteorology, space research, etc. Among them were the *"I. Kurtchatov"* Nuclear Research Institute in Moscow, the *"M. Bauman"* Aviation Academy, also in Moscow, and even the Russian Space Corporation *Energia.*

Together with our colleagues from another department of IMS (who later established *PARAFLOW* Company), the *Proel* staff designed the system architecture and basic software of the simulator of the Soviet space shuttle *Buran* (the application software itself was designed by a Russian team). In fact we completed the task as a private firm – *Prol Co.* The first contract with *Energia* Space Corporation was valued at USD 28 million.

Comment of S. M: "In order to be able to carry out such tasks, the Bulgarian government invested about 2.5 million USD in our team alone! We were very grateful to the former member of the Communist Party Politburo and Minister of Electronic Industry Stoyan Markov – thanks to him we had almost perfect working conditions. In the mid 1980s here in IZOT Corporation there existed an excellent infrastructure for developing computer technology. All activities were vertically integrated, and there was a person who reported to Politburo and COMECON… This lasted till 1987 when they dismantled IZOT into three smaller industrial combines – 'Disc Memory Devices', 'Micro-processor Systems', and 'INCOMS', each of which operated independently. There was a rumour that when IZOT was dismantled our main competitor in COMECOM – the colleagues in 'Robotron', in the former East Germany, celebrated this event for three days."

Hence till the end of 1980s the team worked at the highest technological level with sheer state funding. After 1990, however, with the economic crises that emerged both in Bulgaria and the former Soviet Union, the situation changed. By 1993-1994 the orders for advanced computer systems ceased completely.

During that period the newly established firm tried to work with Bulgarian plants designing specialised computer systems, provided consulting, etc. Nobody was paying exclusively for R&D activities and the *Proel Co.* had to finance these activities from its (meagre) profit. In 1992 they were still working on a new family of parallel processors, but the project soon faded away since the price of testing the system they needed for the integrated circuits and some other elements was 20 000 DM.

Mr. Y: "When you are used to R&D activities you don't pay attention to the details, but you have to keep in mind that the socket alone of one of our processors cost 500 USD. So when the large projects ceased, we ran into enormous difficulties. The Bulgarian state withdrew completely from this business and suddenly, from being a highly valued R&D firm, the banks treated us like we were swindlers – when we applied for credit, the banks laughed at our processors and proposed to take as guarantee our family apartments!

Hence in order to survive we had to look for applied projects from industry. In 1992 we signed a contract with the Bulgarian Telecom Company (BTC) for a computer system able to check for technical failures in the automatic telephone switches. When an American colleague saw what we were doing, he declared in public "…the *Proel* people use computer systems for space shuttle flight control to operate 1928 model automatic telephone exchanges."

The main problem in our work with BTC was uncertainty – its managers often had rather contradictory requirements, or they were unable to formulate their demands clearly enough. At one point I realized there is a huge gap between their vision and ours about how the contract is to be fulfilled. Eventually we produced the system, but they came with additional requirements, so it had to be redesigned, etc.

Since the BTC was one of the key public companies, our contract suffered enormously from the frequent changes in the Government – every new Government appointed a new CEO and when he came to the BTC office, usually his first task was to annul the contracts signed by his predecessor. Hence our contract stopped and began again several times, until finally we gave up… They still owe us about 12 000 USD, but if you try to sue them, it would take many years… It was a very painful experience and thinking on this contract now, it seems to me there should be some mechanism for the Government to cover (partly) the risks in R&D projects like those we had with BTC.

We also designed an advanced cash register for *ORGTECHNIKA* Company, the main Bulgarian producer of these devices. We worked three years on this task and they paid us about 10 000 DM, but they never implemented it into production. These are funny contracts – when in IMS, we had a budget of 50 000 DM and more for a single computer plate, designed by six people together with external subcontractors in less than a year. But in the time until 1989 those who ordered a project knew what they wanted and what the money was for…

You see, after 1991 it was very difficult and the end result was that most of my colleagues left the company. We were 40 people when we established *Proel*, now we are only eight. In the beginning we were ten partners (co-owners), now we are only four. But what does it mean to be a co-owner – you are the last one to get his salary, first you have to provide salaries for those who are not owners. So when the profit vanishes, some people give up…

(*Comment of M. I, former colleague from IMS:* Many talented engineers departed from *Proel.* Now some of them are key designers in large international companies such as AVI (Canada), CORELL (USA), etc.)

Mr. S.M: There were not so many companies in the 1990s that managed to keep up a high level of R&D activities in-house. Maybe DATECS is one of those companies…

Yes, *DATECS* was a little bit better, since they managed early enough to support R&D with their sales. We have a sales department too, but we established it too late and our sales are small. Yet the two people from the "Sales" department, they bring 60% of our profit. DATECS developed a very strong sales department and they accumulated larger resources.

Mr. Y: " Outlining our activities, I should add that besides the projects with industry we also had international R&D projects. In 1993-95 together with English and Bulgarian universities we developed a system for training students in parallel programming. We collaborated also with a German company on a system of virtual reality to be exported to the USA and other countries. However, the Germans failed to reach an agreement with their American partner. There was also a project with a British partner – we designed a "sensors' head", orienting the industrial robots in their environment. We used sonars – the head possessed 16 such supersonic sonars which, all together, provided a pretty good real-time orientation of the machine.

Yet nothing commercially very serious ensued after the end of each of these projects. All these projects were of the type 'working under the orders and with materials supplied by the client'. You are put in someone else's schemas of work. It is true you get some money for that, but the real profit goes to the customer to whom you work as subcontractor. Many of my former colleagues are doing this, but this is not real R&D, although we are all forced to accept this type of contracts because of the detrimental conditions in which we live.

Today it is possible to carry out R&D in countries like Bulgaria under the following conditions:

- If you have some additional business that is profitable enough;
- If you are moral enough, i.e. you do not put your profit into luxury cars and houses, but reinvest it for development (when we get some extra money, our first task is to buy something for the company, that is why we are still driving our *Lada* and *Moskvich* cars);
- If you respect the work of the experts to some minimal degree. This is not the case in Bulgaria now – we often install some equipment

> for customers and when I put 50 BGN for labour, they are displeased, although they paid thousands of dollars for it. People here are ready to pay thousands for 'iron', but they refuse to pay fifty dollars for the work of a highly specialized expert!

Summing up these three conditions, you see it is almost impossible to carry out R&D here. Maybe there are still some people at the Academy of Sciences who are trying to do it. Recently the Government has been talking again about high-tech parks, but I am skeptical about it, we shall see…

Working on such a limited market for R&D services, we are gradually approaching the threshold below which the quality of our work diminishes sharply. I already feel it – we were more people before working on a given task, and we made fewer mistakes. Now there are fewer people, but we make more errors. The reason is that when you have more people, the different tasks overlap and it is easy to cope in case of some illness, or some other change. In R&D there are certain standards to follow – often they are even not written ones, but people knew them and they respected these standards. It is very difficult to teach a newcomer to be a good R&D engineer. So when there is a single man on each task and he leaves, there is no one to assume his duties…

Now, having been for almost ten years in private business, I found another interesting phenomenon. Here in the business, the rules are simple enough – you get a good salary if you have orders and work hard. But in the public sphere nothing has changed – they have less money, but much more certainty. I noticed many people are leaving us and going back to working for the state – they have less money, but they have larger holidays, fixed social security, they easily get medical leave, etc. So nothing has changed from the Socialist period, although it should have…

What are we at *Proel* doing now? – Generally speaking, we turned from computer systems development to computer communications. For example, there are new electronic ISDN telephone switches, suitable for relatively small offices. The problem is to balance between their resources and the resources provided by a typical LAN computer network. For example, a modern ISDN telephone switch provides up to 64 kB per second connectivity between its users, which is enough maybe for 90% of them. However, the remaining 10% have higher requirements and maybe they need LAN. If you need to connect their computers via an ISDN network, it is very expensive – an ISDN plate for PC now costs about 1000 USD and only banks can afford such an investment. So you need some other solutions and we are working on that.

- *Do you have competitors in this area?*

Yes, the competition is strong and, to be frank, our company is no longer among the best. Yet we have an advantage because of our experience in computer systems development… Recently we found a niche in corporate communications, adding a special design to serial Daewoo-Telecom digital switches so that they are able to support ISDN channels. After a year of negotiations, our company won a contract for selling Daewoo switches on the Bulgarian market. We continue also with our previous activities, such as designing specialized hardware based on Linux operational systems, thus avoiding the problem with licensing Microsoft hardware. We use it to provide Internet services for neighborhood offices. We also design Web pages, trading electronic components commissioned by German producer, etc."

Postscript: By the time of the interview there was not much left of the previous scale of research. Two years ago the firm ceased making strategies. Conducting R&D in the field of high technology needs both serious investment and careful planning. Now they have no money for that and most of the people have left the company. Its strategy, if it can be called such, is to survive.

22. AV Joint-stock company

The First Interview

Interview with I.Z, Director of AV Joint-stock company
Russian Carelia
18.05.2002
Interviewers: I.Alanen, J.Nikula, L.Granberg, interpreter: S.Pasti

S.P:- *Here are professors from the universities of Helsinki and Jyvaskyla. They are sociologists. They are engaged in a study on the countryside and the influence of the last 10 years, the changes in the life of the rural population. They conduct interviews with representatives of different groups of the population occupying different social statuses, representing different trades.*

- Thank you for making it possible to visit you. And, if we may, let's begin with your own history. Who are you? Where were you born? Where did you study?

I was born in Kinelahta in Pryazha district in 1965. I completed 8 grades in Vedlozero. Then I studied at the Suvorov military school in Leningrad and in the higher military tank school in Kharkov. I served as officer in many areas of the former Soviet Union: in Ukraine, in Moldova. My last place of service was Yakutsk. In 1992 I left the armed forces with the rank of captain. I left the army despite the prospects of making a career. I had personal reasons. I was the assistant to the military commissioner of the Republic of Yakutia. Then I arrived in Pryazha. At this time my brother worked as forest guard in Svyatozero. My father worked as director of “Pryazhinskoe”. Together with my brother I decided to establish a small enterprise in timber cutting and sawing. Our enterprise is now 10 years old. This is our history. Should I tell about the 10 years of our history?

- Please, it could be very interesting.

We started with one brigade. There were 8 workers in the brigade. 100-200 cubic meters of timber was allocated for cutting to us. We made houses, bathhouses, with manual labour. Later we drew a loan from a bank and bought the first tractor from the Onega tractor factory. Then we also bought the first timber lorry. At that time I went to courses in management for half a year. The head of the group was the professor from Petrozavodsk State University Anatoliy Shishkin. He organized joint projects at the firm "KarelNOK" and he was head of the training project. I also took a course in business accounting in Finland for two weeks in 1992. In the same place we studied banking and all other questions.

- Where was your training in Finland?

It was a college in Ilomantsi.

- Was it difficult to take the first loan?

I was lucky. The manager of the Pryazha bank branch of Rossel'banka gave on trust and we left our tractor as a stake. He also gave us more money so we could pay taxes from loans. At that time there was very high inflation in Russia. The rate of interest grew monthly. Sometimes it was about 300 % per year. Then we took a private loan for a timber lorry from our friends. In 1993 we organized a joint Russian-Finnish enterprise

"SVIFT". This word is formed from two other names. "Svyat" is our enterprise and "Fintraining" is the Finnish enterprise. In 1996 we reorganized this enterprise as a closed corporation. It stands for names of the founders. And we have been working for 10 years. We have close cooperation. For 10 years we have been working with one partner.

- How did you find your Finnish partner?

We had a common circle of acquaintances. We were looking for each other for half a year. Our partner came to Petrozavodsk when he had another firm. He came here as a buyer of raw material. Then we organized a joint venture. It is the "parent enterprise" of 4 current enterprises with a circulation of about 2 million euros per year. It is only production of our own.

- So, you have a parent enterprise and another 4 enterprises?

They are separate enterprises. My brother and I own them. In 1999 we bought the pig-breeding complex "Vilgovskiy". The second enterprise is our first enterprise "Svyat". It still exists and it is engaged basically in woodwork but doesn't export anything. All the goods go to the parent enterprise. Only AV" is engaged in export. The fourth enterprise is our project for a tourist center "Pinery". Last year we began construction.

- What is the share of the Finnish partner in "AV" enterprise?

50 %.

- Are you satisfied with your cooperation?

Yes. We have been working for 10 years. It has not been interrupted. It means that we are satisfied. Though regrettably the partner is going to retire.

- Many joint ventures have had difficulties.

We can always encounter difficulties. But I think it is possible to find a compromise.

- There are many misunderstandings because partners are representatives of different cultures. They have different histories, different representations about life. How do you resolve such issues?

How do we resolve such questions with the partner? I will go to him. I will join his culture. He likes fishing. We went fishing at the border with Norway. He was with his wife and I was with mine. It is like a junction of cultures. Here I familiarize him with Russian culture. We have traditions too. You have the sauna tradition too, but we do it differently. We like to celebrate holidays with the collective. His children came here too. They could be my partner too, because his children are same age as mine. We have good relations both at work and after work.

- "Pinery" is only a construction project or is it a wider project?

"Pinery" as a ready tourist center will work in the sphere of tourism. "AV" carries out the construction. "Pinery" will work as the independent enterprise. We have trained people in the sphere of management of tourism. We aim to open for the first turn of visitors next year. We are going to provide food and accommodation.

- How do you train the people who will work in this centre? What kind of aims do you set to them? Where did you find these people?

We look for them basically amongst personal acquaintances. We recruit the backbone of the collective from among people we know. These people we retrain, even though they have a higher education. They have taken one-year courses. This is the managing staff. Next year we are going to start training courses for the lower echelons of workers. We will advertise. We had an offer for training programs. It was free-of-charge. But last year we could not find a person/young man 18-20 years old with knowledge of the Finnish language who could work in our enterprise in the future.

- Do you train the managing staff in Finland too?

No. In Russia.

- You construct your center. You probably studied the market and know who will come?

At present we want to be engaged only in accommodation and food. In Karelia we have enough tour operators that have worked about 6-10 years, and they are ready to render services to find clients for us. Later we want to do it ourselves. We can't do all things together.

- *Who are your future clients? Are they Russians or foreigners?*

Both.

- *Is your partner from Finland engaged in tourist business?*

No. He does not build now. He is at retirement age and his children do not want to come here to work.

- *The construction of a new complex demands big investments (both construction, and training of the personnel). Did you receive any credit?*

Yes, we received the state bond loan in December last year. We defended the business-plan. We allocated 35 % of investments for the first turn of constructions. 65 % is our own money.

- *How much was it (the money)?*

8,3 million rubles.

- *The system of granting loans is interesting. Is it necessary to have any guarantees or is it enough that you are ready to invest 65 % of the money?*

At the start, before receiving the loan, we had already invested 20%. Before the loan, the commission came to examine what had been already done. We have a photo. All the top people of the republic came. Second, they studied all the accounting documents, the balance of the parent enterprise, where you can see an increase in turnover and profit.

- *The top people of the republic visited you. This means it is an impressive project and that it is difficult to receive a loan.*

Yes, we are the first to have received such a loan. And also, it will be the first such project in our republic. We traveled around in Germany and in Finland. We saw that at each lake by the road there is a small restaurant and 5-6 cottages. We will have an administrative building, 30 comfortable small houses for 5-6 persons. All buildings will be made of our own materials. There will also be a two-storey building here, with a restaurant and a conference hall on the second floor, with 110 places. All these buildings will be located in the beautiful pine forest on the lake shore 40 km from Petrozavodsk. It will be a comfortable place. It is only half an hour's drive from Petrozavodsk. It will be as good a place as the hotel "Northern" or the tourist complex "Karelia". We have calculated the profitability. At the price of 20 euros per person (room and breakfast) and a level of activity of 70 %, our complex will be a competitive enterprise.

- Do you rent the land or does it belong to you?

At present we rent the land. We have different approaches. During the time of construction of our complex we rent land. In the future we can rent it for 49 years or buy it. I think, you know that there have been discussions about a law on land to be enacted. We draw up documents. Now this area has been an industrial territory for 49 years. We also rent a wood that we have stored up since 1999 and an area, since 2000. You know, only a timber industry enterprise can rent a wood area. We are the first private enterprise that has received the right to rent a wood. Now all enterprises have short-term rent contracts (for 4-5 years). There are about 30 enterprises renting wood in Karelia. In total in Karelia there are about 600 wood cutting enterprises. On the basis of the analysis of the work done during these years, we shall prolong the term of rent to 49 years. At present our enterprise occupies the first place on the following parameters in Pryazha district: profit of the enterprise, paid taxes from one rented cubic meter of wood and average level of the salary. We hope the rent will be prolonged.

- Now you rent the land. Later, the land law will be enacted. But whatever the law, it would not influence your enterprise activity, would it?

No.

- In the last 10 years Russia and Karelia have gone through serious structural changes and probably business development has not been smooth either. There were recessions and rises in business development. What does your analysis show? What fields of activity were more favorable during these years? Was timber cutting the most favorable activity during all this time?

Yes, the fields of activity have varied. In the periods default, in 1994 and 1998 timber cutting was favorable. And in 1996, 2000-2002 we aimed at woodwork. It was more favorable.

- The changes in the exchange rate are very important for your activity. But they were important for all Russia. Do you have any local conditions that influence your work?

Certainly; our basic source of income has been timber cutting for 10 years. In the last 1,5-2 years we began investing money in woodwork. We think this source will pass to the bottom rank. The construction of our tourist center became possible because for these 8 years my brother and I have more confidence in the stability of the Russian legislation. We have more confidence that it is possible to invest money. The money is about 2 million euros for constructions for the tourist center.

- Is it the first time that you are full of confidence and [a feeling of] security?

Yes. It is not only security. The question is not that people from abroad will come to us, but also that our people will begin to earn and they can come to rest in such places. We analyzed everything and decided that the time has come.

- Lately in Finland the tourist centers have many Russian tourists and the profitability of these centers depends on foreigners. Basically there are Germans. In Finland they are involved in fishing. People who like to fish come when other people stay at home.

We have it as an incidental business. We will have hunting and fishing. It is the fifth project that we have begun. It will be the fishing and hunting village Gurkala. It is 20 km from Pryazha. We have rented 39 hectares of forests with lakes and islands for 50 years. There will be a hunting complex in this area. We have 3 small hunting lodges. We put rabbits on the island (300 rabbits), planted berries and various vegetables for the restaurant "Pinery ". Like in Soviet times, children will work and rest at the work camps in the summer time. In spring and autumn we shall earn money from hunters. We already have bears there. It's at lake Pirozero. The most difficult matter is the questions regarding organization. [The difficulty] is connected with the absence of statutory acts. We, being pioneers, are doing this work for the first time. Being tenants of this territory, we try to keep out people from fishing. People have already begun to complain about this. We said that they can fish, but they must choose another time. We are not against fishing, but it is impossible during the spawning. The law forbids it. Now we see to it that people do not fish. It would be possible to ask for a state salary for this.

- Could we ask some more questions? How many people work at the enterprise?

200 people work at the 4 enterprises.

- How many people work in the forest?

About 60 people. Other people work in construction, in the sphere of services, in the security service.

- Could you tell us why you got this pig farm and how it helps the activity of your enterprise?

First, a little later you will go to our dining room. We have revived the custom of feeding the workers like they do in big enterprises. We will have a restaurant with 110 seats. People must be fed with meat. We have calculated that basically a pig farm is not an unprofitable enterprise nowadays. Therefore we may possibly work further in this direction. It is only necessary to take care of our own business and use the funds correctly. We bought a mini provender mill from Moscow and we make fodder with all the additives for the pigs. We went through all northwest Russia and Finland and found 4-5 grades of breeding pigs; we were engaged in breeding. We received help from the Finnish businessmen and Finnish people too. We have a project under the Tacis Programme and there is a well-known farm "Stream" near St. Petersburg. Today we buy technologies and the equipment from Finland. "Stream" is the best pig farm in northwest Russia. They used to buy pedigree sows from Finland. Tacis paid 50 % and we will pay 50% too. And we bought the piglets twice cheaper. We have equipped one pigsty with automatic feeding from Finland. One person manages a pigsty with 1500 pigs. This year we must pay our part, 50 %. Then the new line of automatic feeding will be installed. We can cooperate in different spheres with different people and any culture. If it is favorable and interesting to both sides, I hope that many people from Karelia and Russia will get to know about us. Now we have more investment offers than we can use. Today we are owners of our enterprises and some people don't like this. Russian creditors say they could give money if we sold them some part of our business. They said that we would be able to build quickly. But I don't know those people and I don't want to take their money. I am not afraid, but I just don't want to. We had some offers from Sweden and Finland. And we are ready for them as a tourist center. We are ready to consider any offers. It is in our interest to have a Finnish or Swedish co-founder. They will provide a stream of tourists. It will be favorable and interesting to them. During the winter, the road was better. We will construct the road in the summer.

- You build small wooden houses. It this your basic produce of woodwork or do you have something else?

At present we build small wooden houses only for ourselves. We practically do not export. We have friends in Finland, for whom we make them. The price and quality are suitable for them.

- You think that local people are unable to buy such small wooden house?

They can. Today we are in a condition to provide according to the needs. We started with one machine. Today we have three. The second machine was defective even though it was from Finland. We repaired it.

This is the man on duty. A month ago there was nothing in this place. We will have houses here. We try to make each house different. We have 10 hectares here.

- Is there any other businessman in your district that has the same business?

No.

- So you have no competition?

No.

- It means that the other businessmen are only cutting timber?

There are some businessmen who prepare wood in small quantities in our district. It's only 2-3 thousand. They are really small businessmen. They sell wood. I'm not talking about the medium and big enterprises, but we have them, for example Olonets, Shujales.

- Is "Shuja-les" a private enterprise?

Yes. But they have benefits. It is a former timber industry enterprise. At one time they worked as a town-based enterprise with 1500 workers. Now that enterprise has about 600-800 workers. In other words, the number of the personnel has decreased twice. I had 8 workers, now I have 200. This fact is less taken into account.

- *What kinds of benefits do big enterprises have?*

Forest rent and tax benefits. They can be given a postponement. Today half of the timber industry enterprises are unprofitable. It is possible that they might go bankrupt. But this is a social question.

- *Do you know of any cases when the authorities have a severe attitude toward businessmen and interfere with them?*

I can't say that the authorities have a very severe attitude. They work on the basis of laws, job descriptions. But we might interpret laws differently. I can give an example: in my enterprise the repayment of value added tax is in 3 months. I had prepared all the documents in April. On the fifth of May the tax officer said that everything was all right but they can return the papers not before July. I must pay with my own money and wait for them to return it to me. They have the job description. Three months. They wait until the very last day of the third month. It is a small point, but you find it happening very often.

- *Do you think they do that because they want to get something, for example a bribe?*

No, I don't think so. They really comply with the rules, job descriptions, and laws.

- *The laws change very often and there are many laws. It probably influences your long-term planning?*

Certainly. Let's go. It's about 100 meters from here.

- *Is it possible to see these houses inside?*

Inside there nothing is ready yet.

- *Is it possible to see the size of house? Is it for 3-4 persons?*

We will have different houses. This first house we built last year. There will be small, comfortable, cheap houses for short stays. For a long-term guest (1-2 weeks) we will build bigger and more comfortable houses. When conferences are held, many groups come to us for several days. These first small houses and the conference hall are designed for that. In addition to small houses, there will be different bathhouses (black bath, Russian bath, and sauna) here.

- Is it possible to go to the lake after the sauna?

We will have bathhouses on the shore. We could go and see that area. The boat-station, pavilion, and tennis-court will be there. Everything must be ready by next summer. Therefore there is a lot of work to be done.

- The Finnish tourists would probably be interested in native Karelian culture. Did you take that into account?

We have a small enterprise "The Karelian Room" in Pryazha. The Karelian kitchen will be there. Folk art will be provided too by artists and craftsmen from Pryazha and Svyatozero. Handicrafts will be sold. Let's go. In addition to our workers, who work at the enterprises, home workers, hunters are [also] provided with work. We plan to have game meat in our restaurant. We want hunters to sell us their kill. We have our own fish. The lakes are rich in pike and pikeperch. It is healthy food. And it is our pride. This pine tree is 250 years old. There is a name board here. The air is pure. We shall clear away here, we shall remove the bushes. It is pleasant to breathe the air here in summer and in winter too.

- How many rooms are there in this house?

Three.

- Is this small house designed for one family?

Yes. It could be a small company of 2-3 persons, on a business trip. They can rent a house.

- We had to stop in Petrozavodsk because we did not find any place in Pryazha. At first we had expected we would live in Pryazha for the whole week.

We expect that many people will stop off at our complex.

- What are the most difficult things in the activity of a private businessman? We have heard it said that it is possible to work if the authorities don't impede with taxes.

We must pay taxes. It is normal. I think, it is a wrong opinion that taxes are very big. The question is in the redistribution. It is very important for me. How much money remains here and how much goes to Petrozavodsk? How much money goes to Moscow? I would like to know about my own taxes. I am interested in this question. Only 5 % of the wood cut here stays in Pryazha and the income tax does not stay here. We should we think about the profitable enterprises in our district? We calculated that about 20 million roubles of taxes go to the budget of the district. Our tourist complex can give about 36 million roubles in 4 years. I would like this money to stay here. We can use it for developing local production. I understand that all the taxes cannot stay here. We must send money to the different levels. But I think that most of the money should stay here. People ask me, if you pay so many taxes, how much money do you earn? Local people say that they used to go pick mushrooms and it will be impossible to pass here. But I'm not making this only for myself. 200 people work at my enterprises and earn money. This is really a good thing. And I pay taxes. This money goes to pensioners, teachers.

- Do you have some contact with the local authorities? We heard in Estonia that there are no benefits from local authorities and there is nothing to expect [from them].

We want to elect the kind of authorities that can work for the common good. Therefore this year we went to elections for the first time. We took part in the election campaign in the local regional council.

- In your opinion, are things developing in the right direction?

Yes, but we have some difficulties. It is evident in examining our picture album. You can see what we had when we started and what we have now. It was under the same authorities, with the same taxes that we have now.

- You are head of the big enterprises, where the number of workers has increased from 8 to 200 persons. You had to overcome many difficulties. How did this idea come to you?

You're asking about the tourist center or about all the enterprises?

- We're asking about the organization of work. How can you organize people? So that workers will work well and give good quality.

It is our life. It depends on the labor collective. I study all the time. My parent brought me up well. To trust people, to work, and to set an example, to go forward. This year I will graduate from the Institute of International Law and Economy. My specialty is finance and credit. Many people are surprised, what do you study for? Our group consists of 59 persons. I am the only straight-A student from my group. I have nothing but the highest grades. Many people said that it is a paid institute, where you don't have to study so hard. You must embrace your work, your life. I think it is necessary to take interest in life. That is the most important thing. I won the Petrozavodsk bowling championship this year. Life should be many-sided. It is necessary to find time for all these things. I do not speak about the time I spend at different meetings.

- How much time do you spend interviewing new workers?

We already have a management. They are 6 persons out of 200 workers. They have so much work, but they deserve their salaries. I choose people with the same type of character. They are interested in that work. We have a young collective. We see prospects and everyone is responsible for his own part of the work. For example, we have taken a man with an animal farm. Now he is chief executive of "Vilgovskiy".

- Did you find that person yourself?

Yes, certainly. Pryazha district is very small. Our builder of the tourist center is Victor Vasilyevich. We consider him to be the best builder in Karelia. Maybe if not in Karelia, in Pryazha district certainly. We have competent experts. And it is clear that they will have 5-10 times higher salaries than working for the state. We engage youths. We teach them. At the enterprise we have organized courses on two specialties: drivers (for the children of workers) and....

- How have you solved the alcohol problem? Some people drink. Do you have this problem? How does it influence the quality of work?

It is connected with the selection of people. We have assumed the obligation towards the local authorities to hire 10 people of the unemployed once per quarter. They just drink and do not want to work. We have three football teams and one basketball team. Parents with children play together. A grandfather, father, and grandchild work at the same enterprise. Children play football; they go to competitions in Saint-Petersburg, Petrozavodsk, Finland. We have a cultural programme too. A person that does not smoke and hasn't been ill for a whole year gets a prize. At that time when we organized our enterprise we had a big lumber order. It was in 1993. We worked in Vedlozero. We rented a building because we did not have a base of our own. My Finnish partner asked me: "Why is the lumber not ready?" The brigade leader answered that the people were drunk. What holiday is it? – No holiday. He went on Tuesday. There was nobody there. On Wednesday the situation was the same there.

On Thursday the workers went to the workplace. The Finnish men brought a box of vodka and said that they can drink more. There was such an occurrence here. I cannot understand why it happened. Three days they could not make the order from Finland. They drank for no reason. They had received their salary the day before. They were not my workers. It was another enterprise that had taken our order. We didn't have the time to fulfill that order.

- How do you organize work so as to avoid this problem?

We have the same problem, but not so big. It is impossible not to have it. We can see [a person's] attitude. A person can keep order at home. The biggest problem was that the owner could not feel like an owner during these 10 years.

The Second Interview

V. P., the director of the joint-stock company "Pinery"
Pryazha district, June 12th, 2003
Interviewers: J.Nikula, I.Alanen, L.Granberg, interpreter: S.Pasti

- Thank you for the possibility of interviewing you. We would like to have some more detailed information about the activity of your department and about the situation connected with the development of tourism in the Republic of Karelia. Could you please introduce yourself? What is your position and what is your specialty?

I am the director of the joint-stock company "Pinery". My specialty is tourism management.

- Where did you work before you became the director of the center?

I worked in the forestry.

- In this region?

Yes. I worked at the joint-stock company "AV". "Pinery" is a department of "AV". The idea of developing the tourist infrastructure in Pryazha district appeared three years ago. We chose a place for the center. My education, I… I've got two degrees. I graduated from the Petrozavodsk State University, the department of history. My second specialty is tourism management.

- Did you get this specialty at the same university?

Yes, I did.

- Last year we visited "Pinery". We have some information about the activity of the enterprise. There was construction work being done at that time. Could you tell us what has been done during this year?

Now we are making the interior decoration. It is necessary for the houses in the wooden construction to mature. Such are the construction requirements.

- Why should the houses mature?

The wooden material should dry. Then the interior decoration should be done. Now the project is already finished. We are getting the last parts of the project description of the restaurant and we'll start work on this big site.

- So have the documents been approved anywhere?

The documents were in the project organization. And we are planning to start laying the foundations in just a month. There will be a restaurant for 70 people. There will also be a conference hall for business appointments, then a computer hall, a bar, a billiards room and other entertainments in the building.

- And when are you going to get the complex working?

In October 2005.

- You won't start working before that date, will you?

No, we will not, because building and hosting tourists at the same time is very difficult.

- There was information in the media that the complex would start working by City Day.

Yes, that's true. But unfortunately the economic development is changing constantly in our country. And we are now spending money that we needed to use for the tourist complex on the main production now.

- Don't you use the bank loans for that?

No, we don't. We had one loan but it wasn't enough. The loan system needs to be much better.

- We also have a question about the location of "Pinery". What are you planning to build there besides the main buildings and the tennis court?

Yes, we are planning to build a tennis court and a boat station. Our enterprise makes boats called "Pryazhinskaya". The people call them "Pryazhinka". There are other boats which are built in Karelia and Kalevalsky district. I don't know how to call the boats. The boats called "Kizhanka" are built at Onega Lake. We are planning to make a snow safari. We are going to prepare snowmobiles and ski roads.

- How many people will work there according to your calculations?

There will be 25 people, including the guards.

- You are planning to start the complex working in 2005. Are you going to organize any training courses for the staff?

Yes, we are.

- What kind of courses?

We would like to organize training courses for our staff in Finland. Our complex is like a Finnish or Swedish one. We saw many such tourist complexes. That is why we put our houses in the forest.

- Are your people going to study languages in order to work in the tourist service?

Finnish and English. It is the compulsory requirement. It is necessary for the people who will work with foreign guests.

- Are you sure that you will be able to find the necessary number of qualified workers in your district?

No, we are going to invite people from Petrozavodsk. But there are a lot of people who are studying now. And the children of our workers are studying as well.

- If you plan to invite people from Petrozavodsk, you will have to think about their accommodation.

Yes, we are just doing it now. As I told you, the workers' children study at the university. There are two institutes that are… It is possible to get an additional specialty on the basis of a higher education.

- Did you assess the tourist market? What do you think, where will your tourists come from?

In addition to the bordering states (I mean Finland and Sweden) there is the internal market – St. Petersburg and Moscow.

- Are you planning to do the marketing yourselves or do you have some agreements with tourist agencies?

The main economist of Karelia is doing the marketing. She works at two universities, gives lecture courses. She is a PhD. She works at the Karelian State Pedagogical University, the Petrozavodsk State University, and the Institute of Economics.

- What prices are you planning to set?

According to the business plan for 2001, the price is 2500 roubles, breakfast included. I mean for a cottage for four people. The price is the same if you come alone. That's 85$. We want to include the food in the total price because we have a pig-breeding complex. So we have our own meat. And we also have bread, milk, butter, and potatoes. We solve the problem at the local level.

- According to the economic justification of your business plan, what categories of tourists are you planning to invite? Is it for families or is it for different firms that could hold meetings here?

We can say that the time for holiday traveling is over now. Now it is time for business tourism: conferences and seminars. We pay great attention to that. There is an exemplary schedule of planned events for the coming months. It's all connected with business tourism. But let's imagine the time for students. I mean the holidays. We have seven cottages for that purpose. The prices are much less but so are the conveniences… And there are the business class houses.

- *What is the capacity of your complex?*

120 people in all. We planned the annual load at about 80%.

- *You've said that part of the workers are from Petrozavodsk. And how many local residents will work here?*

There will be about 70% local workers. Because we must have people to work in the kitchen. We need a specialist, a qualified cook who would get a good salary. This is a small example. This person will be invited from Petrozavodsk. Of course, this is something that can be taught. But this person must be gifted, a talented person. There is one very important problem for Karelia and Russia. It is the problem of security guarding. So, the staff should be qualified.

- *What positions are you planning to give your local workers?*

They will work as hotel cleaners. It will be enough. They will work all the year round and all day and night.

- *You would like to teach some of the staff in Finland. Have any agreements been made with any educational institutions?*

No, there aren't any, because I think we will be able to make agreements with the help of district administration.

- *There are many offers in Finland. There are a lot of educational centers where everybody can study subjects in the tourism branch.*

Because the tourism structure is at a quite high level in Finland. I visited Italy and Spain. There are hotels that are evaluated as four-star ones. But I can say that the real level of those hotels is much lower. But in Finland you can be sure that the level of the hotel you chose matches the real level. That's so.

- *You said your prices matched the Finnish ones.*

Yes, that's right.

- *And what about the price for students?*

It is a half the total price.

- The tourists from Finland when using your services would probably pay attention to getting acquainted with Karelian culture. How would you make use of this?

The thing is that our complex is located very appropriately. It is 40 km from Petrozavodsk on the road St. Petersburg – Murmansk. And there is a road to Valaam and Kizhi. It is necessary to supply so that the demand might appear.

- If we turn to the situation in the Karelian tourist infrastructure, what is it nowadays? Are there any companies like yours?

No, there are no such big projects like ours. There are some small ones near Petrozavodsk. That is the situation in Karelia. In Sortavala the situation with tourism business is a little bit better.

- What is your opinion, what are the main problems of developing tourism in Karelia: the high prices or the lack of infrastructure?

First, there are no building projects. The main idea of a project is that you can see every detail. You can't come and buy a typical project and then build. Everybody wants… Besides, there is no financial support. The second problem is purely economic, financial. There are no long-term loans.

- So, there is no program for long-term loans for such projects at the republican level or at the building branch level, is there?

No, there isn't. This topic was discussed many times. But it's necessary to do something. A lot of people have understood that tourism is the great future.

- Have any real steps been taken along this line, apart from talking about it?

Yes. There is a tourist center organized by the tourism and sports committee. Then, there are cases of government financing. It helped the construction. A big complex is opening now in the Marshal Waters. It is a hotel and preventive medical complex for 70 people. It is opening very soon. This place is very famous. Then, the government has been helping agriculture a lot recently. For example, the Kinerma village. I'm giving you examples from our district. And in the neighbouring districts such as

Suojarvsky and Pitkyarantsky. There's the village of Sustamo there. And the farmsteads.

- *What about Kinerma?*

I don't know just what kind of help was given, but it was.

- *We talked to the head of the district recently. He said the administration had made an inventory of the companies and the businessmen who were engaged in the tourism business. There were 47 enterprises and four among them were the local ones. The rest of the enterprises were either from Moscow or from St Petersburg. What kind of activities are they engaged in?*

I can explain the situation. The fact is that every enterprise had its own tourist center or a pioneer camp some time ago. Then the process of privatization started. Well, all those buildings exist today. Some enterprises did not want to do anything with such tourist and pioneer camps. Some of them became deserted. But it is impossible to invite tourists to those camps now. I can say so for almost 90% of them.

- *How many working companies like yours or Kinerma's on the district territory are engaged in the tourism business?*

I think there are probably three or four. But we are the only enterprise in the republic that has such a big project.

- *Could you list these companies?*

Well, there is a place called "Porozhki" at the village of Chalna. It is near Petrozavodsk. It is a former tourist hostel of the university. The next one is near the Topozero village. It was belonged to the university too. There are three centers owned by people from Moscow. They are working now. It is necessary to pull down the remains of the hostels, the former pioneer camps and tourist centers and to build new cottages. As for children's camps, there's the one called "Raduga" and another called "Lesnaya skazka" on the district territory

- *There is the company called "Oma kody" in Pryazha. Did they host tourists there?*

All the conveniences are outside. I mean the toilet.

- Is there a hotel in the center?

Yes, there is. And there are hotels in Medvezhyegorsk and Pudozh too. But one can hardly call them "hotels".

- What about the cafes along the motorways? Is it possible to get R&B service there?

No, it isn't. It is possible to get it in private houses.

- What do you think; do any external companies make investments in the tourism business at the moment?

There are businessmen. You can find the information in the district administration. There is a tourism counselor there.

- Do you think there are businessmen who are able to start such a business?

Yes, I do.

- The administration held a meeting for the businessmen working in the tourism branch. Could you tell us about this meeting? What were your impressions?

It was the first meeting and we had to get acquainted and have discussions. We didn't manage to do that because of another purpose.

- What was the main purpose?

I think the purpose was to make the inventory. Though there is a good document made within the framework of the "Blue Road" project. There are descriptions in it of those sites that had been chosen according to the project. There are a lot of different things. There are full descriptions of all the hotels, the cafés, and the monuments.

- There is a tourism office in the administration. What is it's main role? Is it an activity coordinator?

We don't see any advantages for us.

- Is it possible to organize any coordinating body?

It would be useful to organize Internet cafés. A person could go there and see something new, some new information about the activities of other companies.

- We agree with you. The development of Internet sites would be quite useful. We tried to get such information before our trip to the district.

Yes, of course. There is a website of Petrozavodsk. It is www.onego.ru

- Do you have any strategic partners abroad and in Karelia?

We would like to have such partners.

- And have you ever looked for partners?

No, we haven't, because we can't rely on the Internet. We visited some tourism fairs but we didn't have our own presentation. We went there just as representatives of tourism in January. The companies of Sortavala and Pitkyaranta always make presentations.

***

News from February 2012: Republic of Karelia, The Chamber of Commerce and Industry announces:

Offered for sale: 100% of the shares of the Gurkoila farm, located in Pryazha district, the Republic of Karelia. On the basis of a long-term leasing agreement, the site has access to the forest area with a total area of 21 000 hectares and two natural lakes with a total area of 5 sq. km.

Source:
http://www.ek.fi/ek/fi/yritysten_kv_toiminta/apua_tukea_kansainvalistymiseen/liitteet/venajaverkko/2012/120222-Saate-TPP-investointikohteet.pdf

23. A Private Farmer from Lithuania.

Mindunai, Moletu district, Lithuania
Date: October 31st, 2000
Interviewers: J.Nikula and I.Alanen, interpreter: L.Krisciunaite

- *Could you tell us the main facts about your life?*

I was born and grew up in Vilnius; our family lived there for 38 years. But after Lithuania got independence, we decided to go to the countryside and take back our grandparents' land. We transferred it from another district.

- *How did you make the decision to become a farmer?*

Because my father liked land and farming very much. He used to say that farming is very good and profitable work, because he had farmed in pre-war Lithuania. And I too have always liked land, plants. When we lived in Vilnius, our family used to go to the countryside every summer. We lived in a tent. And then we decided that we could have our own house in a village.

- *Could you tell us about your education and what you did before moving to this village?*

Before that my husband graduated from Vilnius Engineering Institute. I graduated from Vilnius Construction Technical School. Both of us worked at the Construction Ministry.

- *What kind of farm did you get when you came here?*

We took a loan from a bank and bought an old house in this village. My husband's grandparents had land in another district and for 9 years now we have been trying to get it back by restitution and move it here. But until now we have not succeeded. Now we rent a land plot of 5.4 ha, but if we got our land back by restitution, we could cultivate about 30 ha.

- *In what year did you become farmers?*

In 1991.

- *Was it before the big de-collectivisation process? Did you take some specific loans? If I understand correctly, in Lithuania there was a specific loan system for farmers at that time.*

There was a Law on Peasants' Farms and under it a lot of local people and officials got land. But we did not get land under this law. Because we were newcomers and they showed distrust in us.

- *Did you get a specific loan from the bank?*

No, we just got an ordinary loan with 17 percent interest. We took a loan of 90 thousand roubles.

- *Did you have some other money before that or some other sources?*

This loan was the only money at that time. And we paid it back to the bank out of our profit within two years. We grew carrots and the local people were very surprised that carrots could grow here very well. We sold carrots on the Vilnius market, because at that time petrol was cheap. Every second day we sold 3 - 6 sacks of carrots. 5 carrots cost 1 rouble.

- *I think you made a lot of investments. Perhaps you constructed new buildings, bought some machinery...*

We brought here from Vilnius two very good and expensive Japanese cars. We exchanged one of them for an old tractor, made in 1970, and some harvesting and cultivation equipment. It was very good for us.

- *Were you able to continue making investments?*

I understood that we needed a co-operative. I was very interested in agriculture, because I did not have agricultural education. Every week I used to go to the Agricultural Chamber in Kaunas and attended a lot of seminars. I had read a lot of literature and took part in different organisations. I understood that it was difficult for a farmer alone to buy anything. Therefore I established a vegetable growers' co-operative, "Korota", there in Moletai in 1994.

- *Does this cooperative sell products? Do they also collaborate with farmers?*

This cooperative took care of marketing and machinery. When I was going to establish it, I wanted to have processing of vegetables there as well. But this cooperative went in another direction and I left it. We had a project and some Dutch people invested big money in it. After that big corruption started in this cooperative and I left it.

- *When did you leave the cooperative?*

In the autumn of 1997.

- *During the time of the de- collectivisation process economic conditions were terrible. How did you cope with this?*

When we came here, the kolkhoz was still functioning here. Also, there was a nice culture centre, a kindergarten. The head of the kolkhoz was a very wise and good man. This kolkhoz was destroyed in 1993 - 1994. But because we came here from Vilnius, no kolkhoz property was due to us and I do not know how they divided it.

- *Did you get some support from the local people?*

No. In the beginning they also accused us and said that we had bought up everything in Moletai and Mindunai. We tried to be nice with them, but they considered us very bad people. Now, after 9 years, they have changed their view.

- *So, you did not get any support. Did you make everything by yourselves?*

We have done everything by ourselves. The local people just tried to do us harm. Now they have changed their opinion. But now they are envious. They were not used to hard work in the kolkhozes and now they are envious, because we are farming successfully. When I want to employ some people for a short time, they do not want to work. For them it is better to do nothing and live only on social relief.

- *In our interviews people usually say that some people feel it is better to go hungry than to work.*

Yes, that is true.

- *What kind of changes was there in the minds of people, in their feelings, and in the village atmosphere, when the de-collectivisation started?*

We were very happy and thought that everything would be very well. We would work, sell on the market and live on our own and as we wanted.

But for a lot of villagers it was very painful. Some of them perhaps were happy, but the majority of them understood that they would lose their jobs. If the property of the kolkhozes had been divided in the right way, maybe everything would have been O.K. But some people were left without any property.

- *Let us go back to your business. Could you tell us step by step how your business developed? What kind of products did you produce? What kind of machinery did you buy? What was the profitability?*

We work very intensively. When I left the co-operative, I was looking for possibilities to produce vegetables and sell them profitably. But certainly for that we need big investments. So, all the time we borrow some money from the bank, which we pay back, we get a loan once again, and so on. Now our business is almost ruined.

- *What kind of vegetables do you grow now?*

Next year we are not going to grow any vegetables. We will put aside our land. Previously, we tried to grow industrial crops and tobacco. We had an agreement with a tobacco factory in Kaunas, but they did not buy our production. We had big losses. Also we planted quinces when it was popular. But it was not profitable. And because carrots grow very well here, I tried to produce them. But before producing carrots, I also tried to bake rolls. I bought all the necessary equipment and I was baking rolls for two years. But every year the purchasing power of Lithuanians decreases. Therefore, after a while, every business comes to ruin.

- *You mentioned that you have an organic farm.*

Yes, now it is an organic farm. But before that, we also produced carrot juice. But starting each activity cost a great deal of money. And not just for buying equipment, but also for different documents, for enterprise registration, and so on. Because a single farmer cannot produce anything alone. And it doesn't matter that my enterprise is of just one person and I don't have any employees, I have to fill out a very big questionnaires with 25 - 30 pages. We produced carrot juice and sold it to Vilnius kindergartens. But every month we sold less and less. The petrol prices grew. Therefore it became unprofitable. In 1998 experts from "Eko Agros" came here the first time and granted our farm the status of transitional to organic farm.

- *How long did this transitional period last?*

3 years. So, next year our farm will be an organic one.

- *Where do you find a market for ecological products? Do you see a future in it?*

A market chain, "Maxima" would buy it, but we do not want to sell it to them, because they are willing to pay only a very low price.

- *Do you think that small farmers have any possibility of doing profitable business nowadays?*

Now we have 5.4 ha of land and I think that it is too big for an organic farm. An organic farm can be 1 - 2 ha. It depends what is grown on the farm. I visited 7 organic farms in Poland, a few farms in the Czech Republic, in October I was in Switzerland. I was interested in organic farms and understood that small organic farms can be profitable.

- *Is there an association of organic farms?*

A: Yes, there is an organic farms association "Gaja" in Kaunas. I am a member of it.

- *Does it help you?*

The association helps just in education.

- *Could you give a bit more details about your business plan for organic farm?*

I have made a few business plans and I do not trust them. It does not matter who makes the plan, me or some specialists. It would be false [in all cases], because we do not know what prices, what kind of new laws and taxes we will have next year. Everything changes all the time. Business plans are not realized. And it would not be honest to make a business plan for the SAPARD program.

- *What kind of products are you going to produce in the future?*

I think that we have to grow such production that is wanted on the market. I am going to sell it in the store chain "Maxima" because they need various vegetables. But I do not know yet if it will be profitable, because transportation and packing materials are very expensive.

- *Is there some possibility that customers might come and buy products on your farm? Are you going to sell products directly from your farm?*

In the future we are going to cultivate not so big a plot of land. Because here in Mindunai a lot of tourists come and there is a land plot for camping near the lakes, I tried to sell my vegetables from a tent near the road. And passers-by bought a lot of vegetables. So, we will build a small cafe near the road and we will open it next spring. We are going to cook big dumplings, bake potatoes, sausages, and sell juice and organic vegetables.

- *Do you have some additional income that is not from your farm?*

If we did not have some additional income, we would not exist. My husband works in an organisation for land exploitation. But he gets a very small salary. I get a pension of 270 Litas. My son is unemployed. He came to this village because in Vilnius he had a very small salary. He thought that he could earn more on our farm, but now farming is not profitable.

- *Do you have only one son?*

Just one. Another son was killed 6 years ago. Now I am worried about my son and I feel easier in my mind when he lives together with us.

- *Let's go to the topic of tourism. Could you tell us about your activities in tourism as well?*

We want to work in tourism too, but now Lithuania is in such a situation that only very rich people are able to do it. And some support from the SAPARD program would only go to rich people. Because there is competition for getting this support, you have to win projects, which require big investments. And in order to get investment support you need to have 100 percent of the money yourself. Only later will you be paid back 45 per cent of all investments.

- *What kind of tourism would you like to start if you had the possibility?*

I would like to build separate small houses for tourists and a bathhouse. And they could have a meal in my café. Also I would have a small horse for riding around on. And I could teach people popular national business activities. Because I am a national master. I would like to co-operate with neighbours in tourism activities. For example, I could provide one kind of leisure activities, other farmers, other activities. And tourists could stay for 2 - 3 days in different places. I have many ambitions. There are a lot of interesting places in Moletu district. For example, a curative lake, an oak - grove, where oak trees supply people with energy. And tourists could go to these places on horseback. Also, we could rent boats near the lake.

- *When I listen to you, I think that you and your husband are very enterprising people. How do you get your ideas? I heard that you visited Switzerland, Poland, took part in courses in Kaunas and so on. And you have had business activities in different areas - in agriculture and in tourism. Could you tell us how you get your ideas?*

Yes, some people noticed my ideas and therefore I was invited to go to Switzerland. I had suggested many ideas to people and now I am famous in Lithuania. I have done a lot in 9 years. Not long ago one man from Plunges district phoned me and asked for some idea. I began to work so intensively after my son was killed. Because I wanted to escape from my heavy heart.

- *Do you speak German?*

No, I do not. But my son can speak a little.

- *You are changing your activities all the time. You grew carrots, tobacco, baked rolls. How long did every activity last? And how does this transition from one activity to another happen?*

Each activity lasts for about two years, because all the time we think that after a while these activities will become more profitable. But after two years it became less and less profitable and we could not get back our investments for those two years. Because the purchasing power of Lithuanians is decreasing all the time. So, our incomes are decreasing too and after about two years we have to leave our activity. Now I started to produce ecological carrot jam. I presented this product at a fair and people were very interested in it and I sold everything very quickly. I thought I could sell it in the store chain "Maxima". But when the store manager told me the price they would pay me for this jam, I thought it would not justify the expenses. I also need a bar code for a new product. Therefore I have to become a member of the association "EN Lithuania", where the entrance fee is 400 Litas. The membership due is 150 Litas. Also I have to pay for producing the bar code. So, I have to have about 1500 Litas in order to start selling this jam. Now I am ashamed, but I am in a critical situation. I am going to rent premises and to be engaged in the second-hand clothes business during the winter.

- *What are the biggest problems for your business - policy, laws, or money?*

I think that if our policy were changed and we had laws that are more favourable for ordinary people, we would not need any support. We just want smaller income taxes, and maybe enterprises have to be exempt from these taxes for the first 5 years, or these taxes could be smaller in the beginning. And there could be preferential credits with 5 or 7 per cent interest. We need laws that would not frustrate enterprises at the beginning. The members of my family are very active; perhaps only my husband is more conservative. My son always supports my ideas. And my age does not matter for me. If I need to, I would learn a foreign language.

- *What kind of farmers' or political organisations do you belong to now?*

I am a member of the farmers' association. Before I was very interested in politics and was a member of a political party. But now I am not interested in politics any more.

- *Is it a general association or a private farmers' association?*

It is a private farmers' association.

- *I think that it is a peasant farms' association, which was established before Lithuania became independent. If so, you were able to establish new farmers associations. Could you tell me about them?*

I came here in 1991, and there was already a private farmers' association. But I think that this farm association and Agricultural Chamber were established after Lithuania got independence. I am not sure, but think that there were no farmers' associations before Lithuanian independence.

- *What kind of activities does this association conduct and what is your personal role in it?*

I am a member of the council of the farmers' association.

- *It is a council of a local farmers association?*

It is a farmers' association of Moletu district.

- *Are there many women in this council?*

There are five members and I am the only woman in it.

- *How many local farmers belong to the farmers' association?*

I do not know exactly, because at present this organisation is very passive. Earlier, we had meetings every month starting from 1991. Later people became disappointed in agriculture. They started to come to meetings more and more rarely. Now we could say that it is functioning just formally.

- *Why did the activities develop in such a way that the association became just formal?*

Because farmers were disappointed and because they are not successful in marketing their produce. And especially milk prices now are very low. In other districts farmers' associations organised some strikes. Sugar beet growers went on strike too.

- *What kind of strike was it? What did they do?*

This strike was in Marijampole district, so I know only a little about it. They had this strike because sugar factories did not buy their produce. And as far as I know, those sugar factories had been bought by foreigners.

- *Did the farmers leave the sugar beets on the fields or did they go to demonstrations, blocked roads? What kind of action did they take?*

I do not know, because it was far from us and I am not interested in it. All day long I think about how I myself will survive in the future.

- *But I want to go back to the question about the association of farmers. How many farmers in this district are members of this association? What have they been fighting for? How many of them are still farming successfully? How many of them have closed down their farms?*

People are working patiently. There was only one strong farmer, who went broke. Now he is on trial because he did not pay taxes for his employees to "Sodra". Now people are afraid to take loans from the banks. For example, now we pay 500 Litas just as interest to the bank every month. But I do not know when we will be able to return all the loans.

- *How do you see the future of agriculture in this village in three, five years' time? And what possible alternatives can you see? And what would you do differently on your farm now? How do you estimate your career?*

I cannot see a better future for agriculture in the next three years. Maybe if we have new Parliament members, after 5 or 10 years we could feel some changes. I think that only our grandchildren will have a better life. Our children don't have the right way of thinking. And usually children behave as their parents do. So, I cannot see a better future.

- *And if you could go back in time, what would you do?*

I would not go to the countryside. I would rather stay in Vilnius and start a private trade or some other activities. And I think that I would have a better life in Vilnius than here. Sometimes I think about the possibility of going back to Vilnius even now.

- *Do you think that bigger and specialised farms have no future either?*

Yes, so far I think that they have no future. I think that only very big farms could have a future, but not here in Moletu district. We have only 5.4 ha of land, but the soil is very mixed: there is some clay, some gravel, and some sand. This land is also hilly and it is very difficult to cultivate it. In other districts, like Siauliai, were the land is flat, big farms can have a good perspective. In Moletu district I can only see a future for small farms, specialized in growing herbs, or ecological farms. Because I saw small ecological and specialized farms abroad and I know that such farms can be profitable.

- *Are there other organic farms here or are you the only one?*

No, there are about 20 or 21 organic farms in Moletu. The biggest number of organic farms is in Birzu district. Moletu district is in second place by the number of organic farms. But there are some districts in Lithuania where there are no organic farms.

- *And what is the total number of organic farms?*

In the private farmers' association there are about 80 organic farms. But not all organic farm farmers are members of the private farmers' association. So, you could find out the exact number only at the agricultural department.

REFERENCES

Amann, R., Cooper, J., 1982. *Industrial Innovation in the Soviet Union.* Yale Univ. Press, New Haven

Avramov, R. 2003. Socialism on Bulgaria's 20th century (an interview), in: Historical sociology of socialism: special issue of journal *Sociological Problems* 1/2 (in Bulgarian).

Barreto, H. 1989. *The Entrepreneur in Microeconomic Theory*, London and New York, Routledge

Berliner, J. 1988. *Soviet industry from Stalin to Gorbachev: Studies in management and technological progress*, Cornell University Press (Ithaca, N.Y.)

Bourdieu, P. 1994. *Raisons pratiques,* Editions du Seuil, Paris

Brus, V. 1988. Enterprise and Socialism-are they compatible? Lessons from Eastern Europe and China, in: *PRAXIS International* No.1, pp.99-108

Bundzhulov, A. 1995. Heterotopies, Critique & Humanism Publishing House, Sofia (in Bulgarian)

—. 2002. Lecture on historical sociology of socialism, University of Plovdiv (mimeo)

—. 2003. 'What Emerges in the Place Of Artificial Joints and Networks Under Socialism'. In: *Special Issue 2006,* pp. 130-148

Bundzhulov, A. and Deyanov, D. 1992. 'Post-totalitarian Elites'. In: *Izbor* No.5 (in Bulgarian).

Callon, M. 1992. "Sociologie de sciences et économie du changement technique: l'irrésistible montée des réseaux technico-économique". in: *Les réseaux que la raison ignore.* L'Harmattan, Paris, pp.53-78

Callon, M. 1994. Is the Science a Public Good? In: *Science, Technology and Human Values*, vol. 19

—. 1996. "Le statut économique des activités de recherche et développement. Éléments pour une analyse dynamique des réseaux technico-économiques" In: *Représenter, Hybrider, Coordonner.* CSI-Ecole des Mines, Paris.

Callon, M. and B. Latour 1986. Comment concevoir les innovation?, in : *Prospective et santé*, No.36, Hiver 1986, pp.13-25

Simon Clarke, S. and V. Kabalina 1994. Privatisation and the Struggle for Control of the Enterprise in Russia, paper for Conference on *Russia in*

Transition: Elites, Classes and Inequalities, Cambridge, 15th-16th December 1994

Deyanov, D. 1992. 'Third Networks'. In: *Brodie's Report.* Sofia: IKSI (in Bulgarian).

—. 1997. 'Public Space as a Stake of Reflexive Sociology'. Preface to Bourdieu, P. Practical Reason. On the Theory of Activity. Sofia: Critique & Humanism (in Bulgarian).

—. 2003. The Society of Networks as a Problem to Socioanalysis. In: *Sociological Problems 1/2* (in Bulgarian).

Doynov, O. 1989. Letter to The Members of Bulgarian Parliament, December 22, 1989

—. 2002. Memoirs, editor Zoya Damyanova, Trud Publishers, Sofia (in Bulgarian)

Donchev, S. 2000. Industrial Restructuring and the Transformation of Society, in: *Sociological Problems* No.3/4 (in Bulgarian).

Dosi, G., Chr. Freeman, (Eds.) 1988. Technical Change and Economic Theory. London & New York, Pinter Publ.

Feiwel, G. 1977. Growth and Reforms in Centrally Planned Economies. The Lessons of the Bulgarian Experience. Praeger Publishers, N.Y.

Florida, R., Kenney,M. Venture Capital-financed innovation and technological change in the USA, in *Research Policy* 17 (1988), pp.119-137

Foucault, M.1986. Of Other Spaces, in: *Diactrics*, Vol. 16, No.1, Spring

Freeman, Chr. and C. Perez, 1988. Structural crisis and adjustments, business cycles and investment behaviour, in: Dosi, G., Chr. Freeman, (Eds.) 1988. *Technical Change and Economic Theory*. London & New York, Pinter Publ.

Freeze, K. J. 2007. Innovation and Technology Transfer during the Cold War: The Case of the Open-End Spinning Machine from Communist Czechoslovakia, in: *Technology and Culture*, Vol. 48, No. 2, pp. 249-285

Grebel, T. et al., 2001. An Evolutionary Approach to the Theory of Entrepreneurship, JEL

Grossmann, G 1963. Notes for a theory of the Command Economy, in: *Europe-Asia Studies*, 15: 2, pp. 101-123

Hankiss, E. 1988. The "Second Society": Is There an Alternative Social Model Emerging in Contemporary Hungary? In: *Social Research*, Vol. 55, No. 1-2 (Spring/Summer), pp13-42

Hayek, F.A., (ed.) 1935. Collectivist Economic Planning, London, Routledge & Kegan Paul

—. 1945. The Use of Knowledge in Economy, in: *The American Economic Review*, Vol. 35, Issues 4, pp.519-530

Hsu, C.L. 2005. Capitalism without contracts versus capitalists without capitalism: Comparing the influence of Chinese *guanxi* and Russian *blat* on marketization, *Communist and Post-Communist Studies,* 38, pp. 309-327

Ivanov, D., 2004. The Sixth Department, Trud Publishing House, Sofia (in Bulgarian)

Jones, Leroy P. and Il Sakong 1981. Government, Business, and Entrepreneurship in Economic Development: The Korean Case. *Journal of Economic Literature*, Vol. 19, No. 4 (Dec., 1981), pp. 1622-1624

Joseph A. Schumpeter 1991. *The Economics and Sociology of Capitalism*, edited by Richard Swedberg, Princeton Univ. Press, Princeton

Karamanev, G. (ed.) 2001. *The Man Who was Ahead of Its Time. Memoirs for Georgy Naidenov – Geto*, Zaharii Stoyanov Publishing House, Sofia (in Bulgarian)

Kidder, T. 1981. *The Soul of New Machine*, Atlantic-Little Brown, NY

Kivinen, M. 2002. *Progress and Chaos. Russia as Challenge for Sociological Imagination*, Kikimora Publications, Helsinki

Kivinen, M. and J. Nikula 2006. Researching Transition. Mir Rossii, tom XV, No. 1, pp.50-75

Kirzner, I. 1997. Entrepreneurial Discovery and the Competitive Market Process: An Austrian Approach, in: *Journal of Economic Literature*, Vol. XXXV (March), pp. 60–85

Knight, F. 1921. *Risk, Uncertainty and Profit,* Houghton Mifflin, Boston

Knorr Cetina, K.(1994) :. Laboratory studies, in: Jasanoff, S., Markle, G., Petersen, J., Pinch, T. (eds), *Handbook of Science and Technology Studies, Thousand Oaks,* Sage, Thousand Oaks

Kornai, J. 2000. Hardening the budget constraint: The experience of the post-socialist countries, *European Economic Review* Vol. 45 (9), pp. 1573-1599.

—. 2001. La transformation economique postsocialiste. Dilemmes et decisions. Maison des sciences de l'homme, Paris

—. 1992. The Socialist System. Political Economy of Communism, Oxford Univ. Press, 1992 (Bulgarian Edition 1996, Marin Drinov Academic Publishers, Sofia)

Kuura, A 2006. Entrepreneurship Policy in Estonia. MPRA Paper No. 676, Munich

Langlois, R. N. 1987. "Schumpeter and the Obsolescence of the Entrepreneur", Paper presented at the History of Economics Society annual meeting, June 21, 1987, Boston (Working Paper 91-1503,

Department of Economics, University of Connecticut, November 1991; A revised version of the paper published in *Advances in Austrian Economics* 6: 287-302 (2003)).

Ledeneva, A., 1998. Russia's Economy of Favors. Cambridge University Press, Cambridge

Liuhto, K. 1996. Entrepreneurial Transition in Post-Soviet Republics: The Estonian Path, Europe-Asia (Formerly Soviet Studies) Vol. 48. No. 1. Glasgow.

—. 1998. Transformation of the Estonia Enterprise Sector form a Planned Economy towards Market Economy. In Kivinen, M (ed): The Calamari Union: Middle Class in East and West. Ashgate, Aldershot.

Martinelli, A. 1994. Entrepreneurship and management, in: Handbook of economic sociology, pp.476-503

Minev, D. et al. 1996. "Bulgarian Economy: Reforms, Changes and Perspectives", Institute of Sociology, Sofia.

Mozny, I.2003. *Why So Easily...* Sofia: Iztok/Zapad (this edition) (in Bulgarian).

Murrel, P. 1990. The Nature of Socialist Economies. Lessons from Eastern European Foreign Trade. Princeton: Princeton Univ. Press

Mygind, N. 2000. Privatisation, Governance and Restructuring of Enterprises in the Baltics. CCNM/BALT(2000)6, OECD. Paris

Nelson, R. and Winter, S. 1976. In search in useful theory of innovation, in. *Research policy,* No.6

Nikula, J. 2004. Networks, Skills and Trust: Necessary Ingredients of Rural Entrepreneurship in the Baltic Countries? In: Alanen, I (ed): Mapping the Rural Problem in the Baltic Countryside. Ashgate, Aldershot.

Nove, A. 1972. 'Market socialism' and its critics, in: in: *Europe-Asia Studies*, 24: 1, pp. 120-138

—. 1981. Stalinism and After (2nd ed.), George Allen & Unwin Ltd.,

Radaev, V. 1997. Practicing and potential entrepreneurs in Russia, in: *International Journal of Sociology*, Fall 1977, pp.15-50

Raychev, A. 1985. *The Young Person and the 'Small Truth*. Sofia: Narodna Mladezh (in Bulgarian).

—. (1992) 'The Second Network'. In: *Brodie's Report.* Sofia: IKSI (in Bulgarian).

—. (2003): 'Genesis, Mutations and Degeneration of Second Networks'. In: *Historical sociology of socialism: special issue, Sociological Problems 1/2* (in Bulgarian).

Reich, R. 1992. The Work of Nations: preparing ourselves for 21st century capitalism, Vintage Books

Revol, H., 1994. Les enjeux de cooperation scientificque et technologique avec les pays de l'Est (rapport). Office parlamenaire de politique technologuquee et scientique, France

Romsics, I. 2007. Economic reforms in the Kadar Era, in: *The Hungarian Quarterly,* issue 187: 69-79

Rosenberg, N. 1976. Perspectives on Technology, Cambridge Univ. Press, Cambridge

Run, R. and Utt, R 1990. Bulgarian Economic Growth and Transition Project, National Chamber Foundation, Washington

Schumpeter, J. 1934. *The Theory of Economic Development*, Cambridge, MA, Harvard University Press.

Schumpeter, J. 2003. *Capitalism, Socialism and Democracy*, Routledge, London and N.Y. (First published in 1942 by Harper & Row, New York

Shmulyar Green, O. 2009. Entrepreneurship in Russia: Western Ideas in Russian Translation, *Gothenburg Studies in Sociology No.40*, University of Gothenburg

Sutela, P. 1991. Economic Thought and Economic Reforms in Soviet Union, Cambridge Univ. Press

Swedberg, R. 1998. Entrepreneurship – The Social Science View, *Working Paper No.64*, Stockholm University, Dep. of Sociology

Szelenyi, I., in collaboration with Manchin, R. 1988. *Socialist Entrepreneurs: Embourgeoisement in Rural Hungary,* Polity Press, Cambridge.

Szelenyi, I., K. Beckett and L.P.King, 1994. The Socialist Economic System, in: Neil Smelser and Richard Swedberg, eds., *The Handbook of Economic Sociology,* Princeton Univ. Press, Princcton, pp. 234-251

Tchalakov, I. 1997. Innovation in the Non-Exchange Economy. An Essay on Joseph Schumpeter, in: *Sociological Problems*, No.4 (in Bulgarian), pp. 3-18.

—. (2002). La théorie des réseaux techno-économiques et le développement dans les économies administrées, dans: J.Boucher, G. Fotev et S. Koleva (s.d. de) *Mutations de société en quête de sens*, Éditions LIK

—. 2003a. Joseph Schumpeter rethought: the classic ideas on the innovations in no-exchange economy at the light of some resent studies of the communist economy, in: *Theorie Vědy / Theory of Science,* Vol.: XII/XXV/2003, No.3, Prague

—. 2003b. Socialism as a society of networks and the problem of economic development, in: *Sociological Problems, Special Issue 2006*, pp.106-130

Tyson, L. d'Andrea, T.Petrin and H. Rogers 1994. Promoting Entrepreneurship in Eastern Europe, in: *Small Business Economics* 6: 165-184, Kluwer Academic Publishers

Venesaar, U. 2006. "Entrepreneurship and Small Business Research in Estonia: an Overview", in: Mets, T, Andrejevskaja, J., Venesaar, U., Kolbre, E. (Eds), *Entrepreneurship in Estonia: Policies, Practices, Education and Research*, Tartu University Press, Tartu, pp. 270-294.

Ziyang, Z. 2009. *Prisoner of the State*, New York, Simon and Schuster